Kay Simpson
409 N. Elm St.
Momence, IL 6095

MW01120284

Forty years in the church of Christ

Father Chiniquy

Nabu Public Domain Reprints:

You are holding a reproduction of an original work published before 1923 that is in the public domain in the United States of America, and possibly other countries. You may freely copy and distribute this work as no entity (individual or corporate) has a copyright on the body of the work. This book may contain prior copyright references, and library stamps (as most of these works were scanned from library copies). These have been scanned and retained as part of the historical artifact.

This book may have occasional imperfections such as missing or blurred pages, poor pictures, errant marks, etc. that were either part of the original artifact, or were introduced by the scanning process. We believe this work is culturally important, and despite the imperfections, have elected to bring it back into print as part of our continuing commitment to the preservation of printed works worldwide. We appreciate your understanding of the imperfections in the preservation process, and hope you enjoy this valuable book.

Truly yours—
C. Lehrivique.

Forty Years

IN

The Church of Christ

Rev. Charles Chiniquy, D.D.

Author of " Fifty Years in the Church of Rome," etc.

Chicago, New York, Toronto

Fleming H. Revell Company

1900

PREFATORY NOTE

This book, "Forty Years in the Church of Christ," is now offered to the public with the belief that it is eminently adapted to interest as well as to instruct.

For several years before his death, Dr. Chiniquy had in contemplation the preparation of an account of his life and career after he left the Church of Rome, and the last years of his life were largely devoted to this work, so that at the time of his departure it was substantially complete

While it abounds in striking incidents and events in the author's wonderful career, this book is not designed to be a connected autobiography. As may be easily inferred from what himself says in his preface, Dr. Chiniquy aimed to relate only what he considered could be made subservient to the illustration and application of the great truths of the Gospel he so ardently loved Had he lived longer, however, he would probably have added other matter at his command.

In editing this work, there have been no essential changes made. It bears the impress throughout of the author's marked individuality and, as to matter and style, the flavour of his great soul permeates every page.

Although each chapter is substantially complete in itself, there is a general stream of characteristic thought and feeling running through the whole.

The responsibility of issuing this book having been committed to me by the author, my revered father-in-law, I have spared no pains to have the work as near perfection in every respect as possible, and, in this connection, I am glad to acknowledge the valuable assistance I have received from Rev Prof John Moore, of Boston, and Rev. Principal Mac Vicar, D. D., of Montreal.

I feel that this book cannot be better introduced to the readers than by the following character sketch from the pen of Dr MacVicar, which incorporates his address to the thousands present at Dr. Chiniquy's funeral.

J L MORIN.

65 Hutchison Street, Montreal.

INTRODUCTION

CHARLES CHINIQUY: HIS LIFE AND WORK

A Character Sketch, by the Rev. Principal D. H. MacVicar, D. D., LL. D.

The death of Dr. Chiniquy on the 16th of January has called forth in the daily press. both French and English, innumerable notices of his unique career. The general fairness by which they are characterized is in impressive contrast with the treatment he often received in his lifetime, and may be regarded as an encouraging sign of the times.

It need hardly be said that good and great men are often misunderstood and misrepresented. It is a favourite method with the devil and his servants to direct their envenomed shafts against those who prominently represent and uncompromisingly propagate the truth of God So not a few of them are forced to pass through life in a tempest, but the end is peace. So it was with Chiniquy.

His life has been so often sketched that it seems a work of supererogation to offer anything further regarding it. For beauty, for graphic and dramatic effect, I cordially commend the autobiography from his own pen It covers the first fifty years of his life, and the manuscript recording the events of the remaining forty years he completed before his demise and forms the present work If, to some, the record seems unduly voluminous, let them remember that the man and his work were extraordinary. Taken all in all, we shall not look upon his like again.

To put ourselves in possession of the key to his conduct, and to understand the foundation of his training for his great mission, we must begin with his childhood. It is in early years, when the faculties are pre-eminently plastic and receptive, that lasting impressions for good and evil are made. In the seclusion of home, more than in the bustling arena of the outside world, character is determined and moulded It is there that boys and girls receive their life vocation The ministry of "the church in the house" is usually most influential This was the experience of Dr. Chiniquy

He was born at Kamouraska, Quebec, on the 30th of July, 1809 His father passed through a full course of literary and theological training for the priesthood in his native city, Quebec, but never took holy orders He studied law and became notary, and ultimately settled at Murray Bay "That place," says Dr. Chiniquy in his autobiography, "was then in its infancy, and no schools had yet been established. My mother was, therefore, my first teacher." A wise and admirable one she certainly was, and taught him the lessons which governed his course in life, and which, with boundless enthusiasm and singular success, he pressed upon the acceptance of hundreds of thousands, especially during the last half of his career.

Here I use his own words as descriptive of the religious and educational discipline he enjoyed in the home of his childhood:

"Before leaving the Seminary of Quebec my father had received from one of his superiors, as a token of his esteem, a beautiful French and Latin Bible. That Bible was the first book, after the ABC, in which I was taught to read. My mother selected the chapters which she considered the most interesting to me, and I read them every day with the greatest attention and pleasure I was even so much pleased with several chapters that I read them over and over again till I knew them by heart When eight or nine years of age I had learned by heart the history of the creation and fall of man; the deluge, the sacrifice of Isaac, the history of Moses; the plagues of Egypt; the sublime hymns of Moses after crossing the Red Sea, the history of Samson, the most interesting event of the life of David; several Psalms, all the speeches and parables of Christ; and the whole history of the sufferings and death of our Saviour as narrated by John."

He then tells how his mother used to question him regarding the meaning of what he read, and how, one day when engaged in studying the scene upon Calvary, she suddenly burst into tears, and both wept for joy as the love of the crucified Son of God touched their hearts.

"No human words can express what was felt in her soul and in mine in that most blessed hour· No, I will never forget that solemn hour, when my mother's heart was perfectly blended with mine at the feet of our dying Saviour."

The evidence of the sincerity of these words, and of the spiritual light then shed upon his soul, is seen in his subsequent conduct God's Word does not fail in its mission, or return to Him void. Immediately the lad becomes a witness for the truth He imparts to others the good word of life which he has himself received And with the glimpses we possess of the history of the early life of Samuel and Jeremiah and Timothy, and of "the children crying in the temple and saying, 'Hosanna to the Son of David,'" we need not doubt that boys and girls at eight and nine are capable of rendering such blessed services. Hence the narrative in young Chiniquy's case proceeds:

"We were some distance from the church, and the roads, on the rainy days, were very bad On the Sabbath days the neighbouring farmers, unable to go to church, were accustomed to gather at our house in the evening. Then my parents used to put me up on a large table in the midst of the assembly, and I delivered to those good people the most beautiful parts of the Old and New Testament. The breathless attention, the applause of our guests, and—may I tell it—often the tears of joy which my mother tried in vain to conceal, supported my strength and gave me the courage I wanted to speak when so young before so many people When my parents saw that I was growing tired, my mother, who had a fine voice, sang some of the beautiful French hymns with which her memory was filled.

"Several times, when the fine weather allowed me to go to church with my parents, the farmers would take me into their *calèches* (buggies) at the door of the temple, and request me to give them some chapter of the Gospel With the most perfect attention they listened to the voice of the child whom the Good Master had chosen to give them the bread which came from heaven. More than once I remember that, when the bell called us to the church, they expressed their regret that they could not hear more."

In this simple narrative we have the secret of Dr Chiniquy's extraordinary power in after life. The child was father to the man His heart and thoughts were permeated with Gospel truth He received in these early years the education which stood him in good stead to the end of his days, and proved the solace and joy of his heart in the last hour.

This being the case, why should we for a moment yield to the presumptuous folly of those who regard the Bible superannuated, and useless as a school-book? It is nothing of the sort Next to the Saviour, it is God's best gift to men, fitted to enlighten their intellects, their hearts and consciences, and designed by Him to hold the first place in the home, the school and the college It was for this supremacy of the Word that Chiniquy fought his thousand battles.

It is hardly necessary to say that on leaving home for more advanced and literary and theological studies, he entered upon a course of training much of which he afterwards deplored and condemned Possibly some of his best friends were right in thinking that they saw occasionally traces of this bad education in his after life It is no easy task to emancipate oneself fully from the influence of what is incorporated in one's very nature by the efficient drill of the class room And, yet, upon a broad view of the case, this training, which Dr. Chiniquy publicly repudiated in its distinctive features, was essential as a preparation for his subsequent polemical undertakings. He thus gained an intimate acquaintance with—an inside view of—the mighty system he was destined to oppose. It is a great matter to be able to speak of what we have seen and learned by hard personal experience. An experience of fifty years should give weight to any intelligent and honourable man's statement. And, with regard to Dr. Chiniquy, we say only what his Romish co-religionists with practical unanimity acknowledge that while in their communion he was distinguished for purity of life and actuated by lofty motives. And the same can be said of him since he renounced Romanism The *True Witness*, the English organ of the Roman Catholic Church in Montreal, in an article on his death, said "That the late Father Chiniquy had been the author of great good in his time, it would be untrue and unjust to deny, that he crowded into the space of forty years more than any other man in this country—or perhaps in any other one—is equally undeniable."

This is strong testimony and in accordance with facts that have been repeatedly published. It is not possible in the space at our disposal to give even a brief epitome of what is here referred to. A few outstanding instances may be selected without giving details. We mention his great campaign as "Apostle of Temperance." In this he closed nearly all the distilleries, breweries and saloons of the province. In 1850 he accepted the invitation of Bishop Vandeveld, of Chicago, to establish a colony of French-Canadians in Illinois. He set out on this mission with the blessing of the Bishop of Montreal, and was successful in organizing a strong settlement at St. Anne, Kankakee County. Bishop Vandeveld, being removed from Chicago, was succeeded by Bishop O'Regan, of whom Father Chiniquy complained as oppressing the colonists. The rupture between them became serious, and the upshot was the Bishop was deposed by the Pope This was brought about by his opponent soliciting the aid and intervention of Napoleon III, who had powerful influence at the

Vatican   Was this an instance of what has so often occurred
—clerical meddling with politics?   O'Regan was succeeded
by Bishop Smith, of Iowa, and the troubles between him and
Chiniquy, after many keen disputations regarding auricular
confessions, the authority of the church, etc., reached a crisis.
The Bishop pronounced sentence on him in these words,
"You can no longer be a Roman Catholic priest."   Father
Chiniquy raised his hands to heaven, and cried, "May God
Almighty be forever blessed."   He returned to his colony,
told them what had occurred, and soon after was received,
along with over two thousand converts, into the Presbyterian
Church of the United States.   Two years later he visited
Canada and entered the Presbyterian Church, in connection
with which he continued to labour to the end with unflagging
energy and zeal.

During forty years, all along the line of action, he was
privileged to see the abundant results of his strenuous toils
and hard-fought battles.   Thousands upon thousands in this
and other countries joined the ranks of his followers.   In
1874 he became the champion of British rights and liberties
in Montreal.   He began to preach the Gospel in the French
Protestant Church on Craig Street, and was soon driven from
it, narrowly escaping death, all the windows being smashed
with stones by the mob.   It then became almost impossible
to find any church that would allow him to speak within its
walls.   I finally secured for him the basement of the old
Erskine church for one night, and thereafter the pastor, the
late Dr R F Burns, and his elders and deacons, granted him
the use of "The Free Church Cote" for several months.
Thousands pressed to hear him night after night.

The determination was to let the multitudes of French
people who desired to hear the Gospel do so, and thus to
vindicate and secure for all the right of free speech   It was
rough and even dangerous work   We retained the services
of over thirty policemen every night inside and outside the
church.   We were often followed on the streets, and treated

to showers of stones, by thousands who shouted, "Kill Chiniquy!"

Victory was ultimately, not on the side of the mob, but of right and fair play. And who will say that the principles at stake were not worth the trouble and exposure we were forced to encounter?

But what a contrast to these turbulent scenes appeared on our streets and in Erskine Church on the 19th of January! That great and beautiful edifice could not contain half the people who pressed for entrance to do honour to Chiniquy's memory. The funeral procession was the largest witnessed in our city since the death of the Hon. Mr McGee. More than ten thousand French Roman Catholics, and Protestants of all nationalities, lined the streets or moved in the solemn, silent procession that bore his remains to the church At least four thousand, chiefly French Roman Catholics, during three days, reverently entered the home of Father Chiniquy and looked upon his calm and peaceful face, silent in death. One old man walked ten miles to get this last look. Many begged souvenirs of him, and were given such in the form of photographs and tracts and pamphlets written by their deceased friend Some fell upon their knees by the corpse and wept, exclaiming, "How wicked we were to have stoned the dear old servant of Christ." What a change! They had received the Gospel from his lips, and now felt in their hearts that he was fallen asleep in Jesus, for with his latest breath he had expressed his unfaltering trust and joy in His redeeming love.

Truly history repeats itself Centuries ago Paul and Barnabas were unlawfully and brutally beaten at Philippi for preaching the Gospel—the same offense for which Chiniquy was repeatedly stoned. But when the jailer who had thrust them in the inner prison and made their feet fast in the stocks received the word of the Lord " he took them the same hour of the night, and washed their stripes; and was baptized, he and all his, straightway." It was the church thus founded in a stormy conflict that afterwards sent gifts by the hands of Epaphroditus to Paul when a prisoner in Rome. So we have seen it with our own eyes—the people who had denounced and hunted and stoned Chiniquy, when renewed by Divine grace, vying with each other to do him honour. In the face of these facts who will say that his life has been a failure, or that there has not been the most cheering and significant growth of the spirit of toleration in this old province of Quebec? In this all patriotic Canadians should rejoice, and quit them like men and true Christians by seeking to promote the true unity and prosperity of our great dominion by bringing the entire population under the power of the Gospel

I close this imperfect sketch with the words which I uttered before the thousands assembled in Erskine Church regarding the late venerable Dr Chiniquy:

Now that his life-work is done, and he rests from his labours, it may be profitable to ask, how are we to regard him? I answer:

He was a distinguished man, of unique personality and mission, who will not soon be forgotten. In many respects he stood alone, a commanding figure in our country and century His ancestry and education I need not trace. This has been done by his own pen. and his exceptionally high endowments, his literary theological and dialectic skill and genius have been sufficiently dwelt upon by the press His numerous publications, translated into many languages, and widely circulated in many parts of the world, are a lasting monument to his ability and industry

His missionary labours were not confined to one country or continent. His apostolic zeal in disseminating the truth carried him through Canada, the United States, Britain, Australia, Tasmania, the Sandwich Islands, New Zealand and portions of Europe; and by means of his printed works, brilliant and fascinating in style, he has been heard, and will continue to be a powerful factor in the thought and life of regions upon which his eyes never rested "He being dead yet speaketh."

He will be remembered as an enthusiastic reformer. In early manhood, and, indeed, to the end of his own life, this was his proper *role*, not an easy one, as proven by all true reformers—religious, social, and scientific. The qualities required for such a mission are of the highest order—faith in God and man, courage, patience, gentleness, love, indomitable perseverance, a spirit of self-sacrifice and willingness to work and suffer and die for the truth and the vindication of human rights.

It will be too much to say of the deceased, or of any mere man, that he possessed these and kindred attributes in perfection, but the record of his many struggles gives evidence of the high degree in which he manifested many of them; and that he achieved memorable successes has been acknowledged by all This was conspicuously the case in his heroic single-handed battle with the demon of intemperance, when he gained a glorious victory, for which he received marked recognition by the citizens of Montreal, and was publicly thanked by the parliament of the province in 1851 This is but one instance of victory. Need I remind you that he lived to see many other views for which he contended triumphant? We all know how toleration, independent thought and action regarding matters civil and religious, have advanced during the last forty years In these respects Quebec of to-day is not what it was for the preceding century, and, by the blessing of God upon the labours of the deceased and others who will continue his mission, brighter days are yet to dawn. What is needed is a larger measure of his faith and manly fortitude. How often in his multitudinous controversies did he appear hedged in upon all sides—surrounded by frowning, impassible, mountain difficulties, but his courage never gave way. In the face of them all, like heroes of the past whom we delight to honour, his cry was ever, " Who art thou, O great mountain? Who is weak, and I am

not weak? I can do all things through Christ who strength-
eneth me "

What if in the conflicts through which reformers necessa-
rily pass there is more than a little which they and we,
as well as timid, ease-loving. peace-loving onlookers deplore
shall we not in spite of this, and in the exercise of that
broad Christian charity which rejoiceth in the truth, and
thinketh no evil. credit them in the face of convincing evidence to that effect with sincerity of purpose, and manliness
of conduct in seeking to be first pure and then peaceful? I
tell you what you all know, that men of this type are
especially needed in our day, and should be highly esteemed
—men of undaunted boldness and holy rashness, if you will.
who fear not to challenge things as they are and have been,
and who risk everything in the effort to secure to their fellow men the full enjoyment of their God-given heritage of
civil and spiritual freedom This was the practical altruism
by which Dr Chiniquy was largely characterized

Hence, I venture to think, further, that he will be remembered as a true patriot. The fire of loyalty to our sovereign
and country burns with ardour in the breasts of his fellow
countrymen, but in none with greater intensity than was felt
by the heart of him whose remains lie silent before us His
was a patriotism, a love of country, which was thoroughly
outspoken. based upon Christian principles, and therefore
united with a catholicity of spirit which enabled him to
rejoice in the good and prosperity of the many other countries that enjoyed his labours. Hence, with the Master he
could heartily say, "The field is the world," and with the
apostle of the Gentiles he uniformly felt and said, "My
heart's desire and prayer to God for my countrymen is that
they may be saved." With all his love of freedom, and as
the champion of the right of private judgment and free
speech on the platform and in the press. this was the great
impelling motive of his life: that his dear countrymen might

enjoy the liberty with which Christ makes His people free

We do not say that in his strenuous efforts for this purpose he never erred. God forbid None could be more ready than Dr. Chiniquy to confess to God in the closet his weaknesses and failures and sins. And how often have thousands heard him say so in public, and declare that his only hope was in the all-sufficient and infinitely efficacious blood of atonement, which cleanseth from all sins In this faith he lived, and in this faith he died. You have read his testimony on his death-bed to this effect; and were the lips that are now silent once more unsealed they would declare with an eloquence inspired from the kingdom of glory, "It is true—I know by blessed experience that Jesus Christ, and He alone, saves to the uttermost all that come unto God by Him'

It is no exaggeration to say that the strongest wish of Dr Chiniquy's heart through life was that his countrymen, whom he passionately loved, might accept this glorious message

I testify what I have seen. I have been with him in the solitude of his chamber, when he prayed for them with an earnestness which reminded me of what is recorded of Knox, the great Scottish reformer, when he cried to God, "O give me Scotland or I die."

Finally, I venture to think that the memory of Dr. Chiniquy, as a broad-minded, far-seeing, Christian patriot, will have a permanent place in the history of Canada, and prove an inspiration to thousands of his countrymen to cling to the truth and the Saviour he so fervently proclaimed That truth he ever sought to put into the hands of every man as his birthright To its supreme and infallible authority alone, and not to any man or council, he yielded unquestioning submission, and by the preaching of his blessed Saviour, who is "the way, the truth, and life," he was honoured of God in bringing many thousands from darkness to light. These shall be his joy and crown of glorying before our Lord Jesus at His coming, and then it will appear that the struggles and sorrows of life, however painful and prolonged, are not worthy to be compared with the glory that shall be revealed, for "They that be wise shall shine as the brightness of the firmament, and they that turn many to righteousness as the stars forever and ever"

PREFACE

I had no thought of writing this book till the meeting of the General Assembly of the Presbyterian Church of Canada, in 1889 I was then on the eve of celebrating my eightieth birthday, and on the motion of the Rev. Dr. MacVicar, Principal of the Presbyterian College, Montreal, and Rev Dr. Warden, Secretary-Treasurer of the Board of French Evangelization, the Assembly passed a vote of congratulation as a public expression of Christian esteem towards me At the same time, a resolution was unanimously adopted to invite me to write a new book under the name of 'Thirty Years in the Church of Christ," as a sequel to my last book, "Fifty Years in the Church of Rome."

I could not but yield to that request. for I felt that it would not be doing justice to my God and to myself to write of my half-century of bondage under Rome, and not give an account of my glorious liberty under Christ; so I have taken steps to prepare a book containing some of the most striking incidents and events since I came into the possession of the full and blessed light of the Gospel, covering now nearly forty years

During this last period of my life, which has been very eventful, I have traveled in many countries and visited different continents, and I have given thousands of sermons and lectures, and thus in spreading the Gospel I have had the opportunity of seeing human nature in its varied aspects. As these experiences of mine illustrate the saying, "truth is sometimes stranger than fiction," I feel that what I have to say in this work is adapted to interest as well as to impart very useful knowledge.

The Christian readers of this book will wish to know at

17

first some of the ways through which our merciful God has
brought me from the feet of the Pope to those of the Lamb
who has made me free and pure with His blood. In the
first part of this work I aim to satisfy such a reasonable
desire

As history is philosophy teaching by example, I endeavour
to give in the book, as a whole, facts which suggest and teach
lessons, and stir up greater activity on the part of Protestants
to resist the aggressions of Romanism, and to spread the
truth among the benighted dupes and slaves of the Pope.

In an important sense, I have written this book because I
could not help it   The truth I have is not my own—it be-
longs to my heavenly Father, and the treasure in the earthen
vessel I am bound to give to others as far as I can

With this feeling and purpose, I send forth this volume on
its mission, hoping that it will be doing good after I am gone,
and thus, though dead, I still may speak to others

CONTENTS

19

20 Contents

Contents

INVOCATION

MERCIFUL HEAVENLY FATHER.—To obey Thee, when speak
ing to me through Thy Church. I will tell Thy children some
of the things I have seen, heard and done since the blessed
day that Thou hast given me Thy saving light   Do Thou help
me . . . guide my thoughts and my pen in such a way that
everything I say will be for Thy glory and the good of Thy
redeemed ones.   AMEN!

FATHER CHINIQUY AT 50 YEARS OF AGE

CHAPTER I

A Sketch of My Life Before the Dawn of the Saving Light

When relating the story of the mercies of God towards me these last forty years, I cannot ignore that my Christian leaders will like to know something of my priestly life, so I will give them a sketch of the most remarkable events of my life before the dawn of the saving light of the Gospel came in its fulness upon me.

I was born at Kamouraska, on the 30th of July, 1809. My father, Charles Chiniquy, was a notary. My mother's name was Marie Reine Perreault. My grandfather, Martin Et Chiniquia, was a fearless sailor from French Biscay in the service of the king of France. His ship, like many of the ships of those days, being half military and half merchant, was well known by the English war-ships with which he had several encounters. Wolf, on his way to capture Quebec, in 1759, seized and forced Et Chiniquia with other pilots to navigate the fleet through the dangerous St. Lawrence river.

Several times, when a young lad, I heard him telling us how, during the way up the river to Quebec, there were two soldiers with pistols close to his ears, in order to blow out his brains if his ships touched the bottom; but he did his duty so well, though reluctantly, that his new masters, after the conquest of Quebec, rewarded him by putting him the head master of the harbour of that city.

My father went to Murray Bay when I was still young, and died there suddenly. It was in a year when the crops had failed and there was a famine raging all around. Our only support was the milk of a cow which had been given me when a calf by the landlord, Nairn. But the priest wrenched that

27

providential support from my mother on the pretense of taking the soul of my father from the flames of purgatory. We came very near starving to death, fortunately, my mother had a sister married to a very rich merchant of Kamouraska, Mr. Dionne, who came to take me as his own child. My father had studied to be priest before being married, taking a complete course of theology in the seminary of Quebec, and had received as a token of esteem from the Superior of the seminary a magnificent Sacy Bible, half in Latin and half in French As there were no schools near us in Murray Bay, my mother was my first teacher, and the book in which I learned to read was the Bible, and the first word I learned to spell, by the providence of God, was "B-i-b-l-e"

I was exceedingly fond of reading that Book and the time I was not giving to fishing, or catching hares, was spent in reading its marvelous pages. I not only read them, but learned by heart, under the guidance of my mother, the most interesting parts It was not without childish pride that I recited those chapters to the farmers who used to come to my father's office. I will never forget one beautiful Sabbath day, going to church with my mother. A farmer asked me if I would not recite before the whole crowd the chapter he had heard from me the week before in my father's house. Having consented, he took me in his arms, placed me in his *calèche* and there I recited in my best style the story of the Prodigal Son. There was not a dry eye when I finished; but the priest, his name was Courtois, having heard that a child had given a chapter of the Bible to his people, thought it advisable to put a stop to such a *scandal.* The next morning he was early at my father's house to get that Bible and burn it. Trembling by the side of my mother, lest my Bible be given up to be destroyed, I was listening with a breathless attention for my father's answer, and my heart leaped with unspeakable joy when I heard him showing the door to the priest, saying, "You know what door by which you entered, take the same door and go." It was the first and last time I ever saw one of the priests in my father's house, they not being on good terms, though I never knew why.

Not very long after I was at Kamouraska, the celebrated Bishop Duplessis came to give the confirmation. He was a personal friend of my uncle Dionne, who received him as his guest. He had specially noticed me among the little boys in the choir and learning that I was his host's nephew, he called for me in the parlour when surrounded by his priests. He took me by the hand, and said, "Look at me, my little boy How old are you? . . . Would you not like to be a priest?" My mother had asked me that question many times before and I had always answered. "Yes, mother." In my mind there was nothing so exalted on earth or in heaven, after God, as a priest, so with a trembling voice I answered the Bishop: "Yes, my lord, I would like to be a priest" Then the Bishop looking at my uncle said to him, "Mr. Dionne, have you any objection to sending that dear little boy to my college in Nicolet, perhaps we shall make a bishop of him?" My uncle answered: "My lord, I will be very happy to send him to your college," and he kept his word The next fall it was my privilege to begin a course of study in the college of Nicolet which I finished with good success in the year 1829.

After spending four years as a teacher of Belles-Lettres in the same college of Nicolet, I was ordained a priest on the 31st of September, 1833, by Archbishop Sinaï, of Quebec.

The next day I was sent to St. Charles, Rivière Boyer, as vicar of the Reverend M. Perras, where I remained only eight months. The Reverend M Bédard, curate of Charlesbourg, who had been one of my father's teachers in theology, having expressed the desire that I should take charge of his parish during the summer while he would accompany the Bishop in his visits in the diocese, I left St Charles for Charlesbourg in the beginning of June. It was there that God had prepared me one of the most terrible trials of my life. I had hardly been a week in my new charge when my parish was attacked by the cholera morbus. In the short space of a

month I buried more than thirty of my parishioners. Day
and night I had to be about, consoling the sick and preparing
the dying After having spent the day in visiting the sick,
besides the burials, I had to spend the night in hearing confessions As there were no physicians around, I had to take
care of the bodies as well as the souls. And those of my
readers who would like to know anything about that terrible
plague, which made so many victims in Canada during that
year, may read it, in my book "Fifty Years in the Church of
Rome" When M Bédard came back from his visits with
the Bishop, the plague was over, and I, after two months of
deserved rest, was named for one of the vicars of M Tétu,
curate of St Rock, Quebec It was there that I had the
providential opportunity of studying the laws of anatomy in
the Marine hospital of Quebec, under the celebrated Dr
Douglas, and it was there, after studying four years the rav-
ages of alcohol in the human frame, I went on my knees and
swore that I would never drink any more of those deadly
alcoholic beverages, and that I would do all in my power to
persuade my countrymen to do the same thing To day people would hardly believe me, would I tell them the commotion
it created when the next day I refused to take my glass of wine
and beer at the table A few days later the Bishop sent for
me to know if what he had heard was true He gave me a
severe lecture and ordered me to give up that resolution, but
I stood firm as a rock. In vain he tried to persuade me that
it was a heresy, already condemned by the church, to have such
narrow views concerning wine and beer, but to everything
he said I told him that I had studied that question in the
best book, written by God himself, which was the human
body, and that I had seen with my eyes that every drop
which goes into the body is a poison. Among my arguments,
I opened his Bible and read in the twenty-third chapter of
Proverbs, verse thirty-one, " Look not upon the wine when it
is red, when it giveth his colour in the cup, when it moveth itself
aright. At the last it biteth like a serpent and stingeth like

an adder " It was evident to me that the good Bishop did not remember ever having seen those words· he was so amazed at them.

But I must not omit here to say a word about the bloody insurrection of 1837–38 We knew that a conspiracy among our parishioners of St. Rock was organized to upset the English Government and to unite themselves with the United States. In the month of December, a few days before the battle of St Denis, we noticed a great excitement, and we were all in fear that we were fast approaching a terrible crisis. One evening Dr. Rousseau, who had been one of my classmates in Nicolet and who, of course, was very familiar, came about nine o'clock to our parsonage where there were five priests. We knew that he was a leader of the conspiracy against the government and he had evidently come to gain our influence to his views, and, with a freedom which filled me with disgust and distress, he revealed to us a part of their plans. Although we were in favour of reforms we were opposed to a civil war by which we poor, weak French Canadian people would be crushed by the mighty English nation I tried to show him the absurdity of the plans he was just speaking of to us, as hundreds of cannon of the impregnable citadel of Quebec could, in a few minutes, make a pie of the citizens of St Rock.

With impassioned words he answered me, "Ah, the citadel! the citadel! We are sure to get it opened when the day of justice comes The Irish Catholic guards are pledged to open the doors, and then we will put to the sword our merciless English tyrants inside and outside the citadel." I could not restrain myself any longer. I jumped at him saying, "You miserable traitor, you are not satisfied to be a traitor yourself, you want to make us your accomplices," and addressing myself to M, Tétu, I said, "You ought not to allow that man to come here to try and enroll us under his traitorous banner. I see now that they are preparing here a new St Bartholomew slaughter. I have suspected it for some time. but I will

oppose it so long as I have a drop of blood in my veins. I
prefer to be ruled by the noble English nation You ought
to turn that traitor out of here, but as you do not do it, I
will do it for you" Then taking hold of the back of his
neck by my right hand, I pushed him down stairs more
quickly than he had ever gone down before Then coming
up, I said to the priests· "It is evident that they are preparing one of those horrible tragedies which are a shame to our
religion and our nation. They want to slaughter the English
under the pretext that they are Protestants They rely on
the treachery of the Irish Catholics, who, being on guard at
the citadel, will open the doors I will go immediately to
the governor to warn him of the danger" Half an hour
later, I was with Governor Gasford. It was after ten o'clock
at night. "My lord," I said, "I come here on a solemn
errand. I want you to keep my message a secret between
you and me. There is a conspiracy among the Irish soldiers
of the garrison to open the door of the citadel and there will
be a general slaughter of you and the English people of Quebec in a few days if the insurgents of Montreal are victorious
in the first battle which is to be fought there." The governor thanked me and said, "Please give me the names of
the leaders of the conspiracy." I replied, "No, I cannot do
that I do not come here as an informant or traitor against
my own countrymen, I only want to save them from their
own folly as I want to save the English from the impending
danger I hope your lordship will thus understand the deli-
cacy of my position as I risk my life in what I am doing now.
You cannot ask any thing more. I ask on your honour not to
betray me Put only Protestants to guard your citadel"

A few days later the battle of St Denis was fought and
gained by the French Canadian patriots, but the plot of taking the citadel of Quebec had failed because, to the unspeakable dismay of the Quebec patriots, all the Irish guards at
the citadel had been changed.

It was not long after this incident that the Bishop, having

heard that I had given two lectures on the reasons we had to give up the use of intoxicating drinks, called me to his palace to ascertain if it were true that I had given these two addresses. Then, on my answering in the affirmative, he was beside himself with anger and, pacing up and down the room, said, "This teetotalism is only a Protestant affair. I will not allow any of my priests to proclaim those principles in Canada." I answered, "My lord, be calm, please, you are mistaken. Father Mathew now is blessed all over the world for preaching teetotalism in Ireland. It is only a few days since we read that the Pope had sent him his apostolic benediction." "Well," said he, "it may be very well for Ireland to have those doctrines preached, for is it a well-known fact that drunkenness is the great plague of that nation; but it is a different thing with our dear Canada. It is an insult to compare that nation with ours. Read that paper and you will see my opinion about you," and he presented me a sheet of paper written with his own hand, but not signed. What was my surprise and my dismay to read in that paper that he absolutely forbade me to preach teetotalism and if I did not submit to his will he threatened me with excommunication "It is not signed" said he, "but I will sign it the first time you disobey me" I replied: "My lord, evidently, if you had been near Zacharias when the angel came to tell him that his son would be great in the sight of the Lord, and would neither drink wine nor strong drink, you would have excommunicated that angel, and if you had been near the angel when he brought his message to the mother of Samson telling her not to drink wine or strong drink you would also have excommunicated him as you want to excommunicate me" My words fell upon him as a thunderbolt, and with a much subdued voice, he said, "I have not signed that, but will do it if you do not what I say. I am your superior." Then I said, "I will see what I will have to do when you excommunicate me," and I left him, trembling with indignation at his tyranny. A few weeks later the Bishop again called me to his palace and said. "Your father was my personal friend and my pupil. Like you, he had some good, but also some very bad qualities, and you have inherited only his good qualities. You offended me the other day by your stubborn resistance to my will. I want to punish you by putting you at the head of the parish of Beauport which has the reputation of possessing the greatest number of drunkards in Canada If you wish to fight the demon of intemperance you will have opportunities to do it there to your heart's content " Had he told me he would send me to the penitentiary, he would not have distressed me more, but in spite of all my objections, I had to accept the charge

Reverend M Begin, who was my predecessor in Beauport, was one of those good old Canadian priests who had taken his views on temperance from St Ligouri, who says that so long as a man can distinguish a pin from a load of hay he is not drunk. Not to be too long on this question, I found that the parish of Beauport, at the door of Quebec, was one of the oldest parishes of Canada, that its revenues were the richest. Its soil could not be surpassed, the fisheries were then exceedingly rich, their gardens, their limestones, with the forests around gave them incalculable resources. But they expended so much money in their drinking habits that they had never been able to have a school and teach their children, when they had seven taverns doing an immense business in their midst The number of drunkards, old and young, men and women, were so numerous that I do not dare to say. I would not be believed. To make such a people sober was surely above the strength of a man. But what is impossible to man is easy to our merciful God. With tears of sorrow and ardent prayer day and night, I asked God to help me to save that people.

Not long before, a fact had occurred which, though already in my former book, may have again its place here A lady in the highest ranks of society, but unfortunately a desperate drunkard, had killed her only child whilst drunk. Carrying her in her arms, she had fallen, and the head of the little one had struck the sharp angle of the stove with such force that the skull was fractured and the brains had been scattered on the floor   Death was instantaneous.   When called by the unfortunate husband, I found her in the arms of Dr. Blanchet, Coroner Panet, and her bereaved husband, trying to kill herself. She begged for a knife. She filled the house with her cries. "I am lost! I killed my darling, I want to be buried with her!"   Though four men were holding her it was with difficulty that we could prevent her from killing herself At about eleven o'clock at night she slipped from our hands, filling the house with her cries, ran to the cradle, and, quick as lightning, she took her child in her arms, tore the bandage which held the skull in place and pressed her face and her lips in the gaping wound   Then she ran around the room crying. "I am lost! I am damned!" and falling on her knees before me, she cried. " Dear Father Chiniquy, can a drunken woman who has killed her dear child be saved? Dear Lucy, can you not forgive me thy death? O cursed wine! Why did I not follow your advice when so often with tears you asked me to give up that cursed wine! Please take that blood and that brain, go around Canada, and put it on the top of every house in our country   Say it is the blood and brains of a child murdered by her drunken mother. Tell the people never to touch a drop of that wine. It is cursed in hell, cursed on earth, and cursed in heaven."   And when saying this, torrents of blood flowed from her mouth; a vein had burst, and she fell dead at our feet

Was not this a message from my God? The spectacle of that blood and of the corpses of those two victims of wine were stereotyped in a mysterious way into my whole being, and it gave me an energy, a power and eloquence which were not mine   That energy and power were irresistible, for I felt in that solemn hour they came direct from my God to me that I might fulfil a grand and blessed mission in my dear country.

Before a year had elapsed, the people of Beauport were the most sober people of Canada. Not a drop of liquor could be sold among them.

The God of the Gospel had again come to the touch of the dead Lazarus, and looking down in Divine compassion had shed tears of distress on the corpse of His dead friend, and said, "Lazarus, come forth," and Lazarus came out. The great God of heaven had taken by the hand the noble people of Beauport, and had made them march at the head of one of the greatest temperance reformations that not only Canada, but the whole world, has ever seen. I thought that my duty was to keep the remembrance of that remarkable event. I gave three hundred dollars to M. Leprohon, the best architect of Quebec, to make the column of Temperance which I asked the Bishop of Nancy to bless on the seventh of September, 1841.

This column is still standing and can be seen on the road going to the Falls of Montmorency, about half-way between Quebec and Beauport.

Why is it that the Roman Catholic clergy have not understood that it was an unpardonable crime and eternal shame to them to have allowed that great temperance work to drop since I left their idols to follow the God of the Gospel?

In the year 1842 when I left Beauport it was my unspeakable joy to see the seven taverns had disappeared and in their places seven thriving school-houses were filled with happy children.

When it was announced to me by the Bishop that I must leave Beauport for the parish of Kamouraska, that was almost a death blow to me and to my people. It was in vain that I tried to show the Bishops the injustice and undesirableness of such a change. Without mercy the Bishop told me, "Though Beauport is a very important place, Kamouraska is, in our eyes, still more important." It was then the only summer resort of the people of Quebec and Montreal. "The old curate Varin is dying, and we have no other priest to take his place there   It is the parish where you were born, and we hope you will make no resistance when we ask you to leave your dear Beauport for Kamouraska without any delay. The God who has blessed you in such a marvelous way in Beauport will bless you again in the same way in Kamouraska, and we hope that the triumph of the grace of God will be as great as it has been in Beauport."

Let those of my readers who wish to know the interesting details of my four years sojourn in Kamouraska, read it in the "Fifty Years in the Church of Rome"   Suffice it to say that during that time, by the great mercy of God I had the joy of enrolling under the banners of temperance not only the grand and noble parish of Kamouraska, but all the parishes for more than one hundred miles below.   Also the parishes around Lake Tamiscouata and to Point Levis, on the south shore of the St. Lawrence River, and on the north shore from Quebec to Murray Bay

The year before I went to Kamouraska one hundred tuns of rum had been sold by the merchants, and the debts of the people to those merchants were $250,000   By the great mercy of God the last year I was there not ten gallons of intoxicating drinks had been sold in the whole parish and the immense debt had been reduced to $150,000

At first I had been fiercely opposed in my temperance work by Reverend M. Mailloux of St Anne de la Pocatière, and Quertier of St Denis, but after two years they honourably changed their views and came with great zeal and ability to help me fight the common foe   But I could not stand such herculean work any longer   To fulfil the duties of curate at Kamouraska and establish the societies of temperance was too much for a single man, so, in 1846, I said to the Bishop: "I think it is the will of God that I should fight the demon of intemperance all over the country, and if you have no objection, as the Bishop of Montreal has invited me to establish societies of temperance in the parishes of his immense diocese, I will go and join the good monks of the

Oblats of Mary Immaculate   There are not less than thirty priests there who will help me in my temperance work, and instead of being alone to fight our giant enemy—"Rum"— I will have a real army of true soldiers of Christ to help me "

But, before leaving Kamouraska, I had received a letter from a very dear but very poor friend in Quebec who was blessed with a very large family. His letter drew my tears·—"You know my sad position," he said, "overwhelmed with a family which is absolutely out of my power to give the material as well as intellectual bread to, which every father owes to his children   I have been impressed with a thought several months   You have studied the question of anatomy and all the injuries done to man by all the intoxicating drinks   Your success in fighting the demon of intemperance is marvelous, it seems to me that you could write a book on temperance which would be welcomed into every French Canadian family   That book would bring a great deal of money   I have said to myself, " If dear Father Chiniquy would write that book and give me the benefit of the first two editions, it would not damage him, and it would lift me up, and give me the means to provide for the future of my dear children. Can you do that, M Chiniquy? If you can, there will be a blessing upon you for time and eternity."

I had never thought of writing a book on that subject, but the desire to save that family which was very dear to me came as a flash of light   I went on my knees, and I said, "If it is Thy will, O God, that I should write a good book on temperance, I promise that the first two editions shall belong to that dear friend of mine "

Three months later the book called the "Manual of Temperance" was finished, but I had not the time to copy the manuscript   I rolled it up in its crudeness, went to the captain of a schooner, called Béchard, who was to sail the very next day for Quebec   "Do you know such a man in Quebec?" I asked him, " he has a large family, but is as poor as a church lat." "Well," I said, "when in Quebec, please go and give him this roll of paper, with this small letter," and in this small letter I said, "My dear friend, here is the answer to your letter of four months ago I have worked day and night to write the book you asked for. Make two editions of it for your own benefit Keep every cent for yourself and your dear children, and when those two editions shall be exhausted. give me back my manuscript: and may the Lord bless and prosper you is the prayer of your devoted friend,

C CHINIQUY.'

A week later—this was in the fall—Captain Béchard was knocking at my door. I could hardly recognize him, he looked twenty years older than when I had seen him. His voice was suffocated in his sobs. "Well." I said, "what is the matter, my dear friend, with you?" He replied, "Ah, dear Father Chiniquy, I have lost my precious schooner. She was wrecked in this last terrible storm on the rocks between Berthier and St Valier It is by a miracle that I escaped with the rest of the crew. I have been picked up unconscious on the sand where I had been hurled by a furious wave" "And the little bundle of paper I gave you, where is it?" "It is lost," he replied, "I had put it in my trunk which is now at the bottom of the river. The little money which I had gained this year, and was taking to Quebec to pay my debts, is lost also, every cent of it I am ruined! What will now become of my poor family?" I answered, "My papers cannot be lost, and for yourself, do not despair of the future "

I went to my drawer, took some old papers, put them into his hands and said, "Here are twenty-five pounds to help you from your wreck, and I pledge myself to get twice that amount from my rich uncle Dionne. You know the noble-hearted, farmers of Kamouraska will also help you to get another schooner. Cheer up! Never give up your confidence in God "

We knelt and prayed and we wept together. And then

again I said, "Where do you think I can find your little trunk with my paper?" "It cannot be found," he said, "it was dashed with the rest on the rocks, I spent four days to find all that could be found on the shores." I dismissed him, went to my servant man and said, "Hitch up the horse and buggy. I want to go to Quebec without a moment of delay ' The roads were very bad It took us two days to reach the first house of St. Valier. There I broke one of the wheels of my buggy in a ditch I went to the next house After taking some refreshment and rest, I said to the landlord, "Have you heard anything of the wreck of Béchard's schooner?" "Ah, yes," he said, "it has been a complete wreck It was dashed upon the rocks and torn to pieces " "Have you found anything on the shore?" I asked. "Nothing of any account, except this morning when I saw a little trunk entangled in the mud and branches and I brought it here and gave it to my wife " "Can I see that little trunk?' I said "Oh yes sir " It was there in a corner all dripping wet I opened it and the first thing I saw under the cover was my manuscript I fell on my knees and thanked God for this providential discovery. Then I took it myself to my friend in Quebec Some weeks later I received a letter from Reverend M. Ballargon, curate of Quebec, and who became, later. Archbishop, with these lines which I copy, word for word

"Your marvelous little book, 'Manual of Temperance' is just published I began the reading of it before going to bed, and do you know I was not able to sleep before I had finished it. I went yesterday morning to my Quebec parishioners and I told them. 'After the Gospel, this is the best book you can read. It is written by Father Chiniquy, and I hope in a few days I shall hear there is a copy in every house in Quebec and in all Canada ' The result was that the next three days three thousand copies of your book were sold at fifty cents each, and I hope that ten thousand more will be sold, so that the whole country may bless you "

My friend, by the great mercy of God, was taken out of his

misery to a position of ease, and being intelligent and industrious pushed himself up and now his children are among the first families of Canada for their wealth, talents and respectability. Of course their father died long ago, and if you ask me what those children are now doing to show their gratitude toward me, I will tell you. Ordered by their priests, they curse me because I believe and preach that there is only one name under heaven by which we can be saved.

So I went to Longueuil in 1846 and received a warm reception both from the Bishop of Montreal and the Oblats there. But, after a year of novitiate, I saw very strange things in that institution which proved to me that those monks were only comedians. I will give here only one instance

I had as an associate to advocate the temperance cause in St. Hyacinthe a French monk by the name of Guignes. He had the direction of the first part of the service and, before beginning his address on the evil of drinking wine, he used to say to the faithful in a most pious tone. "Let us pray, dear brethren, the Good Mother of Christ to persuade you of the evil of intemperance;" and as all the people, listening to such an earnest appeal, threw themselves on their knees with bowed heads, the good monk took out from his garb a flask and sipped his wine with great relish and with such zest that I could see he expected more inspiration from his bottle than from Mary.

I cannot help mentioning also here another adventure which proves that some Canadian priests, as well as some French monks, were not sincere in their profession of temperance, but were dragged into that great movement by the enthusiam of the people

When speaking in the same town six months later, the morning after the first address, the curate of the parish, Mr. Crevier, came to me at breakfast wringing his hands with unspeakable distress. I asked, "What is the matter with you, Monsieur le Curé?" He replied, "Have you not heard the awful noise last night when they destroyed my distillery?"

"What," said I, "have you a distillery?" "Yes," he said
"And you invited me to preach temperance when you have a
distillery to spread drunkenness?" "Yes, I thought it was a
good and profitable way to invest money." "In that case,"
I said, "I rejoice that the people have been prompt enough
to see your duplicity and punish you as you deserve" I must
add that the temperance people, without my knowledge as
well as without my instigation, had invaded the distillery
during the night and made havoc with it, breaking all the
machinery.

At the end of my novitiate, when I was about to take the
vows of allegiance to the Society, being asked, according to
usage, by the Superior to mention before all my confreres
my decision as to joining the Oblats, I said, "You will be
disappointed, as I have been myself. After having been
associated with you in the hope of becoming an Oblate, my
conscience tells me that the only thing I have to do is to
leave you and do my providential work alone under the
supervision of the Bishop and the co-operation of the secular
clergy."

After I left the Oblats I carried on during four years
the crusade of temperance with wonderful and blessed
results.

In the year 1850 I received a letter from Bishop Vandeveld
of Chicago, Ill., inviting me to go and help him to make a New
France of Illinois by directing the tide of the French immigration towards the magnificent plains of Illinois which were
then almost entirely a wilderness. Seeing in this invitation
a call of Providence to fulfil another great mission for my
countrymen and my Church in founding a colony, after having
been the instrument in the hands of God to draw my countrymen out of the mire of drunkenness, I gladly accepted it, and
with the blessing of my Bishop and his reluctant consent I
exiled myself to the neighbouring great Republic To my unspeakable joy I saw myself soon surrounded by thousands of
French-speaking people who had responded to my fervent

appeals published both in Europe and Canada.   Soon flourish-
ing parishes of my countrymen gladdened my heart and rewarded my labours as a colonizer

But my new calling was not a sky without a cloud   There
also I had my tribulations and sad revelations about my
Church, which darkened my mind and weakened my faith in
it.   About a year after my arrival, Bishop Vandeveld came to
me with tears in his eyes and announced to me that he had
decided to abandon the diocese of Illinois for the one of
Natchez, because, said he, " I cannot bear any longer the corruption of my priests.   There are only five honest priests in
this diocese, so I asked the Pope as a favour to transfer me to
another place "

Holding in great respect and affection this Bishop, I felt
very keenly his departure, and had I known who was to
succeed him, I would have felt it still more bitterly.

His successor was Bishop O'Regan, the most tyrannical and
shameless rogue that I ever had to deal with

After several years of contest with that Bishop, who was a
notorious defender of drunkenness and immorality among the
priests of his diocese, and who was guilty of simony, theft and
brigandage himself, I wrote to Pope Pius IX, enclosing
documentary evidence of the Bishop's guilt, with the result
that after a full investigation the corrupt prelate was
deposed.

Bishop Smith of Dubuque, Iowa, the new administrator of
the diocese, deputed the Rev. Mr Dunn, Grand Vicar of
Chicago, to seek an interview with me, and thank me for
having rid the diocese of such a depraved man, but at the same
time to inform me that I and my people were suspected of
being more Protestants than Catholics, and to urge me to draw
up a document which would prove to all the world that I and
they were still good Roman Catholics.

As I was considering what form this document should take,
the thought seized me, "Is not this the golden opportunity to
put an end to the terrible temptations which have shaken my

faith and distressed me for so many years?" I determined to
frame my submission in such a way that I might make sure
that the faith of my dear Church was based upon the Holy
Word of God and not the lying traditions of men.

I then wrote down, "My Lord Bishop Smith,—We French
Canadians of Illinois want to live and die in the Holy
Catholic Apostolic and Roman Church, out of which there is
no salvation, and to prove this to your lordship, we promise
to obey the authority of the Church according to the Word
and Commandments of God as we find them expressed in the
Gospel of Christ"

The Grand Vicar thought that the act of submission was just
what was wanted, but I had my grave doubts whether the condition of only submitting to the Bishop's authority according
to the Word of God and the Gospel of Christ would ever be
accepted My surprise was therefore great when Bishop
Smith, having read the document, received it with joy, and
gave me in return, to show to both friends and foes, a testimonial letter which contained the highest expressions of
esteem for me both in public and private character.

But the Jesuits of Chicago were soon at work, and raised
a great storm, saying that I was no more than a disguised
Protestant, and that I must be compelled to submit to the
unconditional authority of the Bishops

I was again sent for by the Bishop, who, as a prelude to the
conversation asked me for the testimonial letter, which when
produced and handed over, was arbitrarily committed to the
flames without one word of explanation. "Mr. Chiniquy" he
said, "I ordered you here because you have deceived me in
giving me a document which you know is not an act of submission; I hope as a good priest you do not want to rebel
against your Bishop. Take away the words—Word of God
—and—Gospel of Christ—from your act of submission, or I
will punish you as a rebel." To this I calmly replied "What
you ask me is not an act of submission, it is an act of adoration. I do absolutely refuse to give it" "If that be so, sir,"

said the Bishop, "you can be no longer a Catholic priest."

I raised my hands to heaven and cried: "May God Almighty be forever blessed." and I left the room.

Such, in brief, are the ways through which God, in His mercy, called me to pass, in order that I might come to the full light of His glorious truth.

So far, I have spoken almost exclusively of the external warfare I had to wage against the representatives of Rome before I could come to the spring whence flows the pure water after which my soul was panting

But the most terrible struggles I had to sustain were within, in my poor heart, bruised by the great conflict of moral and spiritual forces, whose issue is always victory of truth or error, of God or the devil

I will take my readers in my next chapter to this invisible battle-field, and I will relate to them what God has done for my soul.

CHAPTER II

The Light Breaks upon Me. After Much Struggle I Accept Christ and Eternal Life as a Gift. I Present the Gift to My People Who Likewise Accept It.

I remained twenty-five years in the Church of Rome as one of her most devoted priests.

During that whole time I sincerely believed that the Church of Rome was the only Church of Christ, and I did all in my power to extend the authority of that Church in America and other continents

But when in that Church I had to believe and preach, with all the priests that out of the Church of Rome there was no salvation; and my heart was very sad when, looking upon you, Protestants, I had to believe that you were all to perish and go to hell after death.

I thought that my duty was to convert as many Protestants as I could and bring them into submission to the Pope. It seemed to me that the best way to persuade the Protestants to become Roman Catholics was to study the Bible as well as I could, and challenge your Protestant ministers to a public discussion in order to prove to you that your ministers do not know the Holy Scriptures. and that they were deceitful and ignorant men, and that you ought not to pay any attention to their teachings, but that you should come to hear the priests of Rome and accept their doctrines.

With that thought in my mind I studied the Holy Bible more than the priests of Rome are accustomed to do

Many times I spent, not only the whole day, but the night, in studying the pages of the Holy Book, in order that I might be able to show to the Protestants that they were deceived by their ministers, and that their duty was to sub-

46

mit themselves to the Pope of Rome, if they wanted to be saved

I had a great love and respect for the Holy Scriptures   I never opened the Holy Book without addressing a fervent prayer to God to guide me in my study in such a way that I might be more and more every day a good, a faithful and a holy priest of Rome.

But, strange to say, I never read the Holy Book without hearing a secret and mysterious voice, in the bottom of my soul, troubling my faith, and telling me: "Do you not see that, in your Church of Rome, you do not follow the Word of God—but you follow and teach the lying traditions of men!"

That mysterious voice was telling me, "Are you not ashamed to invoke so many names of saints and angels when your Gospel tells you so clearly that there is only one name which must be invoked to be saved?

"Are you not ashamed to say to the Virgin Mary, in your Breviarium, 'Thou art the only hope of sinners,' when the Gospel tells you that 'Jesus is the only hope—the only Saviour of the World?'"

One day that mysterious voice spoke to me as the voice of thunder, after I had said to my people that, after their death, their souls were to go and spend many years in the flames of purgatory to be purified from their sins

"Shame upon you," said the voice, "to speak of a purgatory of which there is not a word in your Gospel!"

"Do you not read," said the voice, "that it is only through the blood of Jesus that the souls of men can be purified?

"Come out! Come out from such a church, where you preach doctrines absolutely opposed to the teachings of the Holy Gospel!"

These voices were evidently the voice of my God! But I had to take them for the voice of the devil, for the Pope was telling me it was the devil's voice.

When studying the theological books written by St.

Liguori, St Thomas, and all the other theologians, I had to believe that my Church of Rome had received from Christ the right to burn, imprison and kill all the heretics and the Protestants when she was strong enough to do so. But my Gospel was telling me with a thundering power that this was the devil's doctrine, opposed to the Gospel For Christ had rebuked His disciples when they wanted to bring fire from heaven to punish those who refused to allow Him to go into their town

So there was, many times, a great trouble in my soul For those two voices were heard, and, to please the Pope and remain in the Church of Rome, I had constantly to take the voice of God for that of the devil, and I had to accept the voice of the devil for the voice of my God

Thus it was that, during twenty-five years, my God with His merciful hand was trying to take me away from a false system of religion But to obey the Pope I had to resist—I had to struggle against my God.

But in that long struggle, my God was to be the stronger —and the blessed day had come when my merciful Saviour was to come to me as a conqueror, with His mighty power

That blessed day, I was alone in my little study room, reading my Bible, when the voice of my God spoke with such power that I could not be mistaken

"Come out! Come out from the Church of Rome!" said that thundering voice, 'You cannot be saved in that church where you make your own god every morning, with a piece of dough' No man can make his god with his own hands. Did not Paul say to the Athenians that God could not be made with gold and silver, or marble? He cannot more be made with a piece of dough' Come out! Come out from the Church of Rome!"

Falling on my knees with burning tears rolling down my cheeks, I was crying to my God. "O my God, if the Church of Rome is not Thy Church, where is Thy Church? Where can I go to be saved? Is it possible, O my God, that the Church of Rome, so grand, so old! the Church of so many mighty nations! the Church of my mother! the Church of my dear country! the Church which has been so good to me, so high in the eyes of my fellow men, is not Thy Church!

"I beseech Thee, O my God, give me some more rays of Thy light, that I may see where is Thy Church, and that I may accept it!"

But for more than one hour I prayed in vain for light!

Instead of light my God was wrapping my trembling soul with the darkest clouds.

But after more than an hour of the most unspeakable desolation I felt that my God had heard my humble supplications

Suddenly before the eyes of my soul there was something very strange, but marvelously amazing

It was a light! And in the very midst of that light, my Saviour was nailed to the cross!

Oh I could not be mistaken! It was my beloved Saviour which was there! The crown of thorns was on His bleeding brow—His hands were nailed to the cross—and His body was covered with bleeding wounds!

And He was coming to me!   .   When very near I heard His sweet voice telling me:

"My dear friend, I have heard thy cries—I have seen thy tears, I come to bring thee eternal life as a gift

"My Father has so much loved thee, that He has sent Me. His eternal Son Jesus, to save thee by dying on the cross!

' On that cross I have paid thy debts to My eternal Father's justice. and I have paid them to the last cent!

"On that cross I have asked and obtained thy pardon! On that cross I have bought for thee an eternal life which I bring thee, just now, as a gift of My eternal love! Look up and see the crown of glory I have brought for thee "

And when my dear Saviour was speaking to me these marvelous words He was giving me grace to understand them as much as a man can do

I looked up and I saw, what I hope every one of my readers will see just now, if you look up with the eyes of your soul. For the crown was not only for me, it was for everyone of you also.

Yes, I looked up, and I saw with the eyes of my soul, a crown! But what a rich, what a precious crown!

And on that crown I saw my name written with the blood of the Lamb!

And my beloved Saviour was telling me, "I present thee that crown as a gift of My love; . . . take it. . . . The only thing I want from thee is thy faith, thy repentance, thy love!"

My Saviour said again, "Look up."

And I looked up again, and I saw what every one of you will see, if, with the eyes of your soul, you look up to Christ. I saw a throne! But what a glorious throne! No! Never any mortal king or emperor has sat on such a glorious throne!

And my name was written on that throne with the blood of the Lamb! And my beloved Saviour was telling me: "I present thee that throne as a gift of My love I have shed My blood to the last drop. I died the most horrible death to buy that throne;   take it

"The only thing I want from you is that you believe in My love—repent and love Me!"

It was then, that more with my tears of joy than with my lips, I said to my beloved Saviour.

"Oh, dear Jesus—Precious Gift—how sweet Thy words are to my heart. Yes, I will love Thee to-day, to-morrow and forever   .   Oh! Precious Gift! Beloved Jesus! Come and abide in my heart to make it pure. Abide in my soul to fill it with Thy love. Oh! Precious Gift! Dear Jesus, abide in me to-day, to-morrow and forever, that I may be one with Thee the few days I remain in the land of pilgrimage."

To make a long story short, I must tell you, my dear readers, that I opened, for the first time, the hands of my soul, and that I took possession of the gift—the precious gift, the immortal gift, which our eternal God had sent to me!

It is then that, for the first time, I understood that great mystery of the love of God, which the Pope ignores, and which is so sadly concealed from the eyes of the honest but so cruelly deceived Roman Catholics, that eternal life is a gift. . . .

No human words can tell you the joy of my heart when, for the first time, I opened the hands of my soul and accepted the gift, the great gift, the immortal gift.

It was then that, pressing that new Gospel to my heart, and bathing it with the tears of my joy, I swore that I would never preach anything but that Gospel, in which I had just found that eternal life is a gift.

It was then that I said to my dear Saviour, "By offering me eternal life as a gift, Thou hast forever taken away from my shoulders the heavy yoke of the Pope. Thou hast saved me. But I do not want to be saved alone! Save my people. Grant me ever more to show them that eternal life is a gift of Thy love; . . . grant me to help them also to break the heavy and unbearable yoke of the Pope

"Oh, that my dear people may know, to-morrow, that Jesus has saved them! That Jesus has paid their debts, that Jesus has bought for them an eternal life, on the cross—and that He wants nothing from them but to repent, believe and love!"

This marvelous revelation was given to me on a Saturday afternoon   I spent a sleepless night.

I was too happy to shut my eyes and sleep. When a man has just received such a gift, how can he forget it and sleep?

Many times during that happy night, with tears of joy, I said with David "Oh, my soul, bless the Lord! and let all that is within me bless His holy name"

The next day was the Lord's day—the weather was splendid—and I had never seen so many people in my large church as on that day.

Addressing them I said in substance.

"French Canadians:—The very night before our adorable Saviour was to die, He said to His apostles 'I will offend you this night!'"

"Now I just tell you the same thing. I will offend you to-day. But as the offense which Christ gave to His apostles has saved the world, I hope that, by His mercy, the offense which I shall give you to-day shall save you.

"I was a priest of Rome till yesterday—and I was your pastor—but, yesterday, at about three o'clock in the afternoon, a new light came to me, and there was an irresistible force in that light!

"Through that light I have seen clearly that the Pope and the Church of Rome are the two greatest enemies of Christ the world has ever seen. Through that fraud I have been deceived, and I have deceived you. But by the help of God, yesterday. I have given up the Pope and the Church of Rome, and I am no more your pastor!"

The last words had hardly gone from my lips, when a cry of desolation went out from every heart. "Dear Father Chiniquy! Is it possible that you have left our holy Church?"

I answered them, "Dear countrymen, I do not come here to tell you to do the same thing. Do not trouble yourselves about me, in this solemn hour do not look to me, but look to Christ alone."

"I did not die on Calvary to save you, I did not shed my blood to cleanse your souls and buy a crown of glory for every one of you   But Christ has done it—look to Him and Him alone in this solemn day!

"Will you allow me to tell you why I left the Church of Rome, yesterday?"

They all answered, "By all means tell us that!"

There was then in the front pew, a most beautiful child about six months old, in the arms of its happy mother. I said to the people

"Look at this beautiful child. See his bright eyes, his rosy cheeks, his smiling lips! See how he is stretching his little arms around the neck of his happy mother, to give her one of his angelic kisses

"Surely there is life in that child!

"But what has he done to get that life? Has he moved a straw to get it? Has the Pope of Rome done anything to give that life to this child? No! that life is a gift of God The child has done absolutely nothing to get it. It is a gift of God. The Pope of Rome has had nothing to do with that life.

"But if the child could speak and say to his mother: 'Dear mother, how happy I feel in your arms. how kind and loving a mother thou art to me. From morning to night thou art busy with me. It is from thy breast that, many times a day, I get the life which is in me   What can I do, dear mother, to show you my gratitude? What do you want from me for that life which is in me from thee?' What would the mother answer?

"She would answer. 'Dear child, I want nothing, but a kiss from thy angelic lips   Press your dear little heart on mine, that I may feel by its pulses that you love me as much as I love thee'

"Mothers, who are here   Is it not the only thing you would ask from your dear child?"

They all answered, "Yes, sir."

Then I said· "Come with me to the feet of your dying Saviour, on the cross. . . .   Look at His crown of thorns.   . . See the nails in His hands and his feet—count if you can the bleeding wounds—hear the agonizing cry,

'Father, Father, why hast Thou forsaken Me?' See the horrible death! And then ask your Saviour 'Why that crown of thorns on Thy head? Why those nails in Thy hands and feet? Why those bleeding wounds? Why that horrible death on the cross?' And He will answer, 'To buy you an eternal life!'

"But ask Him again, 'What do you want from me for that eternal life which you buy at such a price?'

"And He will answer· 'I want nothing but your hearts and your love! That eternal life is a gift I offer you.'

"Now, if you go to the Pope and his priests and ask them· 'What must we do to be saved?' They will tell you —you must go and confess your sins to a priest, very often more guilty than yourself; you must abstain from eating meat all Fridays and Saturdays, and many other days of the year; you must gain or buy indulgences, pray to the Virgin Mary, to the saints, to the angels; . . . you must go into the flames of purgatory or give a great deal of money to get out of them'

"But all those things are deceitful human inventions

"For what did our dear Saviour answer to the young man who asked him what he had to do to have eternal life? Did He speak of Auricular Confession in His answer? Did He speak of abstaining from meat, of indulgences, of purgatory?

"No! He left those inventions and deceptions to the Pope. Our Saviour answered, that day, what He answers you, to-day, in His Gospel For He has not changed His religion or His doctrine. He answered, 'To be saved, my young friend, you have nothing to do but to love My Father, who has so much loved you that He has sent Me, His eternal Son Jesus, to save you. Love your neighbour Repent, believe in Me, invoke My name, and you are saved; eternal life is a gift.'"

For more than one hour I spoke of the gift. I showed its greatness, its value, its beauty.

I soon saw that I was not alone speaking of the gift. My beloved Saviour was with me in His spirit. For my people were beside themselves with admiration and joy when hearing, for the first time, of that marvelous gift

And when I asked them   "Who will give up the Pope to follow Christ. among you?   Who will give up the debasing and so costly religion of the Pope to accept the religion of the Gospel of Christ who offers you eternal life as a gift?"

Without a single exception they were all on their feet.

The heavy, unbearable yoke of the Pope was forever broken and rejected.

CHAPTER III.

My dear Bible Continues to lift Me up above the Dark Atmosphere of Romanism. The First Publication of the Holy Scriptures in Canada.

The Christian reader of this humble volume will never understand the mercies of God towards its author if he does not remember that from infancy, through a miraculous providence, I was raised in the respect and love of the Holy Scriptures

It is only by reading my first volume, "Fifty Years in the Church of Rome," that they will appreciate that fact, and that they will help me to praise the Lord for His infinite mercies

When a priest of Rome, I never could reconcile myself with the restrictions put by the Popes and the councils on the reading of the Divine Messages of God to man through the Holy Bible, and I availed myself of the first opportunity I had to express my mind publicly on that subject.

For time and eternity I will bless my God for having granted me the favour of persuading the Bishops of Quebec to publish an edition of the Holy Gospels for the use of our countrymen.

In my daily conversations with the priests, I had brought many of them to my views by showing them that the very barriers put between the people and the Holy Scriptures would give to the Divine Book the irresistible attractions of a forbidden fruit, and that, sooner or later, our countrymen would ask and receive from the Protestant *Colporteurs* those very Bibles which we were refusing them

During the four years stay in the city of Quebec, before my being appointed curate of Beauport, I had golden opportunities of being acquainted with all the priests of the diocese, and those opportunities had been multiplied, when curate of Beauport, by my going to almost every parish to establish the societies of temperance.

As I was constantly gaining the minds of the priests to those views, my hope was increasing every day, that the hour was approaching fast when we would pull down the granite walls which past ages had put between our people and the inspired Book. That blessed opportunity was to come sooner than I expected.

The French Revolution of 1830, which ruined Charles X., had forced his cousin, Archbishop Forbin Janson, one of his principal ministers, to leave France and come to Canada. I felt at once that, if I could enlist his influence in favour of my schemes of temperance and of the diffusion of the Gospel among our people, 1 would more easily remove the obstacles which were before us for this triumph Having completely, though secretly, at first, persuaded him to help me to fight the demon of intemperance, I opened to him my mind about the desire I had to see the Gospel of Christ read in every family of our dear Canada.

He answered me· "This is a very delicate question; I cannot take upon myself to initiate it, or to urge it upon the minds of the venerable Bishops who rule the Church of Canada, but if I am consulted by them on that matter, I will not conceal my mind In my diocese of Nancy where our Catholics are mixed, as yours are here, with Protestants, we have found it impossible to prevent them from having access to the Bible. We have allowed them the Catholic versions. but with the Commentaries approved by the Church."

In the year 1841, after having blessed the column of temperance which I had erected at Beauport as a public memorial of the marvelous change wrought by that society among my people, that remarkable Bishop was asked to preach a retreat (a revival) to the priests of the diocese of Quebec.

Nearly 150 attended the exercises of those religious meetings in the Seminary of Quebec

This offered the golden opportunity for which I was looking since the day I was ordained a priest. The very first day of that retreat I wrote a short and respectful address to the Bishop, to which I had secured the signatures of all the young priests to the number of nearly one hundred.

In that petition we were simply asking our ecclesiastical superiors if the time had not come when we could safely put the Holy Gospels, with the best commentaries, approved of by the Church, into the hands of our people.

Though at first the Bishop seemed to be taken by surprise, and a little embarrassed, he received us kindly, but with the condition that this grave subject should be discussed in one of our public meetings, and that every one of his priests should be allowed to give his own views thereon.

It was just what we wanted. As I had been selected to write the petition I was also selected to open the debate, which I did in the following words, which I have kept, and which I give here:—

' MY LORD,—VENERABLE BRETHREN.

"After the sending of His eternal Son, Jesus, to save us by dying on the cross, our great and merciful God has never presented to the poor sinful children of Adam greater proof of His Divine love and mercy than by giving them His Gospel.

"But as Jesus Christ was to be the Saviour of every one who would accept Him, so the Gospel was to be the light— the guide—the bread of life of every one who would accept it.

"As every man has a divine right to go to Christ personally, and as that right cannot be taken away by any church authority, so every man has the divine right to hear or to read the Word of God, when it is presented or spoken to him.

"As it was a crime on the part of the priests of Jerusalem to prevent the people from receiving Him, so I consider it would be a crime for me and for every one of us to prevent our people from reading the Word of God—the Gospel of Christ—when they wish to have that privilege"

I had hardly finished that sentence, when I was furiously interrupted by several old priests, who were at the right hand of the Bishop "This is Protestantism, this is the doctrine of Luther and Calvin!" they all cried at the tip top of their voices. I asked the protection of the chair (the Bishop) against these interruptions and insults.

"Let my venerable opponents allow me to finish my short address, I said, and they will see that I am neither a Protestant nor a Luther. This interruption at the beginning of my address was as unfair as it is unchristian. If I say anything wrong, the venerable fathers who have interrupted me will have the opportunity of showing my errors But is it not a sure indication that they find their position illogical, unchristian, when they show such a fear lest we discuss it?"

Then the Grand Vicar Demers (who had several times been the Superior of the Seminary of Quebec), advancing two or three steps towards me, and pointing his finger to my face, answered with a furious voice "Mr. Chiniquy, you are a heretic, and a new Luther. You trample under your feet the decrees of the Holy Council of Trent That Holy Council absolutely forbids the reading of the Scriptures in the vernacular tongue of the people, and you want us to help you in that heretical work! And you are so daring as to promulgate such a doctrine in our presence without allowing us to protest against your errors!"

"My Lord," I said, "Please allow me to answer at once the venerable Superior of the Seminary of Quebec

"I know very well that the Holy Council of Trent has put strange and deplorable restrictions on the reading of the Holy Scriptures not only by the people, but by the priests also. However, I am not here to condemn the ecumenical council or to invite you to revolt against its authority, as I am accused, but let me respectfully ask you, my lord, and through you this whole venerable assembly, to remember the circum-

stance and the times of the Council of Trent Luther, Calvin, Zwingle and a thousand other heretics had raised a
storm against our Holy Catholic Church such as the world
had never seen. The spotless sails of the sacred ship were
torn into fragments by the hurricane.

"The roaring and furious billows of the raging sea were
striking the sacred ship from every side and even more than
in the terrible storm spoken of by St. Luke,—Christ seemed
to sleep and let the storm rage . . Whole nations had
been swept away from the deck, and many more were threatened to disappear under the roaring billows.

"What was to be done in that supreme hour of anguish and
peril?

"Have you not heard what is often done in the midst of
destructive hurricanes, by the fearless and skilful mariners, to
save the ship? Do they not throw overboard many of the
most precious parts of the cargo in those hours of peril?

"Is it because they find those objects bad in themselves or
because they have a peculiar detestation of them, they throw
them overboard? No

"It is often the contrary; they often throw overboard what
they consider the most precious part of the cargo, the very
objects they love the most But do you not know what more
than once the honest and intrepid captain with his fearless
crew have done after the storm was over and the ship was
saved?

"Have you not seen them, after, going back to the place
where they had been so near to perish to pick up as many as
they could of the precious objects and treasures they had
thrown overboard? And when they had picked up and saved
as much as they could of the precious objects which were yet
seen floating on the surface of the calmed waters, have you
not seen them making for the port of safety? And did they
not bless God for having given them the opportunity of
wrenching from the raging waves the very objects they had
thrown overboard to obey the laws of a cruel necessity?

"My lord, and my venerable and dear brother priests There is no use of shutting our eyes to the sad realities of our present condition. We cannot read the history of the Council of Trent without shedding tears on the precious and sacred things thrown overboard to save the ship in those days of furious storms.

"I am not here to criticise and condemn the pilots and the illustrious, learned fathers of the Council of Trent. Nay, my tongue be forever silent and mute rather than condemn the holy men who were manning the sacred ship in those stormy days! Nay, my right hand be paralyzed if it is raised in condemnation against them.

"But now that the dear Saviour, as when on the furious sea of Samaria, has awoke from His mysterious sleep; now that He has stopped the raging waves and bidden the storm to cease, is it not the duty of every one of us who are forming the crew engaged by the Master to man the ship; is it not our duty to revisit the sea, when it is calmed, to pick up and save some of the precious things which are still floating around us, before they entirely disappear from our sight, and forever sink under the treacherous waves?"

The last words had hardly fallen from my lips when a burst of applause from the great majority of my hearers told me that I had touched the right chords of their intelligence.

But it was easy to see that the old priests, for the greater part, were still furious against me. However, not feeling hampered by their visible ill-will, I continued

"My lord, among the precious and divine things thrown overboard in those days of trouble, which we must try to save is the unquestionable right which every Christian has to read the Holy Scriptures and interpret them according to his own honest conscience, guided by the Holy Ghost who is never refused to those who ask Him.

"For instance, who among us would dare to say that the admirable Epistle of Paul to the Romans was not the property of every Christian of Rome? Had not every Christian of Rome the right to read and keep that letter thirty years after the death of Christ? And where do we find an authority to say that any council had the right to take away that Epistle from the hands of the Christians of Rome in those days?

"How could that letter, sent by the Apostle Paul as bread of life to the Romans of his time, be considered such a deadly poison by his successor, Paul IV, that it would be absolutely forbidden to taste it to-day by the same people of Rome?

"Are we really determined to continue to say to our people that that Saint Paul, who was so visibly guided by the Spirit of God had not common sense enough to write a letter to that people which they could understand? Can we find a single word in that letter of Paul to give us to understand that the people of Rome could not make use of their own personal intelligence and conscience, but that they had to borrow the intellect and conscience of their neighbour to understand him?

"What I say of the admirable Epistle of Paul to the Romans, I say of all the Scriptures. I thank God that I am a Catholic priest. I would not exchange the honour and the privileges of that title for all the gold and silver in the world. I do not revolt against our holy Church, I do not condemn the fathers of the Council of Trent for having done what they did to save the ship in the dark hours of the most terrible hurricane.

"But now our magnificent ship is sailing on a calm sea. Is it not the time to take again on deck the untold spiritual, intellectual, moral and Divine treasures, which Christ has brought from heaven to save the world?

"Ah! I wish my feeble voice could go all over the world and be heard by all those whom the dear Saviour had redeemed in His blood and who have accepted Him as their only hope, their only joy, their only life for time and eternity! Let them be called consecrated priests of the Lamb, or the redeemed of the Lamb, it is the same in my mind   To every one of them I would say· 'Is it not time to enter again into the inheritance of the treasures we have lost? Is it not time to hold in our own hands and press to our bosoms the untold treasures which the Son of God has given us in the Gospel?'

"For remember this, the day you have sworn or promised in any way not to interpret it according to your own intelligence, your own conscience, guided by the Spirit and the grace of God, that Divine Book is an empty cistern; it is a cistern without water, it is water without substance, without taste, without life.

"You have not forgotten, my lord, that when I was ordained a priest, you asked me to make a most solemn promise, in the presence of God and His people, that I would never interpret the Holy Scriptures according to my own intelligence, conscience and common sense.

"With my hand on the Holy Bible, you made me swear that I would interpret it only according to the unanimous consent of the holy fathers.

"Now, I solemnly and respectfully ask your lordship to answer me   If I am too stupid, too ignorant, too much deprived of Christian intelligence to understand St Matthew, St. Mark, St Luke. St. John when speaking to me in the name of my Saviour, Jesus Christ, how can I be intelligent enough to understand Tertullian, Jerome, Augustine, etc., who are infinitely more obscure?

"Please, my lord, tell us, if St John, St Luke, St Peter, St. Paul, etc.. have not received from my God the light, the grace to speak to me in an intelligent way. when surely filled with the Holy Ghost, how is it that Origen, Justice Clement etc., have surely received from my God, a degree of lucidity and clearness refused to His ambassadors, His apostles and His evangelists?

"If I cannot rely on my own private judgment and conscience when studying, with the help of God, the Divine pages of the Bible, how can I rely on that private judgment when studying the holy fathers?

"If you answer me that I have nothing else but my private judgment and intelligence to lead, understand, and follow the holy fathers, how is it that I shall be lost if I make use of that same private judgment when I am at the feet of my Saviour, Jesus Christ, listening to His eternal and life-giving words?

"Nothing distresses me so much in our holy religion as this want of confidence in God when we go to our Saviour's feet to hear or read His soul-saving words, and our so perfect self-confidence, when we go among sinful and fallible men, even called holy fathers, to know what they say.

"Would it be possible that, in our holy church, the Word of God means uncertainty, darkness, night, death, and the words of men light and life?

"When you, our venerable Bishop, did put the Holy Scriptures into my hands and commanded me to study and preach them, I understood what you meant, and I promised to do it with my best ability with the help of God You gave me a most sublime work to perform, and by the grace of God, my whole life shall be consecrated to it. But when you ordered me to swear that I would never interpret the Holy Scriptures except according to the unanimous consent of the holy fathers, have you not forced me to be a perjured man by swearing to a thing which I could not do! Have you not made me, with every priest here, swear to do a thing as ridiculous and impossible as to take the moon into my hands!

"For it is very probable that there are not two chapters of that Divine Book on which there have not been some differences of views among the holy fathers The writings of the holy fathers fill at least 200 volumes in folio, and it would require more than ten years to know on what text they are unanimously of the same mind, and on what texts they differ.

"If, after that time of study, I find that they are unanimous on the question of orthodoxy on which I have to preach, all will be right with me, I will walk to the gates of eternity with a fearless heart. But if among fifty holy fathers there are forty-nine on one side and one of opposite views, in what awful distress I will be plunged! I shall be like a ship in a stormy night, after losing her mast, her sails, her compass and her helm! I shall be lost!

"If I were allowed to follow the majority there would always be a plank of safety to secure me from the impending wreck But my oath, my terrible oath, has tied me and every one of you, my venerable brethren, to the unanimity. If our faith and the doctrine we preach is not that of unanimity, we are perjured, lost men!

"What a frightful alternative is put before us by that strange oath!

"The holy prophet, speaking of the Word of God, tells us: 'Thy Word is a lamp unto my feet and a light unto my path' (Ps. 119:105.) But what are we doing with that Divine lamp and that bright and precious light?

"We put it under the bushel that it may not be seen! We are sworn to ignore and deny its power and authority. 'I am not ashamed of the Gospel of Christ,' said Paul, 'for it is the power of God unto salvation, to every one that believeth.' (Rom. 1:16.)

"But, by our conduct, do we not really make the people believe that 'The Gospel is the power of the devil to damn the world?'

"Not only we prevent our people from having any access to the Divine Book, but we violently take it from their hands and destroy it under their eyes when we have opportunity to do it.

"By my advice, two years before I was curate of Beauport, four of the principal families of that parish had purchased, in Quebec, as many Bibles of Sacy, approved by the Cardinal Archbishop of Paris.

"But my predecessor, Rev Begin, who is just sitting here, at my right hand, having heard of it, went without an hour of delay, wrenched the sacred volumes from their hands, and threw them into the fire, in the presence of the whole family

"What we respectfully ask from you is, not only to put an end to these sacrilegious acts, but to show our love and respect for the holy Gospel by giving it to our people with the commentaries approved by the Church

"It is evident that the fathers of the Council of Trent made those stringent laws against the reading of the Holy Scriptures almost in spite of themselves—with the understanding that those restrictions were deplorable things, and only to be in force for a short period of time. They wisely gave to every Bishop the right and power to destroy those barriers and to restore the natural right the people had to the Holy Book when they find it advisable

"Then, it is not a revolt against the holy council we demand, it is only a favour which the holy council has allowed your lordship to grant, that we demand, in allowing a Canadian edition of the Gospel And, relying on the zeal, the piety and the high Christian intelligence of our Bishop, it is our firm hope that he will grant us that favour."

The way my address had been received by the great majority gave us the assurance that the God of the Gospel was on my side. Rev. Grand Vicar Demers, ex-President of the Seminary of Quebec, was the only one who tried to refute me   But he did not dare to touch a single one of my arguments   His address consisted in the hundred times repeated prophecy that Mr. Chiniquy, the young curate of Beauport, would soon become a Protestant if he were not yet one.

Thanks be to God, he was a good prophet

Rev Charles Baillargeon, then curate and some years later Bishop of Quebec, defended my position and in a splendid address on the right of the people to read the Scriptures, he closed the discussion

When the votes were taken, only five dared to oppose us. The victory was complete. The Bishop at once named a committee to prepare the first Canadian Edition of the New Testament which was not finished until 1846.

CHAPTER IV

The Darkest Hour of the Night Before the Bright Rays of the Day

The 10th day of January, 1846, the large parlour of the Right Rev. Bourget, Bishop of Montreal, was filled by a great number of priests, to whom he said, in substance, "I have invited you here to ask your advice on a most important and sad subject

"You all know the efforts made recently by the Protestants to destroy the faith of our dear people. At first, their perfidious and underground work was so universally looked upon with horror by our countrymen that we hoped we had nothing to fear from those miserable apostles of error and irreligion.

"But to-day a dark and threatening cloud is in the very heart of one of our most interesting parishes.

"I have just learned that more than fifty young boys and girls, all children of our Catholic families, have been entered into the Protestant college of La Pointe aux Trembles at the very door of Montreal.

"If, every year, those fifty or sixty young men and girls poisoned by the errors and impieties of Protestantism are sent back from that school into the midst of our honest but illiterate population, who cannot see that they will scatter the poison of heresy and Protestantism into hundreds, even thousands of families of our good but so unlearned country people? Every one of those perverted boys and girls will be like sparks of fire which will soon be spread all over our dear Canada, and cause the ruin of our holy Church

"We must not lose a moment in extinguishing those threatening sparks of fire.

67

"It was to ask you the help of your wisdom on the best way of counteracting the first efforts of those heretics that I have invited you to meet here to day"

As I had been working then only a few months in the diocese of Montreal, I felt that my duty was to let my elder priests give their views and I kept silent, listening to what was said, for more than an hour   Then the Bishop told me, "Dear Father Chiniquy, though you have been among us only a few months, you have worked four years within the city of Quebec, four other years in the grand parish of Beauport, and as long in the still more important parish of Kamouraska

' In every one of those places, I know that you have met a great many Protestants, and I have even learned from the Bishop of Quebec that you have laboured with such zeal and success among those heretics that you have persuaded ninety=three of them to give up their errors and submit themselves to the holy Church   We want the benefit of your experience. We would like to know your views about the best way of paralyzing the efforts of the Protestants in their diabolical project of spreading their errors in the midst of our dear Catholic people"   Though this request took me by surprise, I was pleased with it. No words can give an idea of the prejudices, the contempt, nay the hatred which my theological studies, and my personal natural wickedness had accumulated in my mind against Protestants from the very day I had entered the college of Nicolet to that very hour of the 20th of January, 1850

Though I am ashamed to do it, I really think it is my duty to confess that I was hating with a supreme hatred every English man and woman, for the simple reason that they were Protestants

Such was, in the days of my youth, the impressions of the education given in the family, in the schools and in the colleges, that every Protestant was looked upon by me as a monster, born enemy of my religion, of my God and my country.

The books I had read, the lessons of my teachers in the college, and of my theologians in the Seminaries were all converging to the same result. These dark, infamous and diabolical sentiments made such an impression on my young mind, that, to-day, I am still filled with disgust and horror against my teachers as against myself when I think of them

Under the full pressure of those sentiments I reminded the Bishop that the dangers ahead for our dear country and our holy Church were greater than many suspected I added, "This is a war to death between those infamous heretics and our holy Church. It is a hand to hand battle, every one of us has to fight against those soldiers of hell if we want to save our country In all her councils and through all her theologians of our holy Church, has she not forbidden us to have any communication with the heretics? Has not our holy Church told us that we must deal with them as with wolves which cross our fields to devour our lambs and our sheep? Does not our Jure Canonico tell us that it is not a sin to kill them, when we have our opportunity? What can I say on our duties and rights in reference to those miserable ambassadors of hell which you do not know?

"Let every one of you listen to the word of his intelligence as well as to the voice of our Church about the best way of saving our dear Catholic people from the jaws of those roaring lions. I will say please let me go and preach to the people of La Pointe aux Trembles three or four days. Give me carte blanche to act and fight in my own way against those miserable ambassadors of hell, and, with the help of the blessed Virgin Mary, I will give you a good account of my humble efforts against them. My hope is that after those three or four days of crossing the sword with those ignorant and fanatical followers of Luther and Calvin, we shall not have much to fear from them."

My short address was received with the most frantic applause from the whole assembly.

After a few approving remarks, Bishop Bourget told me,

" Go, and remain not only three days, but much longer, if you wish to confound and pulverize those heretics   We will pray the Virgin Mary and St. John the Baptist, the patron Saint of Canada, to help you.   But be prudent, do not expose yourself in any way which might put you in the hands of the law

" Do not forget that our misfortune is that we are a conquered people ruled by Protestant England, and we have no fair play nor any justice to expect from those heretics "

A week later I was the guest of the curate of La Pointe aux Trembles, who at the demand of his Bishop, had invited me to deliver a course of three days lectures to his people against Protestants.

During the next three days the church of La Pointe aux Trembles was crowded to its utmost capacity, not only by the people of that parish, but by hundreds from the neighbouring parishes who wanted to know what I had to say against the *Suiss*, as the first French Protestants used to be called in Canada, because, likely, some of the first missionaries were Swiss.

My memory and my mind were stuffed in a marvelous way with all the ridiculous, abominable, diabolical lies published against Luther, Calvin. Zwingle, etc , and against all those who had accepted their reforms.

All those lies and calumnies were sincerely believed by me as Gospel truth (as they are generally believed even to day by the priests of Rome).   I gave them to the people with all the epithets and expressions of contempt and wrath that fanatical and blind zeal could inspire me.

My readers would hardly believe me to-day were I to tell them the historical lies which I gave those poor people as Gospel truth.

For instance, I told them how the Protestants of France, after having slaughtered thousands and thousands of defenseless priests, nuns and honest farmers, had sold their country to English Protestants who were coming to cover France with blood and ruin, if the good, honest, peaceful, French Catholics had not been forced in self-defense to slaughter those bloody and treacherous Protestants in the St. Bartholomew night.

For, let the Protestants of Canada and the whole world know that this is one of the Romish historical lies and calumnies invented by the Jesuits, and accepted as Gospel truth by the great majority of the Roman Catholics

" Look at the miserable heretics," I said to the people, " how they look peaceful, charitable, humble, to-day. Their voice is like the voice of the dove in their manners when they visit with you with their falsified Bible under their arms, they look like lambs. But let them grow in number, and they will do here what they did in France, England, Scotland, wherever they are strong enough: they will turn your houses and your churches into ashes, and they will slaughter you to take possession of your beautiful farms, if you dare to resist them!"

Really, the devil had taken possession of me, when I was proclaiming those horrible Jesuitical lies, which I believed then very sincerely.

For, let the Protestants who read these lines remember that this is the history as the Jesuits and the greater part of the Roman Catholic writers have given it.

What could be the feelings of my poor countrymen after three days of such horrible historical lies given them with a burning zeal by a priest in whom they had confidence?

Shall I tell it again? Yes! The devil had really taken possession of my heart. I was breathing nothing but hatred, vengeance and death against those defenseless and humble ministers of the Gospel. My hope was that I would make the ground so hot under their feet, in that parish and everywhere in Canada, that they could not dwell any longer in our land.

The last address was hardly finished the third day, when I saw five or six of those humble and zealous ministers of the

Gospel, or *colporteurs*, who had patiently and bravely attended all my meetings, with their Bibles in their hands, coming to meet and challenge me to have a discussion with them, promising to refute me before my people.

I was overjoyed when I heard them challenging me to a public discussion. It was just the trap in which my hope was that they would fall.

Instead of accepting their challenge, I turned towards the multitude, that had just come out of the church,—and I said· "Do you not see those miserable heretics, who come to challenge and insult you and me, at the very door of your church? Why do you not give them a lesson which they will never forget?"

A thought had evidently come from hell into my heart, in that hour, the darkest of my life

I do not like to confess it, but I must. The intelligent reader understands that my intention was to have them so cruelly beaten, that they would either die there, on the spot, or be so cruelly treated that they would run away from the place, never to come again.

My cruel and cowardly intention was so well understood by the multitude that the words had hardly fallen from my lips, when forty or fifty young men, like furious tigers, threw themselves on those few defenseless men, and struck them without mercy.

In a moment their clothes were torn into rags, and their bruised and bleeding bodies were rolling in the snow, which was two or three feet deep on the ground. Very soon the snow was reddened with the blood of several of them.

With a word of my lips or a movement of my finger I could have put a stop to that horror.

But, alas, I was a true, a devoted priest of Rome!

The blood of those heretics was the most pleasant thing I had ever seen!

I was saying to myself, "Surely if they are not killed they

will run away, never to come again!" Very probably they would have been killed there, if the God of the Gospel had not come to the help of His heroic messengers.

A noble Roman Catholic French Canadian farmer, moved with compassion at the horrible spectacle which was before his eyes, cried out, " It is a shame to beat so cruelly defenseless men—I cannot bear that "

Then quick as lightning, throwing his coat and overcoat on the snow, he struck the nearest of the would-be murderers with his terrible fist, and sent him rolling down bleeding in the snow.

In less time than I can say it, he had applied his terrible fist on the bleeding noses or the blackened eyes of half a dozen of his cruel and mistaken Roman Catholic countrymen And who will not praise the Lord with me, to-day, when I say that this heroic action was applauded by most of the people? The wounded and bleeding. but heroic, servants of Christ were at once left free to pick up their ragged clothing and run back as fast as possible to their lodgings.

Then, falling on their knees (as I learned ten years later from their own lips), they raised their supplicating hands to the Mercy Seat, and said to the dear Saviour as much with their blood as with their lips, " Dear Saviour, Thou seest our bruised bodies and bleeding wounds, and Thou knowest the one who has caused us to suffer as we do. We beseech Thee, look down on him in Thy mercy. Show him the error of his ways. Give him the saving light of the Gospel, that he may know and love Thee as his only Saviour; change that stone of the wilderness into a child of Abraham. Grant him to see the ignominious chains which tie him to the feet of the idols of Rome, that he may come with us to invite his poor Canadian countrymen to accept Thee as their only hope and Saviour for time and eternity "

And, blessed be the Lord, the prayers of those modern and heroic martyrs were heard at the Mercy Seat.

There has never been any doubt in my mind about the fact that, in the admirable providence of God, I owe my conversion to the fervent prayers of these six humble but admirable Christians, who had been so cruelly beaten at my instigation in January, 1850, at the door of the Church of Pointe aux Trembles.

The night after I had committed that criminal and shameful act, was spent in the parsonage of Longueil where I used, then, to reside with my intimate friend, Rev. Mr. Brassard. It was a sleepless night.

I was hardly in my bed when a voice more terrible than the roar of thunder was crying within my soul "Are you not ashamed of what you have done to-day? Though by a real miracle those defenseless and honest men have not been killed, the blood they have lost, the cruel wounds they have received, cry for vengeance to God against you "

To silence those voices and excuse myself in my own eyes, I rose three or four times to read the theological books of my church and see again what she was teaching about the right of the Roman Catholics to persecute the Protestants.

I read in St. Thomas Aquinas, Vol. 4, page 99, that not only we should "not tolerate them, but that we must deliver them into the hands of the secular power to be exterminated." When reading these doctrines of the best and most approved theologians of my church. which were unanimous in assuring me that the heretics have no right to live. I persuaded myself that, after all, I had not committed any sin when only beating men whom we had the right to kill

It was then, that, for the first time, I heard a new voice within my soul which caused me unspeakable distress from that night to the day of my conversion.

"Do you not see that in your Church of Rome you do not follow the Word of God, but you follow the lying traditions of men?" It was for the first time in my life that the suggestion of leaving the Church of Rome had come to me with great force

There was no doubt in my mind but that all the powers of hell were combined for my perdition. I fell on my knees and prayed to God to silence these voices which were shaking my faith. From the bottom of my heart I swore I would live and die in the Church of Rome, out of which (I sincerely believed, then) there was no salvation.

But, to prove to myself again that I had done well to get those heretics punished, and that my holy Church was right to teach us to hate, maltreat and even kill them, I took my Bible, with the hope of finding some of the texts which would prove to me that such were the teachings of the Scripture. Where can I find words to express my surprise and emotion when, on opening the Divine Book, my eyes fell on these words in Luke, Chapter 9·

"And it came to pass, when the time was come that He should be received up, He steadfastly set His face to go to Jerusalem. And sent messengers before His face; and they went and entered into a village of the Samaritans to make ready for Him. And they did not receive Him because His face was as though He would go to Jerusalem. And when His disciples, James and John, saw this, they said, Lord, wilt Thou that we command fire to come down from heaven, and consume them, even as Elias did? But He turned, and rebuked them, and said, Ye know not what manner of spirit ye are of. For the Son of Man is not come to destroy men's lives but to save them." I had hardly finished reading this last sentence when as formidable a thunderclap as I ever heard, before or since, struck the ears of my soul, saying, "Do you not see that in your Church of Rome you do not follow the Word of God but the lying traditions of men? Where do your Popes and theologians find the right to punish, beat, imprison and kill the heretics, when Christ says the very contrary?"

What could I answer to my troubled conscience when hearing those awful rebukes from the very lips of Christ? I felt stunned and more than ever confounded. While sitting at the breakfast table the next morning, Rev. Mr. Brassard told

me. "Your eyes are swollen as if you had spent the night in
tears .   . What does that mean?" "You are not mistaken when you think that I have wept, last night." I answered "I have just passed through the most dreadful hours
of my life   The cruel beating of those poor defenseless men
has come to my mind and conscience under such colours
all night, that I am really horrified at myself. In order to
silence the voice of my guilty conscience I left my bed
several times to read the pages of our most approved and learned
theologians   Of course I have found them unanimous in
telling me that the heretics are not worthy to live, that they
have no rights which we are bound to respect, that it is the
duty of the Catholic Church to deliver them into the hands
of the secular power to be exterminated, that it is forbidden
to speak to them, to work with them, or encourage them in
any way

"In your volume of Jure Canonico I have read again, that,
not only is it not a sin to kill a Protestant, but that such a
holy action gives the assurance of the pardon of all his sins
to the murderer. More than that I have found that the killing of a Protestant by a Catholic is not murder. But this
has not silenced the cry of my conscience.

" But to my unspeakable confusion my eyes have fallen on
the ninth chapter of Luke, where our Saviour is absolutely in
opposition to the doctrines and practises of our church on
that subject. Then a voice more terrible than that of a
hurricane had shaken my very frame, when crying in my ears,
'Do you not see that in your Church of Rome you do
not follow the Word of God, but the lying traditions of
men?'

" What could I answer when my conscience was telling me
that this was the truth, the sad truth! But how can I picture
to you my distress and desolation, when it seemed to me that
God Himself with all His angels was crying to me· 'Come
out, come out from that Church of Rome, whose hands are

reddened with the blood of ten millions of men she has slaughtered to establish her power over this enslaved, blind, perishing world.'"

Mr. Brassard answered me: "My dear Chiniquy, with the hope. nay, the assurance, that you will never betray me, I must tell you that there are many things in our poor Church of Rome which I cannot believe; for they look to me not only against the teachings of the Gospel, but against common= sense. The right which our Church assumes to command the civil power to hang, burn, torture and kill the heretics cannot come from Christ. I am always struck with sorrow when I read the bloody pages of our Church history, which tell us how she has filled her dungeons with not thousands, but millions of honest men and women, and where they were starved to death or had to suffer tortures which would have horrified the savages of our forests. It is a fact that our Church has put to death millions of Protestants, because they could not believe certain doctrines which they, wisely or un- wisely (God only knows), thought contrary to the Scriptures. To my mind and conscience, this is such a dark spot on the face of our Church that all the waters of our vast rivers and bottomless oceans cannot wash it away.

"I tell you my mind, my dear Chiniquy, far from admiring or approving you, when yesterday you told me how you had caused those brave and honest (though mistaken) Protes- tants to be so cruelly beaten, I silently condemned you from the bottom of my heart.

" Continue to spread your admirable views on temperance, but let the Protestants alone. Convert them if you can, with scriptural arguments, but give up forever the idea that we Roman Catholics have any right to beat them or shed their blood, because they cannot see many things just as we do."

When uttering these last words, the voice of my noble friend was trembling, yes, there were tears in his eyes, and, unable to conceal his emotion, he abruptly left the table and ran to his room.

This friendly rebuke found such an echo in my troubled conscience that I remained speechless, and then I also took to my priest's room   Leaving the table, I retired with the words ringing in my soul:

"Do you not see that in your Church of Rome you do not follow the Word of God, but the lying traditions of men?'

CHAPTER V

A Macedonian Cry from Chicago. Auricular Confession

Many are the opportunities we have had to understand what Paul felt, when, in a vision, he heard the cry from Macedonia, "Come and help us" Hundreds of times we have heard that cry coming from Chicago to New York, from New York to San Francisco; from San Francisco to the Sandwich Islands, Australia, New Zealand, Tasmania, England, Scotland, Ireland. and more than five hundred towns and cities in the provinces of Manitoba, Ontario, Quebec, New Brunswick, Nova Scotia. Prince Edward Island, Cape Breton, etc.

Several large volumes would not suffice to tell the interesting episodes, the narrow escapes, the sorrows as well as the joys of our heart, when, to answer that cry, we had to pass through the most crushing humiliations, or we had to rejoice at the great triumphs of the Gospel over its implacable enemy, Popery, in those different places these last forty years

The first Macedonian cry, after our conversion, was from Chicago.

There was then, in that city, a French Canadian, by the name of Ducharme, keeping a very respectable hotel. A Roman Catholic by birth and education, his faith had been shaken by the scandalous lives of the priests of Rome in that city.

From him came the first Macedonian appeal Come and help us!

His invitation came to me as an order from heaven. To my unspeakable joy, I found that not less than five hundred of my countrymen had been gathered by him in a very large and decent hall, near the Haymarket, to hear the Gospel message I had to give them

After the most hearty reception by that multitude, and a prayer addressed to our heavenly Father, I told them

"I do not come here to address to you any long speech My only intention is to give you the explanations you want, and to answer your questions about our new religious position."

After a few moments of silence, the President rose and said: "Dear Father Chiniquy, the news of that last religious event at St. Anne has come to us as an earthquake, which has shaken our religious views to their foundations. Yes, in many families, our religious convictions have not only been shaken, but they have been destroyed, completely ruined! To-day, many of us stand before the religious ruins you have made! But what does an intelligent man do when his house has been ruined, shattered, demolished by an earthquake? Does he remain with folded arms, motionless and discouraged before his demolished house? No. After the first hour of desolation, he looks to the best way he can build up a new home on those ruins Nay, he looks how to make a better home with the very ruins which the earthquake has left.

"It is with that in view that we are met here You confess that you are the cause of these ruins. Have we not, then, the right to ask you to help us gather what we can from the ruins you have made to give us a renewed home, and more solid foundations?

"In the name of this large assembly, I will ask you why you have abolished Auricular Confession Is it not a Gospel institution? Has not Christ said to His apostles, ' What ye bind on earth shall be bound in heaven ' ' The sins ye shall forgive on earth shall be forgiven in heaven. The sins ye shall retain on earth shall be retained in heaven?'

"What have you to give us to reconcile us with our God after we have sinned?"

"To answer your questions from the Scripture, history,

and common-sense," I replied, ' I would keep you here not only the whole night, but during all the hours of to-morrow. I cannot do it. I will then present only a few common-sense arguments against Auricular Confession, and with the help of God, you will be forever delivered from that degrading and infamous yoke.

" Please tell me, is your wife still living?"

"Yes, sir, thanks be to God, and she is just here sitting by me."

" Have you any daughters?"

" Yes, sir, I have two. You see them at your right hand."

" Have you any boys?"

" Yes, sir, three, and they are all here to hear you."

" Now please allow me to address you a few other questions. How long is it since you have been to confession?"

"Well, well, you ought not to ask me that. I am ashamed to acknowledge that I have not been to confess for seven years "

" And your boys, do they like to go to confess?"

"I am sorry to acknowledge that they follow my bad example. They do not go to confess more than their poor father. '

"And your wife and daughters, if it is not an indiscretion to ask that question, do they go to confess very often?"

" Yes, thanks be to God, my wife and daughters are very pious; they never let a month pass without going to confess to their priest. And I think if I had not objected to it they would go to confess every week "

" Now, my dear sir, I must thank you for your answering me. But I have another question to ask you, and though it is of a very delicate nature, I hope that you will continue to deserve the respect and gratitude of this large meeting, by your honourable and truthful answer Suppose that instead of a man in that confessional there were a young lady to hear your confessions, would you be seven years without regarding her pressing appeals to come and confess to her?"

My question was followed by such a burst of laughter as I have never heard before nor since. My honest interlocutor answered me

"I'll let you guess my answer by what you know of the human heart"

"Yes, yes, you are right," I told him, "it is useless to insist; any one who has some knowledge of human nature, would easily understand the consequences that would naturally follow from such a mode of Auricular Confession. Yet why would it be worse than the mode which is now practised?

"Women are more shrewd than men in these affairs. There is not a lady among you who would allow her husband to go and confess to a young lady. If a Roman Catholic lady saw her son going once a month, or once a fortnight, to the feet of a young lady, to speak to her for hours about all that is going on in his poor heart, and to tell her all his thoughts and desires, she would go and take him away, and tell him that it was not proper for him to be there. She would not permit her husband to go to the feet of the most respectable woman and tell her all his thoughts; and if the husband urged that there was no danger, and that the lady was as pure as an angel, and that he was highly respectable, she would only laugh at him, and bring him out of the confessional box. But it is strange that the husband is not so shrewd. He is a stupid being, compared with his wife. He sees his wife going to the feet of that bachelor, and remaining alone with him for hours, telling him all her secret thoughts, but he says to himself that there is no danger as his wife is honest! And where is the difference between a man confessing all his sins to a woman, and a woman telling all her bad thoughts and actions to a man? You would not tolerate the former It would be considered an offense against society, a public immorality. And in the latter case it is also a public immorality. It is an offense against the laws of God, and it ought to be an offense against the laws of man

"A Bishop, who was first cousin to the king of France,

Charles X., and also his secretary, came to Canada. His name was Forbin Janson, and he had been Bishop of Nancy, Lorraine, France. After confessing to me one day, he told me that there was a book I should have which would guide me in putting questions to the priests in the confessional; it is in relation to the sins of priests. He gave me a copy which I have brought with me to-day, and I ask some of you to come forward and read a portion of it, bearing on the subject we now consider. It is a question the priest must ask to himself in his examination of conscience after he has been hearing confessions."

Then the chairman read the following extract·

"When hearing the confession of females, have I put to them questions about their sins, which brought answers by which my imagination has been filled with thoughts which have led me into great temptation and sin? The priests in general do not pay sufficient attention to the bad effect which is produced by hearing the confessions of females By these confessions, they are constantly tempted, and these temptations weaken the soul of the priest to such a degree that his purity is entirely destroyed."

"That is pretty clear," I said "You see, it affirms that the priests are constantly tempted and induced to fall into sin through the confessional

"Napoleon I., Emperor of France, knew so well, by his personal experience, the corrupting influence of Auricular Confession on the minds of young people, that when his only boy was old enough to make his first communion, he wrote himself the questions which the priest would be allowed to put to his young son, and he absolutely forbade that priest to put the immoral questions usually put to the young as well as to the old people

"If left to himself, the priest of Rome, as a general thing, would not put those infamous questions. But the priest of the Pope is not a free man who can act according to his honest conscience—he is a miserable slave, obliged to obey his Church.

And that Church obliges him, under pain of eternal damnation to put those demoralizing questions to the old and the young, to men and to women, to the boy and the girl who come to confess to him.

"Has not the whole of France been struck with horror and disgust at the declaration made by the noble Catherine Cadière and her numerous young female friends, against their Father Confessor, John B. Girard, a French Jesuit?

"The details of those villainies practised by that Father Confessor and several of his friends, Jesuit priests, with their penitents are such that I cannot tell them here.

"Who among you has not read the history of Father Achazius, Superior of the nunnery in the city of Duren, France? The number of his victims was so great, and their ranks in society so exalted that Napoleon thought it was his duty to take that scandalous affair before him.

"The way this holy (?) Father Confessor used to lead the noblest girls and married women as well as the nuns in the city of Aix Lachapelle, was revealed by a young nun who had escaped the snares of that confessor and had married a superior officer of the army of the Emperor of France. Her husband thought it his duty to direct the attention of Napoleon to the performances of that priest, through the confessional But the investigations which were directed by the state councillor, Leclere, were compromising so many other priests and so many ladies of the highest ranks of society, that the Emperor, though not over-scrupulous, was absolutely disheartened and feared that their exposure before the whole of France would cause the renewal of the awful slaughters of 1792 and 1793, when so many Roman Catholic priests had been mercilessly hung or shot as the most implacable enemies of morality and liberty.

"He abruptly ordered the court of investigation to stop the inquiry, under the pretense of saving the honour of so many families whose single and married women had been the victims of their Father Confessors. He thought that prudence and shame were urging him not to lift up more of the dark and thick veil behind which the Father Confessors conceal their hellish practises with their fair penitents. The Emperor of France found it was enough to confine Father Achazius and his co-priests in a dungeon for their lives.

"But it is not only the Emperor of France with the law courts of that great country who tells you and me that Auricular Confession is the most demoralizing and degrading institution, the Popes of Rome themselves have been forced by the providence of God to be the witnesses of that demoralizing agency. Yes! The Popes themselves have given to the world the most unanswerable proof that Auricular Confession, far from helping the young and old girls and married women, is a school of perdition.

"Not very long after Auricular Confession had been instituted, rumours of the most horrible scandals between the Father Confessors and their penitents, spread everywhere. In order to put a stop to that state of things the Pope, Pius IV., in 1560, determined to make a public enquiry and to punish all the guilty Father Confessors, who would be accused by their fair penitents. A bull was published by him, by which all the girls and married women who had been misled by their Father Confessors, were ordered to denounce them. And a certain number of high church officers of the Holy Inquisition was authorized to take the depositions of the fallen penitents   The thing was, at first, tried at Seville, one of the greatest cities of Spain

"When the edict was first published, the number of women who felt bound in conscience to go and depose against their Father Confessors, was so great that, though there were thirty notaries, and as many inquisitors to take the depositions, they were unable to do the work in the appointed term Thirty days more were given them   But the inquisitors were so overwhelmed with the numberless depositions that another period of time of the same length was given. But this again was found insufficient! In the end it was found that the number of priests, who had their penitents through the confessional, was so great that it was impossible to punish them all without destroying the church. The inquiry was given up and the guilty confessors remained unpunished. Several attempts of the same nature have been tried by other Popes with the same effect

"But if those honest attempts on the part of some well-meaning Popes to punish the confessors who destroy the purity of their penitents have failed to touch the guilty persons, there are, in the good providence of God, infallible witnesses to tell you that Auricular Confession is nothing else but a snare to the confessor and his penitents. Yes, those bulls of the Popes are irrefragable testimonies that Auricular Confession is one of the most powerful inventions of the devil to corrupt the heart, pollute the body, and damn the souls of confessors and penitents

"Auricular Confession was invented by the priests of Bacchus five hundred years before Christ came to save the world by shedding His blood for poor sinners. Those priests of Bacchus had to swear never to marry, just as the priests of Rome And they made use of Auricular Confession, just as the priests of Rome, to make their celibacy a most easy thing by the knowledge they have of the personal disposition and weakness of their penitents Through the Auricular Confession they know those who are strong and those who are weak among their penitents—and you understand the consequences of that knowledge by your own common-sense.

"When, at the beginning of Christianity, the priests of Bacchus had introduced themselves into the church and tried to establish Auricular Confession, they were courageously opposed by all the holy Fathers of the first centuries of Christianity St Basile, in his commentary on Psalm thirty-seven, speaking against Auricular Confession says: ' I have not before the world to make a confession of my sins with my lips; but I close my eyes and I confess my sins in the secret of my heart.   Before Thee, O God, I pour out my sighs, and Thou alone art the witness, my groans are within my soul: there is no need of many words to confess my sins sorrow and regret are the best confession.   Yes, the lamentations of the soul, which Thou art pleased to hear. are the best confession.'

"St Chrysostom, in his homily 'De Poenitentia,' Vol. 4, Col 901, says· 'You need no witness of your confession Secretly acknowledge your sins, and let God hear them.'

"In one of his homilies, he says· 'Therefore I beseech you always to confess your sins to God only   I, in no wise, ask you to confess them to me.   To God alone you must show the wounds of your soul. and from Him alone you must expect the cure   Go to Him, then, and you shall not be cast off, but healed   For, before you utter a single word, God knows your prayer '

"And in his commentary on Hebrews 12, he further says: 'Let us not be content with calling ourselves sinners; but let us examine and count our sins, and then I do not tell you to go and confess them to a man, according to the caprice of some but I will say to you with the prophet: Confess your sins to God acknowledge your iniquities at the feet of your Judge: pray in your heart and your mind, if not with your tongue, and you shall be pardoned '

"In his homily on Psalm 1, the same St John Chrysostom says: 'Confess your sins every day in prayer   Why should you hesitate to do so?   I do not tell you to go and confess your sins to a man, a sinner as you are yourself, who might despise you if he knew your faults.   But confess your sins to God, who alone can forgive them '

"The same St John Chrysostom, in his admirable homily 4. says· 'Tell me why should you be ashamed to confess your sins?   Do we compel you to confess them to a man who might one day throw them in your face?   Are you commanded to confess them to some of your equals who could publish them and ruin you?   What we ask of you is simply to show the sores of your soul to your Lord and Master, who is also your friend, your guardian, your physician '

"In a small work of that St John Chrysostom 'Cathechisis ad Illuminandum,' we read the following remarkable words: ' What we should most admire is not that God forgives your sins, but that He does not disclose them to anyone, nor wish us to do so What He demands of us is to confess our transgressions to Him alone that He may forgive them '

"St Augustin, in his beautiful homily on the 31st Psalm, says· ' I shall confess my sins to God, and He will pardon them all. And such confession is not made with the lips, but with the heart only I had hardly opened my mouth to confess my sins, when they were pardoned; for God had already heard the voice of my heart.'

"I would keep you all the night should I repeat to you all that the holy Fathers have said to show us that Auricular Confession was not practised in their time and that they were opposed to it We know the year and the day when it became a dogma in the Church of Rome, as we know the year and the day when the idolatry of the wafer-god and the other recent idolatry of the Immaculate Conception of Mary were invented.

" When our Saviour said to His disciples, ' What ye shall bind on earth shall be bound in heaven and what ye shall loose on earth shall be loosed in heaven;' or when He said, 'The sins you forgive on earth shall be forgiven in heaven, and the sins you shall retain on earth shall be retained in heaven,' He was speaking of the sins committed against each other

"St. Peter understood Him well, when, hearing our Saviour saying admirable words, he said 'Good Master, how many times shall I forgive my brother the sins he has committed against me, shall it be seven times?' He answered, 'I do not say seven times but seventy times seven.' And He finished that address which was given to a multitude of people, by saying· 'So will my Father do to you, if, from your heart, you do not forgive the sins your brother has committed against you.' Do you not say every day the admirable prayer which our Saviour Jesus Christ has brought from heaven for every one of us? Well, what are we taught to say about our sins in that prayer that God may forgive them? 'Forgive our trespasses, as we forgive those who have trespassed against us.'

"You see our Saviour does not teach us to say, 'Forgive our sins as we confess them to the priest.' No! But He wants us to say, 'Forgive our trespasses, as we forgive those who have trespassed against us,' and He adds, 'If you forgive those who have offended you I will forgive your sins.' Yes, if you forgive the sins of your neighbour against you, God Almighty will forgive your sins It is Christ Himself who made that promise, and when God has forgiven you, what is the use of going to a priest to get your pardon?

"Has our dear Saviour told us to go and confess our sins to a priest? No. never! When speaking to the poor sinners, Jesus said to them, 'Come unto Me all ye that labour and are heavy laden and I will give you rest.' 'I did not come to save the righteous but the sinners.'

"Our Saviour has said and He does say it this very night to every one of us, 'All those who believe in Me and invoke My name shall be saved!' Saved! and that without going to confess to a priest.

"Then let us go to Him, believing in His love and His mercy, and invoking His name this very night, and our sins are forgiven, we are purified and saved by Him alone!

"What does our merciful God say to every one of us this very night, by Isaiah? 'Let the wicked forsake his ways and the unrighteous man his thoughts; let him return to the Lord and He will have mercy upon him, and He will abundantly pardon' (Isa 55· 7, 8.)

"What does the prophet David say? 'I confess my sins unto thee, Oh my God, and I have not concealed my iniquities. I have said I will confess my iniquities unto the Lord, and Thou forgavest my transgressions.' (Ps. 30· 1-5.)

"What does our beloved Saviour tell you and me this very moment? Please listen to His sweet, saving, merciful words·

"'As Moses lifted up the serpent in the wilderness, even so must the Son of man be lifted up.

"'That whosoever believeth in Him shall not perish but have eternal life' (John 3 15.)

"Read the fourteen epistles of St. Paul and you will see that that great apostle never thought of Auricular Confession He has not a single word about it. When speaking to the sinners about the best, the only way to be reconciled to his God, he absolutely ignored that panacea of the Popes of Rome. He always sent the sinners to Jesus and Jesus alone for their pardon

"And St. John, that beloved one of Jesus, what does he say to the poor sinners to get their pardon? Here are his words: 'These things we write you that your joy may be full. This then is the message which we have heard of Him, and I declare unto you, that God is light and that in Him there is no darkness at all.

"'If we say that we have fellowship with Him, and walk in darkness, we lie, and do not say the truth.

"'But if we walk in the light as He is in the light, we have fellowship one with another, and the blood of Jesus, His Son, cleanseth us from all sin.

"'If we say we have not sinned we make Him a liar and His Word is not in us.

"'My little children, these things I write unto you that ye sin not. But if any man sin we have an advocate with the Father, Jesus Christ, the righteous.

"'And He is the propitiation for our sins, and not for ours only, but also for the sins of the whole world.' (St. John, 1st Ep Vr. 1.)

"You see how the Apostle John has absolutely forgotten to advise the sinners to go and ask pardon from their father confessors. It is to Jesus and Jesus alone that he sends them. So that is what I do, to-day. Let us go to Jesus, let us invoke His name, repent and wash our souls in His blood. Then and then alone we shall be forgiven, absolved and purified from our iniquities. Yes, let us go to Jesus and Jesus alone, and we shall obtain pardon and peace in this world and eternal life in the next. But I will not separate myself from you without asking a great favour. Please let those of you who are determined never to go to confess their sins to the priests of Rome, and who will go only to their Saviour Jesus Christ for their pardon raise their hands"

And with tears of joy I saw that every one of that great multitude had forever broken the heavy and ignominious yoke of the Pope to accept the blessed and sweet yoke of Christ.

CHAPTER VI

The Temptation

I was not a little surprised, when, at the beginning of the second week of November, 1858, on opening my door to some one that was knocking, I found myself face to face with the Rev Mr Mailloux, the grand vicar of the Bishop of Quebec, who had led Bishop O Regan to our town on the never-to-be-forgotten third of August of the year before.

After the preliminary exchange of expressions of common politeness, he asked me if we were so absolutely alone that he could give me a confidential message from the Bishops of Canada. I gave him the assurance that we were absolutely alone, and that nobody would hear him, beside our God, myself, and our guardian angels. "Then," he said, "I feel happy to be the bearer of a message which I hope will put an end to the awful scandals and sad divisions of the last two years. . . .

"You have not forgotten how dear you were to those Bishops, nor how kind they were to you. After the Bishop of Quebec had put you at the head of the two most important, beautiful and rich parishes of his diocese, Beauport and Kamouraska, the Bishop of Montreal gave you the greatest favour ever given to priests by allowing you to go and work in his whole diocese, whenever you liked, in union with his curates That same Bishop of Montreal. after having obtained from the Pope the magnificent crucifix you keep as a public token of the personal esteem of the vicar of Christ, has given you the official title of 'Temperance Apostle of Canada,' not only that, but it is from his advice that the city of Montreal has given you the gold medal you carry on your breast

"Well, these venerable Bishops, who have overwhelmed you

92

with honours and dignities, when you were working with them, have sent me with the promise that they will do still more for you, if you come back and submit as a dutiful priest to our holy church! Oh, do not rebuke them. Do not rebuke me, for I am still your friend, as I was when you were in our midst. Forget and forgive what may have been wrong in what the last Bishop of Chicago, as well as myself, may have done against you. Come back, dear Father Chiniquy, to that Catholic Church of Canada, which has taken you in triumph from the lowest parts of the St Lawrence river, to the shores of Lake Huron. We are ready to do still more for you! Come and dry the tears which are flowing on so many cheeks Come back and rejoice so many friendly hearts which are so sad on account of your separation from us."

When saying these last words, he took my hands into his, pressed them in the most friendly way and bathed them with his tears

I would not be honest were I to deny that his words and his tears made a profound impression on me. My poor human and sinful heart was not indifferent to the honours, dignities and riches which were there in store for the rest of my life, if I would only accept the message of peace from the Roman Catholic Bishops of Canada. I would have fallen a prey to the Tempter had not the dear Saviour come to my aid But He was there to succour and save His poor, weak, half-conquered servant. In that moment, a grand, solemn, divine spectacle struck the eyes of my soul. I saw my Saviour "on the summit of that high mountain, where the devil had taken Him to show Him all the kingdoms and the glory of the world." It seemed to me that I was hearing the devil's voice, saying, "All these things I will give thee if thou wilt fall down and worship me" But the answer which I had heard from the lips of Jesus, thrilled my soul. "Get thee hence, Satan; for it is written. Thou shalt worship the Lord thy God and Him only shalt thou serve." As a flash of lightning it passed through my whole body, trans-

forming me into quite a new being. I felt strong as an unconquerable giant, though I knew that the strength was not my
own strength, and I answered· "My dear Mr Mailloux, I am
much obliged to you for the interest you show me, and I
appreciate the sincerity of your motives in bringing that
message from the Bishops of Canada   I would surely accept
your friendly offer, if I had left the Church of Rome from
any worldly motives.   But my God knows that it is only for
His sake and to obey Him, that I am what I am to-day
Please pardon me the disappointment I give you.   Tell the
good Bishops of Canada that I am very grateful for this last
friendly effort they make to persuade me to return to the
Church of Rome; but tell them also that though they should
offer me all the dignities and the incalculable treasures of the
Church of Rome, I would not take them in exchange for the
treasures I have found in the Bible"   And when saying
these last words, I presented him with the Divine Book

My last words had hardly fallen from my lips when his
head fell into his hands, and he wept as a child for a few
minutes which seemed to me an hour, for I felt exceedingly
sad at such a strange and unexpected grief

After he had eased his feelings of disappointment with his
tears, he raised his head and looked at me.   But his look was
not the same as before, his face was like the face of a furious Iroquois (I have been told since that there was Iroquois
blood among his grandmothers).   That Mr. Mailloux was by
nature one of the most ugly specimens of humanity which
can be seen   His lips, naturally too thick and large for a
man, were rendered still more repulsive by a large black
piece of raw flesh on the right part of the upper lip, his eyes
were unsettled, and his very smile was nothing but an idiotic
grimace

Rising suddenly on his feet, he made a step towards me
and brandishing his fists near my face, he said "Miserable
apostate! You sign your sentence of death by refusing the
message of peace I have just delivered to you.   You know

the rights, the laws, as well as the duties of our holy Church Our best theologians tell us that you have no right to live from this fatal hour And our holy Popes in the compendium of our most sacred laws, in our Jure Canonico, tell us that it is neither a murder nor a sin to take your infamous life. If you have forgotten those laws, there will be someone who will make you remember them very soon. You have not ten days to live!"

And his rage was such when uttering these threats, that there was foam on his lips I answered him, "I am not more shaken by your bloody threats than I was by your glittering promises of human glory and honour. I am the servant of a God who can protect me against the malice of all the Popes, the priests, and the slaves of Rome. If it is His will that my blood should be mixed with the blood of the millions you have already slain, I am ready to shed it for the cause of the Gospel"

He was out of the house before I had uttered my last words. Taking his hat and cane he had left at the double quick, and he soon disappeared.

Though I might write a volume to tell what I felt when alone after that dark hour, those who have never passed through such an awful experience could never understand me.

When alone I fell on my knees to pray for more wisdom and courage at the approach of the terrible impending conflict. On the table was the ninth volume of the theology of St. Thomas. I opened it and read that the Roman Catholics had as much right to kill me now, as to kill a wolf which was crossing their fields to eat their sheep! A little farther on, on the same table was the "Jure Canonico" where the Church of Rome says that it is neither murder nor a sin to kill me now; nay, I read that it was such a holy action to take away my life that the sins would be forgiven to the Roman Catholic who would risk his life in taking away mine.

o

The next day, just when going to take my dinner, two of our dear converts came to tell me, "Dear Mr Chiniquy, a rumour is spreading this morning against your character, more quickly and more disastrously than the prairie fires which came so near destroying the village some years ago You must stop it at once, if you cannot do it. we come to tell you in the name of many that you will have to leave the colony"

" What is the rumour"? I asked.

"You know, we suppose," they replied, "that when Mr Mailloux left you yesterday, he went directly to John Bélanger's to spend the night and say his mass and preach to his people, this morning   Well, the few Roman Catholics of the place went to spend the evening with him; they remained till twelve o clock hearing the most shameful and scandalous stories against you   Among other things Mr. Mailloux told them that you had many illegitimate children in Canada; that you had been interdicted and forced to leave the country on that account.   Those who were there last evening, to the number of thirty, are publishing that story this morning against you   It goes with the rapidity and destructive power of a hurricane   As soon as we heard it, we thought it was our duty to come and acquaint you of it   Now you know what you have to do through respect for yourself and your numerous friends here"   I answered them, "Dear Mr. Mailloux is very hard on his old friend!   He ascribes to me gross immoralities   Yesterday he told me that I should soon be murdered   Now I see that before taking away my life the Romanists wish to take away my honour.   With the help of God, we must show to the Roman Catholic ambassador, once more, that he is not in the land of the Holy Inquisition, where injustice and cruelty have full sway against those called heretics   There are laws here to protect our honour as well as our life   Please, come with me to John Bélanger's. where we shall probably find Mr. Mailloux, and then we shall see what we have next to do in the matter."

Five minutes later, we were face to face with the Rev. Mr. Mailloux, whom we found, as we expected, in the company of John Bélanger.

Before any salutation, I said, ' Mr. Mailloux, please tell me, before these two witnesses and Mr. Bélanger who is here, if you know that, when in Canada, I had a great number of illegitimate children and if you have ever told that story anywhere." At this question he became as pale as a dead man and with a trembling voice, he replied, " No, sir, I have never said such a thing. I know that you were a good priest and that you never committed such crimes " These words were hardly uttered when John Bélanger, with a terrible oath, said, " Mr. Mailloux, are you not ashamed to deny such a thing? Last night in my presence and in the presence of about twenty witnesses you said that Father Chiniquy had about twelve illegitimate children in Canada " Mr Mailloux then replied, " I did not say that he had, I said that I had been told that he had "

Bélanger, with another oath, said, "No, sir, you did not say that you were told, but you affirmed that it was so. You ought to be ashamed to deny it, this morning Go away, and never put your foot in my house any more." "Now, Mr Mailloux," I replied, " Tell me before these people if you believe or know that I have been guilty of such crimes in Canada as you allege " He answered, " No, sir, I do not believe that. I believe you were a good, honest priest." " Now, sir, can you say in my face that I have been interdicted and turned out of Canada by the Bishops? " With a voice half suffocated with shame, he said, " I cannot say that, for I know the contrary. I know the Bishop has given you, as a token of his esteem, a silver chalice to say mass." Then Bélanger again said, with another oath· " You are a d—— liar, for you told us last night that the Bishops had turned Mr Chiniquy out of Canada " " Then," I said, " that is all I want to know Good-bye, sir "

When coming back with my two friends, they advised me to prosecute him, saying that they 'could find at least thirty witnesses who had heard him say it. "No, my friends," I answered, "this is not the Christian way to act with my enemies. I prefer to follow the advice of Christ—to forgive

"Besides that, such calumnies of my enemies do not injure me at all   They do more harm to their cause than to ours. Those calumnies bear their refutation with themselves and they bring disgrace only to their authors. You see how he was confounded and trembling in my presence, and how he has been turned out from the house of his best friend "

Just four days later the judge of Manteno, a town six or eight miles north of Bourbonnais Grove, came to visit me. "I think it is my duty, my dear Mr Chiniquy," he said, " to come and tell you that there is a formidable conspiracy among the priests and the Catholic people of Bourbonnais to take away your honour. Yesterday, I was, in my capacity of judge, the witness of a fact that proves it   You know Madam Brosseau, who has the reputation of being the handsomest lady of the town? Well, yesterday when her husband came home for his dinner, he found his wife in tears in her parlour. 'What is the matter with you, my dear, are you sick?' 'No, my dear husband, I am not sick but I am sad,' she answered. 'I have on my conscience a burden which is heavier than a mountain   I ought to have revealed it to you long ago, but I never dared   You remember when you were in California some years ago, Father Chiniquy was our priest in Bourbonnais, and I had to go to confess to him. But instead of acting with me as an honest priest, he did things which I am ashamed to repeat: but now that he is an apostate, and tries to destroy our holy religion, I think that it is my duty to reveal the truth.' Brosseau of course was furious against you. He said to his wife, I must have that infamous Chiniquy punished   I am just going to Judge Baby to know the best way to prosecute him.'

"When with me Brosseau related the story he had heard from his wife   I told him he was doing well to punish you as you deserved, but, I said, 'I must go with you to get the deposition of your wife.' When with her, in the presence of her husband, she not only repeated what she had told him, but she added many things more. I congratulated her on her courage, and I said, 'Madam, I will now write down your deposition in the presence of your husband. Give the details of Chiniquy's infamous conduct, for it will be necessary to have that presented to the court.' And I began to write. I covered three sheets with the most infamous acts that a man can do and that a woman can reveal. Then I took from my pocket this Bible, and I said, 'Now madam, you must swear on this Bible that what you have just said is the truth, for, as a Justice of the Peace, I must have your oath before taking another step in this matter.' Looking at me with a distressed countenance, and trembling from head to foot, she exclaimed: 'Is it possible that I will have to swear to these things?' 'Yes, madam, we cannot take another step in this matter without your oath.'

"Then bursting into tears and concealing her face in her hands, she exclaimed, 'I cannot swear that.' 'Why not?' I replied. 'Because it is a lie from beginning to end,' she said. With a terrible imprecation, her husband said, 'Why have you told us such abominations against Father Chiniquy when it is not true?' 'Because my Father Confessor, the last time I went to confess, asked me to do that,' she said.

"Now, Mr. Chiniquy," said the judge, "if I had any advice to give you, it would be to prosecute the priest at once."

I answered, "No. I prefer to follow the advice of my Saviour. When I left the Church of Rome, I knew the cost The prophecy of Christ must be fulfilled in me as it has been in those who have fought Rome before me. Our Saviour warned us of these things when He said:

"'Blessed are ye when men shall revile and persecute you, and shall say all manner of evil against you falsely for My sake. Rejoice and be exceeding glad: for great is your reward in heaven: for so persecuted they all the prophets which were before you.'"

CHAPTER VII

Father Brunet. A Prisoner in my Stead

Curam habe boni nominis

The calumnies of the Reverend Mailloux and Mrs Brosseau were still ringing in my ears when a new storm burst on my head which would surely have destroyed me had not my merciful God come to my help

A revival (a retreat) had been preached in Bourbonnais by Reverends Mailloux and Brunet previous to their departure for Canada, and the whole population had been induced to go and confess their sins to those two priests Among the sins they were asked to confess was that of having gone to hear the address of Father Chiniquy. They were then warned against committing that sin any more by being assured that Chiniquy was an apostate—a monster. To this many times the penitent replied. "We know nothing bad about Father Chiniquy, except that he has left our holy church. but this is his business. We do not want to follow him. How can we promise never to speak to him, when he is in our midst, and that very often our daily business obliges us to meet him for advice and often for help"

To this the Father Confessor had invariably replied "Chiniquy is an excommunicated priest; he is a monster, he has set fire to your church and turned it into ashes."

"But how do you know that it is Father Chiniquy who has set fire to our church?" generally replied the penitent.

"You must believe me, as I am your Father Confessor," had answered Father Brunet . . . "I advise you even to tell it to your neighbours and friends that they may avoid his company, that he may be forced to leave the place."

A goodly number of those honest, though cruelly deceived countrymen, left the confessional box indignant at the malice and calumny of their Father Confessor They spoke to each other of the evident plot of those priests to destroy me, and they came to the honest conclusion that their duty was to warn me

Remembering that my Saviour, when struck by the coward officer, had answered him· "If I have spoken evil, bear witness of the evil but if well, why smitest thou Me" (John 17:23), and that Paul had appealed to Caesar, I felt that it was not only my right but my duty to bring my implacable, cruel and cowardly enemy before my country to ask him to prove what he had said, or to repair the injury he had caused me to suffer. I could not do the work which the good Master had entrusted to my feeble hands without a good name.

The next day more than one hundred carriages were at the door of the parsonage of Bourbonnais in order to accompany Father Brunet in triumph to the depot of Kankakee, where he was to take the train for Montreal Numberless gay banners were floating to the breeze, with the mottoes: "Honour to Father Brunet," "May God bless Father Brunet," etc.

The good (?), the holy (?) Father Brunet was sitting at a rich table loaded with the most exquisite dishes, and surrounded by many priests and friends gathered there to thank and honour him for the glorious battles he had fought, and the glorious victories he had gained against the infamous apostate, Chiniquy. the last six months. Two o'clock had just struck. It was the moment the choice and excellent desert was being brought before the holy (?) priests

Suddenly the door of the dining-room is rudely opened, and a , tall man, with a most threatening face steps in. Without saluting anybody, he glances severely over the whole company, and with a stern voice, says: "Is Father Brunet here?"

Who was that strange personage whose rude appearance

and stentorian voice was chilling every heart? It was the Kankakee sheriff, I Burns

His first question, "Is Father Brunet here?" having received no answer, he raised his stern voice and said, "Is Father Brunet here?" With a trembling, stammering voice, and with cold drops of sweat rolling on his forehead, Father Brunet answered, "Yes, sir, Father Brunet is here; I am Father Brunet"

Quick as lightning the heavy hand of the sheriff was on the shoulder of the confounded and trembling priest, with this sharp sentence "You are my prisoner; come at once to the court-house. I will put you into gaol if you do not give me securities for $10,000 for your appearance at the next court, to show you are not guilty of a great crime which is laid to your charge"

And the worthy ambassador of Rome had to leave there and then his delicious preserves and follow the sheriff to the court-house.

The reader can understand the dismay of the multitude, who had come there with their fine carriages and their banners of triumph flying to the breeze, when they saw their Father Confessor in the hands of the sheriff, taking the road to the gaol This was an hour of distress and desolation such as the poor Catholics of Bourbonnais had never before seen, and which they will never forget

To make a long story short, I must say that my prosecution of Father Burnet began the 15th November, 1858, and was ended only the 23rd April, 1861. when he was sent to gaol for having refused to pay the $4,625 which the jury had condemned him to pay for his lying slanders against me

He had brought seventy-two witnesses to prove that I had set fire to their church, but it became evident to the jury that every one of those witnesses perjured himself to please and obey his Father Confessor

When asked the question. "Did you see Mr. Chiniquy

when he set fire to your church?" they all answered "No";
and when asked if they were there on the spot when Mr.
Chiniquy destroyed your church, they all said "No", and
when asked, "Where were you when your church was
burned?" the greater part of them answered, "We were at
home"; and when asked to say if their homes were near the
church, they answered "No"; and when asked to say the
distance from their home to the church, two answered, "Three
miles," and one, "Seven miles." And when the judge himself asked those witnesses how they could swear that Mr.
Chiniquy had set fire to their church when they were so far
away from the spot, they answered, "We know it because our
holy Confessor has told us that it was so and we have sworn
that it was because our holy Father Confessor has told us that
it was our duty to swear as we have done." The Protestant
judge, as well as the members of the jury who heard those
testimonies have told me many times since that they would
never have believed me, had I told them the degree of
ignorance, immorality and dishonesty which are the great
result of Auricular Confession

The fact is that that suit has done more than all my addresses and books to show the people of Illinois that Auricular Confession is one of the masterpieces of the devil to
corrupt the hearts of men, enslave their intelligence, and
damn their souls.

The day after poor Father Brunet was put in gaol, I was
crossing one of the streets of Kankakee city when a Roman
Catholic lady met me. She was just coming from a visit to
the unfortunate prisoner to whom she had brought some comforting words, I suppose, with a basket filled with comforting
delicacies.

Furious with me, she said with a very loud voice, "Shame
upon you for sending to goal such a holy priest!"

I answered her, "It is not I who has sent him to gaol, it is
the people of Illinois through the judge and the jury."

"Shame upon you," she replied again, "but if you think that you have made that holy priest miserable by you malice, you are mistaken, for he is happy."

"Who told you, madam, that he is happy," I asked.

"He has just told me so himself, yes, as he said to me just a moment ago, 'I am glad to suffer for my holy church, for it is for the sake of our holy religion that I came here to fight against that apostate priest '"

"Well! well! madam," I replied, "I thank you for that information, it is really precious to me."

Then entering the store of a friend I asked for a pen and some paper to write the following letter:

"Rev. Father Brunet:—

"I am just receiving the news which does exceedingly gladden me A lady who has visited you has just assured me that you were happy to be where your are Then allow me to tell you that there are two men very happy, to-day, in Kankakee, for I am also happy to see you there in that very gaol where you wanted to send me, by inventing the calumny that I set fire to the church of Bourbonnais.

"Wishing you to continue to be happy to the end of your twelve years of reflections,

I am, your devoted,

(Signed) C. CHINIQUY."

It appears, however, that the good priest of Rome was not to be very long happy. There was a multitude of rats in that gaol which were troubling his peace during the day and prevented him from sleeping during the night by mercilessly biting him

He then began to think how he could manage to get out of this new and happy home

It will be interesting to the reader to know that the order of the Oblats, to whom Father Brunet belonged, had made a successful appeal to the French Canadian Catholics and had received the whole sum of money which he was ordered to pay me by the jury, as an indemnity for his calumnies, but the order of the Oblats and Father Brunet preferred rather to commit a new crime than to give the reparation ordered by the court to me. They gave the money to a band of Roman Catholic brigands, some say to the sheriff who had succeeded Mr. Burns, and during a stormy night, the doors of the jail were broken and the black bird escaped to Canada, where he published that during a dark night, the Holy Virgin Mary dressed in a white robe had come to the door of his gaol, opened it, and said to him, "My dear son, come out!" and he had gone out in that miraculous way.

Since the day that my merciful God has opened my eyes to the errors of the Church of Rome and given me the evident mission to show the dark system of lies, duplicity, corruption of that masterpiece of Satan, nothing has helped me more to fulfil my mission than the calumnies, the perjuries, the robberies and the ridiculous fables to which Rome has had recourse, to fight her battle with me, around Father Brunet.

There is no exaggeration in saying that more than one thousand honest Roman Catholics are now walking in the blessed light of the Gospel from what they have heard with their own ears and seen with their own eyes in that celebrated suit; for that suit has been a truly celebrated one in Illinois

And let those who suspect that we are exaggerating, when we say that the action of Father Brunet was endorsed by the Roman Catholic clergy, read in the "Répertoire général du clergé canadien, par Mgr Cyprien Tanguay," page 251, and they will find in a note at the bottom of the page, these very words: "Le père Brunet combatit pour la foi avec un zèle tout apostolique—et ses combats lui valurent six mois d' incarcération dans une prison malsaine des Etats-Unis." Translation: "Father Brunet fought with a truly apostolic zeal and his battles gained him six months confinement in an unhealthy prison of the United States"

Here is a man who invented the vilest calumnies against an old friend, who had seventy-two false witnesses perjure themselves to sustain his calumnies, who used the confessional as means of spreading his calumnies, who got several thousand dollars from him whom he had injured, by keeping the fine to which he had been condemned, who broke the door of the prison where justice held him for his public crimes, and yet this very same man is canonized as a saint and offered as a model of apostolic zeal to the Canadian people!

CHAPTER VIII

The Famine

The years of 1858 and 1859 were disastrous ones for our colony at St. Anne. Two terrible frosts in the summer of 1858 and a real deluge of three weeks in 1859 had completely destroyed our crops, on the low lands.

In order not to perish, we were forced to mortgage our lands and borrow money from land sharks, who made us pay between 20 and 30 per cent. interest.

Of all the words of human language, the most terrible is *famine*.

The first Sabbath in May, 1859, a young woman had dropped dead, when on her way to church. In the afternoon, when in the midst of her desolated family, I learned from her husband that, for the last three months, he and his wife had not taken more than a meal a day in order to prevent their three children from starving!

It was evident that she had died from want of food. No words can tell my desolation in those dark days—the darkest days of my life.

In order to help my poor people as much as possible, I had not only sold my two horses and my buggy, but I had mortgaged my watch, my gold medal, everything I had, even my house and my dear chapel, to get food and clothing for the most destitute.

More than that, I had borrowed from several brokers about $1,000 for which I had given what is called "Cutthroat mortgages," relying on several sums of money due to me, to meet those notes when due. But when the day of payment had come, I had not been able to collect a single cent to pay them.

The priests of Rome foreseeing that, had bought my notes with the hope of ruining me and putting an end to what they called our scandalous schism.

At their demand, the sheriff came and seized everything which could fall into his hand in order to sell them at the door of the court-house of Kankakee city. My last cow was taken, my chairs and table, the piano, even my bed and my library were taken from me. I could see everything go with dry eyes and unmoved heart when I remembered for what cause I was losing them. But I could not retain my tears when I saw my dear and precious books go. Laying my hand on my big Bible, I said to the Sheriff. "I hope you will allow me to keep this Bible as the only thing which I possess to-day," and he granted me that favour.

That night, having no bedstead, not even a pillow to rest my head on. I lay down on the naked floor. But I am mistaken—I had a pillow! Yes, and the most precious pillow upon which a man has ever rested his head—my Bible! I never got such a sweet rest than during that never-to-be-forgotten night when my head rested on the Divine Book!

The next morning my knees were the only table I had to hold my dry and hard biscuits. But if I could not give a very rich food to my body. it was not so with my soul. for I fed it with the Bread of Life. I read in my Bible

"Lay not up for yourselves treasures upon earth where moth and rust doth corrupt and where thieves break through and steal, but lay up for yourselves treasures in heaven, where neither moth nor rust corrupts and where thieves do not break through, nor steal."

After my frugal breakfast, I went to the postoffice. There was only one letter to my address, but. to my great surprise, it had the mark of Charlottetown, Prince Edward Island, a place from which not a line had yet ever been addressed to me. When I opened it. a little piece of paper fell on the floor. I picked it up, and, to my great surprise and joy, that little piece of paper was a check for $500.

Here are the contents of that short letter, signed by the Rev. George Sutherland. "We have heard of your heroic battle against our common foe—Rome You must not be left alone when so bravely fighting in the gap. . . . A few Gospel friends in Charlottetown and vicinity, send you this small sum to strengthen your hands and cheer up your heart. Please accept it with the assurance of our sympathies and admiration. Truly yours, George Sutherland." Five hundred dollars was surely a big sum in itself, and I had to bless my merciful God for it. But what was it, when I was surrounded by at least 500 starving families? It hardly lasted two days!

When this Providential help was gone, and I felt I had nothing but my tears to give to my people, the thought came to my mind that my duty was to go to some place not visited by the calamities which had ruined us, and ask the Christian people to come to our help.

I proposed that plan to the Rev. Mr. Staples, pastor of the Presbyterian Church of Kankakee city. Having approved it, he gave me a letter of introduction to the Rev. John Leyburn, D. D., then editor of the *Presbyterian* of Philadelphia, Pennsylvania, and, without any delay, I started for that distant city.

Having secured a decent room in a respectable hotel, I went to the office of the *Presbyterian*, and presented my letter of introduction to its editor. He received me as politely as he could, but I felt him as cold as an iceberg.

It was the first time in my life I was begging. As a priest of Rome. I had always plenty, not only for myself, but for all those who were in need around me.

After reading my letter, he said "It is a real misfortune that Mr. Staples has addressed you to me, and advised you to come to Philadelphia for help Not a month ago, another priest of Rome, a fine looking man, came to me saying, that he was disgusted with the errors of Rome and desired to become a Protestant. I received him well, and, with many of the ministers of the city, I gave him a helping hand. We even introduced him to our families, and did all in our power to make his new existence as comfortable as possible. But we soon found, at our cost, that he was the vilest of men, a beastly drunkard, a thief and the most impudent liar we ever met. Now, my dear sir, you understand that your coming to us so soon after that ex=priest, is a most unfortunate thing for you. However, I do not want to discourage or rebuff you, the dishonesty of that priest does not mean that you are also a dishonest man, but you are intelligent enough to understand that it puts a mountain of prejudices against you and your mission of charity towards your starving people. Then do not raise your expectations of success too high, but as you come to me to get my advice, I will give it.

"First   To-day, go to the noonday prayer=meeting, at Sansom Street Church, and introduce yourself to the great crowd of Christians you will meet there, giving your name, position, trials, as well as you can, but be as short as possible and throw yourself entirely into the hands of God for the result."

Just at twelve, I was in one of the front pews of the vast and absolutely crowded church, and as soon as I could find my opportunity, I was on my feet to speak on the first six verses of the fifteenth chapter of John.

But I had not yet entered into my subject, when the president rang his bell to stop me, saying, "We are not allowed here to speak more than five minutes."

Disappointed and confused, I had to sit down with the conviction that I had made a fool of myself before that refined English=speaking multitude. I could see on the faces of many the badly concealed expressions of pity for my poor broken English language. My conviction was that this, my first appearance before the Philadelphia people, was a complete failure. In the afternoon with a heavy heart, and confused mind, I went again to Rev. Dr. Leyburn's office. He seemed disappointed and displeased to see me again. But when extending his hand to shake mine, he kindly said: "I was much vexed by the rudeness of our president at the noonday prayer-meeting in so abruptly silencing you before you had any reasonable time to present your subject. As you are a stranger, and a Frenchman, not yet quite familiar with our English language, he ought to have given you at least ten minutes to speak. But do not be discouraged. The Lord rules behind the darkest clouds. What do you propose to do now after your first trial has been such a sad disappointment?"

I answered· "My object in coming again to you, this afternoon, is to ask you to give me the addresses of your principal ministers, with a few kind words to each of them from you, asking them to allow me to present to them my case and the terrible distress of my people.·"

"Well, my dear sir, the only thing I can do is to give you the names and addresses of our principal ministers. But you must give me your word of honour not to say that I have done that. You must not even mention my name. How can I give you the letter you ask when you are a perfect stranger to me? Here is the letter of introduction sent to me by the Rev. Mr. Staples. Take that letter with you as an introduction to the ministers you want to visit. It is the only thing I can do for you just now. May God help you," and with these words, he dismissed me as abruptly as if I had the smallpox with me.

It was too late to begin my visits that afternoon. There were no street cars in those days, and I had only $4 in my pocket to pay my hotel expenses; it was impossible to think of taking a carriage. The whole traveling from minister to minister was to be a walking affair. And in that immense city of Philadelphia, many of those ministers were at a great distance from each other. When alone in my room, I had plenty of time to consider the difficulties which were before me. At every part of the horizon towards which I turned my mind, I could see nothing but dark clouds, unsurmountable difficulties and obstacles of the most formidable nature. But the more I saw there was no hope of success from men, the more I felt the need of going to my merciful heavenly Father and putting my trust only in Him I opened my dear Bible and, in the marvelous providence of God, my eyes fell on these words of God, addressed to Elijah, "Get thee hence and turn thee eastward, and hide thyself by the brook Cherith   . . I have commanded the ravens to feed thee." (1 Kings 17. 3, 4.)

I fell on my knees, and, as much with my tears as with my lips, I asked my God to look upon me and my poor starving people in His compassion.

I could not shut my eyes a single minute in that awful night It seemed that I was hearing the cries of desolation of my poor starving people when there was no one to help them There was before my eyes an awful vision of thousands of starving children asking for food from their heart-broken parents who had nothing but their tears to give them!

Even to-day when I think of that awful night, I cannot understand how I did not die during its endless and dark hours My heart was so broken! And though comforted for a moment by the words I had read, my faith was not strong enough to shake off the fear that my supplications and prayers for the next day's success were to be received by a cold and contemptuous rebuke

At last the long and dark hours of night passed away, and one of the brightest suns I ever saw began to shine. But it could not bring rays of hope to my soul. I could hardly eat anything at breakfast My throat was choked by the bread I tried to take when I was thinking that my poor people were starving I was ashamed to sit at such a rich table when so many dear friends were shedding bitter tears in their desolated homes.

At last the hour of the awful trial had come. I had been told that I could not present myself to the doors of the ministers before eleven o'clock As I had to walk two miles before reaching the first one on my list, I left the hotel at ten, after having given nearly all my money to the hotel keeper.

The day was oppressively warm, 90 in the shade, not a breath of a refreshing breeze through those streets, ten and fifteen miles long, bordered by houses from three to five stories high. I had not walked more than a mile in that fiery atmosphere when I came near fainting. I entered a house and asked for a glass of water, which was very kindly given me This did me good, though the next mile seemed ten miles long

At last I arrived at the door of the Reverend Mr X, and I rang the bell. After waiting a long time, nobody coming, I rang again. Every minute of waiting seemed to me an eternity, for the burning sun was wrapping me with an atmosphere of 90 degrees I was nearly fainting when a negro girl came at the third ringing.

"What do you want, sir?" she asked

"I want to see Rev Mr. X" I replied

"Please give me your card," she said

"I have no cards with me," I replied.

"Then please give me your name."

"Chiniquy is my name," I answered, and a moment later I heard the girl saying to her master—"Mr. Niquichiche wants to see you sir."

"Niquichiche! Niquichiche!" answered the minister "What a strange name! It is some beggar again, I suppose Go and tell him I am busy Let him come to-morrow."

And the negro girl had hardly given me her message, when she abruptly shut the door and left me outside in the burning sun

I had more than a mile to go to the next minister Many times on the way, I came near fainting I had to stop three or four times and ask a glass of fresh water at the grocery stores which were on my way.

It was half past one when I saw the name of Rev. Mr Y on a silver plaque on the door. The servant girl came at the first knock, but she seemed out of breath and very impatient. "What do you want?" she asked. "I want to see the Rev. Mr. Y." "You cannot see him before three o'clock. He is just at his dinner." "Please give him this card (for I had bought a few cards and had written my name on them on the way) and ask him if I cannot sit a moment and take some rest in the shade, inside the door in the corridor." The girl went with my message and soon came with a cold, "No, sir, you cannot sit here, but come back if you like at three o'clock," and she slammed the door and left me out as if I had been a mad dog

I had again to turn my face towards the burning sun and walk another mile to meet the next minister. But I felt so completely disappointed, humiliated, and discouraged by the rebukes I had received at the doors of these two ministers, that I remained some time as paralyzed and unable to go one step further. I sat a few minutes on the stepping stones to rest My head was aching under the burning rays of the sun and I think I would have been killed with a stroke of apoplexy had not a torrent of tears flowed from my eyes . . . Let me confess it to my shame, in that awful moment, I came very near cursing the day I was born

But thanks be to God, that terrible temptation was of a short duration. Suddenly the memory of my Saviour, forsaken and overloaded under the burden of my sins in the garden of Gethsemane, came to my mind It seemed I was hearing His cries, when, in His agony, He said: "Father, if Thou be willing, remove this cup from Me: nevertheless, not My will, but Thine, be done" Strengthened by this solemn remembrance, I reached the house of the Rev Dr Y at about three P. M., but absolutely exhausted To my other bodily and mental sufferings was then added one of which I had heard spoken but had never yet experienced — blisters to the feet. They who have never suffered those horrible pains will not understand me Suffice it to say that it is simply horrible Accustomed as I had been, seven years to walk on the soft grass of the prairies of Illinois, my feet were not prepared for the new trial in store for them. In several places the skin was gone and the blood was running in my boots. At every step I suffered a real torture. It was as if nails had pierced the flesh, or as if burning coals had been applied to them. It was with this new addition of pain that I reached the splendid parsonage of the Rev. Dr Y. This time I was determined to walk into the corridor, and sit a moment in the shade, to breathe some fresh air and recuperate my strength, for I felt absolutely worn out

As soon as the servant opened the door, without saying a word, I entered and sat, or rather fell, on a chair which was there. I presented my card, and said, ' Please give this to the Rev. Dr. Y, and tell him that I have some important thing to communicate to him." The girl went and soon came back, saying "Dr Y is busy, he cannot see you to-day, he is to leave for the country this afternoon "

I answered: "Please tell Dr. Y that I want to see him only two or three minutes on a most important business. It will not delay him."

The servant took my message, but she did not come back.

I waited about five minutes, when the lady herself with her bonnet on her head and her shawl on her arm, presented herself to me suddenly from the parlour. Without saluting me she said, ' Has not the servant told you that Dr. Y was busy and could not see you? If you were a gentleman, you would know that your business was to go. Well, sir, I come to tell you that Dr. Y cannot see you. We are just starting for the country, the carriage is there at the door. If you have any business with my husband, do it by letters; you cannot speak with him to-day. Please leave this chair when nobody has invited you to sit on it."

If I had not gone promptly, it was evident that she was prepared to push me out of the door herself, or call her servants to render her that service I walked out at the double quick to prevent my being forcibly ejected by the servants, whom I saw approaching evidently by the order of their mistress.

But I could not go far. The few minutes of rest rendered a hundred times more painful the blisters of my feet Besides that, my moral as well as my physical strength was completely exhausted

I was as a man who is drunk. The body was too heavy for the enfeebled legs

After a sleepless night, I had not had a breakfast of any account, no dinner—and had been walking for the last five hours under a burning sun in an atmosphere of 90 degrees.

Suddenly, all the objects around me seemed to turn as spinning tops

I walked a few rods, but soon my eyes could not see enough to guide me. My feet struck on a stone at the corner of a street, and I sank down on it unable to walk a step farther With my head resting on my hands, I began to cry: "Oh my God! my God! what will become of my poor people! Thou knowest it, I cannot consent to go back to see their tears and hear their cries of desolation, if I cannot save them from their terrible distress. I am ignominiously turned out from every door of the so-called ministers, absolutely without a friend in this city, without a cent remaining to pay my lodging, unable to walk a step farther, the only favour I ask from Thee is to put an end to my miserable existence just now "

My hope was that God had granted my prayer, for I had hardly finished it when I lost consciousness How long I remained unconscious I do not know.

When I came back to myself, and opened my eyes, I saw several people around me, and a tall lady dressed in black, who was shaking my head and saying "What are you doing here, sir ?"

I was, for some time, unable to answer or to understand my position. It seemed, at first, that I was dreaming.

The kind lady took my hand, and said again, "What are

you doing here, sir?" With a feeble voice, I answered. "I am sick, and unable to walk any farther."

Then the good lady, gazing at my face, exclaimed: "Are you not Father Chiniquy who addressed the noonday prayer=meeting of yesterday, at the Sansom Street Church?"

"Yes, madam, I am."

"And you say you are sick and cannot walk Why is it so?"

"Because my feet are blistered, my boots are filled with blood, and I am exhausted from having walked in the burning sun since ten o'clock this morning."

"O my God!" exclaimed the good lady. And then. calling a cabman who was near by with his carriage, she told him "Please take that gentleman to my hotel; I will pay you"

She helped me to stand on my feet. and the cabman helping me into his carriage, drove me to the hotel.

A few minutes after my arrival the kind lady, with a doctor she had taken with her, was by my side in that comfortable hotel The name of that good Samaritan, of whom we will hear more in this book, was Miss Rebecca Snowdon.

CHAPTER IX

The Angel of Mercy and the Manna from Heaven. God is Our Father, We are His Children

Miss Rebecca Snowdon was the angel of the mercy of God in the city of Philadelphia. Having inherited a large fortune, which she had almost completely given for the support of the poor, and the different Christian work of the churches, she had an unparalleled influence among the ministers as well as among the people. She was the soul and inspiring genius of a large part of the Christian work of that great city. The poor and the unfortunate from every class were looking to her for help and consolation. At the same time the treasuries of the rich were always open to her calls.

Not satisfied with taking me to her hotel and engaging one of the best doctors to give me his care, she spent several hours of the night with him at my bedside.

At first the doctor feared there were symptoms of sunstroke in my extreme prostration, and he did not conceal his anxiety. He asked for another physician for advice. But they concluded that my prostration was due only to anxiety of my mind, the want of sufficient food, and too much walking in the burning atmosphere of the city.

Both doctors did all that could be done to restore me, and my merciful God blessed their efforts in a marvelous way.

The next morning they declared that I was well enough to attend the noonday prayer-meeting of the next day. Miss Snowdon then said: "As the doctors hope that you will be able to-morrow to attend the union prayer-meeting of the Sansom Street Church, I will go to see Mr. George H. Stuart and ask him to arrange a special meeting of the ministers, and you may trust in the Lord for the rest. Through the press I have followed your steps since your marvelous conversion with your people I have secretly written to several ministers in your neighbourhood, and Mr. Stuart has done the same. The best reports about your conversion and your genuine evangelical work are in our hands, as well as the sad history of the complete loss of your crops; Mr. Stuart knows more about you than you suspect. All that can be done by us to help you in your difficult work, will be done. Be of good cheer, and trust in the Lord.

"There are millions of idle dollars in Philadelphia, New York, Baltimore, and in the cities of New England. By the grace of God some of those idle dollars must be unearthed and go to save your starving people. There are thousands of Christians who will be happy to share with you and your people what the Lord has entrusted to them."

God only knows what balm these words were to my soul. . . . After she had spoken, I asked her to read the 103rd Psalm of David "Bless the Lord, O my soul! and let all that is within me bless His holy name." This she did After that she humbly knelt and sent to the Mercy Seat, for me and my poor people, one of those ardent supplications as she only could do.

That George Stuart of whom Miss Snowdon had spoken, was known to me only by reputation I knew he was one of the greatest Christian philanthropists of our time, that he was at the head of one of the rich banks of Philadelphia, and the founder of the Young Men's Christian Association

The next day he kindly took me, with Miss Snowdon, in his carriage, to the noonday prayer-meeting of Sansom Street Church, and he helped me to walk to the front pew, for I was still quite weak, and my feet were not yet completely healed.

The pressing invitation sent to all the ministers to attend that meeting had spread the rumour that George Stuart and Miss Snowdon had some very interesting new facts to present about Father Chiniquy and his people. The church was crowded to its uttermost capacity by the élite of the city. Not less than sixty ministers had come to the appeal.

As soon as the first preliminaries of the meeting were over, Mr Stuart having asked and obtained permission to speak twenty-five minutes instead of five, gave the history of our conversion by reading half a dozen interesting letters of ministers who had visited us. And he depicted the spectacle of our sufferings from the loss of our crops with such a burning eloquence that there were no eyes dry in that large audience.

He concluded by saying: " It is one of our wisest regulations not to beg any money in our noonday prayer-meetings, and I will not break that law, but in the name of our Saviour Jesus Christ, I ask all the ministers who are here, and those of you my Christian brothers and sisters who can do it, to remain in order to hear from me and Miss Snowdon what we consider to be our duty in this solemn hour."

Only very few left the church after the benediction.

At the invitation of Mr Stuart, the ministers came to the front After a fervent prayer from one of them, the assembly was organized into a new one under the presidency of George H. Stuart, in order to put to me the questions they desired about our colony and myself One of the leading ministers then asked me if I had joined any denomination

I answered, " No, sir, not yet. After we had accepted Christ for our only Saviour and the Gospel for our only rule of faith, we publicly gave up our allegiance to the Church of Rome and we called ourselves Christian Catholics " " Why did you not connect yourselves with one of our great Christian denominations?" asked that reverend gentleman. " That denomination would have taken you by the hand, and they would have helped you through your present difficulties "

I answered, " The joining of one of your denominations is a more difficult thing than you suspect. You have no idea how your unfortunate divisions look to the eyes of a new convert from Rome. As you want me to speak plainly, I will tell you the truth on that subject Your divisions are a frightful scandal to us they make us unspeakably sad. There we see the grand Episcopal Church so much opposed to what she calls the dissenters, that she will not allow a single one of their ministers to speak in her pulpits, or receive the communion at her altars. Here we find the Presbyterians divided into several camps fiercely fighting against each other. Every one of you knows how the United States are just now filled with the deplorable scandals of the war between the two grand sections of the Presbyterians under the names of Old School and New School A little further we find the Lutherans with their crucifixes and so many other ways of Romanism, assuring us that they are the best branch of the Church of Christ. But at a little distance further we see and hear the fiery and pious Methodists telling us a very different story. I have many reliable volumes in my library showing me that there are more than 100 different denominations of Protestants, many of them fighting each other like wild cats! How can we find which is the best, the most evangelical, the most really Christian among that multitude of denominations, when they, more or less, condemn each other? Have you ever thought of the amount of study required to know which is the surest, the shortest way to heaven among so many roads which lead into such different, not to say opposite, directions? Do you not see that this is a most intricate, difficult, not to say impossible thing. for a man just coming out from the dark dungeons of Popery? Oh' dear Christian friends, why are you not one? Your divisions, your animosities, your quarrels are a terrible stumbling-block to us. When will come the happy day when the Episcopalians, the Presbyterians, the Baptists, the Methodists and the Congregationalists, etc , will embrace each other and forget their differences at the dear Saviour's feet! Then the world will be saved. Then and then only this world will be brought by an irresistible, a Divine power, to the feet of the Lamb who will make the people pure with His blood, and free with His Word!

"You advise me, my dear and venerable brethren, to join one of your denominations! It is my prayerful desire since the happy day I found my dear Saviour Jesus Christ, who washed my soul in His blood. But the more I study your different books of explanations about your peculiar articles of faith, the more I find it difficult, not to say impossible, to make a choice And the more I think that we, the new converts of Rome, do well to accept for the only rule of faith the answer of our Saviour to the young lawyer who asked him, 'Good Master, what must I do to have Everlasting Life?' 'Love God, My Father, who has so much loved you, that He has sent Me to save you Love your neighbour as yourself, repent, believe, invoke My name, and you will be saved.' Is that not the very platform brought from heaven by the Son of God to save the world? My heart is sad when you invite me to join one of your denominations For I want to join them all I want to embrace them all and press them all to my heart as equally being the children of God. Beloved of Christ, I do not want to reject a single one of you, so long as you love our Saviour Jesus Christ and believe in His atoning blood to save us. But if I unite with the grand Episcopal Church for instance, will I not then be deprived of proclaiming my Saviour's love in the other churches? Will it not be a sad necessity to consider myself above the rest of my Methodist, Baptist, or Congregationalist brethren? If I unite with the Baptists, after being immersed, will I not be forbidden to sit at the Lord's table, as a brother, with the Presbyterians and the rest of the Christians? Will not the rest of the disciples of Christ be as excommunicated, profane men, and strangers to me?

"Are you prepared to tell me that that platform built by the hands of Christ Himself, 'Love God and thy neighbour, repent, believe in Me, invoke My name' is not large enough to keep us all: or that it is not holy enough to save us all?

"But I do not come here to teach you, my beloved and venerable brethren, I come to be taught by you. It is my desire to follow your advice and if possible join with one of your Christian denominations. For I feel that if we do not, our newly converted congregations will soon form, as a new division, a new denomination, under the name of Chiniquy's church—a thing which we must avoid at any cost. That appellation of Chiniquy's church has already been given us, to my great distress, by the Roman Catholics. But this choice of the denomination with which we will unite requires a great deal of attention, study and prayer. Please tell us how much time you give us to make that choice?"

The reverend gentleman who had been selected to address me, said, "As you have already read and thought much about that matter, we think that you could give us your choice to-morrow. We answer, I pledge my word of honour, that the denomination you will join will take you and your converts by the hand, and help you to go through the difficulties by which your faith is so much tried."

And turning his face towards the ministers surrounding him, he said: "Do you not sanction what I have said, and do you not promise Father Chiniquy that you will do all in your power to persuade your church to help him when he will have connected himself with one of our denominations?" They all answered, "Yes! we do promise that." I then said, "I cannot sufficiently thank you, venerable and dear brethren, for this unexpected, unmerited, and so great kindness towards me. You give me one day to consider which is the most evangelical Christian denomination among you, and if I join that denomination, my dear people and myself will be delivered from the terrible calamity which is upon us! This is very kind, very liberal indeed! But allow me to show you that I am still more liberal than you are. I do presently give you three days to consider and solve that great question of the most evangelical Church

"If it is an easy task for me, as you say, to find out that great and marvelous secret in one day, it will be more easy for you all to find it in three days. I am here alone, without experience, and without knowledge of the great questions involved in that finding whilst you will not only be sixty against one to resolve that great problem, but you are among the most learned men of the United States, being also well versed in all the questions and the difficulties involved in that work. Yes! I ask you again, please take three days for your researches, and the moment you unite in finding what I want to know, tell it to me. I solemnly promise here that I will connect with that denomination at once."

The last word was not yet out of my mouth when a burst of enthusiastic applause shook the very walls of the vast edifice Every one seemed to be beside himself They were clapping their hands, striking the floor with their feet, waving their handkerchiefs in sign of approbation, and crying, "Bravo! Bravo! That is right! That is right!"

Mr. Stuart, who had been among the most enthusiastic in applauding, rose, and said, "The lesson Father Chiniquy has just given us, is one of the best we ever had· it is worth a million of dollars. I wish all the echoes of our vast plains and high mountains would carry them over all the Protestant Churches of the five continents. Father Chiniquy has put us Protestants into a bag out of which we cannot escape. Yes! our miserable, ridiculous divisions are a shame! How can we ask him to do a thing which not one of us can do—nay, a thing which cannot be done by sixty, by a million of us! Would to God that we were *one* as our Saviour Jesus Christ wants us to be one, that the world might see that He is really the Saviour of our world Without that unity, I fear much that our Christianity is a sham! Would to God that our theologians would have kept the Christian nations on that platform on which Father Chiniquy and his people stand to-day!

" I move that no more effort be made to ask him and his converts to come down from that large and divine platform which he has so wisely chosen and on which he so nobly stands! Is he not safe on it? Who will second my motion?" And the whole assembly—ministers and people—were on their feet to second it.

" I move a second motion," said Mr Stuart, "which is, that we respectfully ask the ministers and officers of every denomination in Philadelphia to invite Father Chiniquy to address their people every evening of next week, including the Sabbath, and that collections should be taken at each meeting for him and his people to save them from their great tribulation."

. That motion was seconded with thunders of applauding voices. "Here is my third and last motion," said Mr. Stuart. "I move that just now, a collection be taken by Miss Snowdon and other ladies she will choose, to help Father Chiniquy and his people. I have had small cards put in the pews that you may write your names with the sums you wish to give, if you have not the cash with you; and to give a good example, I put these $200 into Miss Snowdon's plate "

This motion was again seconded by the whole people The collection was immediately taken by Miss Snowdon and the other ladies, and $1,500 were put into my hands, in good promissory notes and cash, before I left the church!

The Israelites perishing in the desert from the want of water, were not more filled with admiration and joy when they saw the fresh water coming from the rock at the touch of Moses' rod, than I was at the strange, unexpected and marvelous spectacle which was before me

The great Christian, George H. Stuart, had touched the rock, and the fresh waters were coming to quench the thirst and save my dear people. I was unable to speak only with my tears of joy and gratitude. My emotion was too great to utter any intelligent expression.

What I heard and saw that day was as marvelous to me as the manna which had fallen from heaven at the prayer of Moses.

I remained twenty days in Philadelphia addressing the people in seventeen different churches. Then I went to New York, where a still greater success was in store for me. Then to Boston Three months later. I was invited again, not only by the ministers of those cities, but by those of Chicago, Washington, Baltimore, Pittsburg, Montreal, Toronto, Springfield and many others. The churches were never large enough to hold the people who wished to hear what I had to say of the mercies of our God towards us.

Wherever I went committees were formed under the name of "Chiniquy's Committee," to raise money enough to pay the mortgages, and buy food and clothing for the people. On my first return home a committee was formed of six of our principal converts of St. Anne, who selected me for the president, and Mr Staples for the secretary, to correspond with our Christian benefactors, spread, I dare say, over the whole world, for abundant help came from England, Scotland, Germany and even from the Australian colonies.

Before the end of the year, all the mortgages, to the amount of $56,000, were paid. Two hundred barrels of flour had been distributed, with as many bushels of potatoes, and thousands of pounds of meat necessary to make the people forget the terrible calamities which had struck them.

Besides that one hundred and fifty large boxes of good clothing had been sent to be distributed

When the last cent of mortgage had been paid, and the numberless cutthroat mortgages given by our dear converts had been torn into fragments, with our own hands, and thrown into the fire; when every one had been fed and clothed and the tears of distress had been changed into tears of joy, I gathered my dear countrymen into their humble chapel, to ask our merciful God to bless our benefactors, and to thank Him for His mercies toward us With the holy prophet we sang together, " O give thanks unto the Lord, for He is good: for His mercy endureth forever. Let the redeemed of the Lord say so, whom He hath redeemed from the hand of the enemy; and gathered them out of the lands, from the east, and from the west, from the north, and from the south.

"They wandered in the wilderness in a solitary way; they found no city to dwell in. Hungry and thirsty, their soul fainted in them. They cried unto the Lord in their trouble, and He delivered them out of their distresses And He led them forth by the right way, that they might go to a city of habitation.

"Oh that men would praise the Lord for His goodness, and for His wonderful works to the children of men! For He satisfieth the longing soul, and filleth the hungry soul with food. Because they rebelled against the words of God, and contemned the counsel of the most High· Therefore He brought down their heart with labour; they fell down, and there was none to help.

"Then they cried unto the Lord in their trouble, and He saved them out of their distresses. He brought them out of darkness and the shadow of death, and brake their bands in sunder.

"Oh that men would praise the Lord for His goodness, and for His wonderful works to the children of men!" (Psalms 107.)

CHAPTER X

A Lesson of the Mercies of God in Disguise

The terrible calamity by which our colony of St Anne had been visited in the year 1858-1859, was almost entirely concentrated on the fertile though low lands of our dear converts.

By the mysterious providence of God, the farmers of the surrounding country had generally been blessed with crops almost as rich as usual. Of course the priests of Rome had availed themselves of the fact to publish everywhere that this was the visible punishment of God.

Though we knew very well that it was not so, we were humiliated, embarrassed and confused when we had to speak on that matter with those of our former friends who had remained in the Church of Rome.

When considering that strange fact, in the presence of God, more than once I had wondered in my desolation, "Why it was that we have been visited by these calamities just after we have heard and obeyed the merciful voice of our God, and given up the idols of Rome to follow His holy Gospel?"

It was only when among our Protestant friends that I understood that mystery of the love of God towards me and my people Without those calamities we would have remained as strangers to the Protestants of the United States and Canada There would have been no intercourse between them and us, and we would have had no opportunity to understand the unfathomable abyss which separates the unfortunate Roman Catholics from the regions of light, intelligence, liberty and true charity which come from the real promised land inhabited by the Protestant

128

nations   Yes! though reading our Bibles and walking in their saving light, there would have been no opportunity, I dare say no possibility, for myself and my converted countrymen to rid ourselves of the prejudices in which we were born, and in which we had lived and grown till then, if the apparently rude, though mercifully tender, hand of our heavenly Father had not forced me, in spite of myself, to go out from among my own people, and to live for a considerable time among the Protestants

What was not the pleasure of Caleb and Joshua when, at the orders of God, they went to explore the Promised Land, after the many years spent in the burning sand of the wilderness!   How their eyes gazed with delight on the green pastures, the gardens, the orchards and the vineyards along the brook of Eshcol!

How amazed they were, when looking upon the magnificent and succulent clusters of grapes which were hanging everywhere from the vines!   How pleased they were, when, bent under the burden of the grapes, the pomegranates and the figs, they turned their steps towards the tents of their own people to show them the incalculable richness of the new land which God had given them!

But my joy was not less, when, after the several weeks spent among the new brothers and sisters I had found in Philadelphia and the New England States, I was coming back to my dear but so tried people of Illinois, loaded with the fruits I had gathered on the way

Surely the $56,000 I was carrying were not less precious than the branch cut down with the cluster of grapes which Joshua and Caleb brought to the Israelites in the wilderness.

However, these large sums of money and the great value of the food and clothing I had secured were nothing to me and my people when compared with the value of the moral treasures I had found wherever my merciful God had directed my steps.

It was then, that, for the first time, I could compare the lives of the Protestant ministers with the lives of the priests of the Church of Rome It was then, only, I could see the immeasurable superiority of the moral, literary, social, Protestant education over that of the Roman Catholic. It was then also for the first time I could compare the home life, the private life, the manners and the daily habits of the Protestant ministers with those of the priests of Rome. It was then, in a word, I could compare the unspeakable misery and degradation of the bachelor priests of the Pope, with the beauty, dignity and holiness of the married life of the ministers of the Gospel

One of the first things that struck me was the high tone of conversation of the Protestant ministers Wherever I went among them, I had to admire not only their learning on all the greatest questions of history and Scripture, but the constant application of their time to the study and discussion of what could improve, ornate, enrich and sanctify their minds and characters.

What a difference between the conversation among the Protestant ministers and what I had heard while among the priests of Rome!

For the readers would refuse to believe me were I to tell them what I know on that subject. I still blush when I remember the silly, the foolish, the degrading, the obscene things I heard from the lips of those poor slaves of the Bishops and the Popes

Many times the most depraved tramp of our streets would have felt ashamed to hear the filthy things which flowed from their tongues as from their natural source.

How many times, after having vainly tried to silence them, I was forced in disgust to leave the room, and to let them alone to finish their unmentionable stories!

But how can it be otherwise when those forced bachelors are obliged to spend the greatest part of their time in hearing the infamies of the Auricular Confession? Their minds are

absolutely filled with impurities so that there is no room left
for any honest thoughts.   The daily, the hourly occasions
the priest of Rome has to speak with his penitents on the
most impure, immoral, unmentionable matters, destroy in
him the natural laws of modesty which separates man from
the brute.

Even the most honest priests cannot avoid hearing, every
day, or many times a day, the recital of the most impure, de-
filing stories.   The natural, the irresistible tendency of
Auricular Confession leaves impressions in the mind and
memory, which, though resisted at first, soon become irresistible for the greatest number of priests.

Can you keep your hands white and clean, if ten, twenty
times a day you plunge them into black ink or dirty pitch?

Thanks to God there are exceptional cases here as well as
in everything else in this world.   But these exceptions are
few and scarce.

Yes, through the defilements of Auricular Confession and
the degrading yoke of their diabolical celibacy, the priests,
as a general thing, have their minds, their hearts, their memory, their whole being so debased and degraded, that their
conversations (with exceptions) have an unbearable odor.
One of the most humiliating trials of my life when a priest
of Rome, was the hearing of their conversation.

After having spent several weeks in the Christian company
of those ministers and having remembered the tortures I had
suffered, when forced to hear the silly, disgusting, stupid or
childish conversations of the priests, I felt as having passed
from darkness into light, from death into life, from the doors
of hell to the mansions of the saints in heaven, and I blessed
my God for His mercies towards me and my people.

Another thing which made me understand that the dire
trials through which we had passed were among the greatest
favours of our God to us, was the opportunity it gave me, for
the first time, to see the blessed influence of the wife of the
minister not only in the parsonage but in the church.

It was when in the presence of those angels of the mercies of God, at the side of the minister of the Gospel, that I understood the sophisms of Rome about the celibacy of her priests

Everywhere, but particularly in the parsonage, the power of the wife is like the influence of the sun in the world

As the sun gives light and life to the world, so the wife of the minister is a focus of light and life in the church. Not only she adds to the moral strength and influence of the minister by her presence, but she is herself a tower of strength for her husband and his people

She helps him to console the afflicted and to feed the poor. More than the minister himself, she finds out the secret trials of the families, and she knows how to apply the remedy. She is his best counselor in the hours of anxiety as well as his surest aid in the darkest hours of trial.

As the sacred duties of the minister of the Gospel are numerous, and as it is very often impossible for him to see and do everything he would like to see and do, she supplies him with a will, zeal, and a success which nobody else can equal

As the warm and shining rays of the sun expel the damp atmosphere and the darkness from the house, so the presence of the wife of the minister expels the chilly and dark atmosphere which turns the house of the poor bachelor priest into a hell on earth

Our great God knew well what He meant when He said, "It is not good for man to be alone," and Paul understood well also, the meaning of this sentence, when he said, "Let every man have his own wife."

Marriage is not a human institution it is a Divine one, in this sense, that it has been instituted by God Himself. The vows of celibacy are an insult to God This is the reason why we do not find a single word in the Bible in favour of the vows of celibacy. Vows of celibacy are a Pagan institution The priests of Bacchus, just as the priests of Rome, were

bound by vows of celibacy.   To-day, again, the priests of Vish-
nu, in India, like the priests of Rome, are tied by the impious
vows of celibacy before becoming the priests of their ugly
idols.

To keep his fatal and criminal vow of celibacy, the priest
of Rome has to fight against one of the most sacred as well as
against one of the strongest laws of his own nature, and in
that law implanted not only in his heart, but in his nerves, in
his flesh, in his bones, in every drop of his blood

It is not against a giant man, nor against one of the angels of God, man has to fight to keep his vow of celibacy,
but it is against his great God himself, he has to fight!

And that urgent fight has to be renewed every hour of the
day as well as every hour of the night!

I have known honest but deluded priests successfully fighting all their lives and gaining a doubtful victory against their
God, on that terrible battle-field   But for one who had conquered in that desperate battle, of his whole life, I have seen
ninety-nine miserably defeated and destroyed!

Yes, go around all the parsonages of the 3 000 priests of
Canada, the 10,000 priests of the United States and the 30,000
priests of France and I challenge you to find more than one
in one hundred of those parsonages in connection with
which there is no bad rumour.   And if you can find one in
one hundred free from evil report I pledge myself to show
you ninety-nine parsonages in respect to which scandals have
come out if not to day, the day before

Let those who think that this is too general and too strong,
read the last mandement of one of the Bishops of Louisiana.
They will see that 'No priest in his diocese shall be allowed
to preach except he has accepted the law promulgated that
No servant girl shall be kept by him in his parsonage, except when she will be in a room where no door will be placed
in such a way that the priests will be able to communicate
with her through it ' "

This shows you that the Bishops of Rome know pretty well

how their priests keep their vows of celibacy, when they have the chance to break them. And why is it that this law of the Church of Rome is that no priest shall keep any servant girl in his house younger than forty years old?

Though very few priests ever keep that regulation, it proves to the most blind on that subject, that the Church of Rome herself knows that the vow of celibacy is a sacrilegious blind, a sham, a fraud for the great majority.

A Princess of Italy, who was a nun for several years, Miss Henrietta Carrociallo (she is still living), in her famous book, "Mysteries of the Neapolitan Convents," tells you the same thing.

Within my own personal knowledge, one of the late Superiors of St. Sulpice Seminary of Montreal, Rev. Quiblier, was forced to leave the country after his guilt had been proved in relation to very many of his penitents, among whom were some of the first ladies of Montreal.

The Rev. Guyhot not long since was denounced and forced to leave Canada, where he left many victims, having used largely the confessional to carry on his satanic work.

Only wilfully blind people, to-day, in the whole world, ignore how the priests of Rome make their vow of celibacy an easy matter through the dark mysteries of Auricular Confession.

I had been the sad witness of those hellish mysteries for twenty-five years, when a priest of that Church. How I blessed my God when I could see the Christian dignity, the blessed joys, the gospel and heroic virtues and zeal of the married Protestant ministers! How happy and thankful to my God I was when I could compare the calm and Christian dignity of their ministerial lives in the midst of their families, with the ignominious solitude, the almost constant scandalous, though half-suffocated rumours, the hell on earth, of so many unfortunate priests of Rome!

I then blessed God with all my heart for the calamities which had forced me to leave my sad wilderness to come and explore that Promised Land which was then mine In the midst of that land, how many marvelous things I had found to fill the minds of my people with admiration and joy! With the spies sent by Moses to explore the Promised Land, I could say to my people on my return: "Surely the land whither you sent me floweth with milk and honey and this is the fruit of it. the people that dwelleth in the land is strong; the cities are walled and very great. And there we saw the giants, and we were in our own sight as grasshoppers, and so we were in their sight" But I had not to add. "The land through which we have gone to search eateth its inhabitants." It was the contrary, for, after all, I had found nothing but kindness and heroic charity among its Christian people Surely I had found giants in that land But we had nothing to fear from those giants. I had found them all enrolled under the banners of the Lamb whose blood has been shed to save the world, and they had put their mighty arms at our service to help us to fight and conquer the common foe.

CHAPTER XI

The Debts Paid

" He was wounded for our transgressions, He was bruised for our iniquities· the chastisement of our peace was upon Him, and with His stripes we are healed.

" He shall justify many, for He shall bear their iniquities " (Isaiah 53.)

" He that spared not His own Son, but delivered Him up for us all, how shall He not with Him also freely give us all things?" (Rom 8: 32)

" And as Moses lifted up the serpent in the wilderness, even so must the Son of Man be lifted up: that whosoever believeth in Him should not perish, but have eternal life (John 3: 14, 15)

" And I, if I be lifted up from the earth, will draw all men unto Me." (John 12:32.)

As I dated the blessed hour of my conversion from the moment that my Saviour came to me as the one who had paid my debts and delivered me from the burden of my sins by taking them upon Himself, the only object of my humble labours and prayers since, has been to present that truth to my dear countrymen so clearly that they might accept it, and be happy as I was in its possession. What was then my joy when I found in the present marvelous mercies of God for us, the most admirable arguments and comparisons to make them grasp and understand that mystery of the love of God. as much as man can understand it

The second time I came back from the East, loaded with the donations of our Christian brethren to our new converts. they had come to receive me at the Kankakee station in a tri umphal way, in order to give me a public expression of their grateful feelings More than one hundred buggies and waggons overloaded with people, old and young, with flags in their hands, preceded my carriage on my way home After saluting them and on reaching the town of St Anne, I requested them to stop at the chapel that we might spend a few moments in singing some of our beautiful French hymns, and bless our heavenly Father for His mercies towards us.

After giving them some interesting details about the success of my last efforts in collecting what we wanted to save their properties from the hands of their creditors, I asked and obtained permission to put a few questions to them Addressing, then, one of the most intelligent among them, I asked him if he had any objection to tell us what was the amount of his debt to the money lenders of Kankakee. "The amount of my mortgage," he answered. "was $350 two months ago." "And had you anything to pay that?" I asked him. "I had not a cent," he answered "You know how I lost my crops by the frosts and the deluge which visited us these last two years. My horses and my cattle had perished as well from the bad quality of the food as from the want even of that food" "Now, do you owe anything yet, to-day?" I asked him. With a voice half suffocated with emotion, he answered, "No, sir, I do not owe a single cent; my whole debt is paid The broker whom I visited last week, to my great surprise and joy, told me that before starting for your last trip to the East, you went to his office and paid all that I owed He added, that after paying the last cent, you had taken the note I had given him from his hands, torn it into pieces, and thrown the fragments into the fire in order that nobody could ever come against me with it "

Addressing the same dear convert again, I asked him " Are you very sure that this is not a fish story and a deception? How is it possible that your debt is paid to the last cent, even before you knew it, when you had not given a cent?" He answered. "I am sure that there is no deceit,

no imposture, in that affair. The broker who told me that
has no interest to deceive me. Besides that, I know that
you have done the same thing for many others here around
me   It is a well-known fact that our mortgages have been
paid either by yourself or by the committee of which you are
president, and that our colony does not owe a single cent
more to the lenders of Kankakee, and we have no words to
tell you our joy, our gratitude to God, and to the benefactors
who have thus saved us from a sure and complete ruin."

After this honest man had given his views and expressed
his gratitude in his simple language, I asked him if he did
not find any comparison between this fact and the great mystery of the salvation of the world through Christ, which
was the fundamental truth of the Gospel religion we had
lately accepted   "Yes, sir," he quickly answered, "there is
a great similitude between these two facts   For, just as our
Christian friends of the East have paid our debts to the
last cent, through you, so our heavenly Father had sent His
Son Jesus to pay our debts to His eternal justice, by shedding His blood to the last drop, and dying on the cross   In
both cases the debts have been paid, and the debtors saved
from their creditors without paying a farthing. Our new
Christian brethren of Philadelphia, New York, and Boston,
have done for us in a material way what our Saviour Jesus
Christ has done in a spiritual way for this perishing world."

Then one of the crowd in the back seats said· "The comparison is not quite correct, for when our Saviour paid our
debts, He did not ask us to sign any obligation to repay that
to other people, but the committee (called Chiniquy Committee) has forced several of us, and I, one of them, to sign a
paper by which we promise to give a certain rent according
to what was given us, to support a high school or college in
our midst."

These unexpected remarks came as a thunderbolt in a clear
sky and they seemed to make a deep impression.

I thought it my duty to answer and explain the mistake of

that good brother. "Do you not remember," I said, "that in the beautiful parable of the rich man who had remitted the debt of his poor debtor there was the secret but binding condition that the one to whom the debt had been remitted, was obliged to do the same thing to his debtors? So it is with you, my dear friends: do not think that the marvelous favours our heavenly Father has granted you do not impose any obligation upon you. The admirable Christians of the East are Protestants as you are to-day. With you they protest against the religion of Rome, which deceives the world by teaching that the sinners are relieved from their sins by going to confess to a priest and by doing penances, abstaining from meat on certain days or by gaining indulgence, etc. These new brethren believe, like you, that they were sinners. Through their sins they had contracted a heavy debt to the justice of God. They even believe that that debt was so great, that it was impossible for them to pay it. . . . But they believe, as you do to-day, that God so much loved them, that He sent His eternal Son, Jesus, to pay that debt, by suffering the most terrible humiliations, agonies and death. However, these admirable Christians of Philadelphia, New York and Boston, do not rest there They believe that Christ has put upon every one of them an obligation to love you as He loved them, to help you as He helped them. They believe, in a word, that they have only performed one of their Christian duties in doing for you in a material way what Christ had done for them in a spiritual way.

"Now do not forget it By accepting Christ and His Gospel for your guide, you have accepted the obligation to do to each other what Christ has done for you. You must bear the burden of each other. Your life must be spent in doing good to each other The strong must help the weak, the rich must help the poor The fathers, more than ever in the past, must consecrate their resources, not only to the material, but to the moral and intellectual advancement of their children. This is why the committee has wisely invited you to take the public obligation to consecrate the interest of the large sums of money sent you, to the support of a high school or a college where your own children will learn to become good citizens and good Christians. Remark that it is not in favour of strangers and people at a long distance, but that it is in favour of yourselves (for your children are surely a part, if not the better part, of yourselves) that you have contracted that sacred obligation. It is the knowledge and practice of that law that makes the Protestant nations so superior to the Roman Catholics. It is to the knowledge and practice of that divine law of mutual love and charity that you owe to-day, the marvelous change of your position and the unspeakable joy which fills your hearts Surely you cannot regret that the committee has invited you to accept that loving favour for yourselves and your children "

When I saw that these remarks had been well understood, I said: "This humble house of prayer, after witnessing our tears of desolation, is to-day the witness of our joys· I hope it will soon be the witness of our perfect consecration to the service of God and the salvation of our countrymen who are still under the heavy and ignominious yoke of the Pope. Wherever I have been, through the Eastern and New England States, I have seen an incredible number of French Canadian emigrants working in the factories The greatest part of them has been forced to leave Canada to escape the tyranny and the rapacity of their Roman Catholic priests. For as soon as they have a cent in Canada, you know it well, they must give it for the souls in purgatory, scapularies, medals, images of saints—or they must give it to sing masses to get rain if the weather is dry, or to stop the rain if there is too much of it. What then remains of their money is given to build splendid cathedrals with the palatial parsonages and nunneries which cover the country

"Though still nominal Roman Catholics their faith is much shaken Many are free thinkers and infidels, for they have already too much intelligence to believe the mummeries of the Church of Rome. But they know nothing of the Gospel, for they have no one to give them its Divine and soul-saving doctrines

"Many of those dear countrymen have come to me and I could not refrain my tears of compassion when some of them have said, 'Can you not come to teach us the Gospel as you have done in Illinois, or can you not send some one to do it in your place?" The thought then came to me that it was an obligation to all here to grant them their petition. In the midst of so many new converts we must hope that the God of the Gospel has already chosen some to go and give the bread of life to those perishing souls. Are there not here some mothers and fathers who will offer their sons to the Lord for that holy work? Are there not here among you, our dear young men, some who will be happy to say to their Saviour, · Here, I am ready to go at any risk and peril to preach the Gospel to those who do not know it yet' Let some prayers go to the Mercy Seat in every family, from to-day to next Sabbath, in order to know the will of God on that solemn question. Though I have not a cent, to-day, in hand, for that great and glorious work, my trust in God is so great, that I pledge myself to find the means we want for the young men among us who will hear and obey the voice of heaven when calling them to spread the light of the Gospel among our Roman Catholic countrymen "

And with a short prayer and the singing of a hymn I dismissed the people

CHAPTER XII

New Labourers in the Lord's Vineyard

"The harvest truly is plenteous, but the labourers are few, Pray ye therefore the Lord of the harvest, that He will send forth labourers into His harvest."

The Lord of the harvest had heard the humble but ardent supplications of our dear converts during that memorable week.

There was not a father who, from the bottom of his heart, had not secretly asked the Good Master to take one of his sons to work in His blessed vineyard. There was not a mother who had not offered some of her beloved ones on the altar of her Christian love to spread the Gospel. And many of our boys had said· "Beloved Saviour, here I am command, and I will obey."

Twice during the week we had had public meetings in the chapel, to pray the "Lord of the Harvest" to make His own choice among our young men, and to fill the hearts of those whom He would choose with His Holy Spirit.

At the morning assembly of the next Sabbath we had an immense meeting The weather was splendid, and our large chapel was crowded to its utmost capacity

I had taken for my text the first verses of the sublime one hundred and fifth Psalm, "O give thanks unto the Lord, call upon His name. make known His deeds among the people.

"Sing unto Him, sing psalms unto Him: talk ye of all His wondrous works·

"O ye seed of Abraham, ye children of Jacob His chosen '

After bringing to their memory the marvelous things the Lord had done, by breaking the chains which had kept them

142

so many years tied to the feet of the idols of Rome, I made them remember their desolation at the ruin of their crops, which had forced them to mortgage their properties at such conditions that they could not be saved from a complete ruin without a miracle of the mercies of God.

"But you understand, dear brethren," I added, "that when our great God performed that miracle of His mercies, He imposed upon you the sweet obligations of gratitude. Your own consciences as well as your intelligences tell you that you have something to do, even before the world, to show that you understand what has been done for you   Now let me mention some of those obligations.

"First, with Joshua, let every one of you say from his heart 'As for me and my house, we will serve the Lord'   Yes; let that great God, who has brought you out of a slavery a hundredfold more degrading and oppressive than that of the Egyptians, be your Ruler, your King, as He has shown Himself your merciful Father.

"Second, let every family of St Anne be as a tower of light, so bright that it will be seen from a far distance, to expel the dark night of the errors of Rome from our colony. . . . But there is another obligation of which I said a word the other day on my return from the East.   Some of your sons must be called to preach the Gospel.   O! let them obey the appeal!   Let them heroically be ready to give up home, father, mother, brother, and sister, to follow Christ and help me to spread the Gospel truths among the multitudes of our countrymen who are scattered everywhere in the cities as well as in the country places of the United States.   This is the third and most sacred obligation we have contracted towards our God when we have accepted the great and many tokens of His mercies"

My whole address was then on the privilege and honour of being associated with the Apostles of Christ when preaching the Gospel, and saving the precious souls for which He shed His precious blood on the cross.

I ended by saying "Let us spend this whole day in humble supplications to the throne of mercy for those whom the beloved Saviour will choose, that He may give them the courage to follow His voice, and consecrate themselves to His service This evening, at the end of the meeting I will call those who have heard the voice of the Good Master to come forward bravely and publicly, that we may know and bless them, and that we may offer them to the Lord, as the most precious offering we can present Him"

My request had been well understood. The hours between the two public services of that day were, almost everywhere, spent in fervent prayer At last the hour of the evening service arrived The crowd was so great that the chapel could hardly contain them all. Every one was anxious to know who among our young men would come forward and offer themselves to preach the Gospel This was a secret known only to God; for not a single one of them had said a word about it to anybody—not even his parents. I, myself, was as ignorant as the rest of the people on that affair The subject of my evening address was "The Church of Rome was the great Babylon which had corrupted the world with the cup of her enchantments, idolatries, and impurities But the time was approaching when the Lamb would destroy it by calling those for whom He had shed His blood out of her walls" I showed them that. in the marvelous providence of God, we were the first people who, as a whole community, had been called out of that Babylon, on the continent of America; but I assured them that we were not to be the last Our example would be followed.

I gave the names of many places where Roman Catholics. by hundreds. had already expressed to me their desire to break the yoke of the Pope I told them that they were only the vanguard of an army called by the great Captain of our salvation to fight and destroy Rome on the continent of America, that we had only to keep ourselves faithfully united around the blessed banners of the Gospel, and the God of heaven would soon give us the most glorious victory, etc

After the address, I said "Let us kneel and pray silently our merciful God to make the choice of His own ambassadors, and give them the courage to come forward that we may know and bless them." And we knelt.

The silence of that vast multitude, humbly prostrated, was very solemn   After three or four minutes, I broke the silence by saying· "Dear young men of St. Anne, who have given your hearts to Christ, the beloved Saviour, after washing your souls in His blood, and who wish to spread the knowledge of His mercies and His love among those who do not know them. please come forward around me, that we may know and bless you."

A pretty long silence followed my appeal; but many mothers' and fathers' hearts were beating hard within their breasts in the anxiety to know if one of their boys was to be among those called to be the blessed minister of that Gospel which was now so precious to them

At last we heard a little noise in the back seat. It was one of our dearest young men, who, rising up from his knees, was walking with a slow step and a face beaming with all the marks of true piety and courage. All along the way, the people had to rise from their knees to let him pass through the aisles. From every side we heard whispers· "May the Lord bless you " He had hardly been half a minute near me, when another one from another place in the church came and took his place by the side of the first one. and then another and another, till thirty-three fine young soldiers of Christ were forming a line between the people and me.

No pen can give a true idea of the sentiments of joy and surprise of the people at the sight of that numerous band of brave boys coming to enroll themselves under the banners of the Gospel Tears of joy were flowing on every cheek. But the most happy of all were the loving fathers and mothers who saw their beloved boys marching, with a firm step, to join the recruits of the armies of the Lord.

Beside myself with joy, I took every one of them by the hand, and I presented them, in the name of the whole people, to the Divine Conqueror of souls as the best offerings we could present to Him in return for what He had done for us

The rest of the evening service was a thanksgiving one It was very late at night when we left our humble but dear chapel, our souls embalmed with such feelings of gratitude to God as no human words can express.

Before dismissing our dear young Christian recruits, I invited them to come the next day and spend the afternoon with me, that I might give them my plans for their future

The hope of having, in the near future, so many helpers in my evangelical labours was opening new horizons before me New blood, I dare say, was put into my veins. I felt a new courage and Christian strength in my heart

Already more than two hundred heads of Roman Catholic families, all French Canadians, had given me their names, in Chicago, as renouncing the errors of Rome to accept the Gospel for their only rule of faith; forty-five in Ottawa, fifteen in Joliet, forty in Middleport, one hundred in Kankakee City, and more than two hundred in the surrounding cities in Illinois, Indiana, and Michigan had done the same thing, though I had visited them only a few times. What could I do, if left alone, to cultivate such large and promising fields? But with the hope that my merciful God would give me so many helpers, the future was suddenly becoming as bright as it had been cloudy till now. The first thing I had to do was to give them able, Christian teachers, and in the good providence of God we soon found them, and I soon got the means I wanted for that.

But before long I found that the absence of one or two of their young men was too much for our farmers, who were obliged to engage strangers to take their places in the fields

I engaged myself to give $8.00 a month to help each

family in getting a supply for the one whom I retained in our modest preparatory college, which we called, "The Saviour's College"

I do not want the reader to believe that every one of these young men became a minister of the Gospel, for some of them had to give up their classes for want of health, some were killed in the Civil War. where they had to go and fight the Southern army, a few changed their minds and took other positions; but we always tried to keep the same number in that company. As in the war, when one falls on the battle=field, his place is as soon taken by another one, so we succeeded, in the good providence of God, to find new ones to take the places of those who were missing from the rank and file We now count fifteen ordained ministers of the Gospel from among the young converts of our first congregation of St Anne. One of them, the Rev. Mr. Boudreau, is the pastor of our congregation of St. Anne, which I put into his hands in my eightieth year of age.

To push these young men through their studies till their ordination to the ministry, we had to meet terrible obstacles and to overcome the most formidable opposition from the very men who ought to have helped us But with the aid of God we have gone through all difficulties, and pulled down all the obstacles. Suffice it to say that after these dear young men had studied two, three and four years in our preparatory modest Saviour's College, we sent them to the colleges of Montreal, Toronto or Chicago to finish their course of philosophy and theology. It is now my unspeakable joy to see fifteen of them working with me with great zeal and success for the conversion of the Roman Catholics in their respective fields.

CHAPTER XIII

A Macedonian Cry from Canada

"And a vision appeared to Paul in the night There stood a man of Macedonia, and prayed, saying Come over to Macedonia and help us " (Acts 16 9)

Two very important letters had been addressed to me from Quebec and Montreal in the beginning of January, 1859 The first was signed by about five hundred well-known names,—the second by about one hundred of the principal Roman Catholic French Canadians of the latter city.

Both letters were pressing invitations to go and address them on my reasons for leaving the Roman Church.

Many times before receiving these letters, the thought had come to me that it was my duty to go to Canada and attack the Church of Rome there, in her very stronghold. But I had postponed that work on account of the formidable difficulties and dangers connected with it. No two other places, probably, in the whole world, could be found, where Rome is so strong as Quebec and Montreal To go and attack that giant power where it was surrounded and protected by its most impregnable citadels and armed with its most terrible weapons seemed to me a foolish thing,—a sure suicide

Such was my way of reasoning till I received these two letters. But my views had to be modified and changed after their reception. How could I shut my ears to the cries of those precious, but perishing souls, who were so pressingly asking me to go and give them the bread of life?

At the voice of one Macedonian, heard through a vision of the night, Paul had left everything to meet the appeal. Was it not my duty to go, when, not called by only one voice through a night vision, but by so many hundreds, and in such

148

a public and solemn way? Having been assured by Mr
Gustave Demers, our ablest young evangelist, and Mr
Gauthier, our principal high school teacher, that they would
give the Sabbath instruction during my absence, I determined to start the last week of January to go and work one
or two months in Canada

I will not speak of the distress of the people of St Anne
when I told them that resolution from the pulpit the next
Sabbath   With tears and sobs they asked me not to go and
expose myself to such evident dangers in Canada. I answered them that I felt it was the will of God that I should
go; that my trust was in Him for protection   They would
pray for me, day and night, during my absence, and I would
come back to them full of a new strength, after sowing the
good seed in our dear Canada, where the good Master would
bless it, and make it grow one hundred fold in the hearts of
their brothers sisters and friends who were longing after it.

When on my way to Montreal I had to spend a day in
Toronto   I was not there three hours, when I received a letter
from the provincial Sub. Secretary, Mr. Parent, telling me.

"His Excellency, the Governor, in an informal conversation yesterday about you, has expressed the desire that I
should try to dissuade you from going to the Province of
Quebec to preach against the Church of Rome   Your presence there for such an object will probably bring riots
which the government will not be strong enough to pre
vent or to stop   You know how Gavazzi, not long ago
came very near to being murdered, and how many were killed
and wounded around him   Let this deplorable fact teach
you to be more prudent, please do not raise difficulties or
conflicts in the Province of Quebec, of which you may be the
first victim.   Allow me to give you the same advice   Do not
shut your ears to the voice of
                    "Your most devoted friend,
                              "ETIENNE PARENT
                                   "Sub. Secretary."

I answered:

"My Dear Mr. Parent.—

"Please accept for yourself and give to his Excellency the assurance of my gratitude for the interest you take in my safety. But remember that I am now a soldier of Christ. enrolled under the sacred banner of His cross. If I have to shed my blood and die when fighting for its triumph over its enemies, in our dear Canada, that blood will not have been shed in vain, and my death will be the most desirable one I can wish for

"Truly yours,
"C. Chiniquy"

When on my way from Toronto to Montreal, at several stations I received threatening telegrams, telling me that I was to be attacked on my arrival. But as these threats were not signed by any known persons, I did not pay any attention to them, thinking they were only designed to frighten me

I was, however, to see the reality of the danger when the train arrived at the Montreal station, the first of February A dense but silent multitude, such as I had never before seen at any station, was there, evidently looking with anxiety for the arrival of somebody

Suspecting that I was the object of these anxious lookers-on, I thought that prudence required me to conceal myself as much as I could I had a fur overcoat I raised it in such a way that my face was perfectly concealed, my eyes only could be seen

With the hope that no one would recognize me, I went down from the cars, and walked two or three steps through the dense crowd where everyone was whispering around me, "Where is he? Where is he?"

The accents of the voices, as well as the features of the multitude, told me that I was in the midst of a mob of furious and bloodthirsty Irishmen All of them were armed with sticks, which they were brandishing over their heads.

Of course this made me more determined than ever to keep incognito. I pushed as hard as possible through the crowd, but it was so dense that it was difficult to move on. My anxiety was increasing with the incessant demands, at first whispered but soon loudly uttered: "Where is he? Where is he? The d—— apostate!"

At last a loud voice was heard at a pretty long distance from me, in French, "Le Père Chiniquy est-il ici?" "Is Father Chiniquy here?" I confess it to my shame: that voice sent a thrill of terror through my whole frame, when I felt sure that the multitude which surrounded me was composed of Irish Roman Catholics (many of them drunk) evidently there to murder me.

My only chance of escape was to remain incognito, till I could find a sleigh to take me to my hotel.

The first cry, "Le Père Chiniquy est-il ici? "Is Father Chiniquy here?" had been followed by a deadly silence; but bloody eyes, such as I have never seen, were looking sharply on every side, when the lips, now more free, were filling the air with enraged voices· "Where is he? The d—— apostate!"

Praying my God to protect and shield me, I was more and more trying to make my way through that unpleasant crowd, when another voice was heard asking, with a very strong and energetic accent, "Est-ce que le Père Chiniquy n'est pas là quelque part?" "Is not Father Chiniquy somewhere here?" But by this time the voice was very near, not two feet distant from me. Though I had no idea that the voice was a friendly one, and, though I was still under the impression that that whole crowd was composed of people thirsting for my blood, I felt so ashamed of my cowardice that, with a still louder voice I answered, "Oui, le Père Chiniquy est ici. Que lui voulez-vous?" "Yes, Father Chiniquy is here. What do you want of him?" The last syllable was still on my lips, when, as quickly as a flash of lightning, I saw a great number of people rushing around me from every side. But they were pushing themselves with such energy that no one could stand before them Those who were not in the secret of this movement, were falling on every side like the grass when the irresistible torrent suddenly rushes from the mountain.

Absolutely unable at first to understand what this new noise and tumult meant, I stood a moment amazed and bewildered But the mystery was soon explained, when a friendly voice whispered in my ear "Ne sortez pas de nos rangs Nous sommes des amis accourus pour sauver votre vie menacée par une troupe d'Irlandais ivres et furieux qui veulent vous assassiner." i. e, "Do not move out of our ranks. We are friends coming to protect you against a band of Irish drunkards who want to kill you" In less than a minute, I found myself surrounded by three circles of brave and well armed French Canadian countrymen

Knowing that there was a plot in the lowest classes of the Irish Catholics to take away my life when I would arrive at the station, seventy-five intelligent and fearless young countrymen had formed a secret association under the name of "Francs-Frères," and they had drilled themselves in the most perfect way for several days, in order to be able to go through the crowd with the swiftness and power of an irresistible hurricane, and to form three impenetrable rings around me.

I felt that my merciful God had looked in His mercy on His unprofitable servant He had chosen those dear young countrymen as the angels of His mercy to save my life in that hour, when so many were engaged to take it away I blessed Him from the bottom of my heart I felt absolutely safe in the midst of those three rings. I would have pitied the poor Irishmen who would have tried to go through those circles to strike me.

My generous friends had in readiness a number of sleighs to take us to the St Lawrence Hall where they had engaged the best rooms for me, including the beautiful large parlour, for the price of $50 00 a day.

One of the leaders of that band of dear countrymen, was Guibord, whose burial was to make so much noise a few years later.

What was my surprise and joy when those friends giving me their names after our arrival at the hotel, I found that they were the élite of the literary as well as the cream of our best and wealthiest French Canadian families of Montreal. With only one exception they all belonged to the Church of Rome.

To understand better my feelings of admiration and gratitude, let the reader remember that the previous Sabbath, the Bishop of Montreal had ordered a mandement to be read in all the pulpits, forbidding the Roman Catholics to have anything to do with me. To speak to me or hear me was a damning crime, for which they would be excommunicated. And that mandement had been published in all the French daily papers.

The actions of those dear countrymen who, in spite of such a threat, had exposed their lives to protect mine, and who were surrounding me in that splendid parlour, and overwhelming me with all the tokens of their respect, was already the assurance of a more glorious victory over Rome than I had ever expected. They remained with me till twelve at night, then left me after having concerted the plans of campaign for the rest of the month, with the utmost prudence and wisdom. But before leaving, they granted me the favour I had asked, to read the one hundred and third Psalm· 'Bless the Lord, O my soul! And let all that is within me bless His holy name."

And when alone I read again the so simple and sublime expressions of the gratitude of David for the mercies of his God. In fact, where could I find words more appropriate to express what I felt, after such narrow escapes and such marvelous protection in the very hour of danger? My heart was filled with the hope that, though this evangelical mission was to be connected with great dangers for my life, it was to be a most blessed one. All the echoes of the plains and the mountains of Canada, were bringing to the ears of my soul the dear Saviour's words, "Fear not . . . I am with thee."

The last thought of my mind and the last words of my lips, on that memorable night, were. "The Lord is my shepherd; whom shall I fear?"

CHAPTER XIV

The Gospel Preached to Thousands of Roman Catholics in Montreal. I hear the Priest of Napierville Denounce me from his Pulpit

The Lord of Hosts is With Us, The God of Jacob is Our Refuge.—Ps 46·2

My heart would have fainted within me, the morning of the second of February, 1859, had not the words of the prophet, read at the head of the chapter, come to strengthen me.

Very early the tempter had whispered in my ears, "What can you do here, when alone. cursed by the whole clergy. and absolutely forsaken by the Protestants. For have you seen anyone of their ministers or people here last night to shake your hand or to give you a welcome? No! The seventy-five French Canadians who saved your life are freethinkers who do not care a straw for the Gospel you want to preach.

"They like you because they think that you will help them to demolish the power of the priests whom they hate and fear. But they are night-birds, you will not see them during the day. They are ashamed of you. They do not want to be known or be seen among your friends.

"The ground on which you stand here is cursed by the Bishops and priests as well as by their faithful Roman Catholic people . . . cursed by the Church of Rome, despised by the Protestants, you will be left alone in these large parlours as if infected with the smallpox. You have made a fool of yourself by coming back to Canada after your apostasy from the Roman Catholic Church. You have to go back to your colony covered with shame and followed by the execrations of your French Canadian fellow countrymen. Far from converting them from their errors. you will make them stronger in their faith by your miserable failure."

There was so much common-sense in those thoughts that I had no answer to give them. I felt for a time overwhelmed by their weight. Those thoughts were to my mind what the dark clouds are to the sun in a stormy day; they had taken away the light. I felt surrounded by such a desolating mental darkness, that I could not see where to put my feet, or on what side to turn my face. Alone in that large parlour of St Lawrence Hall, which my friends had engaged for me at such a high price, it seemed that my position was so ridiculous and so compromising, that the people would speak of sending me to the lunatic asylum before the end of the day.

Whether pacing that large parlour, alone, or sitting in one of the fine chairs or sofas, without anyone to exchange a word of friendship, or inquire about me, I was asking myself, "What shall I do here? Why did I come to Montreal? Where are those who invited me to come and speak to them of the Gospel?" There was no answer to my inquiries—no echo to my fainting voice. At the breakfast table I had tried to exchange a few words with the two guests nearest me, but they had refused to answer; the servants were keeping as far as they could from me as if I had had the plague.

Ten o'clock had struck and I was still alone! Every moment of that solitude seemed to me as long as an endless night looks to the poor sick when devoured by a deadly fever. My heart was filled with an unspeakable sadness. My poor soul seemed to be crushed under a mountain of lead. I fell on my knees, and as much with tears as with my lips I prayed to the only One from whom help, strength and life can come. But my merciful God had heard my humble supplications even before I had uttered them. For I was hardly on my knees to pray, when I heard three knocks at the door. The waiter was come to say that several persons wanted to see me. "Let them come in," I answered. And it was my unspeakable joy to see a band of thirty farmers from the vicinity of Montreal, who had been among my most devoted friends when

I was preaching temperance, enter to give me a hearty shaking
of hands with the assurance that the whole people all around
Montreal were pleased to hear of my coming again to spend a
few weeks in Canada.

I had not finished offering them the chairs and the sofas to
sit on, when a still larger number followed, and so on till the
large hall was so filled that there was no more room to sit or
to stand. I was beside myself with surprise and joy.

"My dear friends," I said, "I have no words to tell you
how I thank God for the privilege He gives me to see so
many of my dear countrymen here, around me, to-day . .
You remember how happy we were together, some years ago,
when I was establishing the societies of temperance all over
Canada I see by the expression of pleasure on your friendly
faces, that you remember those happy days. I was then
going among you with a drop of the waters which flow
from the fountains of eternal life—temperance You tasted
that drop and you found it sweet You accepted that temperance as one of the greatest blessings God had ever given
to your families and to our dear country. But it was in this
Bible that I found that blessed drop of water. To-day I
come to offer you not only a drop, but the whole fountain of
the waters of life, by presenting you this Bible, as the most
precious gift heaven has ever given to earth Yes! I am
coming back into the midst of my dear countrymen, to ask
you to accept this Bible as the most precious treasure God
has ever given to man. You will accept it, I hope, as the
bread of your souls, as the light to your steps, as the key
which opens the gates of heaven to those who possess it "

For about one hour I spoke on the Bible and on the
necessity to accept, read and study it in every French Canadian family, as the only way to make our dear Canada
happy, great, prosperous and free

Never have I seen anything like the attention, respect and
pleasure of my auditors as in that happy hour when one of
the chief policemen in the city came and interrupted me by

saying, "The street before the hotel is absolutely crammed with such a multitude of people, who want to see and hear you, that the circulation is completely stopped. Though it is against the law to let such a crowd fill the street, we did not like to be hard on them, when they tell us that their only desire is to see and hear you once more, if it were only for a few minutes. Would you be kind enough to grant the request they have asked me to ask you, which is to show yourself at the window and address them for a few minutes?"

Asking the crowd around me to pardon me if I would leave them alone for a few minutes, in order to grant the petition of their friends, who were in the street, I opened the window To my unspeakable surprise I saw that the policeman had not exaggerated The street was absolutely crammed by such a compact multitude, that the usual circulation was impossible.

The noisy expression of the joy of that crowd when I put my head outside of the window was such that I became almost mute by the sentiments of emotion which filled my heart My address lasted about fifteen minutes—on the text· "I am not ashamed of the Gospel of Christ: for it is the power of God unto salvation to everyone that believeth "

After exhorting them to read and follow the Gospel, as the surest guide to an eternal life of happiness, as the only way to become a happy, great and free people, I thanked them for the joy they had given me by coming, some of them a long distance, to hear the Christian message I had to deliver to them, and addressed a short prayer to our merciful heavenly Father to bless them all with their families.

Then a voice from the crowd said, "Would you be kind enough to give me one of those Bibles of which you have said such beautiful things?" "Yes, my dear friend," I answered, "come this afternoon and you shall have as many as you want "

It was then nearly twelve o'clock, I had spoken over an hour and a half, a part of the time in the open air, through the window, and I was feeling the want of rest; so, after a short prayer, I dismissed the crowd which was filling the parlour But many of them had questions to put to me, and they asked permission to come again, after expressing gratitude for what they had heard.

Where can I find words to tell the sentiments of admiration and gratitude I felt towards my God when alone, thinking of the marvelous things that I had seen that morning?

Peter could not have been more astonished and grateful at the enormous quantities of fishes he had hauled in his nets, at the voice of the Saviour, than I was at the incredible number and the respectful attention of the people who had come to hear the messages of peace I had delivered to them.

What had just occurred that morning was not less miraculous, to me, than the hauling of the fishes, to Peter Both occurrences were true miracles of the mercies of God.

Two o'clock had not struck before not only the large parlour was again crowded to its utmost capacity, but the street before the St. Lawrence Hall was so filled with the people of the city and the surrounding country, that it was rendered impassable At the request of the police, I began by addressing from the window my friends in the street. After I had spoken to them for half an hour, and had dismissed them, I gave an address of one hour to those in the parlour But when I had closed that address, a new crowd, as large, which had gathered in the street and in the corridors filled again the large hall and it was nearly five when, absolutely exhausted, I was left alone to breathe

I soon, however, forgot my fatigue, when one of the greatest Christians of Canada, Sir William Dawson, with Mr. James Court, one of the founders of Pointe aux Trembles College, was kind enough to visit me and invite me to dinner with him at his residence, McGill University. The élite of the Protestants of Montreal, the Dougalls, the McKays, the Redpaths, the Lymans, etc., were there to give me the first as well as the most earnest Christian welcome I ever received from my Protestant brethren of Montreal

But I could remain with them only till eight o'clock, when my French Canadian friends came with sleighs to take me to the Mechanics Hall, where 2,000 of my Roman Catholic countrymen were waiting for a lecture on the reasons why I had left the Church of Rome. In order to keep the rowdy class from our meetings my friends had determined that no one should enter the hall without paying twenty-five cents to help me to meet my expenses.

But will not the readers help me to bless the Lord with the old prophet, that the works of His mercies are above all the works of His hands, when I tell them that the story of this my first day in Montreal, is the history of the following four days, with the only exception that the next day I took dinner with Mr. Lyman and the third with Mr Redpath? By the good providence of God, though we were in the coldest season of Canada, those four days spent in Montreal were so mild and the sun so bright, that the snow was melting all the time. We had not any trouble in any of the meetings except that on the Saturday night, when a few men, sent by the priests, tried to make some noise, but they were stopped by the police and turned out of the hall

During those four days it had been my privilege to present the Bread of Life to at least 10 000 hungry souls and to distribute 500 Bibles and Testaments. Eternity alone will reveal the good done during those four days. The Church of Rome lost her power over many who began to see the light of the Gospel and to love it, and though the fruits were not ripe to be gathered immediately into the granaries of the Father, the good seed was not lost. To day we see the fields, everywhere, covering themselves with a rich crop which will soon be ripe

The night of Saturday had been chosen by my friends to drive me to Napierville, which was the first parish we wished to attack

Though I was very tired, I traveled all night, in order to be in that village at the dawn of the Sabbath. It had been found less dangerous to select that time.

It was about four o'clock Sunday morning when I could take some rest in a dear friend's house The sleep from four to eleven that morning was sweet indeed For my heart was filled with such a joy! And the expressions of gratitude of the thousands I had preached the Gospel to, the last four days, were like music from heaven to my soul

When the hour of dismissing the Roman Catholics from their church, after mass, had come, I dressed myself to go and meet the people at the door of the church My host tried to dissuade me from that project, by showing the evident danger I was running to be insulted, or even beaten if not killed by the people. "It is to-day," he said, "that the letter of the Bishop against you will be read in the church you will be shown there under the darkest colours. The people will be furious against you when they will have heard their priest calling you 'a devouring wolf' Do not go into the midst of such a people when there will not be any one to protect you." I answered him, "You are mistaken when you think that I am alone. I do not come here in my own name, or for my private interest and pleasure. There was no pleasure for me last night to travel through the three feet of snow and the frost of one of your coldest nights of a Canadian winter; and I have no personal interest, surely, to go into the midst of that poor deluded people. But I am the ambassador of Christ and I am sure He is with me to protect and shield me as He protected Daniel in the den of lions."

And I went to the door of that large church. When there, without noise, I opened it a little to see if the service was near the end. The priest was in his high pulpit, just beginning to read the long and terrible letter of the Bishop against me. I was represented as the ambassador of the devil, a monster, a devouring wolf among defenseless lambs The people were forbidden under pain of excommunication and eternal damnation, to hear me, shake hands with me, to lodge and receive me into their houses, etc

When the priest had finished reading that interesting letter from his superior, he added his remarks, and said, that the eternal fires of hell would be the abode of those of his people who would listen to my seducing words, or talk with me or even shake hands with me "That monster has already sent to hell thousands of precious souls," he said, "and he is coming into the country only at the instigation of the devil to destroy and damn you. Though I hope that he will not come to soil our dear parish of Napierville with his infectious presence, I hope that, if he comes, you will give him such a reception that he will not be tempted to come again."

After these words he finished his mass by blessing the people and dismissing them.

I had closed the door before any one could suspect that I was there hearing every word of their priest against me, and I had withdrawn to the northern corner of the high platform which the people had to pass from the church down the stairs

No words can tell the surprise of that people, when, coming out of the building, they perceived and recognized me standing there. They could hardly believe their eyes I appeared to them as a phantom (as some told me after), others thought that they were dreaming As I had many times visited that people when a priest in Canada, passing whole weeks in their midst, preaching, hearing their confession, and giving them the pledge of temperance, they had all known me and loved me till that day, as if I had been their own father

Their eyes had hardly met mine, when they had all forgotten what they had just heard from their priest Many, pressing my hands with the warmest expressions of respect and friendship, were saying· "How happy we are to see you again in our midst." Many others, unable to approach me on account of the dense crowd, which, coming as an irresistible tide, was driving them down the stairs in spite of themselves, were crying to each other with unmistakable expressions of joy· "Father Chiniquy! Father Chiniquy here! Is it possible? How glad we are to see him again!"

Only two or three said, "Father Chiniquy has no business here. Our duty is to drive him away."

But their voices were drowned by hundreds of people saying, "If you do not like to hear or see Father Chiniquy, shut your eyes and run away. For us we like to see and hear him again"

I do not really think that there has been another circumstance so strange and solemn in my whole life. I felt more than ever in that strange hour that "the Lord was my keeper and that He was with me."

As the people were going down the stairs, carried by the irresistible tide of the multitude coming out of the church, they were turning their faces towards me, and in a few minutes I stood alone on the high platform, having at my feet more than one thousand of those dear, honest fellow countrymen evidently waiting to hear what I had to say. As soon as the last ones had taken their position at my feet, I said "My dear friends and countrymen, you have just heard in your church what your priests and Bishops say against me Now would you not like to know what I have to say in my defense? You are too honest and Christian to condemn a man without hearing him, even if he is accused by priests and Bishops. God has given you two ears that you may hear both sides of every accusation. I do not come here to say one single word against your venerable Bishops and pastor. I respect them I only ask you to allow me to say a few words in my defense to explain to you my present position. Will you grant me that favour?" The whole multitude answered with one voice· "Yes, Father Chiniquy, speak—speak —we are glad to hear you!"

Then I said, "Many of you are fasting, for some of you have received the communion this morning, I know it. Many good mothers are in a hurry to see their dear little ones at home. And we are all in the open air where it is not safe to talk much   I ask you all to grant me the favour of coming to hear me at three o'clock this afternoon in that large hall which is there in your beautiful village.

"When I came here I was sure that I would be among a noble and most intelligent people, and I was not mistaken The way you have received me here, just after what you have heard, is the assurance that your minds are as bright as your hearts are noble—not condemning me before hearing me.

' Wherever your admirable present conduct towards me will be known there will be a cry of admiration for your high and honest intelligence, and you will be blessed

"May the God of the Gospel bless you all, and may He bless our dear Canada forever."

The whole crowd had only one voice to say, "May God bless you also, dear Father Chiniquy!" And they quietly dispersed.

CHAPTER XV

My Missionary Tour Continued. The Dagger of the Assassin on My
Breast at Quebec

The first Sabbath of February, 1859, at 3 o'clock, the large
hall of the village of Napierville was filled by the intelligent
Roman Catholics of that interesting town, who wanted to
know why I had left the Church of Rome. Far from following the advice of their priest by giving me such a reception
that 1 would never be tempted to come again, they overwhelmed me with all the marks of respect and friendship
which they were able to give. It was the same thing next
morning when their hall was again crammed by an audience
to hear why a man could not make God with a wafer

In the afternoon the doctor of the village was sent by the
priests to argue against me and to defend Auricular Confession. He tried to show us that our Saviour had established
that sacrament of penance (Auricular Confession) as the
only way to get pardon for our sins. But he was soon at
the end of his arguments, and I asked him to tell us how long
it was since he had gone to confess his sins to the priest
He was forced to answer, "Ten years." The people laughed
at him to their hearts' content. This threw so much cold
water on his fiery eloquence, that he found the only way to
save his lost cause was by making use of a dozen rowdy
Irishmen to drown my voice every time I tried to speak
Though the immense majority of the people wanted to hear
more, we had to stop the meeting. But much of the good
seed had fallen on that well-prepared soil. The Rev. Mr
Lafleur, Revs. Cyr and Roussy had faithfully worked before
me in that precious part of the Good Master's vineyard. A
good number of its families had already given up the errors of

165

Rome and formed a very interesting congregation of Protestants.

It was my joy in the evening meeting, in my host's house, to get, from ten heads of Roman Catholic families, the assurance that they had also taken the resolution to accept the Gospel as their only guide and Jesus Christ for their only Saviour.

The next day, Tuesday, it was my unspeakable joy to meet the honest and intelligent farmers of Lacadie, in their interesting village. For more than an hour they listened to the address I gave them on the Gospel as the only solid foundation on which a people should stand to become strong, happy and free.

A notary having been sent by the priest to interrupt me was politely taken to the end of the village on the shoulders of six sturdy farmers and requested to be quiet, there, if he would not fare worse.

I was not surprised at the friendly reception I received from the people of Lacadie, when I remembered that it was in the midst of this town that the Grande Ligne Mission was spreading floods of Gospel light and truth for the last ten years. There, again, a good number of families accepted the Gospel.

From that place I came back to Montreal. in order to take the train for Quebec. where I was expected the very next day.

In the Quebec Gazette of February 11th, 1859, was the following

"ARRIVAL OF MR. CHINIQUY.

"This gentleman reached Point Levis on Wednesday evening by the train, and was waited upon by a large number of the inhabitants of that locality, and also of this city, who went across for the purpose of receiving him. He remained at Frazer's hotel for that night, and came over to the city yesterday forenoon, and took up his residence in Crown Street, St. Rock.

"We are informed that the number of persons who have visited him since his arrival cannot have been less than four thou-and Twice he was obliged yesterday to speak to the multitude from his window. The people flocked from all the neighbouring parishes, and many had stayed since Monday to see him Some on hearing of his arrival at Point Levis, the night previous, came up from St Anne Chateau Richer and the Orleans Island. Not an offensive word was used by any one, but all evinced the extreme pleasure of having amongst them once more one for whom they entertained the most sincere affection.

"Mr. Chiniquy addressed a public meeting in the lecture hall, St. Anne's Street, this afternoon, but the hour is too far advanced to admit of our giving particulars to-day.

"We would just say, however, that the building was crowded to its utmost capacity, principally by his own countrymen; and that, up to the time that we left, the greatest decorum prevailed, the remarks of the reverend gentleman being frequently applauded with great enthusiasm"

Just as the Quebec Gazette gives it, that address of Thursday was a glorious Gospel success, as well as those of Friday, Saturday, and Sunday, which were all given at 2 P. M., for I did not like to wait till the night to address the people There were not sufficient lights in the streets of Quebec to prevent the rough element from playing their mischief.

The Quebec Gazette tells it, in the intervals of the addresses the large room I occupied was filled with friends and enquirers, and the street before the house was so crammed with the multitudes of kind friends who wanted to hear the Gospel message I had to give them, that two or three times a day I had to address them in the open air from the window

Of course the priests were furious. You could have seen them running through the streets to stop the multitudes that were coming from every side to see and hear me, and asking

them. "Where are you going?" The answer was, invariably
" We go to hear Father Chiniquy." " But don't you know
that it is a crime, an abominable sin, to hear him? Don't
you know that you are excommunicated if you speak to that
abominable heretic?" "Yes, we have been told that," said
the crowds, " but have you not told us hundreds of times
that you have the power to forgive all our sins?" "Yes,
yes," answered the priests, "our Saviour has told us· All
the sins ye forgive on earth shall be forgiven in heaven."
" Well," rejoined the people, "after hearing dear Father
Chiniquy, if our conscience is too much in trouble, we will
go and confess to you again, and you will forgive the new sin
with the rest." And the priests had to go to another corner
with that sarcasm in their ears

The second day a band of brave men who were all among
the five hundred who had invited me to come, told me that
the priests were evidently preparing a mob to kill me during
the night, and they offered themselves to guard the house

I answered them to do as they pleased in that matter. As
it was at their invitation that I was in Quebec, it was their
business to prevent this trouble they were in fear of   And a
guard of fifteen well-armed, intrepid young men was organized to watch, during the dark hours of the night, around my
lodging.

The Sabbath address was, "Our Salvation Through Christ"
Though the most terrible fulminations and excommunications had been launched at the morning service against all
those who would come to hear me, or would even talk a single
word with me, the crowd was so great that we had to open
the windows of the large hall, so that the multitudes who
stood outside from the want of room could hear

The joy that filled my heart was such that, though I was
exhausted, when the night came I did not feel the fatigue.
The sight of those multitudes who were hungry and thirsty
after the bread of Life, and to whom I was permitted to
give that bread and that water, was such a marvelous thing

to me, that very often I could not speak to them except with my tears of joy.

But at 10 P. M. two very respectable friends came to tell me: "Dear Father Chiniquy, you will surely be killed this night if you do not leave the city We have just come from a meeting of the most desperate rowdies of the city which has been addressed by two of our priests. They have so inflamed their brutal passions, that more than fifty have sworn to set fire to your house this night, and to kill you when you try to escape; please leave the city. We have a good sleigh in readiness to take you to a safe place eight or ten miles away." I answered them. "I thank you for your kindness, but I cannot follow your advice When I left the Church of Rome, as well as when I came to Quebec to preach the Gospel, I knew the cost.

"I did not come here to run away. If it is the will of God that I should shed my blood this night for the cause of His Gospel, I shall have the whole eternity to bless Him for that favour" "Then," said my friends, "you cannot prevent us from putting a double guard this night to protect you." "Do as you please in that matter," I answered. And they left me alone.

The few hours before a man expects to die, under such circumstances, are too solemn to allow him to sleep. The shores of eternity are so near, look so bright and grand, that one can hold his breath at their aspect. At about three o'clock in the morning one of my night guards came to me and said: "As the night is much advanced, and the first rays of the day are very near, we think that the danger of an attack from the mob is over. If you have no objection we will go home and take a few hours of rest, for we are all working men, and we must be at our different posts by seven this morning."

"All right, my dear friends, go and rest a few hours; may the dear Saviour bless you for your kindness towards me," I answered. And they left.

I then went to the good waiters, who were also watching, to ask them to give me a cup of coffee   As I had not shut my eyes, I felt the want of some food to keep up my strength.

I was just going to take that cup of coffee when we heard a terrible noise at the door.   That door was evidently broken down, and a multitude of men were running upstairs to the parlour

They were the very ones who had prepared at the evening meeting of the priests, to set fire to the house, and to kill me when I would try to run away   Every one had a mask on his face.   Too cowardly to approach the house when it was guarded by my thirty young friends, they had concealed themselves in a building at a short distance, waiting for the moment that my guardians would leave, at the dawn of day.   I asked them. "What do you want here at such an hour of the night?"   The leader, who had a long butcher-knife in his hand, answered. "Miserable apostate! we come to put an end to your infamous life, if you do not swear that you will never preach your d—d Bible any more." And seizing my right arm with his left one, he planted his knife on my breast.   The half of his companions, armed with sticks and daggers, made a circle around me, and repeated what their chief had said "D—d apostate! if you don't swear that you will never preach your d—d Bible again, you are a dead man "   During that time the rest of the band filling the room with terrible imprecations, were breaking the chairs and threatening to kill the good man, who, with his wife, consented to lodge me during my stay in Quebec.

I told them. "Let those people alone—if it is a crime to preach the Gospel of Christ here, I am the only guilty one— kill me—death has no terror for me, but do not molest those people."

In that moment I felt the dagger so hardly pressed on my breast that I thought at every moment it would go through and through. Raising my supplicating hands towards heaven, I said. "Dear Saviour! For my sake Thou hast shed Thy blood on the cross, if it is Thy will I should mine for Thy sake, may Thy will be done: but come and receive my soul into Thy hands."

These words were hardly said when the would-be murderer, with a most awful imprecation, said: "Infamous apostate! We do not come to hear your heretical prayers, we come to put an end to your infamous life, if you do not swear that you will never preach your Bible" He then pressed his knife so hard that I felt blood running on my breast Expecting every moment to fall a corpse, I again raised my hands towards heaven, and said: "My God! In a moment I will be in Thy presence and I bless Thee for it. But as they want an oath before I die, they shall have it, I swear that, as long as my tongue can speak, I will preach Thy Holy Word as I find it in the Holy Bible." And then opening my vest with both hands, I said, ' Now, strike the last blow." But my dear Saviour was there to protect His poor, helpless soldier.

The would be murderer began to shake from head to foot The dagger fell from his hands on the floor, and with a trembling voice he said, " Well, Father Chiniquy, if you promise to go away we will not kill you."

He evidently meant that I would promise to go away from the city But I thought it was not very wrong to deceive him, when saying the truth. I answered, "Yes, I will go away," secretly meaning, '' I will go away from your bad company" And he left me alone.

The snow had fallen more than two feet deep in the street during the night, and I had a pretty long distance to walk to reach the house to which I wanted to go I felt my bodily strength pretty much exhausted by the trials of that night, and I thought it prudent, before leaving. to take my cup of coffee, which was there on the table. Besides that, I wanted to gain some time, in the hope that some of my friends or night-

guards would know my position and come to my help, for
I had seen one of the servants running away, probably to
give the alarm.

I told the mob, which was then silent, though their bloody
eyes were watching me closely· "I have to walk quite a long
distance in the snow to my knees; you will not find fault
with me I hope, if I take a cup of coffee, with a mouthful
of bread." And I sat at the table But I had not drunk
half of the cup when a furious voice, which I had not yet
heard, cried out "Do you not see that he is deceiving us?
He takes too much time And he means to remain here."
Saying that he upset the table, broke the cup and plates,
and with a fearful blasphemy said, "Infamous apostate!
Go away at once! No delay! Go Quick!" And he nearly
brought me down with his fist

I felt I had to go Putting on my overcoat and my cap I
took my bag and walked to the door. It was still very dark
and, as I said before, two feet of snow had fallen in the streets,
during that night. I was not without anxiety how I could
walk the long distance which was before me. But, by the
good providence of God, a carter was just passing before the
door with his sleigh. I asked him, "Can you take me to the
pro mayor, Mr Hall?" "Yes, sir," he answered. And
soon I was safe under the roof of that noble Scotch Protestant.

For, by the marvelous mercy of God, the mayor, Langevin,
a most fanatical Roman Catholic, was absent for the few days
I was in Quebec

I showed my bleeding breast to Mr. Hall, and I told him:
"Sir, I am just escaping from the hands of a furious Romanist mob who have sworn to kill me if I continue to preach in
Quebec. As I promised yesterday to give, to-day, my last
address on the Bible and the right which every man has to
read it, I will fulfil my promise even if I have to die for it.
I come to put myself under the protection of the British flag,
for the enjoyment of my rights and liberty."

" If you can swear upon that," said Mr. Hall, "I will protect you   But I have a favour to ask of you.   Please do not speak of the wound that you have on your breast, nor of the blood you have lost.   You do not know the terrible effect that sight has upon me   Blood calls for blood.   If it were known that you had received such a wound in Quebec, and that you have had to shed your blood from the hands of the priests, it might have the most terrible results   It might be difficult, if not impossible, to calm the rage of our Protestant soldiers and the other Protestants whom I must call to protect you   For I must put the city under martial law and gather all the powers I can lay my hands on, if I want to save your life, and perhaps my own, to-day, against the mighty and bloody power of Rome "

Half an hour later the city of Quebec was proclaimed under martial law, and more than 1,000 English soldiers with their bayonets were around me to protect my life.   It was between the two ranks of those soldiers of British liberty and fair play, that the mayor drove me, at noon, in his own sleigh, to give the last lecture I had promised on the Bible.

When on my way to the hall between the two ranks of bayonets glittering in the sun, it was quite amusing to see the priests of Rome, half dead with terror, running through the crowds of their poor slaves who were massed all along the streets, saying   " Do not make any demonstration, do not make any noise, do not move a finger against Father Chiniquy.   The city is under martial law!   The soldiers will fire at you and slaughter you at the least appearance of trouble   For God's sake, be still!"

The large hall could not contain half of the people who wanted to hear what I had to say about the Holy Bible and the right of every one to have and read it.   Several thousands who could have no place in the hall, were standing around and listening with breathless attention, through the windows which were opened.   The day was splendidly bright and mild as a summer day.

I had large boxes containing six hundred New Testaments which I distributed, to the last one, to my dear Roman Catholic countrymen, after the meeting.

Thanks to God. the good seed sown in those days has not all been lost, and the blood shed has not been shed in vain. The modest evangelical work which our Protestant societies had begun there, some time before, under the Rev Mr Tetreau and Normandeau, two converted priests, has taken a new and rapid extension

Not far from that very spot where I was so cruelly wounded, a fine stone French Protestant church, for the Canadian converts, has been built. That church would be much too small to day, if our dear French Canadian converts from Rome could have remained in their own country. But, alas! many have been forced to take the sad way of exile. The cruel and unmanly persecutions they are subject to from the priests of the Pope have made it impossible for many to remain in their own country Thousands of them are now eating the bitter bread of exile in the United States.

CHAPTER XVI

How Roman Catholics Understand Liberty of Conscience. My Letter to the Bishops of Quebec and the Priests of Canada

"I saw a woman sit upon a scarlet coloured beast . . . and decked with gold and precious stones, . . . having a golden cup in her hand full of abominations and filthiness of her fornication· and upon her forehead was a name written, Mystery, Babylon the great, the mother of harlots and abominations of the earth.

"I saw the woman drunken with the blood of the saints." (Rev. 17: 3–6.)

If it were possible to awaken the Protestants of Canada from their deplorable and mysterious slumber, and to make them understand the anti-Christian and anti-social principles of the Church of Rome, the events of the fourteenth day of February, 1859, would have done it.

Of all the daily and weekly papers edited by the Roman Catholics of Canada, not a single word was written to blame the rioters for having attacked violently and driven me from my house. They all said that I had no right to preach doctrines contrary to the doctrines of Rome in Quebec, because the majority were Roman Catholics.

Though unable to find a single word of abuse fallen from my lips, they, however, said that they had the right, it was their duty, to kill me if I refused to go away.

They all declared that Mayor Hall was wrong to come to my help and protect me. They all proclaimed that he had no right to employ the civil and military forces to save my life and protect me. His duty was to let the rioters come, break everything in the house where I was staying, pull it down, if I refused to obey them.

175

Here are the very words of Mr. Audet, one of the council-
lors of the city of Quebec, reproduced and approved by the
Roman Catholic press of Canada on this subject

"I acknowledge Mr Chiniquy's liberty of speech when
coming to speak against our holy religion, as I acknowledge
the liberty of a thief to steal, and the liberty of an assassin
to kill

"When I deny the right of the robber to rob and of the
assassin to assassinate, of the sacrilegious to commit sacrilege,
I also deny Mr Chiniquy the right of coming here to insult
and outrage us"

Let us now come to the affair of Monday last

"That day Mr Chiniquy was to lecture in the hall of St.
Anne St, and you, Mr. Pro-Mayor, you had received deposition affirming that there were to be disturbances at that lecture   Accordingly, by your order, all the civil forces were
under arms! You knew that Mr Chiniquy was the cause of
all those troubles, and notwithstanding that, you, the first
magistrate of the city, went yourself in search of Mr. Chiniquy to deliver that lecture to you! Suppose, Mr. Pro-Mayor,
that there had been a riot and a bloodshed, would you not
have been the cause of it? The Canadians have always respected every religious faith; but be assured that we will
exact for ourselves the respect we bear towards others.

"We demand protection, and let it be distinctly understood
that if it be refused to the 45,000 Roman Catholics of this
city, they will know how to protect themselves; and then evil
be to those who dare attack them   This will interfere somewhat with the Bible societies, but I warn them to seek some
other field for the exercise of their zeal.

"Have they not, for instance, India, China, and Japan
where they can go and throw their Bibles?"

These are some of the reflections of the "Quebec Mercury'
concerning the above harangue of Mr. Audet

"Mr Audet has not only publicly uttered, but deliberately
put on record, a declaration of war against the British popu-

lation of this Province. His appeal to the 45,000 Roman Catholics of Quebec is a cry for blood. And in what a cause? This agent of the priesthood has deliberately propounded the principles of the Spanish Inquisition as applicable to those who boast themselves (however erroneously) the free Protestant subjects of a Protestant sovereign

"Mr. Audet boldly announces that *opinion* is a crime,— and that the magistrates are bound to restrain it

"A man, he says, has the same liberty to lecture against Romanism, as to be a robber!

"The meaning is clear. He may be as liable to punishment in the one case as the other   The language of 'The Univers,' the Ultramontane organ in France, is nearly identical with that of Mr. Audet. it distinguishes liberty from right He declares a man has no more right to be a Protestant than to commit a murder or a theft!

"Liberty of speech is to be forbidden, lest those it offends should deliberately break the law, and direful misfortunes for the whole world which must be subjected to the consequences of doing so!

"Mr. Audet concludes his speech by calling on his Roman Catholic hearers to make a new St. Bartholomew's day of their Protestant neighbours! And he finishes by a threat to the Bible societies, to which the treatment formerly received by Mr Papin, gives the utmost significance "

When I went back to Montreal, I thought it was my duty to address a letter to the Bishops and priests of Canada. In the first part of that letter I gave a faithful history of the riot, which I will not repeat here. I will give only the second part.

"To the Roman Catholic Bishops and Priests of Canada:

"You have thus an abridged but faithful history of your own work of the fourteenth of February   But before leaving Canada, I owe it to my fellow countrymen, I owe it to the cause of truth, to address you a few words more.

"Within three years, look at the four riots you have caused

to rid yourselves of those you call 'Protestants, apostates and enemies of your holy church.'

"Incapable of meeting your opponents on the ground of argument, worthy descendants and supporters of the Holy Inquisition, you have recourse to violence, to oppose and destroy the truth which makes you afraid; you have recourse to bloody riots to prop up your tottering power. It is well, continue, accustom the people to use the stick and the club for an argument. Discipline your adepts to shed the blood of those that you call the enemies of the holy Roman Church, applaud the murderers who knock down their victims, with cries of rage, and the robbers who violate the most sacred right of nations, that of the domestic hearth; you will then prove to all that you are the worthy successors of those who slaughtered thousands of their brethren on the night of St. Bartholomew, you will open the eyes of the blindest to the spirit and tendencies of the Romish Church, you will demonstrate to the most incredulous that you have completely renounced the Gospel which tells you not to do to others what you would not like done to yourselves, you will show to the most ardent of your zealots that you are the enemies of Him who said to Peter 'Put up the sword in its sheath, for those who make use of the sword shall perish by the sword.'

"You do not wish that those who differ from you in religion shall have the right to speak, you excite against them the rage of riotous men; you cry for their blood. But really do you think that the people will leave you long in the possession of this power?

"Do you not see that the shoulders of this poor people are bruised and bleeding under the heavy and odious yoke you lay upon them? Do you not hear the low and threatening murmurs that come from the breasts of this people, when they see you drag from them their last farthings, for the souls of your insatiable purgatory? Yes, all these confraternities, all these medals, these indulgences of five twenty, forty *sous*, but for which you extract the money from the poor as well as the rich, will open the eyes of the people. Already many are persuaded that if you really did believe in the fires of purgatory, you would not wait until you got twenty=five cents to take a poor suffering soul out of that purgatory, no more than you would demand twenty=five cents to save a person drowning before your eyes. There are even those that blush for you, when they hear you say. in speaking of such a person, deceased, 'He is probably in purgatory, give me $10.00 $20.00, and I shall immediately try to get him out'

"This shameful traffic begins to be understood and to be despised The people see that the enormous sums they give you for the souls in purgatory remain at the bottom of your purses and that the good souls do not get a fraction. Continue your infamous commerce in prayers, indulgences and medals, build for yourselves with those funds, sumptuous palaces, rear up gigantic cathedrals, robe yourselves in purple and the finest garments; load your tables with delicate viands; knock down those who disturb your repose; and continue to elect in every country the enemies of the people. But mark well what I tell you. the people will soon awake from the profound slumber in which you have kept them. In spite of you, their eyes will be opened to the light which is coming in upon them on every side.

" But this waking up will be terrible, like that of the lion. This people who till the ground, with the sweat of their brow, have not a cent left; the poor people are nearly naked, and their children are trembling with cold Many are obliged to leave their own country to go and eat the bitter bread of exile, and to be the servants of other people. But they will soon awaken, and they will say, 'I have now nothing left, I am naked, hungry, without shelter' Where are the goods that God gave me?' And a voice from heaven shall say to them, 'Behold them, there, in those magnificent palaces. there is the price of your hard labours, and the bread of your children Under the cloke of religion, your priests have ruined you and made you their slaves. They have snatched away a thing more precious than earthly treasure—the Word of God—the Divine Gospel that Christ has sent you to succour you in your wretchedness'

"And then a disturbance will take place, but a terrible disturbance, and a frightful disturbance, such as is rarely seen on the surface of the globe What you have done to others will be done to yourselves and in the same measure. In those days of agitation, of vengeance and retribution, the Canadian people, like the French people in 1792, will settle their accounts with you, and will make you pay dearly for your frauds, your impostures, your intolerance, and your tyranny You will be dragged with violence from your palaces; and your mournful cries will be but the echo of the cries and desolation of your victims Your blood will be mingled with the blood you have shed Your reign, the reign of man, will be at an end, and the reign of Christ, the reign of God's Word, shall have begun."

CHAPTER XVII

A French Officer Saves My Life at Beloeil. Grande Ligne and Longuevil Visited. Rev. Theodore Lafleur

To throttle the Church of Rome, which means not only to dare her fury but to bring down her sceptre into the dust in the greatest citadels of her power, Quebec and Montreal, could not be the work of Chiniquy, it must be the Lord's work.

The mighty hand of my God was so visible in the complete humiliation of the haughty tryants under the feet of whom the people of Quebec and Montreal were crushed for almost three centuries, that there was no possibility for me to be tempted by the the demon of human pride. I had only to be humiliated and amazed when considering that such a work had been wrought through such a weak instrumentality.

Protestants as well as Romanists were amazed that those so dreaded weapons—excommunication, interdicts, etc., fulminated from all the pulpits, which, till then, had kept the French Canadian people at the feet of their haughty tyrants—had suddenly been turned into ridiculous child's play, and had become powerless and been thrown by the people into the muddy ditches, along the public roads.

It was the first time, on the continent of America, that the Roman tiger had been so well shut up in his own den, and that the monstrous snake of Romanism had been so roughly handled without being able to bite the hand that was striking it.

No words can give an idea of the humiliations of the Roman Catholic clergy, when they heard that I was determined to spend another month in Montreal and vicinity in exposing their frauds, their idolatries and their corruptions.

Superhuman efforts were made by Bishop Bourget to bribe me, but he lost his time   He felt more and more every day that I was not only terribly in earnest, but absolutely proof against his threats, his perfidious flatteries, and his impotent rage.

By his orders, the priests invented and published the most horrible calumnies against my character.   But in the good providence of God, these calumnies were invariably destroying themselves by their own absurdity and want of every one of the elements on which their fabrication could stand.

The gold medal they had put on my breast, the title of " Apostle of Temperance of Canada," they had so solemnly given me, the sacred silver vases they had presented me with the very day I had left Canada for the United States, the echoes of my voice which were still vibrating within all the walls of their cathedrals, the tears I had dried, the hearts I had consoled, the marvelous reformations I had wrought all over our country, the giant enemy of Canada, intemperance, which, by the help of God, I had conquered, were facts which, not I, but my God, was bringing to the memory of my countrymen, as an infallible antidote against the poisoned arrows thrown at me by the Bishop and priests, which poisoned arrows were wounding only those who were throwing them

The whole week I spent in Montreal, after my return from Quebec, it was my unspeakable joy to see again my parlour constantly filled by the élite of my dear countrymen, who wanted to hear the Gospel message the Good Master was sending to them   I had also to bless God for the daily marks of Christian regard and kindness I received from the Protestants of all denominations   The evening lectures continued also to be attended by as many people as the large hall could contain, and this, without a single mark of public bad feeling from any quarter

Friends and foes, Protestants as well as Roman Catholics, were equally astonished and glad at such an unexpected triumph of the great principle of liberty against slavery, of fair play against brute force, and of truth against error, since, till then, the most deplorable as well as the most bloody riots had so often been a dark spot on the fair name of Montreal.

To the many who asked me how such a change could be seen, I answered, "This is the Lord's work   The hour is coming fast when the dark night of Popery will have to disappear before the shining sun of the Gospel.   What you see now is the dawning of that blessed day.   This is not my work. it is our merciful heavenly Father's work.   Let us bless Him for it"

It would be too tedious to give the details of the different evangelical missions of the next month, in the district of Montreal.   I will only mention two or three on account of some interesting circumstances connected with them.

A great number of Beloeil, Chambly, and St. Mathias people had requested me to give them a week of my time, and they had selected the splendid hotel of Beloeil Mountain for the place of the meetings, for that hotel had a very large parlour where several hundreds of people could easily be accommodated.   Its manager was a true gentleman who had been an officer in the French army   He had attended several of our meetings in Montreal, where he had bravely and publicly given up the errors of Rome to follow the Gospel.   I was then sure to find in that hotel the protection I wanted for myself and those of my dear countrymen who would come to hear me.   I was not mistaken   The success of those meetings was again above my most sanguine expectation   The large and splendid parlour was filled from morning till night, by inquiring people of every condition, coming from every point of the compass

But on the last days a respectable farmer came from St Mary to tell me that one of the priests had said in his presence to some of his people: "Just as you have a right to kill a wolf when crossing the prairie to slaughter your sheep, so you have the right to kill that miserable apostate, Chini-quy, who is destroying our holy religion."

"Do not betray me," said the good farmer, "but be on your guard when you see a man with a red collar around his neck He will have a pistol to shoot you if he finds his opportunity, for he is a good shot."

I thanked him, and I gave my secret to the fearless French ex-officer, that he might see the best way of protecting my life, though I asked him not to do any harm to the would-be murderer, if possible.

Among my hearers that evening (it was Saturday), I noticed a strong, tall man just before me not more than ten feet distant, with a red collar around his neck. His manners indicated that he was half drunk, and several times he made so much noise that I had to stop speaking on account of him. I had hardly given the last word of my address, when he made a quick movement through the crowd and stopped when not more than five feet distant from me. Then, with a horrible oath, he said, "This is your last heretical address."

Drawing then a pistol from his coat pocket, he pointed it towards me, uttering a new blasphemy.

But the French officer had watched all his movements and had remained close by him since he had entered the room. Quick as lightning, he drew his sword, and struck such a blow under the pistol that it flew almost to the upper floor from the hand of the would-be murderer, after the ball had gone and broken a pane of the opposite window

This rash and daring act was followed by an indescribable confusion Some of the women fainted, some were crying, but I had a number of friends who did not lose their presence of mind. With the sword at his back, that miserable tool of the priests was quickly driven, or rather roughly carried away to a long distance, where he received such a lesson that he was not tempted to come again.

The next few weeks were given to St Pie, St Mary, St Athenase, St Gregory, with the same crowds of Roman

Catholics who were trampling under their feet with the utmost contempt, the fulminations, excommunications and interdicts of their religious tyrants in their eagerness to hear the preaching of the Gospel.

At St. Mary it was my joy to address the large and so admirable congregation of converts which the zealous and fearless Baptist ministers of the Grande Ligne Mission had gained from Rome. That congregation, composed of thirty families, was then under the care of the late Reverend M. Roussy, whose name will be blessed as long as there will be a disciple of the Gospel in Canada

I could not contain my tears of joy when I saw so many of my dear countrymen who had broken the yoke of Rome gathered in their comfortable chapel. These interesting converts, with their pastor, were among those I had most cruelly abused and persecuted when I was a priest of Rome How happy I was, then, to have the opportunity of asking and obtaining their pardon! And how my heart was filled with joy when I could unite my feeble voice with theirs to bless the dear Saviour for His mercies towards us all.

The last place in Canada I laboured in before leaving for my dear colony of Illinois, was Longueuil.

In the midst of that important village, the Baptists had, then, a thriving mission school for Protestant and Catholic young ladies, under the superintendence of the Reverend Théodore Lafleur.

In the good providence of God, the Reverend Mr. Lafleur had been brought to the light of the Gospel many years before me, when he was quite a young man; and some wealthy Protestant, admiring his piety and his rare talents, had sent him to Switzerland to pursue a complete course of study

Having returned to Canada several years since, he had consecrated himself to the preaching of the Gospel to our countrymen, with remarkable success. Though I had bitterly persecuted him, when I was a priest of Rome, I had become the object of his fervent prayers at the Throne of Mercy. He had addressed me several letters full of Christian logic in the beginning of my public conflict with the Bishops, to show me that the only way to possess the glorious freedom and the Divine truths, which Christ had brought from heaven to save the world, was to entirely break the yoke of the Pope and accept the Gospel.

More than that, his burning zeal for my conversion had induced him to cross the thousand miles which were between us, in order to come to St Anne, Illinois, and spend several days in friendly discussion with me

Among the many gifts which Mr Lafleur has received from God, is a wonderful treasure of kindness and affability to which his terse logic and truly admirable Christian spirit gave him an irresistible power over me.

When alone, after having spent one or two hours with him, I had to confess to myself that there was, in that so-called heretic, a perfume of piety I had never met in my church   I was also confounded by the irresistible power of his arguments, and the teachings of history to which I had nothing to oppose

I am happy to say that the letters and the private conversations of the Rev. Mr Lafleur are among the providential things which, by the mercy of God, helped me much to accept the truth when it came to my mind with its splendour

I was, then, happy to have an opportunity of showing the Christian esteem and the gratitude I felt towards that true servant of God, in the two days I was his guest in his literary and evangelical institute of Longueuil

Many citizens of Longueuil availed themselves of my presence in their village to come and ask me a thousand questions about what they called my new religion, and this gave me the golden opportunity of presenting to them the saving truths of the Gospel

During the first night, a few Roman Catholic boys, sent by the priests, had caused us some trouble, by throwing stones through the windows and breaking the glasses. But the respectable part of the population were indignant at that act of brutal cowardice The next evening they came in great numbers to hear the address I gave them, in the large hall of their village. And though they were excommunicated and thrown out of the Church of Rome by that very fact, they were so pleased with the proofs I gave them that their Pope, with his cardinals, bishops and priests, was a fraud, that it was twelve o'clock at night when they consented to be dismissed. Very few of that large meeting left the hall without shaking hands with me and heartily thanking me for what they had heard And the perfect silence and tranquillity of that whole night, told us clearly that we were in the midst not only of a respectable and intelligent people, but among true friends. when in the village of Longueuil.

So it was that, alone, and, humanly speaking, without protection, I had been able to dare the power of Rome in her strongholds, Montreal and Quebec, for two months. But I was not alone No! For the protecting hand of my God had been a visible shield over my head all the time

The Gospel of Christ had been preached to at least 50,000 people, many of whom had never heard it Several thousand Bibles or New Testaments had been distributed to people who had never seen them before. And the Holy Book was to remain there to feed the hungry souls. and quench the thirst of my dear countrymen

Where could I find words to express my gratitude to my God for such a visible and constant protection through so many dangers and obstacles?

When going back to my dear mission of Illinois I could say with the prophet·

"1. If it had not been the Lord who was on our side, now may Israel say;

"2. ` If it had not been the Lord who was on our side, when men rose up against us

"3. Then they had swallowed us up quick, when their wrath was kindled against us:

"4   Then the waters had overwhelmed us, the stream had gone over our soul.

"5.   Then the proud waters had gone over our soul.

"6.   Blessed be the Lord, who hath not given us as a prey to their teeth.

"7   Our soul is escaped as a bird out of the snare of the fowlers· the snare is broken, and we are escaped.

"8.   Our help is in the name of the Lord, who made heaven and earth."   (Psalm 124.)

CHAPTER XVIII

Admitted into the Presbyterian Church with the Bible Alone in My Hand

The fifteenth of April, 1860, ought to be a day never to be forgotten by the French Canadian disciples of the Gospel at St. Anne.

After we had broken the fetters which had kept us chained to the feet of the idols of Rome, in order to become the happy followers of Christ, we felt that we could not honestly continue to call ourselves Roman Catholics. We had to change our church name.

In a general meeting of all our dear converts, where every one was invited to give his views, we unanimously adopted the beautiful name of Christian Catholics, and we determined to give the hand of fellowship to all the different denominations of Protestants who would tell us that they were looking to Christ as their only Saviour. that they accepted the Gospel as their only rule of life.

From the beginning of our religious change, my fear was that we were to make a new branch of the Christian Church and that sooner or later the new branch would be called Chiniquy's Church as had occurred more or less in the days of Luther and Calvin

I was horrified at the thought and possibility of such an occurrence, and we determined to avoid it at any cost. We felt that there were already too many separate branches in the Church of Christ.

It was not long before we saw that our fears were too well founded; every one, even amongst the Protestants, instead of calling us by the beautiful name of Christian Catholics, called us Church of Chiniquy. The only remedy to this threatening drawback, was to connect ourselves with some of the neighbouring venerable churches, and we soon made our choice of the Presbyterian Church.   For our intention was to form a sacred link with the martyred Christians of France known and blessed all over the world as Huguenots for having so heroically shed their blood for the Gospel cause.   I showed to our dear converts that many among them were bearing the very names of those heroic soldiers of Christ, that probably the blood of many of those blessed martyrs was running in their veins

Six elders were chosen to accompany me to Chicago, in order to respectfully ask the Presbytery of that grand city to give us the hand of fellowship and allow us to connect ourselves with that noble Presbyterian Church whose branches extend from one end to the other of the earth and whose shining Christian faith is a terror to Popery all over the world

How happy every one of those venerable ministers felt, when, after the many questions everyone of them had to put to us, they found that our religious views were perfectly correct, and that the great religious movement we were inaugurating was perfectly Christian.   They unanimously consented to receive us into the great Presbyterian family and offered their Westminster Confession of Faith for us to adopt, and thus declare ourselves faithful children of the Presbyterian Church

They were, however, not prepared for the disappointment they were to meet, when I respectfully requested them to withdraw that book and to put the Bible in its place, as the only standard of our faith and life.

With an emotion which he could not conceal the moderator answered me, " My dear Mr Chiniquy, we cannot do that.   Our custom is that our venerable Westminster Book of Faith is the standard to which the new members we receive subscribe as the pledge they give us that they wish to become Presbyterians.   We cannot change that rule "

I answered him, "Mr Moderator. please do not forget that you have here to deal with babes in the faith. You must bear with children when they request you to give them the food which you are not accustomed to give to full-grown people. We do not come here to teach you any lesson, we want to be taught by you. However, we respectfully ask you to allow us to give you the reasons why we want the Holy Bible to be the only key which will open to us the gates of that Church of Christ of which He is not only the corner stone, but which is the blood of His blood and the flesh of His flesh. When we ask you to grant us the honour and privilege to become Presbyterians. it is not in a narrow, sectarian sense of the word, it is the large, broad sense of Christianity. We do not want to press only the Presbyterians to our breasts, we want to press all those who love and serve our Saviour Jesus Christ, and look upon Him as their only hope and their only Saviour, by whatsoever name they may be called We do not want to be on the narrow platform, for instance, on which the Old and New Schools stand, and on which they fight against each other as wild cats We want to belong to that large, Divine platform which our adorable Saviour presented to the young man who asked him, 'Good Master, what must I do to have eternal life?' We want a platform, in a word, on which we shall love as brethren, and press to our breasts as brethren and sisters, all those who, repenting of their sins, look to Christ and love Him as their only Saviour. Allow me to tell you that after reading many of the books published by the most learned men of your different denominations, we have come to the conclusion that your differences are more in appearance than reality. Do not find fault with us, if we respectfully ask you to allow us to believe that our adorable and merciful Saviour was indicating your different denominations when saying, 'I am the vine; ye are the branches; and My Father is the husbandman' There is no need at all that the branches should be of the same form and the same size to bring good

fruits   The only thing necessary is that they should be well
united with the vine   I got that assurance a few days ago,
when reading that marvelous fifteenth chapter of St. John,
under the shadow of a splendid vine which I have planted in
my garden, and which I cultivate with my own hands   After
reading with a prayerful attention these marvelous and
mysterious words addressed by Christ to His disciples, 'I
am the vine. ye are the branches,' I observed for the first
time that there was not a single one of the branches like the
other branches.   I noticed for the first time a branch, a very
near one, which was very large, just as your noble and great
English and American Episcopal Church, and just at a very
short distance I saw a small branch resembling your modest,
though much to be admired Congregational Church   A little
farther on there was a fine branch going straight up towards
heaven, our ardent enthusiastic Methodist brethren, and just
by its side I much admired another branch which was de-
scending like our Baptist friends when they go down in their
water baths   And last, though not the least, I had to admire
some very crooked branches, as the beloved Presbyterians
with whom we want to unite ourselves   But I remarked that,
though all the branches of that vine were quite different in
appearance, they were all loaded with splendid grapes, for
they were all perfectly united with the vine!

"Evidently there are some varieties of views between the
many different denominations which form the Church of
Christ.   But so long as Jesus, and Jesus alone, the Son of
God and the Saviour of the world, is their only hope, their
only refuge, their only life, and His Gospel their only rule of
faith, we want to press them all to our hearts as our brethren
on earth, and our co-citizens in heaven.

"This is the reason that, though we entertain great respect
for your Westminster Confession, we ask you as a favour to
allow us to lay our hands on the Bible as the only door
through which we wish to enter the grand and noble Presbyterian Church."

No words can give an idea of the attention and kindness with which my address was received and my request granted. The next morning found every one of the members of that Presbytery on their way to Kankakee City, by the Illinois Central Railway. There they found good carriages in waiting to drive them to the village of St. Anne, about twelve miles distant. The day was splendid and the grand scenery of the boundless and rich prairies, spreading on every side as far as the vision could extend, was magnificent. Our large chapel was more than crowded.

Multitudes of our dear converts had come from all the surrounding towns and cities, even from Chicago, to the number of more than 2,000.

It was as much with their tears of joy as with the words of their lips that the members of the Chicago Presbytery addressed them and received them all as the new-born children of the great Presbyterian family.

Words are inadequate to express the sentiments of joy and gratitude to God which were filling every heart in that solemn and never-to-be-forgotten day.

A new and glorious page in the history of the Church of Christ was written. The melodious voice of our bell was proclaiming far and wide the new victory of the Gospel. The angels of God were again singing their harmonious chorus—their hymn of joy:

"Glory be to God in the highest, and on earth peace, good will toward men!"

CHAPTER XIX

Muskegon—On the Borders of Lake Michigan

If you want to have an idea of the marvelous lumber industry of the United States, go and see the numerous saw-mills which are around the city of Muskegon, and count, if you can, the piles of lumber, of every size, which stand like giant sentinels along the shores of Lake Michigan.

In the year 1862 the greatest number of those saw-mills were manned by our French Canadian emigrants who, to the number of hundreds of thousands, had to leave the country of their birth, in order to go and eat the bitter bread of exile in the United States

The Archbishop of Quebec, Bishop Baillargeon, had a near relative among those emigrants, who addressed me the following letter at the end of September, 1862

"Dear Father Chiniquy —

"Though I have not met you for several years, I hope that you will remember me when I tell you that I am the near relative to the present Archbishop of Quebec, Bishop Baillargeon, who visited you in the autumn of 1843 when you were curate of Kamouraska. Obliged, as so many of our countrymen, to exile myself, I am keeping a large boarding house here in Muskegon, on the borders of Lake Michigan Many of our countrymen have emigrated here with me Like yourself, we were born and raised in the Roman Catholic Church, but you understand that our faith has received a serious shock by your so public and solemn step of passing to the side of the Protestants. However, I would not be honest if I were leaving you under the impression that our own faith in the Church of Rome had not been shaken before you left it.

194

"Our last two priests have done more here than yourself to cause us to suspect that the religion of the Pope of Rome is not the religion of Christ

"One of them was almost constantly drunk. Several times it has been my sad duty to pick him up when lying drunk along the streets

"We complained to the Bishop, and, at our request, he gave us another one. But we fell into bad hands again, for this last one was making use of the confessional to corrupt his female penitents. His life was a public scandal which forced us to blush. The shameful conduct of those priests is, to many of us, a sure indication that they do not believe in the religion they preach, and we ask ourselves Is it not a supreme act of folly to believe in it?

"There is no need to tell you that the scandalous lives of those priests, with your public exit from our church, have so shaken our faith that many of us have absolutely ceased from attending any religious services However, that state of things cannot last long We want a religion for ourselves and our children. But how can we make the choice of the true religion of Christ, without the help of some one who is wiser than we are?

"Please do not rebuke us when we ask you to come to our help in these days of supreme anxiety and distress In the name of our common Saviour, come and give us the benefit of your experience and knowledge in the choice we must make of the religious way which will lead us to a happy eternal life, after the sad experiences of these few days of tribulations through which we have to pass in this land of exile and misery."

The only answer I could give to that so pressing request was to go without any delay to the help of those dear, but so distressed, countrymen A few days later it was my privilege to be the guest of my old friend, Baillargeon. and to shake hands with the multitude of my dear countrymen by whom he was surrounded

The news of my arrival had been quickly spread, and I was hardly half an hour in the hall of the hotel, when it was crowded to its utmost capacity.

I saw at once that I was in the presence of a great difficulty   Every one of that multitude had his private and personal difficulties   Some wanted me to tell them how it was possible that a priest could make God with a wafer, others wanted to know how it was possible that a drunken priest, whose name was connected with sins, could forgive the sins of his penitent, whose life, very often, was more moral than that of his Father Confessor   I told them.

"My dear friends, we should avoid a very fatal mistake. If you speak all together with the hope of getting the answers at once, we shall have a renewal of the confusion of the builders of the tower of Babel   Please let only one of you alone put his questions. and when I shall have answered him, another one shall have the same privilege"   This being agreed, Mr Baillargeon said   "As it is my privilege to have you in my humble house, I will take the liberty of opening the meeting by calling attention to the article of our religion which I consider the most puzzling of all   We are told that when our Saviour Jesus Christ took the bread in His hand at the supper with His disciples, 'After He had given thanks, He brake it and said, Take, eat; this is My body, which is broken for you   this do in remembrance of Me.

"'After the same manner also He took the cup, saying, This cup is the New Testament in My blood   this do ye, as oft as ye drink it, in remembrance of Me.   For as often as ye eat this bread, and drink this cup, ye do shew the Lord's death till He come'   (1 Cor. 11 24–26)

"Our Roman Catholic Church teaches us that, by this ceremony and these words, our Saviour Jesus Christ not only changed the bread and the wine into His body, soul and divinity, but that He gave to His apostles and to all our priests the power to perform the same stupendous miracle.

"Now, Mr Chiniquy, you had to believe that, and to teach

it, before you left our church—but we know that you do not
believe it any longer. Now please give us the reasons you
had for changing your faith on that subject."

"Yes! yes!" repeated every one of the multitude which
surrounded me. "Tell us why you have changed your views
on that solemn question."

I replied, "Before answering you, let me read you the first
and second commandment of God as they were given to
Moses on Mount Sinai

"'And God spake all these words, saying·

"'I am the Lord thy God, which have brought thee out of
the land of Egypt, out of the house of bondage. Thou shalt
have no other gods before Me. Thou shalt not make unto
thee any graven image, or any likeness of anything that is
in heaven above, or that is in the earth beneath, or that is in
the water under the earth: Thou shalt not bow down thyself
to them, nor serve them for I the Lord thy God am a jealous God, visiting the iniquity of the fathers upon the children unto the third and fourth generations of them that hate
Me, And showing mercy unto thousands of them that love
Me, and keep My commandments'

"In the second commandment our God forbids to take a
created thing,—to make an image of it—to make a god of
it,—and adore it.

"But what does the Pope of Rome order his priests to do
every morning? He orders them to change those wafers into
gods! Does he not give them the power to make as many
gods as there are wafers before them? But do you not see
that this is an imposture? The very moment that you have
said that there is only one God, you are sure that the Pope is
an impostor when he says that the priest has the power to
make as many gods as there are wafers about him! Surely
our Saviour, when holding the bread, said, 'This is My
body,' but He immediately added. 'Do this in remembrance of Me,' that we might understand that it was not His
body, but only a remembrance of His body.

"In the Gospel of St. John, chapter 10. 9, Christ says, 'I am the door,' and in chapter 15. 1, He says, 'I am the true vine.' Will the Pope make us believe that our Saviour was really a door and a vine? No. Our Saviour was neither a vine nor a door. When He called Himself a vine, a door, it was only in a figurative way, it was to show us that it was through Him alone that we could have any hope to enter into heaven.

"St. Paul, speaking of the rock which Moses struck with his rod in order to quench the thirst of the Israelites in the desert, says, 'That rock was Christ!'

"Will the Pope persuade you that that rock was really Christ? You understand that it was only through a figure of language that Paul said, 'That rock was Christ.' It was only to make us understand that it was only to Christ alone we must go to find the spiritual favours we are in need of for our salvation So our beloved Saviour called the bread of the holy communion His body, that we might, when receiving the bread of the communion, forever remember that His body was nailed to the cross, and He died the horrible death of Calvary, that by His sacrifice we might have our sins forgiven.

"Is it necessary to address you a long speech to prove to you that the Pope and his priests are impostors the very moment that they assure you that they make as many gods, every morning, as they have baked wafers before their eyes? Transubstantiation is an imposture; the mass has been invented to make money Paul, speaking to the Athenians, said, 'God cannot be made with gold and silver' If the great apostle had been questioned on that subject, he certainly would have denied that God Almighty can either be made with the cakes baked by the servants of the priests. The ceremony of the masses, for which you have to pay from twenty-five cents to one dollar, or more, is an imposture invented to fill the purse of the Pope and his priests.

"The moment our Saviour has said 'I do not come to break

the commandments of My Father, but I come to fulfil them,'
He could not take a created thing, a wafer, a small piece of
bread, into his hand and make a god of it We see that the
doctrines as well as the practices of the Church of Rome
about the Communion are not the same that we find in the
Gospel; for, in that Holy Book, we see that the apostles, and
Christ Himself, received their first communion after supper.
But, according to the teachings of the priests, it is a mortal sin
to receive the Holy Communion after breakfast, and still
more after supper. If the teachings of the Pope and his
priests are correct on that subject, we must believe that
Christ and His apostles were guilty of a mortal sin for daring to receive the great sacrament after supper! And, as they
never repented of that sin, we must believe that they are forever lost for having made such a sacrilegious first communion."

It pleased the Good Master to give such a blessing to my
few clear and simple arguments that it was evident the huge
fabric of the teachings of Rome on that subject had crumbled down before their candid minds

It was then nearly ten P M , I added:

"You have all worked hard to-day, you want some rest.
Come again to-morrow evening, and with the help of God I
will continue to answer your questions and to show you some
of the errors of Rome "

And I dismissed them after a short prayer.

CHAPTER XX

Second Day at Muskegon. A Narrow Escape

The bright sun had hardly spread its rays on the peaceful waters of Lake Michigan the second day of my evangelical work at Muskegon when two of my dear countrymen knocked at my door to warn me of an imminent though unsuspected danger.

"Among your hearers last night," they said, "there was a young man called Bowker who, though half drunk, knew well what he said. He had not walked fifty feet out of the door last night, when we heard him swearing that your address against his Church was the last one you would give. He swore that he would shoot you dead, this evening, if you dared to continue to speak as you did last night. We come to warn you before it is too late But please, when you will make use of our warning to protect yourself, do not speak to anyone of the friendly message that we bring you, this morning, for there is Indian blood in that young man. His great-grandmother was an Iroquois squaw, and he is as cruel, merciless and blood-thirsty as his savage ancestors were. He will kill us if he is aware that we have warned you against his vengeance" I answered them: "No doubt he has got from his priest the notion that it is his right and duty to kill me In authentic Popish books it is positively said that it is not a sin for a Roman Catholic to kill a Protestant. More than that, it is said that it is such a good and holy thing to kill a heretic that all the sins of the man who would kill me would be forgiven instantly. When I left the Church of Rome I knew the cost. They have already tried several times to murder me, but they have failed. My hope is that the same

200

merciful heavenly Father, whose mighty hand has protected me, will be still my shield to-night. However, we must be prudent and take the precautions of common sense and wisdom against the threatening danger. I see that you are among the few soldiers who have been honourably dismissed from the army after serving your time. Please grant me the favour to follow my advice. I have been told that you have a half-dozen young French Canadians, honourably discharged from the army in this town. Try to meet two or three others of them as friendly to me as you are, carry your guns well concealed under your coats when you come this evening to the meeting. Put yourselves around that young man and watch him closely. If you see that he makes any demonstration to do mischief, as quickly as a well-drilled soldier can do it, put the muzzles of your guns to his face, and sternly tell him, 'You are a dead man if you move a finger against Father Chiniquy or anyone else here!'

" You will see that the vision of those guns so near his face will soon change his mind; you will at once turn that wolf into a lamb. Do not do him any harm, but wrench his pistol or his dagger from his hand, and deliver him into the hands of one of the magistrates of the town, whom you will engage to come to the assembly for that purpose. Follow my advice with wisdom and see that he may not have any suspicion of what you are doing."

Those brave young countrymen followed my advice to perfection. In the evening the meeting was, if possible, still more crowded with my dear fellow countrymen who wanted to know why I had left the Church of Rome. My object that evening was to show them the sacrilegious and idolatrous worship of Mary in the Church of Rome.

After telling them that we should respect the memory of the mother of Christ as the most blessed woman who has ever existed, we ought not to call her the mother of God. I showed them that God being eternal and having no beginning could not have had any mother. That she was the mother

of Christ only as a man.   That He had really taken His
flesh from her flesh and His blood from her blood—but He
could not have taken His Divine nature and His Divine
person from her.   No woman can be the mother of her father   The father must be born before the daughter.   And
Christ, as God, had no beginning—He had created this
world   He was the creator of Adam and Eve.   Christ could
not be the son of any man or woman   "It is a remarkable
thing," I added, "that in the Gospel Christ never, never
called Mary His mother   When addressing her or speaking of her, He always called her woman.   More than that," I
said, "in two of the most solemn circumstances of His life, He
refused to acknowledge her as His mother.   There is that
strange fact as narrated by St. Matthew and St. Mark   .
Here are the very words of the Gospel of Christ   When
Jesus was speaking to the people, His mother and His brothers, who were outside, wanted to speak to Him   Someone
told Him, there are your mother and your brothers standing outside who want to speak to you.   But He answered
the one who had told Him that, Who is My mother and who
are My brothers?   And stretching His hands toward His disciples, He said, here is My mother and here are My brothers.
For any one who shall do My Father's will, is My brother, My
sister, My mother   (Matt 12. 46–50; Mark 3. 31–35)

"If it is such a holy thing to worship Mary as the Roman
Catholics do to obey their Church, how is it that Peter, speaking of our Saviour Jesus Christ, said: ' He is the stone which
has been rejected by you '   He is that principal corner-stone
which you have rejected   There is no salvation by any other
one   For, under heaven, no other name has been given
through which man can be saved

"When the Holy Ghost, through Peter, tells us that the name
of Jesus is the only name through which we can be saved,
what right has the Pope to tell you that the name of Mary
must be invoked to be saved "

These last words had hardly fallen from my lips when the

whole assembly was convulsed by the furious cries, " Infamous apostate: those are the last blasphemies which will fall from thy cursed lips!"

No words can give an idea of the terror and the confusion which followed, when the people heard these threatening words and saw the muzzle of a pistol aimed at me at such a short distance, that it nearly touched my face "

"My God! My God' Stop him! Stop him!" was cried from every corner. But quick as lightning the would-be murderer saw the muzzles of four guns so near his face that some of them even touched his skin, he heard at the same time voices telling him, "You are a dead man, if you move a finger Let that pistol drop from your hand immediately, or your brain will be scattered to the four winds." These words were hardly heard by the would-be murderer when the pistol was dropped on the floor and putting his hands to his face, he cried with a supplicating voice. "For God's sake do not kill me! O My God! O My God spare me!"

My four young, brave friends putting their hands on his collar told him, "You are our prisoner Here is a magistrate who has been the witness of your criminal intention. We deliver you into his hands that he may deal with you according to law "

Trembling from head to feet, the young criminal answered. "For God's sake, do what you please with me, but spare my life. I confess that I am guilty of a great crime against you, dear Father Chiniquy, but I ask your pardon Do not get me punished as I deserve." I answered him, "I do not want you to be punished as you deserve But you cannot find fault with us if we ask the protection of the laws of our country to save our lives."

In less time than I can say it, by the order of the magistrate the hands of the young criminal were tied, and he was ordered to be marched to the common jail to wait for the course of the law about his criminal action

The pistol having been picked up by the magistrate, it was

found that it contained four bullets which were to be lodged in my breast, if my merciful God had not protected me in such a visible way

Of course the indignation of the crowd knew no bounds, and the unfortunate young man would not have gone back with his life, if I had not pleaded for mercy and stopped the arms of those who thought that the proceedings of the law were too slow for such a visible and public crime   It was only through exerting my influence to the utmost I had on that multitude that I prevented a deplorable new case of lynch law   I had with me the ninth volume of the Theological works of St. Thomas   I opened it at the page ninety and I read them the following words of that author, which are nothing but the expression of the Church of Rome

"Though heretics do not deserve to be tolerated we must wait till they are twice admonished, but if after a second admonition they refuse to repent and submit to the Holy Church, they must not only be excommunicated, but they must be delivered to the secular power to be exterminated."—St. Thomas Aquinas, Vol 4, p 90.

After reading this law of the Church of Rome, I told my dear countrymen, "It is not against that unfortunate young man that you must express your just indignation to-day, it is against the Church of Rome   It was only to obey his Church and follow its teachings that he wanted to take away my life.

"I know on good authority that he spent the greater part of yesterday with his priest.   There is no doubt that his nerves were strengthened to commit that crime, even at the risk of his life, by what he heard from him.   He was told, what all the priests say of me, that I am a monster, unworthy to live, a cursed man, condemned to hell by Almighty God as well as by his holy Pope   He was probably promised the forgiveness of all his sins if he would put an end to my life.

" Whenever the Church of Rome has the power to do it she has persecuted the Protestants to her utmost capacity.   She

has sent them to jail, she has confiscated their goods, she has
sent them into exile, or even put them to death. Before the
conquest of Canada by the English, it was forbidden to
Protestants to live in that country. They had the choice
between going to gaol or becoming exiles, if they persisted in their Gospel religion. In France, thousands have
lost their lives, and have been forced to go and die in exile
for becoming Protestants In a single night, and the four
or five months after the St Bartholomew massacre, seventy-
five thousand Protestants were slaughtered in France by the
order of the Pope.

"The whole night would not be long enough to tell you the
tortures, the persecutions, the slaughters of the Protestants, by
the order of the Pope, in Italy, France, Spain, England,
Holland, and all other countries where the Church of Rome
was strong enough to execute the laws of blood and death she
had passed against those who refused to worship her idols
and prostrate themselves at the feet of her Pope and Bishops.
You have seen with your own eyes, this very evening, one
of the acts engendered by the bloody and cruel laws of
Rome. Is it your desire to continue to belong to such a
church?"

There was a universal cry "No. We do not wish to be
any longer the slaves of such a system of tyranny and intolerance."

It was my unspeakable joy to see the whole crowd of my
dear countrymen give up the heavy and ignominious yoke of
the Pope in order to accept the Gospel of Christ for their
only rule of faith.

CHAPTER XXI

The Assassination of Lincoln

Several years ago in my book " Fifty Years in the Church of Rome," I had a chapter on the assassination of President Abraham Lincoln. I charged that on the Jesuits, which took the world by surprise Many of my best friends thought that that was the weak point in the book They thought that it was hardly possible that the emissaries of Rome should commit such a horrible crime. The Jesuits, for three hundred years, have been guilty of many black crimes, but it was thought that to charge this to them was more than they deserved. But I had most conclusive evidence of the truth of what I alleged, and felt confident that I stood on solid ground I did not arrive at my conclusion hastily, and was not warped by my hatred of the papal system and by my conviction that Jesuits were capable of anything, according to the principle that the end justifies the means.

There is no man living who has had so good an opportunity of knowing Mr Lincoln, under most trying circumstances, as I had. There was no man who had taken so much pains to investigate and understand the real circumstances and facts relating to his murder I procured documentary proof at an expense of $2,000, which I have now in my possession, before I reached a positive conclusion, and announced it to the world.

I add here on this bloody tragedy a few considerations to be followed by a statement of facts brought out under the most searching investigations by others, all of which go to confirm the truth of what I had written on the subject.

At the time of the murder of Lincoln the American Republic had just passed through the most terrible civil war in the world's history. Slavery was the cause of the conflict, which held in its grasp a vast multitude of human beings. Abraham Lincoln was President when the conflict broke out, and to its end. He seemed to be the man raised up by providence for the time that tried men's souls. He foresaw with prophetic eyes that slavery must come to an end if the national life would be preserved. After waiting for some time till circumstances became favourable, he issued the proclamation of the emancipation of 4,000,000 human beings from slavery. The captives thus liberated were more in number than had ever been liberated at any one time in the history of the world. The negroes often called Lincoln their Moses, before and after their freedom On the first of January, 1863, the commanding officer of the Union forces appointed a meeting in a grove on old Fort Plantation, Port Royal, S. C, at which the declaration of emancipation would be read. There was quite a programme marked out, but which was somewhat interrupted by a remarkable incident. When the proclamation was read, the many negroes present suddenly broke out singing the national hymn. "My Country 'tis of Thee; Sweet Land of Liberty." That hymn they could never sing before, but now that they were free they sang it with swelling hearts; but how they learned it was unknown. Their hearts thrilled with joy at the thought of being free, and rose in gratitude to God. In their joy and gratitude they did not forget Lincoln, their Moses, who led them from bondage to liberty.

In the United States, slavery was a controlling power, which was confined to what was called the Southern States The aim was, on the part of the slaveholders, to make slavery national and to extend it into new territories which would be gradually added as states. They saw that their plans were likely to be thwarted by the opposing sentiment in the free states. They determined to secede from the Union and set up a nation where slavery would be the corner-stone.

Several of the leaders of the conspiracy, including Jefferson Davis, were officers under the federal government. They were thus the more favourably situated to frame and prepare to carry out their plans   They had taken the oath of loyalty and were drawing their salaries from the treasury of the United States, while at the same time they were plotting to break up the nation   Davis and other conspirators, while concocting their diabolical conspiracy, could make Union speeches and loud professions of loyalty.   Davis came to Boston and spoke in Faneuil Hall at a union meeting while at the same time he came on from Washington for the purpose of dismantling forts and making other preparations for the prosecution of his nefarious plans

It was well known that the Roman Catholic Church was in sympathy with slavery and with the political party chiefly representing it.   The hierarchy never raised its voice against the system, but gave it their countenance and practical support.   The general sympathy between the Romanists and the rebels was manifest, and the slaveholders knew it, and relied much on that fact to help them in accomplishing their object.   The Democratic party of the country, as it was called, was known as the pro-slavery party, and Roman Catholics, mainly through the influence of their clergy, were almost exclusively the members of that party   Thus Popery and the slave system by affinity and through policy became allied. Any professions that the Roman hierarchy might make at that time of course were not sincere, but intended to blind people's eyes, so that the end might be more readily gained. The union of Popery and slavery came closer as time went on and the rebellion progressed.

When the war broke out Archbishop Hughes professed to be a friend of the Union   President Lincoln thought that he might render valuable service abroad in favour of the North, which he gave assurance he would render   He went abroad, but evidently with the object in view the direct opposite to that he professed. He saw the Pope and we know what soon after followed. The Pope addressed a letter to Davis, couched in the most friendly and endearing terms. This was in fact a recognition of the slave-confederacy. Let it be remembered that the only foreign potentate that recognized the Confederacy with Davis at its head was the Pope.

Soon after this the Roman Catholic soldiers of the Union army began to desert by wholesale, as they soon learned that the voice of the infallible pontiff must be regarded.

In the document received from the pension department, which was published in the papers, it appeared that there were 144,221 Irishmen that enlisted, and 104,000 had deserted making the percentage of Irish Roman Catholics who deserted during the war, seventy-two, while that of the natives of the United States was five per cent, and of Germans ten per cent. "This,' as a prominent living writer has said, "is a sufficient basis of the charge heretofore made, that a good Roman Catholic can be loyal only to the Pope, and can never be loyal to our government and to our institutions"

Soon after the visit of Archbishop Hughes to the Pope, the terrible riots occurred in New York, when it became necessary to fill up the ranks which had become thinned largely through desertions. The rioters were made up of Irish Roman Catholics, and it was evident that they were acting under the auspices of their chief clergy. For three days and nights there was a reign of terror right under the shadow of the palace of Archbishop Hughes It was evident that he had proved himself a traitor and was informed by President Lincoln that for the continuance of the bloody riot he would be held responsible He then became concerned for his own safety. Then he broke the silence and gave a short address to the mob, calling them his friends, and the rioters dispersed and order was restored. Thus it was evident that Hughes was carrying out the orders of the Pope and was at the bottom of the whole trouble.

Before I speak directly in regard to the assassination of Lincoln, there is another subject to which I must invite attention, pointing in the same direction

During the civil war in the American Republic, the French Emperor Napoleon and the Pope conceived the idea that during that conflict there was a good opportunity to establish an empire in Mexico. The expectation was that such an empire would be a great Roman power in this continent, and be likely to become part of the slave and Romish nation to be founded on the ruins of the Republic of the United States, and the ultimate control of North America.

Maximilian, an Austrian prince, came over to found an empire in Mexico. He came over directly under the auspices of Napoleon and the Pope He and his wife Carlota went to Rome immediately before leaving for Mexico, where they had an audience with the Holy Father, and received his blessing to help and give them success in their undertaking After they arrived in Mexico, Maximilian found the way to the dazzling empire before his mind to be a hard road to travel; matters were going against him

Maximilian seems to have been naturally amiable, and not being of a strong mind he could be easily influenced and controlled by Napoleon and the Pope for their own purpose   The historian, John Lothrop Motley, who at that time, 1863, was the American ambassador at Vienna, in his correspondence with Dr O. W. Holmes thus wrote:

"There is no glory in the grass nor verdure in anything In fact, we have nothing green here but Archduke Maximilian, who firmly believes that he is going forth to Mexico to establish an American Empire and that it is his Divine mission to destroy the dragon of democracy and re-establish the true Church, the right Divine, and all sorts of games Poor young man."

Maximilian's tastes and religious notions were such as might be expected from his mother and his priestly advisors. Mr. Motley further writes.

"Maximilian adores bull-fights, rather regrets the Inquisition, and considers the duke of Alva everything noble and chivalrous and the most abused of men It would do you good to hear his invocation to that deeply inspired shade, and his denunciations of the ignorant and vulgar Protestants who defeated him. You can imagine the rest "

It is true he had just been at Rome and had just received the papal benediction. Pius IX. felt highly gratified with the recognition of his approbation and blessing in a cause which he thought would result in much for the holy Church. By "Divine right" he could originate a dynasty, and promise "perpetuity" to it, and "secure to it the blessing of heaven upon his enterprise "

The Pope had done a great deal of blessing and cursing in his time, but the results showed that his blessings were worse than his curses. Such was the results in this case. Popes have been very successful in getting people into trouble, but never did much to get them out of it, this finds a striking illustration in the case of Maximilian

The time had now come for the United States to take a decided stand. On the seventh of March, 1864, Mr Seward wrote to the American ambassador at Paris, for the information of the French government: "A resolution passed the House of Representatives by a unanimous vote, which declares the opposition of that body to a recognition of a monarchy in Mexico." He adds in his letter these decisive words· " I remain now firm as heretofore in the opinion that the destinies of the American continent are not to be permanently controlled by any political arrangement that can be made in the capitals of Europe "

The Confederate States looked with a great deal of interest on the French intervention Napoleon had a strong desire to recognize the Confederacy, and urged the British government to join him in such a move. Jefferson Davis said 'Napoleon was anxious to go beyond this, and so was the Pope of Rome; and they alone entertained those views on that question.   Napoleon's efforts looking towards the breaking of our blockade met with refusal from England, the country whose artisans were the chief sufferers by the cotton famine "   The letter of Mr Seward representing the determined position of the United States, produced a weakening and frightening effect on Napoleon.

The French emperor had announced that he would withdraw his troops from Mexico, which, with other drawbacks, made the cause desperate for Maximilian.   Carlota left very suddenly for France and Rome to secure help in the trying circumstances.   When she arrived in Paris and visited Napoleon, she met with a cold reception, and was told that he could do nothing.   She then hastened to Rome to see the Pope, but he promised no practical help, and she, seeing that ruin was inevitable, became suddenly insane, and has remained so

Maximilian, as a last resort, after the surrender of Lee, attempted to strengthen his position by offering large inducements to the Southern rebel leaders to colonize Mexico, and join him.   The idea struck very favourably many of the confederates.   It was noticeable how readily they could become the adherents and champions of monarchy and the Pope. Maximilian utterly failed in his enterprise, and was executed by being shot.

It was as evident as anything could be that a gigantic conspiracy had been formed for the destruction of the American Republic, the two chief movers of which were Jefferson Davis and the Pope   As that had thus far been an evident failure, it was concluded to take the most desperate measures to accomplish the end   It was decided to strike directly at the head of the government, the President to be put out of the way, and the other chief officers to be assassinated, so that everything would be in confusion; none at the head of the government and the army, and the way blocked for a new election   Then the conspirators would step in and have their way, and Davis and the Pope rejoice.

In my "Fifty Years" I gave an extended statement of facts in regard to the assassination of Abraham Lincoln. In that work I stated that I had warned Mr. Lincoln long before the assassination that such an event was likely to take place, and to be on his guard. The conspirators, including Booth and John Surratt, were accustomed to meet at the house of Mary Surratt, in Washington Romish priests were frequent visitors there. Those who met there were known as enemies of the government, and rebels. The assassination had been announced some hours before it actually occurred, in a town in a distant state, showing that the plot was known among certain Romanists beforehand John Surratt was specially looked after and harboured by the priests while a fugitive from justice.

After I had published to the world my account of the assassination of Abraham Lincoln, a full history of it was published, written by General T M Harris, who had been a member of the military commission, before which Mary Surratt had been tried and convicted Through a certain chain of circumstances this gentleman had been led to write a full history of that event.

There is no man in America who has so extensively investigated the subject as he. He availed himself of all the sources of information within his reach. His work is a volume of over 400 pages It is a perfect Gibraltar, and the Romanists have not attempted to challenge its statements Since the publication of that work, Gen Harris prepared a smaller book bearing the title, "Rome's Responsibility for the Assassination of Abraham Lincoln."

I have held an extensive correspondence with the author while preparing his books and I found that there was a complete agreement between him and myself on the subject His investigations and their results go to confirm what I wrote in my "Fifty Years" I quote extensively from his books, which I feel assured my readers will appreciate not only for the information, but as confirming what I had previously published on the subject, and the proof of the truth of the terrible charge which I first publicly made amounts to an absolute demonstration

I now proceed to quote from the writings of Gen. Harris.

"It is my purpose now to review the facts connected with the assassination of President Lincoln, and the attempted assassination of Mr. Seward, and the purpose to assassinate Vice=President Johnson, Secretary Stanton and General Grant The object of this scheme of wholesale assassination of the civil and military heads of the government, was to throw the country into a state of chaos, and thus retrieve the fast failing fortunes of the Confederacy These facts, as developed on the trials of the conspirators before a military commission, and on the trial of John H. Surratt two years later, before a civil court, together with evidence secured by Father Chiniquy, and given to the world in his book, 'Fifty Years in the Church of Rome,' show conclusively the hand of Rome in this stab at our nation's life I will now proceed to pass these facts in review, in their proper order, and to show their significance

"We will take as our starting point the fact well established, that the headquarters of the conspiracy in Washington City was the house of a Roman Catholic family of which Mrs. Mary E. Surratt was the head: and that all of its inmates, including a number of boarders, were devoted members of the Roman Catholic Church This house was the meeting place, the council chamber of Booth and his co=conspirators, including Mrs Mary E Surratt and her son, John H. Surratt, who, next to Booth, were the most active members of the conspiracy in the preparation of the execution of the plot

"Booth, the ring=leader, was born and reared a Protestant. He was only a nominal Protestant, however.

"He was a man of the world, a drunkard and a libertine, and utterly indifferent to matters of religion

"That, under the influence of his associations in the conspiracy plot, he had become a pervert to Catholicism, was shown, however, by the fact that on the examination of his person after his death it was found that he was wearing a Catholic medal under his vest and over his heart.

"The wily Jesuit, sympathizing with him in his political views, and in the hope of destroying our government, and establishing the Confederacy, which had already received the Pope's recognition and expressions of good will and sympathy conferred upon it, had been able to pervert him to Catholicism, and to deceive him into the belief that this medal would conduce to his personal safety, and to the success of his enterprise. He had, no doubt, been baptized into the Catholic Church. This medal at once marked and identified him as a pervert to Catholicism.

"Now we have Mary E. Surratt, John H. Surratt, J. Wilkes Booth, Dr. Samuel Mudd, and Michael O'Laughlin, five of the leading spirits in the execution of the plot to assassinate, belonging to the Roman Catholic Church.

"My impression is that Herold and Spangler were also members or adherents to that church. Be this as it may, they, together with Atzerot and Payne, were the mere tools and hired agents of Booth and Surratt, and so stood ready to serve their purpose; and so it boots not to inquire into their faith or want of faith.

' Our inquiry then, thus far, has established the fact that five of the conspirators were members of the Roman Catholic Church, and that these five were its leaders to whom the execution of the plot had been confided. We have also seen that their meeting place, or council chamber, in Washington, whilst engaged in perfecting their arrangements for the assassinations that had been determined upon, was the dwelling place and under the control of Mrs. Mary E. Surratt and John H. Surratt, her son, both of whom were zealous slaves of the Pope, and clearly proven, by the evidence given before the commission and by that given two years later, on the trial of John H. Surratt in the civil court, to have been leading and active members of the conspiracy. Mrs Surratt was a faithful and diligent attendant upon church services; and, from the evidence given by three or four priests in her behalf before the commission, she had established, in their estima-tion, a high character for devotion and Christian piety

"It was a noteworthy fact, however, that of all these priestly witnesses but one of them admitted that he had been on specially intimate terms with her during the five months in which the plans and preparations for the assassinations were being made

"Most of them had been acquainted with her for many years, and seemed to be well acquainted with her church reputation, but they had only seen her casually during these latter months   One of these, Father Wiget, was noted for his disloyalty, and could hardly been supposed to have spent many hours with her, at different times, without having heard her express her views in relation to the one all-absorbing topic of the time, that was uppermost in the mind of all, and formed the chief topic of conversation. He could only say that he did not remember having heard her utter a loyal sentiment since the beginning of the rebellion, nor could he remember having heard any one speak of her as notoriously disloyal, until since her arrest   He said he had become acquainted with her through having had the care of two of her sons as his pupils, one of these was serving in the rebel army, and the other, John H Surratt, had been a rebel emissary and spy for three years. passing back and forth between Washington and Richmond, and from Richmond to Canada and back, as a bearer of dispatches, and yet the Jesuitical priest endeavoured so to shape his testimony as to leave the impression that the topics of conversation between himself and Mrs. Surratt, whilst all this was going on, and much more, was confined to such topics as the state of her health, the weather, etc   He was very positive as to her good Christian character, which he had been summoned to prove, but had very little recollection of anything else

"Father Boyle, resident at St. Peter's Church, Washington City, had made the acquaintance of Mrs Surratt eight or nine years previously, but had only met her three or four times since. He had always heard her well spoken of, never had heard anything to her disadvantage, had never heard her utter any disloyal sentiments.

"Father Stonestreet, pastor of St. Aloysius Church, Washington City, had made her acquaintance twenty years before, had only occasionally seen her since; had scarcely seen her at all during the last year or two; had always looked upon her as a proper Christian matron. At the time of his acquaintance with her (which he was locating twenty years back), there was no question of her loyalty. Replying to a question by the Judge advocate· He did not remember having seen her, though he might have done so transiently, since the commencement of the rebellion; and knew nothing of her character for loyalty, only what he had seen in the papers.

"Father Lanihan, a Catholic priest living near Beantown, in Maryland, testified that he had been acquainted with Mrs Surratt for about thirteen years; intimately for about nine years; that he had been very familiar with her, staying at her house. He regarded her as a good Christian woman, highly honourable, he had frequently talked with her about current events and public affairs, since the rebellion, but could not remember ever having heard her express any disloyal sentiments; neither had he heard her reputation for loyalty spoken of

"Finally, Father Young, of St. Dominick's Church on Sixth Street, Washington City, was called in her behalf; he had been acquainted with Mrs. Surratt about eight or ten years, but not intimately, he had occasionally seen her, and visited her; passed her house about once a month, and generally called there, staying sometimes an hour. He, like the the others, was a good witness for her as to her character, but could say nothing as to her loyalty, or disloyalty, he had never heard her speak as to current events one way or another.

How can we credit the testimony of this witness? Is it credible that he could have spent an hour in conversation with a rebel woman of such positive character and convictions, once a month, during the heat of the conflict, and yet never have heard any expressions from her on the subjects that filled the minds and hearts of all, and formed the chief topics of conversation, in all classes of society? Such silence between a rebel woman and a rebel priest, who were on intimate and confidential terms, is too incredible to be believed. We cannot help thinking that all these holy or unholy fathers testified under the understood mental reservations of the Jesuits Father Wiget was, as we have said, her pastor, and so, we take it, was her confessor. We cannot think it at all probable that she would have engaged in a conspiracy fraught with so much danger to her, and such grave consequences hereafter, without having confided to him her terrible secret, nor without his approval. It certainly is rather strange that she should have broken her relations with him after her conviction, and taken Father Walter for her confessor and spiritual guide in her preparation for death.

"There must have been some grave reasons for this change; and it was made for her, by these Jesuit priests, for some very important reasons. It is not at all likely that at such a time, and under such solemn circumstances, she would have made this change from her pastor to another priest with whom she had not had any previous acquaintance of her own volition Had she been innocent, her trusted pastor would have been the one to whom she would naturally have looked for consolation. But Wiget had no doubt told her that she would incur no guilt in aiding the conspiracy, and so to Walter she could declare her innocence, having the faith of a Catholic in Wiget's power to grant her this dispensation. Father Walter could say 'that whilst his priestly vows would not allow him to reveal the secrets of the confessional, he could say, that from what there came to his knowledge, he knew her to be an innocent woman.' There was to be a great effort made to get a commutation, or reversal of her sentence, and the strong plea of the Father was to be based on this assertion of her innocence Failing in this, Father Walter for thirty years persisted in his efforts to fix upon the government the stigma of having murdered an innocent woman

"In its uniting with Father Walter to fix upon our government the stigma of a great crime, to its eternal disgrace, the Roman Catholic hierarchy assumed, with him, the responsibility of perverting the well-established truths of history, and of thus manifesting their hatred of our government, and their chagrin and bitter disappointment at the failure of their efforts for its overthrow

" So deep and bitter was their disappointment at the signal success of the government in the vindication of its authority and its right to exist, that, for a quarter of a century, it never ceased its efforts to fix upon it the stigma of this alleged crime, and it was only stopped from this effort by the publication of my "History of the Great Conspiracy" to overthrow our government by a series of assassinations, when, fearing that its further agitation might tend to give publicity to my book, and that thus the facts of this conspiracy would become more widely known and the truth of history vindicated, that the agitation of this charge and contention against the government were dropped as if it had become a hot potato We must not forget that, in all this they acted under a full knowledge of all the facts in the case These had been fully displayed to the world through the evidence produced by the government on the trial of the assassins in 1865, and two years later, still more fully, on a trial of John H Surratt in a civil court. These things were not done in a corner but openly before the world Their sympathy with the conspirators and assassins, and their enmity toward the government, were thus openly proclaimed before the world, and the attitude of the hierarchy toward the assassination of the nation's head was made clearly manifest. It is Abraham Lincoln, it is true, that was slain, but it was the life of the nation that the blow was aimed at. The scheme to aid the rebellion by the assassination of the President, the Vice-President, the Secretary of State, and Secretary of War, and the General in command of our armies, was concocted by the emissaries of the rebel government, who kept their headquarters in Montreal, Canada These emissaries held a semi official relation to the Confederate government The whole run of the evidence makes it clear that the Roman hierarchy kept itself in close relation with these emissaries; and it is highly probable, from a consideration of all the facts, with the head of the government in whose service they were employed also. It kept itself in these close relations for a purpose, and was most likely the original source of the inspiration of the assassination plot. These rebel emissaries were Jacob Thompson, of Mississippi, Clement C. Clay, of Alabama, and Beverly Tucker, of Virginia. These had associated with them as helpers, George N. Sanders, Dr Blackburn, and others; men who preferred to fight in the field of political strategy rather than on the field of battle

"These agents of the rebel government entered into a contract with J. Wilkes Booth and John H Surratt to carry out their scheme, and also aided them in the selection of their subordinates. Whether these emissaries were Protestants or Catholics, I am not informed. My impression, however, is that they were nominally Protestants They were all, however, wicked men, evidently accepting the maxim that, 'all is fair in war,' and having no conscientious scruples as to the means that they employed to give aid to their cause. That the Jesuits had their ear and aided them with their suggestions, is made probable by the fact that in his efforts to enlist as a helper to Booth and Surratt, a young man who was sent before the commisson as a witness on the trial, Thompson used the Jesuitical argument, that to kill a tyrant was no murder; and so, assuming that President Lincoln was a tyrant, it would be a glorious and praiseworthy act to take him off

"That the assassination plot was known to the Bishop of Montreal (Bourget) and a number of his priests before its accomplishment, and received their sanction, was made plain by their subsequent conduct. As soon as the assassination of the President was flashed over the wires, Fathers Boucher and La Pierre kept themselves on the lookout, and ready to help any of the conspirators who might make good their escape to Canada. John H. Surratt and a companion, whose identity was never discovered returned to Montreal on the early afternoon of the 18th of April, the fourth after the assassination The unknown conspirator then sank out of sight Surratt was spirited away from the hotel within fifteen minutes after he had registered, on his return He had registered on the same book on his return from Richmond to Canada, on the 6th of April, had gone back to Washington and played his part in the conspiracy on the night of the 14th of April, and now, on the 18th, had gotten back to Montreal, and was so carefully watched for, that almost at the instant of his arrival he was spirited away and kept hidden carefully in the house of Porterfield, one of Thompson's assistants, who, for his greater security, had relinquished his American citizenship and had taken the oath of allegiance to the British crown. Porterfield told him that the detectives were on the alert, and lost no time in hiding him away.

"Porterfield, deeply exercised for the safety of his charge, as also for his own, only kept him until he could communicate with Father Boucher, a Roman Catholic priest, who lived in an out of the way country parish, forty-five miles from Montreal. Father Boucher immediately sent his servant to bring Surratt to his place for further hiding Du Tilly, Father Boucher's man, arrived before the house of Porterfield late in the evening of the 21st of April, and, taking

Surratt into his carriage, drove him away under the cover of darkness, and placed him in the keeping of his master, Father Boucher. Here he remained for two months, under the most careful watch and guide of his keeper. Whilst here he was frequently visited by some of his friends in whose employ he had incurred his guilt; and by another Father, La Pierre. This La Pierre was canon to Bishop Bourget, ate at his table, and was the same to him as a hand and arm.

"A circumstance having occurred that made it necessary for Father Boucher to unload his charge, he sent him back to Montreal, as secretly as he had taken him away from there, and placed him in the care of Father La Pierre.

"This Father provided Surratt with an upstairs chamber in his own father's house, right under the shadow of the Bishop's palace. Here he kept him for three months, never permitting him to leave his room in the day time, and never at night but in company with himself and in disguise. Thus was Surratt kept hidden away for five months, in the care and in the charge of the Roman Catholic Church; two of its priests keeping watch and ward over him, with a full knowledge of his crime, thus making themselves accomplices, after the fact, as they also no doubt were before its accomplishment. But how about Bishop Bourget? He stands behind the scenes, it is true, but was he not equally guilty? The organization of the hierarchy is a complete military despotism, of which the Pope is the ostensible head; but of which the Black Pope is the real head. The Black Pope is the head of the order of the Jesuits, and is called the general He not only has the absolute command of his own order, but directs and controls the general policy of the church. He is the power behind the throne, and is the real potential head of the hierarchy. The whole machine is under the strictest rules of military discipline. The whole thought and will of this machine—to plan, propose and execute—is found in its head. There is no independence of thought, or of action, in its subordinate parts Implicit and unquestioning obedience to the orders of superiors in authority is the sworn duty of the priesthood of every grade, just as it is the duty of officers in the army; and as much the duty of the laity to their priest as it is of the rank and file in an army to their immediate commanders. There is a complete chain of responsibility, extending from the head all the way down to the membership. Thus the whole vast organization can be wielded, as a unit, to accomplish the plans and purposes of its head. The priest is virtually an intellectual slave to his bishop the bishop to his arch-bishop, and these again to the cardinals, and all finally, to the Popes, white and black. This being the case, it is clear that no priest would have dared to take on himself such grave responsibilities as did Fathers Boucher and La Pierre, involving so much danger to themselves, as also to the character of their church, without the knowledge and assent of their Bishop It would have been held to be an act of insubordination, fraught with the most serious consequences to themselves But the canon occupies a peculiar relation to his bishop, and is supposed to have no other duty but to carry out the order which he receives from his superior. In this view of the case, which represents truly the relations between Bishop Bourget and his canon, La Pierre, can we rationally come to any other conclusion than that Bourget was, in a moral point of view, also a member of the conspiracy? Neither would Bishop Bourget have dared to give his consent to this crime on his own independent responsibility. He knew he was acting in harmony with the desire and purpose of the hierarchy for the destruction of our government.

"The Jesuits plan with the utmost art and cunning, unhampered by any moral restraints, and always with the utmost secrecy, and carry out their plans in the dark. We think, however, that in this case we have succeeded in tracing the Jesuit through all the devious wanderings of his dark and slimy path, and in fixing upon him the responsibility for the assassination of President Lincoln.

"But we are not done yet. In the early part of September, 1865, these unholy fathers thought it safe to unload their charge to their brethren in England; and so made arrangements for sending Surratt across the Atlantic, under an assumed name, and in disguise

"For this purpose they arranged for his passage on a British steamer, the Peruvian, which was to sail from Quebec on the 16th of September, 1865.

"A physician with whom Boucher was well acquainted, by the name of McMillan, had just gotten the position of surgeon to this vessel, and they arranged with him to take under his especial charge a man by the name of McCarthy, who for certain reasons wished to cross the Atlantic under an assumed name and in the most secret manner. The day before the Peruvian was to sail from Quebec these two unholy Fathers conveyed Surratt in a covered carriage to the steamer that was to carry passengers for the Peruvian from Montreal to Quebec They had disguised Surratt by colouring his hair, painting his face, and by putting spectacles over his eyes. Father La Pierre went also in disguise of a citizen's dress Arriving on board the steamer, Surratt was immediately stored away in a stateroom, from which he did not emerge during the voyage, La Pierre remaining in his room with him Reaching Quebec, these two unholy fathers placed their charge in the care of Dr. McMillan, and then took their final leave of him

"They had confided him to the care of their friends in Liverpool by the hands of Dr McMillan, and through whose aid Surratt succeeded in placing himself under the care of the Roman Catholic Church in a foreign land Rome is everywhere, and always the same, and he can feel safe as long as he is in the custody of the church. Here he waited for the Peruvian to make another voyage and return He sent by the surgeon, to his rebel employers in Canada, a request to send him some money, but only to receive the answer that they had no money for him The expense of sending him

across the continent to Italy thus fell on the Church. His
rebel friends had now forsaken him, but his Church stood by
him. He was sent to Italy, and was mustered into the
army of the Pope. Here he remained safely hidden away
for a year or more, but was finally discovered by a government
detective who had been sent in search of him, and who went
voluntarily, hoping to get the offered reward, and who had
enlisted in the same company to which Surratt belonged.
This detective informed our government of his discovery,
and through the agents of our government the Pope was informed that his soldier, who had enlisted under the name of
Watson, was none other than the notorious John B. Surratt, who was a member of the conspiracy that accomplished
the assassination of President Lincoln.

"With a shrewd show of virtuous innocence, the Pope hastened to clear his skirts, and those of his underlings, by ordering his arrest and rendition to our government, without
waiting for its requisition. He was arrested by the Pope's
authority, but was allowed to escape by his guards, and thus
given another chance for life and liberty.

"The story was that he made his escape by a bold leap over
a precipice, at the risk of his life. 'Tell this to the marines;
the old sailors will not believe it.' He was finally captured
at Alexandria, Egypt, and was brought home in chains,
where he was held to answer for his crime.

"Let us here pause for a moment to consider the relations
of the heirarchy to this crime. The testimony given on the
trial of John H. Surratt clearly convicts two of its priests,
Boucher and La Pierre, of being accomplices in the conspiracy; and, by implication. as clearly convicts the Bishop
of Montreal, Bishop Bourget. This testimony was spread
before the world, and so must have been known to the Roman Catholic hierarchy, yet it never called any of these
priests to accountability, or held them responsible for this
crime—the crime of the ages. No one of them was ever
held to have forfeited his standing or good character in the

Church on account of his connection with this conspiracy, and so the hierarchy stands before the world to-day as having given its approval to their conduct in this matter.

"We now come to the trial of John B. Surratt, before a civil court. It is not our purpose to go into a general review of the trial, but only to show the interest taken in it by the Roman Catholic priesthood; the animus of the defense toward the government; and the means resorted to, to make sure of his acquittal. The hand of the Jesuit is everywhere traceable throughout the history of this trial, and, by that hand, one of the most important trials that the history of American jurisprudence records, was well-nigh turned into a farce by the skill and cunning of the defense. The cunning of the Jesuit was exercised in the preparations made in advance to make sure of acquittal of the accused.

"A most noteworthy fact in connection with this trial, as bearing upon the subject of our investigation, was the deep interest manifested by the Roman Catholic priesthood of Washington in this trial, and their sympathy with the accused. There was scarcely a day, during the trial, but that one or more of them was found in the court-room. They also made it manifest that they were there in behalf of the prisoner of the bar; and that they were ready to aid in his defense was very apparent

"Whenever the prosecution brought a witness on the stand whose testimony was particularly damaging to the accused, a witness was always found to rebut his testimony, and was always a member of the Roman Catholic Church. It was also a very significant fact, that no one of all those witnesses was able to pass the ordeal of Judge Pierrepont's cross-examination unscathed It looked as though the task of these priests was to aid the prisoner's counsel by finding the witness that they needed, and stuffing them with the needed testimony. It was thus made manifest, during the trial, on more than one occasion, that witnesses had been hunted up and furnished with a cooked-up testimony to meet the requirements of the case. It is worthy of note that, whenever the prosecution thought it important to rebut any testimony, a witness was always promptly found for them, and was always a Catholic. The manner of these witnesses in testifying, and the fact that they never could stand the test of Judge Pierrepont's searching cross-examination, justly gave rise to the suspicion that they had been suborned, and were delivering a cooked-up testimony. And these facts gave rise to the suspicion that it was the special business of some one to find and stuff witnesses for the occasion.

"John H. Surratt had been a student at St. Mary's college for a year or two, at the breaking out of the war. He had commenced a collegiate course, having the priesthood in view. His sympathies were so strongly for the South that he left the college, gave up his priestly aspirations, and engaged actively in the secret service of the Confederate government.

"As a student he was very popular at the college, and seemed to have won the favour of the president and faculty. The summer vacations at the college occurred during the progress of the trial, and the president took occasion to spend a day in the court-room, and sat, all day, at the side of the prisoner at the dock. His presence there was, no doubt, intended to have its effect on the Roman Catholic members of the jury. It was as much as to say: 'You see which side I am on.' Many of the students of the college took occasion to visit their former fellow student during the trial, and always manifested their sympathy for him by the warmest friendly greeting, taking their places at his side.

One important witness was Dr. McMillan. It will be remembered that this witness was the surgeon of the Peruvian, and that it was to his care that Surratt had been committed, under the name of McCarthy, by his co-conspirators, Boucher and La Pierre.

"The voyage across the Atlantic occupied seven or eight days, and as the doctor was the only man on board in whom Surratt could confide, and as he was carrying in his breast the secret of the great crime that was weighing heavily on his conscience, and being all the time haunted by the spectre of detectives, it was natural that he should seek relief in the confidential companionship of McMillan. He became very communicative, and related the difficulties that he experienced and overcame in making good his escape from Washington, and in getting back to Canada after the assassination; the parts taken by Porterfield, Boucher and La Pierre in keeping him hidden away in Canada for five months, and many other things relating to the conspiracy; and, finally, he revealed to him his identity. The testimony of this witness was entirely conclusive as to his guilt, and so he was particularly obnoxious to the prisoner's counsel.

"He was treated by them, from the start, just as they would have treated a witness who had been convicted of perjury, although they were unable to discredit him by the legal methods. They could not look at him, or speak of him, but with the air and language of scorn and contempt. So important did it seem to discredit this witness that Priest Boucher voluntarily came all the way from Canada to rebut his testimony. His man, DuTilly, was also brought; but notwithstanding the fact that they showed themselves to be swift witnesses, of the most ready kind, they failed to discredit this witness. Under the searching cross-examination of Judge Pierrepont they were made to corroborate the testimony given by the doctor in all of the most essential and important particulars, and the unholy father was made to convict himself of being equally guilty with the prisoner.

"It would seem that the Jesuits had had it in mind, from the beginning of the war, to find occasion for the taking off of Mr. Lincoln. Early in the war they set a paragraph going the rounds of the press, as far as they had it under their control, to the effect that Mr. Lincoln had been born in the Catholic Church, and had been made a member of the Church by his baptism into it, and that he had apostatized, and became a heretic. Mr. Lincoln had seen this statement going the rounds of the press, and believed that such a gross falsehood would not have been published without a purpose. On the occasion of a visit from Father Chiniquy about this time Mr. Lincoln called his attention to this paragraph, saying he had been greatly perplexed in trying to discover the object of its publication; and asked him if he could give any clue to the motive that had inspired such a falsehood. I will give Father Chiniquy's own account of his interview with the President on this subject:

"'The next day, I was there at the appointed hour, with my noble friend, who said, "I could not give you more than ten minutes yesterday, but I will give you twenty to-day; I want your views about a thing which is exceedingly puzzling to me, and you are the only one to whom I like to speak on that subject. A great number of democratic papers have been sent to me lately, evidently written by Roman Catholics, publishing that I was born a Roman Catholic, and baptized by a priest. They call me a renegade and an apostate on account of that, and they heap upon my head mountains of abuse. At first I laughed at that for it is a lie, thanks be to God, I have never been a Roman Catholic. No priest of Rome has ever laid his hand on my head But the persistency of the Romish press to present this falsehood to their readers as a Gospel truth, must have a meaning. Please tell me as briefly as possible what you think about that" "My dear President" I answered, "It was just this strange story published about you that brought me here yesterday. I wanted to say a word about it; but you were too busy. Let me tell you that I wept like a child when I read that story for the first time For, not only my impression is that it is your sentence to death, but I have it from the lips of a converted priest that it is in order to excite the fanaticism of the Roman Catholic murderers, whom they hope to find, sooner or later, to strike you down, they have invented that false story of your being born in the Church of Rome, and of your being baptized by a priest.

They want by that to brand your face with the ignominious mark of apostasy   Do not forget that in the Church of Rome an apostate is an outcast, who has no place in society, and who has no right to live   The Jesuits want the Roman Catholics to believe that you are a monster, an open enemy of God and the Church, that you are an excommunicated man   For every apostate is *ipso facto* excommunicated   I have brought to you the theology of one of the most learned and approved of the Jesuits of his time, Bussambaum, who, with many others, say that the man who will kill you will do a good and holy work   More than that, here is a copy of a decree of Gregory VII. proclaiming that the killing of an apostate, or a heretic, and an excommunicated man, as you are declared to be, is not murder, nay, that it is a good, a Christian action   That decree is incorporated in the canon law, which every priest must study, and which every good Catholic must follow

"'"My dear President, I must repeat to you here, what I said when in Urbana in 1856.   My fear is that you will fall under the blows of a Jesuit assassin if you do not pay more attention than you have done till now to protect yourself.   Remember that because Coligny was a heretic, as you are, he was brutally murdered in the St. Bartholomew night, that Henry IV. was stabbed by the Jesuit assassin, Ravaillac   the fourteenth of May, 1610, for having given liberty of conscience to his people, and that William the Taciturn was shot dead by another Jesuit murderer, called Girard, for having broken the yoke of the Pope.   The Church of Rome is absolutely the same to-day as she was then; she does believe and teach, to-day, as then, that she has the right and that it is her duty to punish with death any heretic who is in her way as an obstacle to her designs

"'"The unanimity with which the Catholic hierarchy of the United States is on the side of the rebels, is an incontrovertible evidence that Rome wants to destroy the Republic, and as you are, by your personal influence and popularity, your love of liberty, your position, the greatest obstacle to their diabolical scheme, their hatred is concentrated on you; you are the daily object of their maledictions; it is at your breast they will direct their blows. My blood chills in my veins when I contemplate the day which may come, sooner or later, when Rome will add to all her iniquities the murder of Abraham Lincoln '"

"The charge that Rome was responsible for the assassination of Abraham Lincoln was first made, so far as I am advised, by Father Chiniquy; and was founded not only on the fact which I have here given, but on facts that came to him as a result of his own personal research His charge is distinctly and explicitly made in his book, entitled, Fifty Years in the Church of Rome' He there shows that Mr Lincoln had incurred the deadly enmity of the Jesuits by foiling and disappointing them in the effort they had made to convict Father Chiniquy of a crime of which they had falsely accused him; and which. had they succeeded in convicting him, would not only have ruined his reputation, but would have secured his incarceration in a prison

"Mr Lincoln defended Father Chiniquy, and being furnished, apparently by a special providence, with evidence that revealed their wicked conspiracy to destroy him, and convicted them of perjury, he was able triumphantly to defeat their wicked scheme, and gave them such a scathing as made them tremble with rage, and slink away with vows of vengeance in their hearts.

'Father Chiniquy in making his warm acknowledgement to Mr. Lincoln could not refrain from shedding tears. Upon Mr Lincoln's expressing surprise at this, and saying to him that he ought to be the happiest man in the world, Father Chiniquy replied that it was for Mr. Lincoln, and not for himself, that his tears were falling. He then explained the cause of his emotion, saying that, knowing the Jesuits as he did, and reading a purpose of vengeance in their murderous eyes, he knew that they would never rest until they had compassed his death

"This occurred at Urbana. Ill , in 1856. In the providence

of God, the duty fell on Mr Lincoln of putting down a formidable rebellion, and of maintaining the authority of the government by its military arm, and Father Chiniquy, realizing that a state of war would afford the Jesuits the opportunity that they sought to at once wreak their vengeance on personal account, and give a stab at the life of the government, made three different visits to the President, during his administration, to give him warning of his danger, and to put him on his guard. As Father Chiniquy has kindly given me the liberty to use his book freely for the purpose of this book, I have given above the result of one of these visits, and shall make still further use of his book in closing up this inquiry.

"We have now traced the history of this assassination as revealed by the testimony given before the military commission, and before a civil court, two years later; and we find ourselves coming in contact with the Roman Catholic Church at every point, and always as a deeply interested party, thus showing its relation to the crime. Its sympathy was always with the assassins, wherever we came in contact with it Its animus toward the government was always seen to be that of the bitterest hatred and scorn. Its manner. that of a lion robbed of its prey. Its every effort was to shield, and give aid to, those on trial; and when it failed in this, to cast obloquy on the government, and to bring it into contempt Thus the history of this great crime reveals to us Rome's responsibility for the assassination of Abraham Lincoln, not as an individual man, however much of personal hatred on the part of the Jesuits might have led them to plan for his death, but as the head of the nation they desired to destroy him But we shall now proceed to give the most positive and unequivocal proof of the complicity of the Romish hierarchy in, and its responsibility for, this crime "

I have thus quoted from General Harris on the subject, to give not only the main facts, but to show that the very extensive research of another goes to corroborate what I stated in my "Fifty Years"

CHAPTER XXII

A Great and Good Institution: The Presbyterian College, Montreal. The Rev. Dr. MacVicar.

During my mission work in Montreal in the winter of 1870, walking one day on St. Catherine Street with a city pastor, a friend of mine, we happened to pass by Erskine church. That friend, knowing the interest I always took in matters relating to education, asked me.

" Would you not like to see the class of students for the ministry which the Rev. MacVicar and Rev. Gibson are teaching?"

"I never heard that there was such a class of students in Montreal," I answered.

"Yes, there is one," said my friend. "Rev MacVicar is so much impressed with the insufficient number of ministers for the Protestant population of Quebec that he is determined to teach all the young men who have a desire to consecrate themselves to the ministry. As there is no college and no place for such a work in Montreal, he has gathered his pupils in the basement of Erskine church."

When inside the basement room, I found it small, low, badly ventilated, badly lighted. But, if the material aspect of this newly improvised class-room was as humble and poor as it could be, it was not so with the appearance of the teacher.

Nothing could be more pleasant than to look at his honest face. He was the very personification of health, strength, intelligence, and Christian enthusiasm.

No king on his throne ever looked more happy than the Rev. D H. MacVicar, in that very first hour that I made his personal acquaintance. His high stature, nearly six feet, his

233

broad shoulders, fine and perfectly well-formed chest, his splendid forehead, the evident dwelling-place of very high intelligence, all the fine and regular but stern lines of his face, were telling me that I was in the presence of one of those few men whose marble statues will some day adorn the public places of their grateful country.

After saluting me in that gentlemanly manner which is his own, he continued his lesson. It was the explanation of the Binomial Theorem of Newton.

When young, the study of mathematics had not only been a pleasure to me, but it was a real passion, and I felt so pleased and so full of admiration for his ease and lucidity in explaining the most difficult parts of that remarkable problem that the sweet remembrances of my college days were revived within my heart

After taking leave of the Rev Mr MacVicar, I said to my companion, "I am filled with admiration for the high capacity of that young mathematical teacher. Sooner or later the Protestants of Canada will acknowledge his unparalleled capacity. Such a treasure of learning and zeal will not be left in the low and obscure basement of this church "

"The Rev. Mr. MacVicar is surely an able mathematician," answered my companion, "but his enormous ambition will destroy him Do you not know that his dream is to have a large Presbyterian college in Montreal? We have already enough, if not too many, of these institutions for the small means of our young and struggling churches The theological colleges of Kingston, Toronto and Halifax are as much as Canadian Presbyterian Churches can support Even Mr. MacVicar would see this if his unquenchable ambition were not blinding him. He evidently aims at being called 'the founder of the Montreal Presbyterian College.' But he will be disappointed. I am very sorry for that, for I like him; he is one of our best working men, full of zeal and piety, but his ambition is almost boundless, and it will destroy him."

"Allow me to differ with you," I answered. "If there is a

thing that is needed in Montreal, to-day, it is a college where our Christian young men will be prepared to spread the Gospel among the French population of this Province of Quebec, as well as among the English speaking people A battle must be fought, to-day, in this province of far more importance than the battle of the Plains of Abraham by the soldiers of the Gospel, if they want to be true to themselves and to the God who gave them the vast regions of the Dominion of Canada. The ambition of the Rev. Mr. MacVicar is a noble one. It is the grand ambition of a true Christian. I hope and pray that the day will soon come, when, in the very heart of this Roman Catholic province, there will be a Presbyterian college, which will be as the lighthouse from which the blazing light will show to the mariners how to save the ship from the rock concealed under the perfidious waves of the stormy sea I would give up, this very day, the blessed evangelical work in which I am engaged among my Roman Catholic countrymen, if I had not in my heart the hope that, before long, there will be a Protestant college where the more intelligent of the young men, whom we bring to Christ, will be trained to preach the Gospel. Before long I will be in my grave with the few evangelists who are helping me and whom I am helping in this precious part of the Lord's vineyard; and who will take our places if there is no college where new recruits will be trained to continue our evangelical work? Surely Mr. MacVicar is too poor to build that college, but the God who has put into his heart the noble and holy ambition of raising it, is rich enough to do it. The gold and silver of the whole world are His and there are enough noble and rich Christian men to do that blessed work, when the hour appointed by the providence of God will sound from the clock of heaven.

And, blessed be the Lord, that great and glorious work is already done

Come and see it! and tell me if it does not look like a miracle. Yes! come and see the magnificent Montreal

college—look at its elegant steeple, pointing to heaven, where
dwells the God whose will is that "every man should be
saved through the preaching of the Gospel!" See the vast
and magnificent rooms prepared for the happy young men
whom the Good Master is calling to work in His blessed vineyard! See the beautiful and vast chapel whose walls resound
with the hymns of praise of those to whom it has been said,
"Go and teach all the nations . . . Lo, I will be with
you to the end of the world!"

That college, whose foundations were laid in 1872, is situated on a most beautiful spot, on the flank of the mountain
whose foot is washed by the waters of the majestic St. Lawrence river, and whose top is crowned with the grandest public park   From the upper part of the college, your vision will
embrace some of the most magnificent scenery the world can
give you.   At your feet is the mighty St. Lawrence river,
rolling its deep and rapid waters as far as your eyes can see.
Count, if you can, the splendid steamers or other ships arriving from Europe, or starting with their rich cargoes for the
different parts of the world.   Will not your mind be filled
with admiration at the sight of the marvelous Victoria Bridge,
two miles long, spanning the giant river from the top of its
twenty-four piers, each one hundred feet high?

If, from the top of the upper part of that college, you raise
your eyes towards the south, you will see the vast and rich
plain, cut in two by the beautiful Richelieu river; and you
will have to admire the mountains of Rouville, Bel-oeil, St.
Pie, which look like giant sentinels to watch over the grand
destinies of Canada.   Now let your eyes survey the nearer
prospects and you will see, a little to your right hand, the
princely palace of the Canadian Pacific R. R. station; listen
and you will hear the thundering cars, which, night and day,
are in motion to pour the incalculable treasures of Asia and
Europe into the bosom of each other.   Look again and you
will see a part of that marvelous steel chain which binds the
Atlantic and the Pacific Oceans together, holding them as

prisoners to the feet of our dear Canada. It is that marvelous railroad, 4,000 miles long, which is destined to make only one nation of all the people of the globe. Yes, it is through that marvelous Canadian Pacific R R. that the divers nations of Asia, Africa, the Islands of the Sea and Europe will now shake hands and embrace each other with the fraternal embrace of peace, common interest and Christian love, on the very spot where you stand.

From those marvels of the work of God, so well blended with the marvels of human intelligence and industry, go and see the library—and there you will not be less filled with admiration at the number of the rare and precious books that it contains, from the magnificent edition of the church fathers to the Codex Sinaiticus.

The value of that college library, though so young, is already more than $100,000, given by the generous citizens of Montreal, and others The college has already endowed chairs to the amount of $300,000, given by Joseph McKay, Edward McKay, Robert McKay, Hugh McKay, James McKay, Mrs Redpath and several unknown Christian benefactors.

The whole value of that splendid college is almost half a million of dollars, the fifth part coming from Mr. David Morrice And that you may better appreciate the noble character of the English Protestants of Montreal, let me tell you that at the same time they were erecting that monument of their Christian zeal and intelligence, they were giving three millions of dollars for the endowments and princely buildings of McGill University, which are only a few rods from the Presbyterian college.

Now, from the material survey of that Christian and so noble an institution, let us spend a moment with the one who is the soul and the inspiring spirit of the whole— the Rev Dr. D H. MacVicar, born in Dunglass, Argyleshire, Scotland. He came to Canada in 1836. He studied in Toronto Academy, Toronto University and Knox College. His first charge, when a minister, in 1859, was Knox Church, Guelph;

his second was the Free Church, Côté Street, Montreal. He became thus, the successor of the eloquent Donald Fraser, who was called to London, England. In 1868, in the humble basement of Erskine Church, he began to gather and to teach the young men who desired to consecrate themselves to the holy ministry.

He was moderator of the session of Côté Street Church when that congregation moved to the west and built the splendid Crescent Street Church, which may be called the first grand monument of his zeal and Christian ambition.

It is to his indomitable energy and zeal, after God, we owe the grand success of the French Canadian Evangelical Society, of which he has been president from its foundation.

His remarkable business capacity and vast literary acquisitions caused him to be chosen as one of the Protestant School Commissioners, which board he has served twenty years, and of which he is chairman. He was sent as a deputy to the Pan-Presbyterian councils held in America and Europe

He has been considered one of the ablest teachers in all the branches of theology and philosophy, and has lectured in other departments, such as classics, ethics and pedagogics. In McGill University, he lectured on logic a whole session He has occupied the position of Moderator of the General Presbyterian Assembly, and there has never been an important subject discussed in those assemblies where his eloquent voice has not been heard and listened to with a profound interest.

He received the dignity of D. D. from Knox College, Toronto, and McGill University conferred on him the honourary title of LL D

Besides the immense details of his various duties as principal, and professor of systematic theology of the Montreal Presbyterian college, he has written several learned treatises on Arithmetic, as well as a large number of very able articles for "The Quarterly Review" and other public periodicals.

For two years he fought like a giant against the infamous theft of the $400,000 given by the government (Mercier) to the Jesuits.

But I would have to write a volume, instead of a short chapter, had I to say all I know about the zeal and Christian labours of Dr MacVicar.

However, I will not omit to say that several times his great learning, eloquence and zeal have so much attracted the attention of the rich congregations of New York and other parts of the United States, that large sums of money have been offered him if he would consent to leave his position in Canada to go and work among them. He has always refused these mundane inducements. He preferred to be poor with his own people rather than rich in a strange land

Dr. MacVicar has understood that there is something more precious and desirable than gold or silver, and he was not mistaken. The 250 ministers of the Gospel who have already come out of his college, with the view of preaching the Gospel, are treasures worth more than all the gold which the mountains of California and Australia have given to the world   The splendid Montreal Presbyterian College is a gem to the crown of Dr MacVicar more precious than all the pearls and precious stones in the crown of the Queen of England   Through that grand Christian institution, Dr. MacVicar has become one of those shining lights which cannot be put under the bushel, but stand on the candlestick, that men may see it and glorify the Father which is in heaven.

CHAPTER XXIII

Antigonish Riot of the 10th of July, 1873

At a meeting of the Synod of the Presbyterian Church of the Lower Provinces, held in Truro in 1873, while the subject of the mission to the French Roman Catholics was under consideration, I was invited to address the Synod, and in the course of my remarks spoke at length on the subject of Romanism, and also of my recent and past work.

At the close of my address I received the thanks of the Synod, and was authorized to visit any of the congregations of the church, with whose pastors I might make arrangements, and to receive one-half of the collections which might be taken up at any of my meetings, the other half to be applied for the benefit of the Synod missions

Under this arrangement I visited a large number of the congregations connected with the Presbyteries of Pictou and Prince Edward Island

I was invited by my kind friend, Dr. Goodfellow, pastor of Antigonish, one of the most thriving towns of Nova Scotia, to give an address to his people. In this invitation he warned me that the great majority of the town was composed of Roman Catholics, but he said, "You have nothing to fear here. There is a Roman Catholic Bishop, a college and a nunnery, and a good number of priests, but they are all my personal friends" I answered him, that I would go with pleasure though I had no confidence in the tolerance and liberality of the Scotch Roman Catholics, and that the Protestants would do very well to be on their guard; but I was ready to face the rioters if we were to have a riot as I expected. Two days before leaving New Glasgow, where I was lecturing, I received a letter dated from Antigonish, with the picture of a skeleton and a coffin, with these words "Infamous apostate¹ this is what you may expect if you dare to come and profane by your presence the Catholic town of Antigonish."

When in Mr. Goodfellow's parsonage I showed him that letter; it made him laugh. "Ha! ha!" he said, "this is some schoolboy's trick to frighten you. The Catholics are all my friends here, priests and people, and many have told me that there is not the least danger."

"You do not know the priests of Rome. They are, in general, the greatest hypocrites and the most deceitful men you can imagine. It is when they tell you there is no danger, that there is the greatest danger; it is when they cry, peace, peace, that you must prepare yourself for war They are not only deceitful men, but they are cowards, they want to attack you only when you are not on your guard, and unprepared to defend yourself." This made him laugh outright.

"I have been told," he said, "that you were brave, but I fear that you are not as brave as I expected, for you see danger where there is no danger at all."

"Well, when the riot comes and the stones fly round our heads, we will see who is the braver, you or I."

We dismissed the subject till the hour of the meeting When it was time to leave, I asked Mr. Goodfellow to give me some strings. "What for?" said Mr Goodfellow. "To tie my hat to my head so well that I will not lose it when the sticks hit it" He laughed to his heart's content and said "I see that you have a terrible fear of the stones. I thought that you were more brave than that." "When the sticks and stones come you will wish to have my strings to keep your hat solid on your head." "Dear Father Chiniquy," he answered, "a brave man is not used to see danger where there is none." "You will understand the meaning of your words when your hat will go I have been in the fire so many times that I know what I say. And no doubt you will be wiser on the subject before the dawn of next day " Then like the old warriors who never went to war without their shield, I took my thick shawl which I always carried with me, and as it was a very warm evening Mr Goodfellow could not understand why I wanted such a heavy garment He only laughed at the reasons when I told him he would understand why when the stones would come on our shoulders "That plaid has already saved my life several times, and it will probably save it again to-night There is nothing like heavy wool to ward off the power of the stones when they strike the shoulders." I never heard a heartier laugh of contempt than his at my unreasonable fear, but I was not disturbed by his jokes and I kept my shawl.

We found the church crowded and evidently one-third of the audience were Roman Catholics.

I had not spoken twenty minutes, when an old woman rose on her feet, and cried out, "At him, boys!" and instantly a number of young men rushed towards me, filling the church with their cries, "That's a lie!" Fortunately there was a good number of Protestants in front of the pulpit who at once formed an impassable wall between me and the rioters.

At the same time cries of "Fire! Fire!" were heard outside and inside the church, and the bells began to ring. Addressing myself to Mr. Goodfellow, I said, "You see, my friend, it is just as I expected, I cannot continue the meeting, the only thing we have to do is to go back home." In vain Mr. Goodfellow tried to show the rioters the infamy of their conduct, his voice was covered with the cries of "Fire! Fire!"

A few friends having come around me, with Mr. Goodfellow, we walked towards the door, in the midst of the cries "You are a liar! kill him! kill him!" At the door were several bloodthirsty Roman Catholics crying, "That is the liar! kill him!"

Then eggs began to be thrown at me from every direction. In a little while dozens had been disposed of. The reader may understand that I looked more like an omelette than a man. I was covered from head to foot, but fortunately they were fresh eggs. Then I said to Mr. Goodfellow "When the eggs are finished, we shall have stones." He answered me, "Oh, I hope not" The words were still on his lips, when a stone struck me on the breast, and I would have fallen on the ground had not two friends prevented me A moment after a Protestant lady, who had stood by me all the time, hoping that her presence would make the rioters less brutal, was struck with such force with a stone that we thought that her leg was broken She was carried into the first house by two friends who were near us

During this time the stones were falling upon me from every side like hail in a storm, but my hat was well secured on my head by the strings, and the shawl, well wrapped around my shoulders, prevented the stones from cutting the skin and breaking the bones.

Then Mr. Goodfellow, frightened by the horrible cries and hail of stones, took me by the arm and said "Let us run, they will kill us" I answered him, "Surely they will kill us We will probably die to-night, but we must die like Christian soldiers, facing the foe. There is no use, they can run as fast as you or I" At that moment a big stone missing me struck his silk hat and it went like a feather before the wind Then his head being uncovered was so badly struck with another stone, that he fell down, his face in the mud, crying: "My skull is broken! I am killed!" We helped him to get up. His face was covered with blood and the skin was torn. I was horrified at the sight and I thought that he would die I turned towards the rioters and said: "You are a band of cowards!" I saw, then, very near us, four priests encouraging the rioters and laughing outright.

We would evidently have been killed there, if providentially we had not been at the door of a Protestant merchant, called Cameron, who, hearing the cries and seeing the rioters around us, opened his door and said. "You and Father Chiniquy come in and save your lives"

Mr Goodfellow could hardly stand on his feet, but. though bruised from head to foot myself, I could with other friends help him into the house, which was immediately closed to the rioters, who began to throw stones in the windows, smashing every pane of glass, and threatening Mr. Cameron to set fire to his house if he did not give me up to be hanged. Mr Cameron said to me: "Do not fear, the cowards will not set fire to my house, for the strong wind now blowing from the sea would turn the whole town into ashes"

We immediately went upstairs on entering the house, and while waiting for the doctor, who had been sent for, I asked one of the elders to read the fifteenth chapter of John.

My soul had never been filled with such joy as then, when, bleeding and bruised for the dear Saviour's sake, we were hearing His sweet voice telling us, "Abide in Me; I will abide in you. I am the vine, ye are the branches I will not call you any more My servants, but My friends The servant is not above his master If they have persecuted Me, they will also persecute you."

And on our knees we were answering Him. "Yes, dear Jesus, we will abide in Thee; come and abide in us, when wounded and bleeding we are suffering for Thy sake."

When the doctor was examining the wound of Mr. Goodfellow and washing off the blood, the rioters fixed a ladder up to the window, and three times came up with a rope to hang me. But every time brave young men with axes repulsed them, telling them that if they came up an inch higher they would split their heads And the sight of the axes brandished above their heads was eloquent enough to persuade them to pass down the ladder.

We were besieged in that way until after one in the morning. Then they began to disperse, and Mr Goodfellow, supported by friends, was taken back to his house, where his poor wife was half dead with fright She had heard the cries and seen the excited multitudes running and crying, "Kill him! kill him!" The fact is that she died not long after from the effects of that terrible night

It will be imagined what an effect such a brutal attempt at liberty of conscience produced on the public mind.

Indignant at such intolerance practised by the Roman Catholics in a Protestant province, nay in a Protestant country, the Presbytery of Pictou, voicing public opinion, protested publicly against that brutal assault, revealing such bloodthirsty hatred, took up the affair and instituted law proceedings, all against my will, for I told them: "So long as you give liberty of conscience to the Roman Catholics, it is their right to stone, persecute, and kill you It is the law of the Church of Rome that they must exterminate the Protestants It is not only their right, but it is their duty to kill you when they have the opportunity. You find this law in the decisions of their councils and their Popes, which has never been repealed Besides you can never get the truth out of a Roman Catholic when his Church is in jeopardy, because he is ordered by his Church to lie, according to the Jesuitical doctrine, that the end justifies the means.

The result of the lawsuit proved that I was right.

The Presbytery took decided action in relation to the matter. The members made a strong effort to have the leaders in the riot legally punished; but it failed, as I foresaw and felt. Of course there were witnesses on hand who were ready to give testimony under oath, such as would suit the purpose of those who aided negatively and positively the cruel persecution. That reacted terribly against the Roman Catholics, and the Bishop and priests saw not long after that they had committed at least a great blunder against themselves The Romanists have felt the disgrace and the bad effects of it ever since, and I venture to say that if I had gone to Antigonish several times since, there would not have occurred a repetition of the scenes I have described. No doubt that riot, and the persecution I suffered in Halifax, which I will give an account of, resulted in preventing any serious trouble of the kind since, in Nova Scotia, and other Maritime Provinces. I may say here that the wrath of man seems in this case to have been overruled for good. Such conflicts may be regarded as so many battles for liberty of conscience and free speech.

CHAPTER XXIV

My Re-Baptism

Baptism is recognized in the Romish Church as an ordinance, and one of her seven sacraments But, like other dogmas of that Church, it has been grossly perverted and corrupted It was originally a simple and expressive ordinance sanctioned by Christ. It was designed as a symbol to represent a fact—the inward spiritual change effected by the Holy Spirit. But in the Church of Rome the reality has been buried and lost sight of in the mere form. There is no spiritual efficiency in the water itself, nor is there any evidence of any necessary supernatural power attending its application Baptismal regeneration is not taught in the Bible, and is a corruption held among Romanists and ritualists In Popery it is taught that when the infant is baptized all the guilt and defilement of original sin are taken away and it becomes as pure as Adam when created. The facts. we see, are against this. for the children who have this excellent start have an unspeakable advantage above others, if Romanist teaching be true, and they ought to be very good, at least much better than others who have not been validly baptized. But we know that this is not the case, as they show the same natural depravity that others do

It is amazing how this Divine ordinance has been abused and perverted I give here some examples of this in connection with the work of the early Jesuit missionaries in Canada. These seemed to be so foolish as to think that some drops of water sprinkled on infants made them Christians, fitted them for heaven, without which they would be lost. Among these missionaries was Father Le Mercier, whom I allow here to speak for himself. In the *Jesuit Relations* of 1637, he writes·

"On the third of May, Father Pierre Pijart baptized, at Anonatea, a little child two months old, in manifest danger of death, without being seen by the parents, who would not give their consent This is the device which he used. Our sugar does wonders for us. He pretended to make the child drink a little sugared water, and at the same time dipped the finger in it. As the father of the infant began to suspect something, and called out to him not to baptize it, he gave the spoon to a woman who was near, and said to her, 'Give it to him yourself' She approached and found the child asleep; and at the same time Father Pijart, under pretence of seeing if he was really asleep, touched his face with his wet finger, and baptized him. At the end of forty=eight hours he went to heaven

"Some days before, the missionary had used the same device for baptizing a little boy six or seven years old His father, who was very sick, had several times refused to receive baptism; and when asked if he would not be glad to have his son baptized, he answered, No 'At least,' said Father Pijart, 'you will not object to my giving him a little sugar' 'No, but you must not baptize him.'

"The missionary gave it to him once, then again, and at the third spoonful, before he had put the sugar into the water, he let a drop fall on the child, at the same time pronouncing the sacramental words. A little girl who was looking at him cried out: 'Father, he is baptizing him!' The child's father was much disturbed, but the missionary said to him: 'Did you not see I was giving him sugar?' The child died soon after, but God showed his grace to the father, who is now in perfect health."

The historian Parkman writes. "Nothing could divert the Jesuits from their ceaseless quest of dying subjects for baptism, and above all, of dying children. They penetrated every house in turn where, through the thin walls of bark, they heard the wail of a sick infant, no menace and no insult could repel them from the threshold They pushed boldly in, asked to buy some trifle, spoke of late news of Iroquois frays—anything, in short, except the pestilence and sick child—conversed for a while till suspicion was partially lulled to sleep, and then, pretending to observe the sufferer for the first time, approached, felt its pulse, and asked of its health Now, while apparently fanning the heated brow, the dextrous visitor touched it with a corner of his handkerchief, which he had previously dipped in water, murmured the baptismal words with motionless lips, and snatched another soul from the fangs of the 'infernal wolf'"

Here was fanaticism combined with deception—a lack of truthfulness which is characteristic of Jesuitism in which the end justifies the means—and thus relying on a few drops of water to save a soul, and that applied by lying, in words and act Yet those Jesuit missionaries are often eulogized and represented as model, self=denying and heroic Christian men, while at the same time practising dark superstition, and that by the most flagrant deception and lying

The false and superstitious use of baptism is carried on at the present time by the Romanists, and this is an essential element in their missionary operations. I give here a marked example of this The apostolic vicar of Su=Tehuen, in China, after reporting the baptism in six years of over 112,815 pagan children in danger of death, and the salvation of two=thirds of these who actually died the same year they were baptized, proceeds.

"We pay faithful persons, men and women, who are acquainted with the diseases of children, to seek and baptize those who are found dangerously ill. It is easy to meet at fairs a crowd of beggars with their children in extreme distress. They may be seen everywhere, in the roads, at the gates of the towns and villages, in the most needy condition Our male and female baptizers approach them with soothing, compassionate words, and offer pills to the little sufferers, with expressions of the most lively interest. The parents willingly permit our people to examine the condition of their children, and to sprinkle on their foreheads some drops of water, securing their salvation, while they pronounce the sacramental words. Our Christian baptizers are divided into two classes: those who travel about seeking for children in danger of death, and those who remain at their posts in the towns and villages, and devote themselves to the same work in their respective neighbourhoods. I intend to print some rules for their direction, and to stimulate them all in their work

"The expenses of the traveling baptizers are 150 francs ($27 90) a year, including his medicines and board, 100 francs ($18 60) are sufficient for a stationary male baptizer, and 80 or 85 francs ($15.00 or $16 00) for a female, and yet the number of baptizers is so great that the whole expense this year (1847) amounts to 10,000 francs ($1,860 00)."

Rev. Jacob Primmer, in his deeply interesting book on Romanism, gives a graphic description of a baptism he witnessed in Rome, which will illustrate the character of the Popish superstition. This I here insert, which presents to the mind of the reader a picture that deserves the name of pagan, rather than Christian·

A BAPTISM IN ST. PETER'S

"On the left, when entering St. Peter's, is a small chapel, called the baptistry. The font consists of a marble cover of a pagan sarcophagus with a bronze top. Everything in popish ceremonial is connected in some way or another with paganism. As we were leaving, at 5:30 P. M , preparations were being made for a baptism. We got near, note=book in hand, as usual, and record as follows Baptism—purses out and payment made to priest, who puts on white cotta, kisses cross on red stole and puts it on—gets his book and goes at it with rattling speed—he remains outside the baptistry rails —blows on the face of the child to drive out the devil—takes spittle and puts it on chin, brow and mouth, goes up to the font, anoints the child's head—this is how Papists are fabricated—continues his harangue at the same high speed—the parents and godmother also rattle away as fast as the priest, holy oil, holy salt, holy crossings, very many; and holy blowing on the face of the infant, in order to dislodge the devil supposed to be in the infant instead of in the priest   The priest changes the red stole for a white one, and the father of the child holds a large bit of candle lit, in his hand, while the priest still harangues with great rapidity, the godmother holds the child's head over the font and the priest pushes it under the water (not sprinkling the head but immersing it)   Responses follow, the whole concluding with 'Amen,' and the Papist farce of manufacturing a Christian is over—another coin is given to the priest and off the parties go. The amazing thing is that the child, while this performance was going on, never cried.   The time taken would be eight minutes   All a farce.   No sincerity, no earnestness.   Evidently the endeavor was to see how quickly they could get through with it."

When I left the Church of Rome I was kindly advised by the Presbytery of Chicago to be re=baptized.   But it seemed to me then, as it seemed to Luther, Calvin, Knox and many others, that my baptism in the Church of Rome was validly conferred   And, after having heard my reasons, the Presbytery unanimously resolved to let me go free on that subject

After that time many venerable brothers in Europe, as well as on this continent, pressed me to be re=baptized; and, though they did not entirely decide me to do it, I confess that they much diminished my confidence in the baptism of Rome   I had many hours of anxiety on that subject for more than three years.   And the dear Saviour knows that I shed many tears at His feet, when imploring Him to give me more of His saving light on that important matter

When I preached in Antigonish, the Romanists determined to kill me, and I was most cruelly stoned by several hundred

of them. Bruised and wounded and staggering, I expected
at any moment to fall down and die by the side of my martyred friend, the Rev. Mr. Goodfellow, who was himself terribly cut on the head, and profusely bleeding; when I heard
in my conscience, a voice telling me, "You die! and you
are not yet baptized!"

That thought distressed me much in that solemn hour. I
escaped from my murderers in a most providential way. I
promised to God to study the question of my baptism more
seriously, with His help; and He knows that I did it. But
though it seemed to me more and more every day that the
reason for being re=baptized was stronger than I thought at
first, the reason for considering my baptism valid in the
Church of Rome was remaining the strongest in my mind.

On the twelfth of August, 1873, having heard that many
citizens around St. Anne were to meet to meditate the Word
of God, pray, and praise Him, it came to my mind that it
would do me good to pass a few hours with them, at the feet
of the dear Saviour, to look with more attention than ever to
His bleeding wounds and to all that He had done and suffered for me, that by His grace I might love Him more and
more.

I had never seen a camp=meeting before, though I had
heard much said against, as well as in favour of, such gather-
ings. But God knows that I went there only with the desire of drinking some drops of those precious waters of life,
which our Saviour never refuses to the thirsty soul who goes
to Him. When I went to that meeting, the question of my
baptism was absolutely out of my mind. I heard several
very good sermons from various Protestant ministers; but
not a word was said, that I remember, about baptism, except
that at 3 P. M we were invited to pray for those who were
to be baptized at 4 P M.

There were between two and three thousand people on that
most beautiful spot; they all knelt and prayed. It was a
most solemn thing indeed to see that multitude prostrated

before the throne of grace and to hear their ardent prayers their sobs; to see the tears of those penitent and repenting sinners crying for mercy.

There was no confusion, as I had expected; there were no contortions, as I was prepared to see   But there was the most sublime and soul-stirring harmony I had ever seen in the humble and earnest supplications of the multitudes. The noise was grand and sublime, as the noise of the deep waters when the winds from heaven blow upon them   All was grand, there, as the works of our God are grand and sublime everywhere.

In the midst of that multitude I was praying with all my heart for those who were to be baptized, when a thought flashed through my brain and chilled the blood in my veins: "You are not baptized, and you pray for others, when you ought to pray for yourself, and be baptized to-day"

I tried to repulse that thought as I used to by saying to myself, "A priest of Rome has baptized me."

But that day the voice of my conscience spoke as it had never spoken   It said as loud as thunder, "The priest of Rome is not the priest of the true, but of the false Christ. He is the priest of the Christ kept in the secret chambers (tabernacle), Matt 24.23-26. The priest of Rome is the priest of an idol of bread made with a little flour mixed with some water, afterwards baked. Have you not made that christ, yourself, with your hands, when a priest of Rome? And that god made with your hands was he not your only saviour and god? Do you think the priests of the idols of China and Japan can administer the sacrament of baptism? Would you believe in the validity of your baptism had that sacrament been administered to you by a priest of the heathen Emperor of China? But what is the difference between a priest of the Pope of Rome who worships a god made with a piece of bread, and a priest of the Emperor of China who worships a god made with a piece of wood? Is it not the same monstrous and damnable idolatry?"

At first, I remained absolutely mute before this new light, for this light had never come to my mind with such an irresistible power. But a moment after, I said, "Oh, my God! I understand that I am not yet baptized. At the first meeting of my presbytery I will receive that sacrament"

But more quickly than lightning the voice of my conscience answered "Will you see the next meeting of your presbytery? Are you certain that you will live to-morrow? Can you not be carried away this very night? And when you know that your God wants you to be baptized *to-day* will you resist His will? Do you want to expose yourself to die the death of a rebel?"

This last thought filled me with distress I could not consent to risk to die a rebel. I determined to be baptized without any delay.

But I was away from my own people, and it seemed to me unorderly to be baptized by a Methodist when I was a Presbyterian. I foresaw so clearly the scornful, the perfidious, the false and unchristian interpretation, the profane remarks which would flow as a deluge upon my devoted head from those who would not or could not understand my exceptional position. For a moment I felt such a distress in my soul at the thought of the unkind and unchristian things which would be said, not only by my enemies, but by my mistaken friends, that I again determined to postpone it to the next meeting of my presbytery.

But my accusing conscience spoke again: "Will you have more consideration and fear for your friends and your foes than for your God? That God says, 'to-day be baptized.' To please the world, will you answer, to-morrow?"

I felt so ashamed at my sorrow that I put my hands on my face to conceal the tears of regret which were flowing on my cheeks, and more with my sobs than with my words, I said, "May Thy name forever be blessed, O! dear Saviour, for Thy long patience, yes, to-day, with Thy grace, I will be baptized But before I receive that baptism of water—Oh! Oh!

do baptize me again with Thy Holy Ghost and Thy blood, fill my heart with more love for Thee."

I rose up, and requested the people to sit for a moment; then, addressing the Rev Mr. Foster, the respected Methodist pastor of Kankakee, I told him, "Can you baptize a Presbyterian without affecting his connection with his own church?"

He answered, "Yes, sir, undoubtedly"

I then said, "Mr Foster, I am a Presbyterian minister, connected with the noble Canada Presbyterian Church, and I hope that nothing will ever break the ties so sweet and so blessed which unite me with that Church. If I were among them, to-day, I would ask them to baptize me, and they would grant me that favour, but I am far away from them And I must be baptized to-day! In the name of our common Saviour, please do baptize me. I was baptized by a priest of Rome, the thirtieth of July, 1809; and till this day I sincerely believed that my baptism was valid But I was mistaken My dear Saviour has done for me what He did for the poor blind man of the Gospel At first I was perfectly blind; He touched my eyes, and I could see men as if they were trees, but Jesus has just now touched my eyes again, and I see the things about the priests of Rome just as they are. The priests of Rome make their own gods and their own christs themselves every morning with a little piece of bread—they shut up that wafer-christ in 'secret chambers' as was prophesied by the Son of God (Matt. 24:23-25). There the wafer-christs are often eaten by rats and mice The priests of Rome carry that wafer-christ and god from house to house in their pantaloon and vest pockets, through the streets in their own private buggies, and in the railroads, to fulfil the prophecy of Jesus, who says, 'beware of the false christs Lo, here is Christ or there; believe it not' (Matt 24 23)

"The priests of Rome eat their christ every morning, and often after they have eaten him, they vomit him out of their sickly stomachs, and they are bound to eat him again. The priests of Rome are idolaters. The Son of God cannot allow them to administer the sacraments of His Church.

" Besides that, the baptism which Rome gives is not the baptism of Christ; it is quite another thing. Christ has ordered that sacrament that, by receiving it, we confess and declare that our souls have been purified by His blood, shed on the cross. But the priests of Rome administer the baptism to take away by it the sins already committed before its reception. Then, the baptism of Rome is not a sacrament, it is a sacrilegious caricature of a sacrament; it is an insult to Christ and His Church."

A few minutes later I was kneeling in front of the multitudes, in the midst of a great number of people who wanted to be baptized with me. And the Rev Mr Foster baptized us all.

I will never sufficiently thank my God for what He has done in me and for me, in that most blessed hour

After we were baptized, the ministers who were there offered most fervent prayers for every one of us; they put their hands on our heads, not as a sacramental sign, but as a mark of fraternal Christian feeling But my emotions were too great and too sweet at that solemn moment to pay any attention to that circumstance. What I can say is that if all the brethren and sisters who were there praying around us had wished to lay their hands on our heads when sending to the throne of grace their ardent supplications I would not have been able to find any fault in that; and even to-day, it is impossible for me to see any impropriety, scandal, or any ridicule, when, under the eyes of God and man, such things occurred in the midst of us children of that great merciful God.

I do not say this as an apology An apology is unnecessary regarding such a solemn and sacred action. My baptism was an affair between my God and me alone—my only regret was that I had postponed it so long, and that uncontrollable and providential circumstances had prevented me from being baptized by one of our Presbyterian brethren But it was the will of God that in this, as well as in many other things of my life, I could not do my own will, but I had to do His will. The ways of God are not the ways of men

Since that time it was my privilege to attend, as a deputy, the admirable (I might say the marvelous) meetings of the Evangelical Alliance in New York.   There the Presbyterians, the Methodists. the Baptists, and the Episcopalians have pulled down, and I hope forever, the walls of division which Satan has raised up among the children of God.   They have all eaten of the same bread, and they have all sat at the same table, that it might be said of them· "They are one bread, one body, one heart, one Church."

And the whole world has blessed the sublime spectacle of that unity   Our dear Canada Presbyterian Church, which has tasted of the delicious fruit of that perfect unity, through her representation at the Evangelical Alliance in New York, will not find fault with her weakest child, if, in one of the most blessed hours of his life, he has thought that there is no more difference or division among the Methodist and the Presbyterian Churches of this land of exile than there will be when, around the throne of the Lamb, they will sing together the eternal Alleluia.

CHAPTER XXV

The Stratagem

In the winter of 1873, all the priests of the city of Montreal had received the order from the Bishop to prove, on the same Sunday, from their pulpit, the proposition of their catechism· "That Mary, the mother of God, is the most powerful intercessor men have in heaven; and we must address ourselves to her, if we expect to receive the favours we ask."

The next Thursday the citizens of Montreal could read on fifty large placards, placed in the most conspicuous parts of the city· "Mary cannot be the mother of God. God has no mother Jesus, and not Mary, is the only one to whom we must address ourselves if we want to receive the favours we are in need of. This truth will be proved next Sabbath evening at the French Protestant Church of Craig Street, by Father Chiniquy "

When on my way to church that evening, one of the head men of the police stopped me on the street, and said· " Father Chiniquy, please change the subject of your address. The French Canadians cannot allow you to speak against 'The Holy Virgin Mary.' There will be a terrible riot this night to silence you, and your life is in great danger."

I answered him: "I will not say a word against The Holy Virgin Mary in my address, I will only refute and protest against the awful blasphemy of your catechism, that Mary is the mother of God, and most powerful intercessor man has in heaven. If there is a new riot to take my life, the Lord will again protect me. My trust is in Him. Let the police of Montreal do their duty, and I will do mine."

I found the church crowded to its utmost capacity. To

the best of my ability I protested against the impious doctrine of Rome about the power of Mary in heaven, and the
title of Mother of God given her

Then I read to them the story of

THE GOOD SHEPHERD AND THE WANDERING SHEEP.

"Then Jesus spake this parable unto them saying, What
man of you having an hundred sheep, if he lose one of them,
doth not leave the ninety and nine in the wilderness, and go
after that which is lost until he find it?   And when he hath
found it, he layeth it on his shoulders, rejoicing.   And when
he cometh home, he calleth together his friends, and neighbours, saying unto them, Rejoice with me, for I have found
my sheep which was lost."   (Luke 15.)

I said, in substance

Let us weigh each of these words of Jesus, and meditate on
them with the aid of His grace

The good shepherd hath counted his sheep; but oh! unfortunately, one of them misses the call; one of them has
wandered away and is lost on the way   This discovery is a
thorn which pierces his heart.   He can no longer rest; he is
uneasy and troubled, and he leaves there his ninety and nine
sheep that he loves so much, he seems no longer to think of
them, that he may think only of the sheep that has gone
astray   He runs after it, he searches every place regardless
of trouble, and neglects no measure that may put him on the
track of his dear sheep.   He is wearied and exhausted in the
search, but no obstacle stops or disheartens him   He loves
his dear sheep so much that he thinks of nothing else.   He
courageously continues to seek until he finds it.   He sees it
at last, but in what a state! Half dead with fatigue, lacerated
with thorns, its limbs torn by the brambles, and not able to
go another step   What does the good shepherd do at the
sight of his guilty, but still dear sheep?   Does he load it
with reproaches?   Does he drive it with a lash to make it
walk and return to the fold?   No, no; the good shepherd has

not one thought of anger, not one bitter word against his dear sheep. Its errors have not in the least diminished his love for it   This guilty sheep has done much to sadden and grieve the heart of the good shepherd; but his heart, though crushed with grief, has remained full of love and compassion.   He would say, on the contrary, that the errors and misfortunes of the poor sheep have only increased the love of the good shepherd towards it.   He sees well that it is too much exhausted to walk and return to the fold   What does he do?   He stoops down to it; he takes it in his arms; he presses it to his heart   Then he puts it on his shoulders. and behold him. bowed under his precious burden, carry back his poor deluded sheep to the fold!   But this is not all   The joy of the good shepherd is so great, his happiness so sincere, that he can no longer contain himself. He shouts, he calls his friends, he wishes that the joy which he tastes may be shared by all the world; he does not allow any one to remain indifferent.   "Rejoice," says he to them, " for my sheep, which was lost, is found."

Behold the Good Shepherd of the Gospel!   Behold Him described by Himself—this Saviour of the world, whose blessed name makes every knee to bow in heaven, on earth, and under the earth!

The Good Shepherd—the crucified Jesus—whose Gospel we preach, is the mercy of God, the boundless and the benevolence of the Eternal, incarnate in the person of the Saviour.   The Saviour of the Gospel is not angry, is not incensed against His flock, even when they go astray.   He loves them with a love so great, so true, that never, no never, will saints, angels or virgins be capable of loving them so much. The Shepherd—the Jesus of the Gospel—never met among His friends any one who could love His dear sheep as much as He Himself does   He has never permitted, either on earth or in heaven, any one to put himself between Him and His sheep to stimulate Him to love them.

The modern doctrine of Rome which tells us that the heart

of the Good Shepherd is so cooled and irritated against His erring sheep that He would forget them or cast them off, if the Holy Virgin or some of the other saints were not there to remind Him of what He has suffered for them, is so absurd and so wicked, that one cannot understand how so many people of intelligence allow themselves to fall into that snare

For what reason does the Holy Virgin interest herself in the salvation of sinners, more than Jesus Himself? Why should the heart of Mary in heaven be more compassionate towards miserable sinners than the heart of Jesus? And why should her ear be more attentive to our prayers than that of the Saviour? We can never find answers to these questions within the laws of common-sense Never shall we be able to find, in the Holy Scripture, a single word that can, in any manner, serve as an excuse or cloak for this monstrous doctrine; and it certainly insults the saints in heaven, as well as Jesus Christ Himself, to believe and say, with the Church of Rome, that our salvation does not depend entirely on the love and mercy of our Saviour, but that this love and this mercy of Jesus Christ, being paralyzed by our sins, must be, as it were, incited and revived by the compassions and by the more active and the more efficacious mercy of the saints.

To render the sacrilegious worship which she offers to the saints acceptable, and to induce sinners to put all their confidence in the Holy Virgin Mary, the Church of Rome assures us that our sins have the effect of cooling the love and compassion of Jesus Christ for us. But, then, the Church of Rome ought to tell us how it is that our sins have not the same effect of cooling the heart of the Holy Virgin and of the saints who, according to the Church of Rome, know all that we do.

If, as is no doubt the case, the saints in heaven are united in will and sentiment with God, that which displeases God, ought also to displease His saints; that which saddens and cools the heart of Jesus Christ, ought equally to sadden and cool the hearts of the saints (always supposing the system of Rome to be true, about the pretended knowledge that the saints have of everything that transpires on the earth), and then, whilst Jesus is excited and angry in heaven, as the Popes of Rome assure us, the saints, and especially the Holy Virgin, ought to partake and approve of His wrath, instead of opposing it and hindering its effects.

Behold the misfortunes of the Church of Rome, having left the Word of God, which is the only guide of the human mind, to follow the fables and traditions of men. She has forgotten that Jesus is our intercessor in heaven, not only the intercessor for saints, but for sinners; she has forgotten that this intercessor is sufficient, and that consequently there is no need for another; she has forgotten that thousands and thousands of times, Jesus has said to sinners, "Come to Me and ye shall be saved." And that He never said, "Come to My mother, or such or such a saint, and ye shall be saved." The Church of Rome has forgotten that the name of Jesus is the only name that we can call on to be saved. She has forgotten that St. Paul, or rather the Holy Spirit, by the mouth of St. Paul, said "For we have not an high priest which cannot be touched with the feeling of our infirmities; but was in all points tempted like as we are, yet without sin. Let us therefore come boldly unto the throne of grace, that we may obtain mercy, and find grace to help in time of need" (Heb. 4: 15, 16.)

The Church of Rome having, then, forgotten that Jesus was always good and merciful, but believing and preaching to the people, whom she had deceived, that Jesus Christ was often angry with the sinner, and seeing that sinners need to have a Saviour always good, and always merciful, a Saviour, in a word, always ready to receive those who come to Him, is bound then, to invent and try to find another Saviour than this Jesus, whom she tells us is always angry.

Then she creates other saviours in heaven; she seeks other friends—other intercessors—other advocates, to whom she has sacrilegiously accorded all the goodness, mercy and unfailing kindness of which she has robbed the true Saviour

But let us hope that our brethren of the Church of Rome will soon understand that they are deceived by their Popes. It is not Mary, but Jesus, who is the "gate of heaven, the hope of sinners, and the salvation of the world"

Nothing could surpass the respectful attention of my auditors, though more than the half of them were Roman Catholics

My hope was that the threatening storm had vanished and that there would not be any trouble. But I had again to be disappointed

When I was just entering into my peroration, I felt as if the ground was shaken under my feet It was evident that a great multitude of furious men were rushing towards the church.

The air was filled with the cries of, "Kill him! kill him!" and a volley of big stones broke almost all the glass of the windows, and fell on my auditors as well as on me.

As at the beginning of the address, I had warned the people that there might be some cries heard outside, and some stones thrown at me, the excitement was not so great as might have been expected I said to them: "Be calm, I am the only one the rioters want to strike, and kill, if they can Do not trouble yourselves They will not molest you if you go out of the church, without any hurry, as fearless men and women Trust in the protection of the God of the Gospel, of whom, I hope, every one of you is a true servant and believer. No doubt you will find some brave policemen at the door who will protect you"

But, as the stones were falling upon us thick as hail in a storm, there is no need to say that everyone was rushing to the doors as quickly as possible

In a very short time I found myelf almost alone in the church with the chief of the police

"You see, Father Chiniquy, that you should have followed

my advice, and changed the subject of your address, or not have spoken at all this evening I do not conceal from you that your life is in great danger Look through this small aperture of the door and you will see that there are more than a thousand furious men whose determination is to kill you. Do not go out of the church, for I have only twenty police-men with me to protect you Remain in the church the whole of the night and I give you my word of honour that nobody will injure you; with my men, well drilled. I can repulse the multitude of rioters, if they want to come into the church; but my men will be powerless to protect you if you go out, they will be overpowered by the thousand blood-thirsty would-be murderers you see in the street."

I answered him, "I see that you ignore that my God is my keeper. He is stronger than all those furious men. He has saved me already from great dangers. He will not forsake me this night.

"That merciful God has just given me a plan which, I hope, will save me and confound my would-be murderers, the priests For I know it—these poor, blind people are sent by their priests

"I cannot consent to spend the night here; though I do not know where I can sleep. You see that I am completely disguised I have changed my fur cap and my fur coat with a friend to more easily fulfil my plan The entire crowd of rioters is behind your twenty policemen, just opposite the door of the church, in the midst of the street My intention is to go straight to them, when leaving the church. They all expect, no doubt, that I shall go right or left of the door and keep myself at the greatest distance possible from them. When I go straight to them, not one of them will suspect that I am Father Chiniquy. They all think I am too wise or too cowardly to throw myself into the lion's jaws. Follow me at a distance of twelve to fifteen feet to protect me, if you see any danger, though I do not expect any. I will go through the crowd of rioters, penetrate their ranks by pushing, and they will open and allow me to pass as one of your personal friends."

The chief of police looked at me with a smile, and said. "You would have made a good general. I think your stratagem is as good as it is daring. Let us try it"

And, without a word more, after asking the dear Saviour to protect me, I left the church at the double quick and turned my face to the rioters who were packed, crying like wild beasts, filling the air with the most awful imprecations against me, brandishing their sticks above their heads, and asking each other, "Where is he? Where is he?"

The first I met was a giant man, swearing like a demon against the Apostate Chiniquy.

I seized him by the arm as roughly as I could do it, shook him and pulled him out of my way, with as much rudeness as was possible, saying, "What are you doing here, you band of fools? Open your ranks to let people pass. What right have you to obstruct the street? What is the matter with you all?"

He answered me with a curse, "We are looking for the infamous apostate, Chiniquy. I want to dash out his brains with this stick. But, the coward; he is probably concealed in the church under some pew"

"Chiniquy! Chiniquy!" I said, "I have seen him going out of the church in disguise. He is laughing at you all You had better let him alone, and go back to your homes." I had to push the next and the next, in the same rough way. and exchange words of about the same kind, till I had passed through the whole crowd, and reached the file of patient hackmen who were peacefully waiting behind the rioters for customers.

Addressing myself to one of them, I said, "Take me to St. Catherine Street, and when there go to the Rev. Monio Gibson. Do you know the number of his house?"

"Yes, sir," said the good hackman, and ten minutes later I was knocking at the door of the Rev. Mr. Gibson, where I met with the most fraternal and Christian reception, and where I spent one of the most peaceful nights of my life.

CHAPTER XXVI

Deplorable and False Liberality in High Protestant Quarters with Respect to the Church of Rome

The general indifference on the part of Protestants to the real character and evils of Romanism arises largely from the idea that there is a sufficient amount of truth and good in that system to justify its being regarded as a Church of Christ. Cardinal Manning truly stated that "the Roman Catholic Church is either the kingdom of the Son of God or the masterpiece of Satan" As it is most manifestly the latter, it is certainly not Christianity. The conviction of this must be deepened before much efficient work is done against the diabolical system. It is sad to see some prominent Protestants taking a wrong position on this subject.

Rev Charles Hodge was a professor in the Presbyterian Theological Seminary at Princeton for about half a century. He was a man of a powerful intellect and undoubted piety; but on this subject he was weak, and as his opinions had very great weight with many ministers and others, his influence in that direction was, to say the least, unfavourable.

Virgil gives us the history of a skilful mariner, who, deceived by the sweet, but perfidious voices of the Sirens, perished on the rocks of Sylla; so, when traveling on the sublime and bottomless sea of Christianity, it has been my sad lot to see more than one shipwreck caused by the sweet but deceptive voices of the Siren of the man of sin.

The venerable Dr Hodge was an example of this. I give here his letter followed by my reply.

"My Dear Sir —

"The question proposed in your letter is one to which wise and good men have given different answers.

265

"Some say that the Romish Church teaches serious error. As the influence of that Church is everywhere, and from its nature, hostile to civil and religious liberty, therefore it is wrong to grant it any voluntary support or direct encouragement.

"Others say that, inasmuch as the Roman Catholic Church teaches truth enough to save the souls of men (of which I have no doubt); inasmuch as it proclaims the Divine authority of the Scriptures, the obligation of the decalogue and the retributions of eternity; and inasmuch as it calls upon men to worship God, the Father, Son and Spirit, it is unspeakably better than no Church at all. And, therefore, when the choice is between that and none, it is wise and right to encourage the establishment of Churches under the control of Catholic priests

"For myself, I take this latter view. The principle cannot be carried out that no Church should be encouraged that teaches error For then we could help none but our own. And the principle involves the absurdity that a little error is more powerful for evil than a great deal of truth for good.

"Of course public men should act on Christian principles, and if it is wrong for a private Christian to help a Catholic Church, it must be wrong for a corporation to do so

"While, therefore, I dread the influence of the Romish Church, and recognize its corruptions in doctrines and worship, I nevertheless believe that it is better that men should be Roman Catholics than infidels or atheists. Romanists teach people to worship Christ, and to regard and acknowledge Him as the Salvator Hominum.

"Very truly your friend, etc.,
"CHARLES HODGE."

" Dear Sir:—
"Since I accepted, by the great mercy of God, the truth as it is in Jesus, and renounced the errors of Rome, I have, now and then, heard many strange things about the doctrines of that Church, but nothing looks to me so strange and sadden-

ing as the letter which Dr. Hodge, of Princeton, has written to approve the Protestants who build up the Churches of Rome. I have just read that letter in your issue of the 24th of August. And though it seems an act of folly, on my part, to publicly protest against the views of such a learned theologian, my conscience tells me it is an imperious duty to raise my voice against the manifest and most dangerous errors contained in the document

"If Dr. Hodge had not so many titles to the respect and gratitude of the Protestant community, if he were not truly one of the most shining lights of our firmament, and if his long and matchless service in the defense of the truth had not given him such a title to the confidence of us all, his error would not be so fatal and deplorable, and I would remain silent

"My humble position, my very insignificance, would be my excuse, in my own eyes, for remaining as a mute dog in the presence of danger. Even to-day I am tempted to say to my alarmed conscience: 'Hold your tongue, be still and quiet—you are in the presence of a giant—with a knock of his little finger he can pulverize you—let these errors go their way and spread—you can't help. these ugly stones, coming down from a high mountain, roll with irresistible force—you will surely be crushed down if you are foolish enough to put yourself in the way and try to stop them'

"I see too clearly the errors of Dr. Hodge. I know too well the incalculable injuries they will do to the cause of Christ, to allow myself to be guided by any selfish fear Though the humblest and weakest soldier of Christ, I have heard Him say, to all those who were enrolled under His banners, 'Fear not' Many times the humblest sentinel, from the ignored outpost, has saved the army by sounding the alarm in time.

"Dr. Hodge gives three principal reasons for approving the Protestants who build the churches of Rome· 1st. The Church of Rome teaches truths enough to save the souls of men. 2nd. It proclaims the Divine authority of the Scriptures—the obligations of the Decalogue, etc 3rd The Romanists teach people to worship Christ and acknowledge Him as the Saviour of the world.

"If these assertions are correct, Luther, Calvin, Knox, etc, would be the most guilty men of modern times, and the millions of martyrs whom Rome has slaughtered would be nothing else but rebels justly punished If the Church of Rome's teaching can save souls, why should we continue to protest against the great soul-saving Church (?) and why do we not go to the feet of the Pope to make our peace with him?

"Dr. Hodge is a mighty logician, I know it, and he has, probably, many brilliant theories in store to support his position But the more arguments he will bring to prove that Rome is a soul-saving Church, and that she is a true worshiper of Christ, the better he will prove that Luther and Calvin, with their millions of Protestant followers, Dr. Hodge included, were, and are, to-day, the greatest fools and the most wicked of men for having made so much noise, caused so much shedding of blood, to get out of the chains of Rome, the more he will prove the verity of the Rev. Mr. Ecker 'Protestantism is a faliure.' And if the learned theologian of Princeton can persuade the Protestants that they do well to build churches for the Romanists, the surer he will make the prophecy of the same Ecker good. 'Before twenty-five years the United States will be Roman Catholic!'

"Had Dr Hodge been, as I have been, a priest of Rome a quarter of a century, he would have spared his friends and admirers the surprise and sadness we have felt at his strange views on the matter

"I do not pretend to say I am perfectly sure of what the learned divine means by 'truth enough to save the soul,' and I would like to know his mind more positively on the subject But before I have that favour. I must bear testimony to the truth, and say, 'After twenty-five years of experience and study as a priest of Rome, I do not know a single truth which that apostate Church has kept intact and un-mixed with the most diabolical and damnable errors.' Let us take the nature, eternity, holiness and independence of God, for instance, as revealed in Christ and by Christ. What is the god of the Roman Catholic Church, seen or known through the doctrine of Transubstantiation? A god made with a piece of bread by a man! Just as Aaron took the bracelets and the earrings of the Israelites, melted them, turned them into a golden calf, and said to the people 'These be thy gods, O Israel, which brought thee out of the land of Egypt,' so the priest of Rome says to his servant girl 'I want to carry the good God (le bon Dieu) to a sick man to-morrow, but there are no more wafers in the taber-nacle; make me fifty wafers or little cakes that I may con-secrate them.' And the domestic mixes the flour with some water, bakes the whole between two red irons, on which there is a cross engraved with the abridged name of Jesus. Then she takes her scissors and cuts those cakes, which are origin-ally about five inches large, cuts them into small round wafers about one inch large, and respectfully hands them to the priest. The next morning that same priest takes those small round wafers to the altar, pronounces five magic words, and showing to the people the wafers, which are now turned into as many gods, he says. 'This is our God: this is the Lamb of God which takes away the sins of the world, adore Him,' and the whole people, with the priest himself, falling on their knees with their faces in the dust, adore and worship the new-born or new-made god.

"I ask it—where is the difference between this modern abomination and the idolatry of the Israelites? The only difference is that the Jewish idolatry was of short duration, they did not stick to it, they gave it up the next day, and shed tears of repentance. But the iniquity, the awful idola-try of Rome is a permanent fact. Their wafer-god, their god made by a priest, with the help of the servant girl, is the basis, the life, the grand, constant and public object of their adoration   I know that the Romanists and Jesuits have very curious though very ridiculous arguments to bind the poor slaves of the Pope, and to prove to them that the adoration of the wafer=god is not idolatry   But I hope that Dr Hodge will not prostitute his high intelligence in attempting to help the sophists of Rome in the efforts they make to prove to the world that a man can make a wafer, turn it into God, and worship that god which he has just made himself, without being an idolater   But if Dr Hodge confesses that the worship of the wafer=god is an idolatrous act, how can he say that Rome teaches truth enough to save the soul?

"Through her sacrilegious and idolatrous sacrifice of the mass, the Church of Rome has not only dragged back the modern world to the idolatry of paganism, but she has added the brutalizing and degrading dogmas of the priests of Jupiter and Venus.

"During the twenty=five years I was a priest of Rome, almost every morning I had to turn into a god a wafer made by my servant girl.   I was assured by my Church that that was my true Saviour and my true God   After that. I had to eat it in the same way that I eat the food which is on my table.   And there are more than 200,000 priests of Rome who, to=day, believe, and do preach. the same monstrous things.

"Nay, you do not probably see a single priest in the streets, or in the cars, who does not carry a dozen of those wafer=gods in his vest or pantaloon pockets.   And we are gravely told that the church teaches saving truth about God!   Well, if the reverend theologian of Princeton really believes that the priests of Rome have the power to change the wafer into his very Saviour and God, why does he not go to worship Him at the feet of their altars?   But if, as I am certain of it, that great Christian man would prefer to be thrown into a burning furnace rather than to adore the wafer=god of Rome, how can he tell us that it is no sin to build temples for such a sacrilegious and idolatrous worship?

"We are gravely told in that letter that the 'Romanists

teach Christ, and regard Him as the Saviour of the world.' Into what strange delusions good and learned men are apt to fall. In writing these lines the celebrated theologian, no doubt, consulted more the kind disposition of his Christian heart than his vast erudition. When the Protestants meet their Roman Catholic neighbours, when they listen to the interesting lectures, or read some of their learned books, when they see their smiling lips, their refined manners, they like to conclude that such amiable and learned men are true worshipers of Christ. It does them good to live in that illusion; they do not even like to hear anything contrary to what they consider the only charitable and Christian way to think of their neighbours

"So Rome has many ways to deceive even the most intelligent and learned ones—she is so expert in the art of entrapping and bewitching souls! Is it not written of that wonderful Church that it will 'come after the working of Satan, with all power and signs, and lying wonders, with all deceivableness of unrighteousness'?

"But the kind and Christian though mistaken feelings of Dr. Hodge and some other Protestants toward the Roman Catholics, will not change the awful truth. The apostate Church of Rome has, long since, forsaken and forgotten the real Divine Christ of the Gospel, and has forged another christ to suit her pride, her lust and her unquenchable thirst of power and human glory

"The Christ of the Gospel is the only corner-stone of His church. The Church of Rome has granted that privilege to Peter. The Christ of the Gospel is the head of His church —but the christ of Rome, said, 'It is the Pope that is the head of the Church.' The Christ of the Gospel had promised His Holy Ghost to all His disciples, even to the humblest ones, to guide them in all their ways and teach them the sense of His holy words. But the christ of Rome has promised his holy ghost only to the Pope, who alone has the understanding of the Scriptures, and the knowledge of the truth. The

christ of Rome says to the sinner, 'Go to Mary and you shall
be saved' The Christ of the Gospel is the incarnate love
toward sinners.   He loves them; He likes to be called their
friend, He constantly prays for them with a love and mercy
that no human language can express   But the christ of Rome
is constantly angry against sinners—he would not listen to
their prayers: he would shut his ears to their humble supplications, if his mother were not constantly reminding him of
the price he had paid and the blood he had shed for them
The Christ of the Gospel is God and man; as God He is as
eternal as His Father, He could have no mother   But the
christ of Rome is quite a modern god, he was born about 1900
years ago, his mother is Mary, who everywhere is invoked
and called the Mother of God by the Romanists

"As Dr Hodge is a good logician, he will easily find that if
Mary be the mother of God. Saint Anne who is the mother
of Mary, and Joachim, who is her father, must be truly the
grandmother and the grandfather of the god of Rome, and
Adam his great grandfather' A most marvelous fact, which.
when well understood, will make it more Christian for the
Protestants to raise temples to a god who has such glorious
grandmothers and grandfathers.

"It is true, as Dr. Hodge says, that the Church of Rome
calls her christ, 'the saviour of the world' But this is just
as when her executioners called Him 'King of Israel' It
is mockery   For, the very moment she has called Christ 'the
Saviour of the world,' she goes to Mary and calls her, also,
the saviour of the world.'

"Rome says most eloquently in many of her books, that
Jesus is the hope, the refuge, the salvation of sinners. But
this is only to throw dust in the eyes of such good and unsuspecting men as Dr. Hodge. Turn the page and you will
see, that, with still more eloquence, she calls Mary 'the only
hope, refuge and salvation of sinners—the door of heaven'

"If some Popes tell you it is through Jesus that every grace
comes to man, and that He is the surest foundation of our

hope, that glorious truth in the Church of Rome is only a blind to deceive—for many more infallible Popes will assure you, in their infallible encyclicals, that it is Mary who is the surest foundation of our hope. I will not insult Dr. Hodge by giving the names of the Popes and the documents which proclaim those plain, clear, blasphemous doctrines, for he knows them very well

"The true Christ was meek, and humble, and merciful He rebuked His apostles when they wanted to punish those who rejected Him He proclaimed liberty of conscience among men But the christ of Rome is a bloody monster, who, through his infallible vicar, the Pope, has approved the slaughter of St. Bartholomew, and covered Europe with rivers of blood and tears

"No! the christ of Rome, with his hatred of liberty, his constant oppression to every human progress, his infallible Pope, his holy inquisitions, his hatred of the Bible, cannot be the true Christ, who is worshiped at Princeton seminary. It is an old, false god, smuggled by the Pope from the old Pantheon of Rome, presented to the world under the name of Christ.

"No! the christ whom I have made, during the twenty-five years, with the help of my servant girl, and with a wafer—the christ, who, through his vicar, the Pope, has made me believe the most monstrous lies, who has persuaded me that his body, his blood, his divinity, could be verily and substantially eaten by me, cannot be the Son of the God of truth He is the father of lies and deception; and the disciples of the true Christ, who raise temples to the spurious christ of the Popes, may be good, honest, sincere Christians, but they are mistaken They give a helping hand to the greatest enemy of the Gospel, they build up the Bible-burning Church; they strengthen those who, after having destroyed the Bible, will not rest until they destroy every vestige of liberty and true Christianity on earth, even if they have to wade up to their knees in the blood of the disciples of the Gospel. The Protestants who build up the Church of Rome give help and strength to the enemy.

"Rev Dr Hodge says of the Church of Rome· 'She proclaims the Divine authority of the Scriptures,' and he takes that as his ground for approving those who build up the churches of the Pope   What would the good doctor think and say were I to go to him with a golden cup half filled with the purest water, but after having put as much arsenic as there is water in the cup, I would tell him: 'Please, sir, drink, this is good and refreshing water'?   Would he not repulse me with horror, and justly call me a murderer?

"Now, what is the Church of Rome doing with the Gospel? Does she not offer it to the people only after she has mixed it with her poisonous tradition?   Does not the Church of Rome, in the most absolute and positive way, say that the written Gospel (which we call the Scriptures) is only a part, an unfinished fragment, of the Gospel?   Can Dr Hodge ignore that the Council of Trent has put the tradition (which they call the unwritten gospel) on a level with the written Gospel, that the one is of as much Divine authority as the other, and that the Roman Catholic is not allowed to drink the waters of life, except when mixed with the deadly poison—arsenical preparations—of Popery?

"The learned theologian says that Rome proclaims the Divine authority of the Scriptures, but he forgets that it is only on condition that we receive the Holy Scriptures in the light of Romish tradition.   For Rome proclaims the Divine authority of the Scriptures, but only with the condition that, under that name, we accept the Divine origin and authority of the traditions about Purgatory, Transubstantiation, Indulgences, Auricular Confession, Immaculate Conception, Infallibility of the Pope, etc   Does he really accept the meaning which that Church attaches to the Word of God—Holy Scriptures?   Does he believe that by rejecting the authority of the one, he rejects the authority of the other?   Then he is a good Roman Catholic, he is all right when he takes the side of the priests of Rome, and approves the Protestants who spend money in building the churches of the Pope. But if he rejects with horror, from his lips, the golden cup which Rome offers her blind slaves, then he is wrong. The mistake of Dr Hodge is very common among the honest and unsuspecting Protestants of the United States They too easily forget that the Church of Rome very often says one thing and means another quite different. When she speaks of the Holy Scriptures with an apparent respect, and proclaims their divinity, many think that she means only that blessed Word of God which is contained in the Holy Bible, such as they have at Princeton College. But it is not so.

"When Rome speaks of the Word of God, the Holy Scriptures, she means the Scriptures transmitted through the written and unwritten tradition. She means the Apocrypha, purgatory, celibacy, absolution, mass, holy water, works of supererogation, worship of Mary, infallibility, etc

"She pretends to have the greatest respect for those two things when perfectly united in one body of doctrine But she does not conceal her implacable hatred of the true Scriptures, the Bible, as Dr. Hodge has it in his hands. That learned man seems to ignore that the Scripture, the Bible, separated from the traditions and the Romish commentaries, is absolutely declared a dangerous, a soul-destroying book by Rome, and the Council of Trent has forbidden the people to read it in their mother tongue. He also seems to have forgotten that the Bible Society, whose object is to give the Holy Scriptures unmixed with traditions, notes and comments, has been, time after time, declared by the infallible Church of Rome to be an instrument of the devil to destroy the souls of men No doubt the book of the *index expurgatory* of Rome is in the library of Princeton. Then let him consult the long list of books forbidden for their *impiety* and *immorality* and he will find that his Bible stands at the head of the list. Let him consult the pages of the history of France, Italy, Spain, Ireland, England, Canada, and even the history of the

United States, and he will see that Rome, as often as she has found her opportunity, instead of proclaiming the Divine authority of the true and unmixed Scriptures, has burned and destroyed them, as we burn and destroy a viper. Yes, let him open the store of his memory and vast science, and he will remember that, not only Rome has destroyed the true and undefiled Holy Scriptures every time she could do it safely, but she has invariably condemned to death those who have been found guilty of reading the Bible

"The memory of Dr. Hodge cannot be so bad as to have made him forget that the Madiai of Florence, and the twelve noble young men in Spain, only yesterday, were condemned to death by the Holy Inquisition for the *unpardonable crime* of having the Bible and reading it.

"That great theologian, following more the instincts of his kind nature and Christian feelings than the teachings of history, assures us that the Church of Rome 'proclaims the Divine authority of the Scriptures'! Yes, by putting the Holy Scriptures in the 'Index,' at the head of the most damnable books which hell ever inspired!

"Rome proclaim the divinity of the Scriptures! Yes, by torturing in her dark and filthy dungeons; slaughtering on her gibbets, burning, in her auto da fé, the disciples of the dear Saviour, who dare to read, love and follow those Holy Scriptures   Rome proclaims the authority of the Scriptures says Dr. Hodge. Yes. says the history of these last thousand years: yes, answer millions of martyrs, she proclaims and acknowledges the divinity of the Scriptures, just as the Jews acknowledged and proclaimed the divinity of Christ, by spitting in His face, nailing Him on a cross as a criminal, and killing Him between two thieves.

"There are many deplorable things to be seen among the Protestants of the United States. But one of the most deplorable is the fatal tendency of so many to ignore the great apostasy and abominations of Rome. In Europe, where Rome is better known, Principal Cunningham called that

church 'the master=piece of Satan'—and surely she is the
master=piece of Satan. But what a sad spectacle we have
under our eyes on this continent! Almost everywhere the
Bible=burning Church of the Pope, instead of being sternly
opposed by the children of God, is petted, helped and
enriched, encouraged, strengthened, and praised by the
greater part of them. Everywhere, with very little exception,
the Protestants, shutting their eyes to the silent but rapid
progress of Rome, sleep when the enemy is raising and arming
his impregnable citadels, training his skilful legions, and
sharpening his sword for the approach of the inevitable
contest.

"But there will soon be an awakening. and it will be
a terrible one. When the Protestants see the extent of
their incredible folly in so betraying the interests of truth
and liberty into the hands of their greatest enemy, it will be
too late! There will be then a Roman Catholic President in
Washington The armies of the Great Republic will then be
commanded by Roman Catholic generals and officers; the
fleets will be commanded by Roman Catholic admirals, and
the fortresses will be in the hands of Roman Catholic traitors
Then the treasure and the immense resources of this magnificent country will be at the mercy of the Jesuits, at the
service of the Pope, and the flag of liberty will be trampled
in the dust Then the American people, who are, to-day, sold
into the hands of Rome by their politicians, and lulled to
sleep by their theologians, will understand that when Rome
speaks of the Divine authority of the Scriptures it only
means that the Bible must be dragged out of the schools, and
torn away from the hands of the old and young, to make a
bonfire

"There are two things which Rome hates with an implacable
hatred.' They are the Bible and liberty At any cost, Rome
is bound to fight down these two things, till they are completely destroyed. But the more she hates our dear Bible
and our glorious liberty, the more she conceals her hatred

under the most deceptive words, and the most fictitious demonstrations of love and respect   It is just when she lays the surest and most perfidious plans to drag away the Bible from the school and the private house that she proclaims most eloquently its Divine authority, just as the murderer puts on a smiling face at the approach of his victim the better to prevent him from being on his guard   Thanks to the betrayals of the politicians, and the delusions of the theologians, except God makes a miracle of it, the Bible and liberty are doomed in the United States.

"Till lately I have had my doubts about that deplorable issue   But these last few years study of things and men here makes it impossible to entertain any doubt about it. Blind, indeed, must be the man who does not see the portentious signs which foretell that the days of liberty are numbered, and will be very short.   With the hundred thousand Protestants, who give their daughters, their sons, and their money to the Jesuits, and with the connivance, the silence, if not the public approbation of thousands of ministers who dare not speak out, Rome is raising her proud banner on every hill, in every valley, of the United States.

"See how Rome is ruling in the midst of all our great cities, from New York to San Francisco; from Quebec to San Jago   It would require the united efforts, the stern energies, of all the disciples of the Gospel to put a stop to the giant power and aggressive work of Rome; but, instead of trying to defeat the public and grand conspiracy of Popery against liberty and the Bible, the Protestants, with few exceptions, are vying with each other who will most efficiently give aid and comfort to the enemy.

"Does Dr. Hodge take the ground that the Church of Rome proclaims the Divine authority of the Scriptures? But there is not a student at Princeton who does not know that the faith of Rome in the Holy Scriptures, and the so-called proclamation of their Divine authority, are founded on what the logicians call a vicious circle.

"Does not Rome boast that she receives the Holy Scriptures because they point to her as the only infallible Church, when, in the meantime, she refers us to those Scriptures to prove the title she has to the supreme respect and submission of the nations? I ask my intelligent readers, what is all that bombast of Rome about her faith in the dignity of the Scriptures, if it is not a castle built in a misty cloud high in the air? Who can believe in the divinity of a thing in favour of which not a single reason can be given which can be accepted by common-sense? Who will believe Rome, proclaiming the Divine authority of the Scriptures, when she has no other argument or reason to our intelligence than a vicious circle!

"Though there is a great deal of show in the Church of Rome there is no real faith even among the priests. The little faith which remains has no more solidity than the building raised on quicksand. From the highest to the lowest ranks of Rome, with very few exceptions, infidelity and skepticism are the rule; very few, to-day, even among the priests of that apostate Church, care anything for the Scriptures

"They do not ask, 'What saith the Lord?' but they ask, 'What saith the Pope?' It is not necessary to be so profound a logician as the celebrated theologian of Princeton to understand that with an 'infallible Pope' there is no need of an infallible Bible. It is just because the Scriptures ceased to be an authority in the Church of Rome that it was found necessary to provide another authority to guide the human intellect. As the Holy Bible had ceased to be the oracle, the source of truth among the Roman Catholics, it was a question of life or death to find or invent a new oracle, a new fountain of truth and life Yes, it became a necessity to proclaim an infallible Pope the very day that the Holy Scriptures had ceased to be an infallible guide. Many have misunderstood the terrible logic which forced the Roman Catholics, almost in spite of themselves, to proclaim the infallibil-

ity of the Pope   To every serious thinker, the proclamation
of the dogma is the most natural and most logical fact. These
last ten centuries the Roman Catholic nations have sternly,
but in vain, tried to resist the logical consequences of the
false and anti-Christian principles which their Church had
accepted as Divine truths.   The proclamation of the infallibility of the Pope is not only the logical consequence of the rejection of the Divine authority of the Scriptures in the Church
of Rome, it is also the last and ultimate effort of that apostate
Church to get forever rid of the Holy Scriptures, in every page
of which she finds her condemnation written.   From the profound thinker, Bossuet, to the learned Montalembert, many
intelligent Roman Catholics had foreseen and foretold that
the proclamation of the infallibility would be a death blow to
the authority of the Scriptures, and would sweep away the
last Christian principle from their Church.

"But logic is stronger than men   When men, in a moment
of blindness, have accepted a false principle to replace a
Christian one, which they have rejected, they are dragged, in
spite of themselves, into its fatal consequences.   By admitting the divinity of traditions which were opposed to the
Holy Scriptures, the Roman Catholics had prepared for the
rejection of the authority of those infallible oracles, and the
necessity of finding some other infallible guide

"From one abyss the Roman Catholics had fallen into a
profounder one, with the same fatal necessity and irresistible
law by which a stone must roll to the bottom of the pit the
very moment the crumbling support on which it rested on the
side of the precipice had been removed

"By proclaiming the Divine authority of the tradition which
gives an infallible Pope, and by accepting that man as equal
to God in wisdom and science, the Roman Catholic Church
has fallen to the bottom of an unfathomable abyss   Human
folly and depravity could not go further.   The last link which
united Rome to the Christian world has been cut.   It is no
more from Christ, speaking to him through the Holy Ghost

in the Scriptures, that the Roman Catholic will receive the truth—it is from the Pope. By taking away the corner-stone, Christ, whom the Father had laid as the foundation of His Church, in order to give place to her infallible Pope, Rome has renewed on earth the awful rebellion of Lucifer in heaven.

"And the Protestants who build the church of this modern Lucifer, like those who approve them, may be honest and learned but they are mistaken men They give help and comfort to the enemy. They are of those for whom Christ said on the cross: 'Father, forgive them, they know not what they do.'

"C. CHINIQUY."

CHAPTER XXVII

A Presbyterian Minister Approves. The Romanists Condemn and Persecute

In 1876 I spent some days in Halifax, N. S., where I spoke in Fort Massey Presbyterian Church.

The Pastor was the Rev. R. F. Burns, D. D., and his congregation was large and influential in the city. He was thoroughly in sympathy with me and my work, and was made up of the stern material which characterized his ancestors in Scotland, the Covenanters. He had no sympathy with the name Protestantism which does not earnestly and practically protest. He was told before the meeting in his church that there would be a disturbance from the Romanists, which he was reluctant to believe, but, let the apprehension of trouble be what it might, he was not going to shrink from having a Presbyterian minister speak in his pulpit, in a city and country where the British flag waves, which means civil and religious liberty.

The people came pouring into the church at the appointed time until it was packed, and there being a large crowd at the the doors, who could not find room, it was concluded to close them. A crowd of Romanists collected around the church for the avowed purpose of preventing the *apostate Chiniquy* from preaching against Popery. During the service there was constant commotion, there was stone-throwing and panes were smashed. Again and again large stones crashed through the windows. The Pastor, Dr. Burns, declared that such attacks were a scandal upon the common freedom of speech and worship. After other plain and pointed remarks from the doctor, I arose and said that what we needed was a dozen of orangemen to go out and clear the street. The disturbance continued, but the meeting. though disturbed, was not broken up, and, after a collection was taken, it closed about ten o'clock. There was intense excitement inside and outside the church. A band of ruffians laid wait by the front door.

Dr. Burns, myself, and several friends passed out by a side door The rioters soon discovered this and followed, throwing stones and snowballs. I was struck several times Dr. Burns with several friends took refuge in a friendly house at the head of Tobin street. The crowd increased and two hundred of my friends, principally orangemen, formed in close order and came to the rescue. We proceeded to the Halifax Hotel, pursued by a howling mob

When we were about half way the rioters resorted to a ruse, and separated, so as to more successfully close in on me and my friends, and if possible hustle and crowd us into the harbour. Near the hotel the cry was raised, "Chiniquy is here!" Then stones and sticks were freely used, by which I was struck several times I entered by a private door, and the stones came showering after me as I went in. An empty bottle struck a young man and cut him badly

My head and arms were bruised, but my injuries were not serious.

No arrests were made at the time.

Of course this persecution, though not openly defended by the Roman Catholic priesthood, was "allowed," and was not frowned down as might and ought to have been, were the priests true friends of liberty and order.

Such is a fine example of the freedom Romanists claim for themselves but deny to others, even in a land where they have full freedom to worship without molestation.

It is with satisfaction I record that public opinion in Nova Scotia so emphatically condemned my ruthless persecutors that, though afterwards I revisited Halifax frequently and addressed many meetings in the city and in very many churches throughout the country, no attempt was ever made to disturb my meetings or to injure me in any way. Even the orangemen have safely marched in procession through the streets of Halifax; and freedom of speech and religious liberty have thus been happily vindicated What is, thus, true of Halifax and Nova Scotia, is true of many other places—cities and rural districts in Canada, in Australia, in the British Isles and even in the United States.

Dr. Burns preached and published a sermon, soon after, called out by the riotous demonstration It was on the text "Be it known unto thee, O king, that we will not serve thy gods, nor worship the golden image thou hast set up" In the discourse he drew a comparison between the Babylon of Nebuchadnezzar and the Babylon of Popery. He proved that there was a close correspondence between them.

This sermon of Dr Burns was so timely and outspoken, that I give several passages from it which I feel sure my readers will appreciate If we had more such fearless and heroic men in our pulpits, Rome would not stalk forth with such a bold front as she now does.

"Even now may the handwriting on the wall of the Vatican be discovered—distinct as that which formerly paled the faces and paralyzed the frames of the giddy and godless revellers in the palace of Babylon. When she is saying—'Peace and safety, sudden destruction will come upon her,' and the world echoes the doleful dirge, 'Babylon the great is fallen, is fallen.' May the Lord hasten it in His time.

"Our subject admits of a ready application to the scenes of Monday evening—a night much to be remembered in the history of our city and Church. How singular the contrast a few brief hours brought round!

"We thought not last Sabbath, when encircling so peacefully and profitably a communion table, that it was to turn out a table spread for us in the presence of our enemies, and that our blood was so near being mingled with our sacrifice.

"Hitherto we had known nothing but peace within and around these walls, but it seemed as if the Lord were coming not to send peace but a sword, and as if judgment were going to begin at the house of God   Should the uppermost feeling with us be, 'An enemy hath done it,' let us feel it right to be taught even by an enemy.   Nor let us be unmindful of the higher uses, for, 'Is there evil in the city, and the Lord hath not done it?'   He permits what He does not sanction   And, 'We have seen the end of the Lord, that the Lord is very pitiful and of tender mercy'   For we have found abundant reason to sing of mercy as well as of judgment, and to conclude that the things which have happened to us will turn out rather to the furtherance of the Gospel

"Very plainly has it been made to appear that the wrath of man worketh not the righteousness of God, and with equal distinctness that God can make the wrath of man to praise Him. while He restrains the remainder thereof.

"We are thankful that the venerable preacher was unharmed during the service, and sustained no very serious injury afterwards.   We are thankful that the audience behaved so well, considering the noisy demonstrations outside and the repeated assaults made on the building.   In circumstances less critical, and with no such dense masses collected, there have arisen panics that have issued in results most disastrous   We feel thankful that the hostile elements inside were kept under control through the force of superior numbers, and the fear of immediate exposure and expulsion.   We are thankful for the part the press has taken, and the determination evinced by our public authorities to prosecute the investigation, and to bring the perpetrators of the outrage to justice. We are thankful for the efficient aid rendered by those outside ourselves, and for the sympathy expressed by the other churches throughout the city   We are thankful that the Protestant pulse amongst us beats stronger than it did a week ago; that the blood flows purer and freer.   We have been at ease in Zion.   We need arousing   In our simplicity, we had thought the voice Jacob's.   We have found the hand Esau's.

"The features of the ancient Babylonians came out in their modern representatives with a somewhat repulsive prominence, especially that spirit of bigotry and intolerance which could not put up with the frank outspokenness of the Hebrew heroes, and their fearless protest against the popular prevalent idolatry.   Wherever our modern Babylon is thoroughly in the ascendant, the minority have no rights which the majority are bound to respect.   The faithful protesters must be hustled out of the way.   Away with them, away with them! The spirit that worked on the banks of the Euphrates is reproduced on the banks of the Tiber and of the St. Lawrence, too, and it is the same that has startled and surprised us here in our fair city by the sea.   Then and there it was three young men.   Here and now it has been one old man. Against them were kindled the flames of the furnace. Against him were directed brickbats and bottles and bludgeons   In both instances, freedom of speech and freedom of action were sought forcibly to be put down   I suppose those lads were looked on by most as fools and fanatics —disturbers of the general peace, and deviators from the general practice. And so by some, even from whom better things might have been expected, our 'old man eloquent' has been regarded. It is easy to criticise him—to take exception to his sayings and doings—to pelt him with paper pellets soaked in vinegar and smelling of brimstone, from snug offices or cosy armchairs; but it's not so easy to run the gauntlet as he has done—to take one's life in one's hand and to face, for nigh a score of years in succession, the kind of weapons that have been wielded against him.   And what has been the head and front of his offending?   Simply this—that ever since complying with the command, 'Come out of her, my people, he' has continued to be a courageous and consistent protester against the sins of our modern Babylon, and ceased not to 'teach and to preach Jesus Christ.'   Simply this—that he has kept ringing out the ancient battle cry. 'Be it known unto thee, O Pope, that we will not serve thy gods, nor

worship the golden image which thou hast set up' This is
true Protestantism. The Protestant who does not protest
against Rome is unworthy of the name.

"The very life=blood of the Protestant faith oozes out when
there is no protesting. For over eighteen years this remarkable man has been in close grapple with this 'mystery of
iniquity,' and it is not to be wondered at if one of his tem-
perament, and with his surroundings, and with the intimate
knowledge which a quarter of a century behind the scenes
has given him of Rome's inner life, and with the rough
handling he has got from those he has left, I say it is not to
be wondered at if he should occasionally 'speak unadvisedly
with his lips.'

"Through all these years the most industrious and insidious
efforts have been made to smirch and to stain his character
in accordance with Rome's customary policy towards those
who abandon her communion. From the fiery ordeal he has
come forth like gold

"He may have been at times hasty in word or deed, but so
were the reformers, and so were the apostles and the prophets
which were before them. Nevertheless, while a man of like
passions with ourselves, and compassed with kindred infirmities, no breath of slander has dimmed the lustre of his
character, or moral stigma been fastened upon his good name.
From 1833, on through the twenty=five years of his priestly
life, his character was of the best. He was a pure priest, and
has in his possession the most undoubted testimonials to this
effect, from the highest dignitaries of Rome He was for
years by far the most popular priest in Lower Canada—the
very idol of the people He was known as the great Apostle
of Temperance—the Canadian Father Mathew Within the ten
years of his wonderful crusade, no fewer than 200,000 of his
countrymen were certified as having received the pledge from
his hands The change thereby effected was without parallel
He had the offer of being made Bishop of the great North=
west, but had the humility to decline it. So devoted was he

however, to the interests of his order, that he received a special commission to gather into one fold those of his countrymen that were 'dispersed among the Gentiles' Going, as he did, from one place to another in the States. he was not a little surprised to find that not less than 150,000 French Canadians had left their native country to live in that great Republic, and he was truly sorry to see that the greater part of them were in deadly danger of losing the Roman Catholic faith, from their being scattered among the Protestants. and from there being so many denominations of Protestants who were trying to convert them to their religious views, and to bring them into what he then called the Protestant net.   On going back to Canada he brought this under the notice of the Bishops, who empowered him to throw himself into this department of missionary work

" In 1851 he settled in the great Prairie State, Illinois, and 12,000 of his countrymen gathered round him. Some seven years later the Damascus scene was repeated. 'There shone a light from heaven above the brightness of the sun, and there fell from his eyes as it were scales' It was principally the entrance of the Word which gave him light   Into this marvelous light he sought at once to lead his people. This has been his life-work since.   He has led out from Rome six or seven thousand of his countrymen in Illinois, and at least as many more in Canada, and other portions of the States.

" During the past six months it is certified that after deducting some 200 who were deemed unworthy, 500 families, embracing 2,000 individuals, have come out from Rome, in and around Montreal.   Considering the unusually strong foothold Romanism has got in Lower Canada, and the uncommon devotion of the French Canadian Catholics, such a result is truly surprising.   When the Lord turned the captivity of these people, we were like men that dreamed.

" It was on the tenth of June. 1862, that Father Chiniquy applied for admission to the Canada Presbyterian Church I had the honour and privilege of making the motion in our

Synod expressive of our deep interest in himself and his work and appointing the committee to adjudicate on his application I was a member of the first committee.

"The following year (on the 11th of June, 1863), he was formally received, amid great enthusiasm, so that he has been for nearly thirteen years a minister of our Church. During my residence in Chicago I repeatedly visited the St. Anne settlement, and, as a member of the Kankakee committee and convener of the French Evangelization Committee (they are now united), I had ample opportunity for forming a judgment regarding him.

"While in Montreal he often occupied my pulpit, and audiences of ten and twelve hundred, principally of his own people, hung upon his lips. His power in French is amazing. No one in our Dominion can come near him in reaching the ear and the heart of the French people. When he came, therefore, to our great city, I hailed him as an old friend, and gladly welcomed him to this sacred desk, in common with my beloved brethren in the ministry

"It seems passing strange to me that such a man, who has had access to the best circles of British and American society, and to the leading pulpits and platforms of Christendom, who led a blameless and useful life for twenty-five years under Papal and for over eighteen years under Protestant auspices, who emancipated 200 000 from the slavery of alcohol and some twelve or fifteen thousand from the slavery of Rome and who has for thirteen years made full proof of his ministry in our Church, should have been here branded as a fugitive and a vagabond, stigmatized as a liar in our pulpits, howled at as by a pack of wolves swarming round our holy and beautiful house, and hooted and hounded for half a mile along our streets, as if he were the filth of the world and the offscouring of all things, under the shadow, too, of a garrison of British soldiers, and beneath the folds of that glorious flag which throws the impenetrable shield of her protection around the obscurest subject and the humblest slave

"It seems passing strange, too, that all this should have occurred in the clear moonlight, and only two or three of these hundreds have been recognized. It seems almost stranger still that those respectable gentlemen, of whose order the old man was once a most distinguished ornament, should not have publicly testified against such cruel and cowardly behaviour, and thrown themselves in the forefront of those who are trying to bring the perpetrators to justice. One of them could have accomplished more than our entire police force, without disparaging its members in the least. Of this I feel persuaded, and I know I can speak for my brethren as well as myself, that were it possible to conceive of hundreds of our people surrounding a Roman Catholic church, breaking many panes of glass, and disturbing by their yells, for an hour and a half, the service going on, and then assaulting, with murderous intent, the officiating priest, we would have been promptly out to try and check them. The first papers of the morning would have published our indignation We would have at once tendered our sympathy, nor slept till we had lent our influence, to the making an example of some of them.

"Let our Protestantism get a healthier tone from this experience. Let our generous youth imbibe the spirit and imitate the example of those blessed young men and say boldly of Roman and every other species of corruption, 'Be it known unto thee,' etc But let no grudge rankle in our breasts, for the religion we profess is a religion of love, and 'Love worketh no ill to his neighbour.' Let us ever keep the line drawn between persons and principles We loath Rome. We love Romanists Let us live as the noble Argyle died—when he said on the scaffold, 'I die with a heart-hatred of Popery' 'Which thing I hate,' as the blessed Master says of the doctrines and deeds of the Nicolaitans With a generosity and magnanimity his enemies would do well to imitate, Chiniquy says 'There are, in the Church of Rome, many millions of sincere and respectable men, and we must seriously pray the

Lord to send them His light—but we cannot go further. We must not abuse them.' How can I more fittingly close my discourse than in the words of his yesterday's letter to me? 'Let every one of my friends unite their fervent prayers to yours to the throne of mercy for the conversion of the multitudes of the blind followers of the Pope, who want to take away my life. Oh, let the dear Saviour look down in His mercy upon them all, to give them His saving light that they may come with us to His feet, to find light, peace and eternal life!'"

Dr. Burns, in an appendix to the sermon from which I have taken these extracts, offers some true and pertinent thoughts in regard to the method of dealing with Romanism. They are certainly in place in this connection. My methods may at times seem severe, and to border on irreverence, but they appear to me to be such as the subject needs. The wafer-god of Rome is so utterly ridiculous, ludicrous, idolatious and absurd, that it should be dealt with accordingly, which I have not hesitated to do. The author of this sermon shows very forcibly that my style in this respect is fully sustained by examples found in the Bible.

"Mr. Chiniquy has been taken severely to task, even by some Protestants, for breaking the wafer in pieces, which, after the priest's consecration, is believed by the Romanists to contain in it the 'body, soul and divinity of the Lord Jesus Christ.' This infallible authority declares that a single consecrated wafer makes only one god, but that if you break that consecrated wafer into a number of fragments, the 'body, soul and divinity' of the God-man is in each separate fragment, so as to contain as many gods. On Rome's principle, 'once a priest, always a priest,' Mr. Chiniquy has still this great power It was to show the folly and blasphemy of such an assumption, that Mr. Chiniquy acted as he did He meant not the slightest disrespect to a sacred ordinance for which, in the true Scriptural view of it, he entertains the profoundest reverence. The irreverence lies with those who

thus desecrate and travesty it   Chiniquy's mode of procedure may not precisely suit our modern ideas of propriety, but
it is an ancient Bible way which has repeatedly 'received
Divine endorsation'   It was substantially the way of Moses
and Elijah, and Isaiah, and Hezekiah, when exposing the
folly and falsity of the idolatries with which they had to com-
bat   When the Israelites worshiped the golden calf, Moses,
their leader, burnt it with fire, ground it to powder, strewed it
in the water and made them to drink of it   (Ex 32 20.)

"Was the calf-god treated thus, then why may not a cake-god
be treated in like manner?   Was Moses chargeable with 'bad
taste' in treating so contemptuously the object of the people's blind veneration?

"Elijah, in like manner, poured contempt on the Baal
worshipers at Carmel and brought the sharpest irony, the
most scathing sarcasm, to bear against them   'Elijah mocked
them and said, Cry aloud, for he is a god, either he is talking, or he is pursuing, or he is on a journey, or peradventure
he sleepeth and must be awaked.' (1 Kings 18.27.)   Was
it counted 'bad taste' in this holy man thus to 'make fun'
of these worshipers who evinced their sincerity by their
continual crying and 'cutting themselves with knives and
lances' (like the flagellants) 'till the blood gushed out upon
them.'

"As a 'take-off' on idolatry, we know nothing to equal the
vivid and graphic portraiture of Isaiah   (Chap 44.9-20.)
The man cutting down the cedar, using part of the wood for
warming himself, part for cooking his food, etc, then em-
ploying the residue in making a god. 'He burneth part
thereof in the fire, with part thereof he eateth flesh; he roast-
eth roast and is satisfied; yea he warmeth himself and saith,
Aha, I am warm; and the residue thereof he maketh a god,
even his graven image; he falleth down unto it and worship-
eth it, and prayeth unto it and saith, Deliver me, for thou
art my god.'—Verses 16 and 17.

"From the standpoint of our modern critics, Isaiah (or the

Spirit of God speaking through him) showed the extreme of 'bad taste' in violating the religious sensibilities of so many, and turning into ridicule their conscientious convictions.

"And how did the good king Hezekiah act towards the brazen serpent? It was the time-honored relic whose preservation seemed pardonable as a quickener to gratitude. But when undue homage began to be rendered to it, it was treated by the king as our modern iconoclast has been treating the wafer; 'He brake in pieces the brazen serpent that Moses had made; for unto those days the children of Israel did burn incense to it; and he called it Nehushtan—a piece of brass' (2 Kings 18 4.)

"The parallel supplied by these four cases is perfect. If Mr. Chiniquy violated the proprieties. he did so in good company Moreover, his action was intended as a test. If Deity resided in that thin, tiny cake and every portion thereof. would He not avenge His own honour thus sacrilegiously insulted by the prompt and signal punishment of the aggressor? That no harm came to him so impressed the beholders that thirty of them. the morning after the wafer was subjected to this test, abjured their allegiance to Rome.

"We are far from saying that Mr. Chiniquy's modes of procedure are always what we or our brethren would adopt. But he knows thoroughly the people with whom he has to deal, and adapts his treatment accordingly. In such matters 'let every one be fully persuaded in his own mind,' and the best criterion, probably, after all, by which to judge his measures, is the wonderful success with which they have been attended."

CHAPTER XXVIII

Rebuked by a Prominent Presbyterian Minister. Approved by His Congregation

My Christian readers would be much mistaken if they were thinking that the lecturer on Romanism is constantly walking among sweet briers and roses, and that he is sure to be fed with sugar plums when working among the Protestant population of America and Europe. More often than is suspected his paths are among thorns, and his bread is mixed with the bitterest gall.

I am, as the dear Saviour was, looked upon as an impostor and a disturber of the peace by many of those very Israelites He wanted to enlighten and to save; so, very often, the brother who is called by God to open the eyes of the Protestant people to the errors and idolatries of Romanism has nothing to expect from many of them but unkind and ungenerous and utterly disappointing treatment.

After I had been, several times, so kindly invited by different Christian ministers of Halifax to address their congregations, it was remarked that I had never been seen within the walls of St. Matthew's Presbyterian Church, of which Rev. Dr. Grant was pastor.

To the question several times asked me by elders of that Church, why I had never addressed them, I invariably answered: "Your good pastor possesses more historical and theological knowledge in his little finger than I have in my poor brain about the errors of Romanism; he feels as I do, that he does not want me to teach you anything on that subject. He can do that himself better than anybody else."

They answered: "You may think and say what you please about our minister, but the fact is that we have never heard a word from his lips against Romanism. It is the very contrary. Not only do we see him in company with the Bishop and priests of Rome, but he is ready enough to show us that he is in sympathy with that Church in many things.

"We would not admire him less cordially, if he were a little more frank in dealing with Rome. Remember that we do not think that our pastor is such a traitor as to try to lead us into the sink of errors of Romanism. We only regret that he is absolutely mute about the past and present errors of that system. As Protestants we want, not only for ourselves, but for our children also, to hear some warning words from our pastor against the snares of Popery

"Now and then we have the sad and shameful spectacle of some of our Protestants in Halifax turning Romanists. This would never occur if our ministers were more attentive to warn us against the snares of those wily and implacable foes of the Gospel. Would you accept an invitation to give us an address in our church, if you were invited by our pastor?" I answered, "I will accept such an invitation from your good pastor with the utmost pleasure, for there is not a Protestant minister in the whole of Canada for whose talents I have greater admiration."

The result of this conversation was, that, later on, in 1876, after the riot of Fort Massey Church, I had the honour to sit at the tea table of Mr. Grant, previous to the address which he had requested me to give, that same evening, on a subject of my own choice, about Romanism Those who are acquainted with the gentleness of Dr. Grant need not be told that nothing could surpass the courtesy with which he presented me to his people before the address.

I took for my text the second chapter of the second epistle to the Thessalonians, where St Paul, speaking of the future enemies against whom they would have to protect themselves, mentioned, "that man of sin, that son of perdition, who opposeth and exalteth himself above all that is called God, or that is worshiped; so that he as god sitteth in the temple of God, showing himself that he is God." (2 Thess 2 3, 4.)

Among other things I said, were these·

"After having been twenty-five years a priest of the Church of Rome, no doubt remains in my mind that that anti Christ, that man of sin, who sits in the temple of God, and who does not only believe but makes the people believe that he is above God, is the priest, the Bishop and the Pope of Rome.

"Yes! Popery or Romanism is the embodiment, the personification of the power, the religion, of the church of anti-Christ.

"Go where you please from one end to the other of this terrestrial globe, and I ask you to show me any persons, who, more than the Pope with his bishops and priests, persistently and publicly say, before all the nations of the earth as well as the angels of God, that they have such mighty power that the eternal and almighty God, who created heaven and earth, is absolutely powerless in their presence

"Please pay attention to what I say here, and understand that which I want you never to forget

"As soon as a priest is ordained by the imposition of the hands of his Bishop, he is to believe that he is more above God than the heavens are above the earth, he is obliged to believe that in his presence the Word of God and God Himself, Jesus Christ, the second person of the Trinity, who with a word of His lips has created the sun which was so bright to-day, with that beautiful moon and those millions of stars which are so bright over our heads to-night, does absolutely lose His power in the presence of a priest. Yes, He must obey the priest more submissively than the vilest slave has ever obeyed his master. He must submit Himself to the will of the priest more quickly, more absolutely, than the little dog need obey you when you have tied a rope to his neck and obliged him to follow you

"I know you are amazed and horrified when you hear me telling you these things You are tempted to think and say that I exaggerate. But please give a moment of attention, and you will see that these are no exaggerations, but that I am telling the simple but the most frightful truth you ever heard.

"Look at these small cakes which I hold in my hands This small one is for the use of the people, and the large one for the use of the priests.

"These cakes are made with a little wheat flour by the servant girls of the priests or by the nuns, between two well-heated irons Every day, some of them, to the number of ten, twenty or sometimes to the number of a hundred, according to the number of communicants, are put by the priest into a silver box, called 'cibarium,' and placed on the altars where he performs, every day, a ceremony called the mass.

"About the middle of that mass, taking that silver box in his hands, he pronounces upon it the following words in Latin, just as I will pronounce them in your presence, 'Hoc est enim corpus meum'

"Then he must believe and every one of his people must believe that there is such a marvelous, such a divine power given him by the Pope, that more quickly than lightning, the second person of the Trinity, Jesus Christ, the Son of God and God Himself, has been forced by him to come down into his hands—and change Himself into those wafers—and change every one of those wafers into body, soul and divinity. He must believe and make his people believe, that there are no more wafers in his hands or in the silver box, but that every wafer has become Christ, God and man, whom you must accept, love and adore as your Saviour and your God.

"As soon as the priest has performed this wonderful miracle, he lifts up this newly created god above his head, and says to his people, 'Come and adore your god; who to save you was made man and died on the cross.'

"And the whole people, falling on their knees, bring their faces to the dust and adore the god whom their priest has just made before their eyes with that wafer baked by his servant girl between two well-heated irons.

"I was an honest man when I was a priest, just as I hope that all the priests who live in Halifax, to-day, are honest; but I was cruelly deceived, as they are, by the devil.

"I made and adored that newly made god every morning of my life during the twenty-five years I was a priest, as all the priests of Halifax made and adored their ridiculous, execrable and contemptible idol, this very morning.

"I do not say these things that you may have any contempt or bad feeling for the Roman Catholics. I do not give you these awful details about their idolatrous worship that you may say to each other when you go out of this temple, after this address, 'How stupid and blind are those poor, ignorant Roman Catholics.' No; our dear Saviour did not come from heaven to teach us to despise our neighbours —He came to teach us how to love and save them.

"The Roman Catholics are no more stupid than you are; but they are in the dark, and it is your fault! Yes, Protestants, it is your fault, it is your sin if your friends and neighbours of the Church of Rome are in the dark regions of Popery! You have the light and you keep it for yourselves. You have the truth about those solemn mysteries of the Gospel and your neighbours have it not! And what do you do to give them the light and the truth? I ask it in the name of the great God you adore: What have you done to show the truth and to give the light to the Roman Catholics on these great and solemn mysteries? If you have done anything, it is so small that it is almost an insult to God

"The Church of Rome would have been a dead thing long ago, if you soldiers of the Gospel had fought it as you should have done Yes; the Roman Catholics would have accepted the light long ago if you had done your duty towards them!

"You have forgotten that you are the soldiers of Christ, enrolled under His sacred banner to silence and conquer His enemies!

"Why has the great God of heaven granted you to conquer Canada if it were not that you might bring its people into the ways of the Gospel?

"Have you done it? All the echoes of heaven and earth answer: No!

"Do not speak of the difficulties which you have to encounter: it is neither British nor Christian to be frightened and paralyzed by difficulties, when the great Captain of Salvation calls you to conquer the French Canadian people to the Gospel.

"Were your heroic ancestors frightened when the Parliament and the King of England said, 'We must conquer Canada?' No! From one end to the other of Great Britain the heroic cry was heard. 'We must conquer Canada!'

"Some people said 'But to conquer Canada we will have to shed rivers of blood—we will have to expend millions and millions of pounds'

"Your heroic fathers answered: 'We must conquer Canada at any cost—let the blood flow—let the millions of pounds go —at any cost we must wrench Canada from the hands of our foe, France' And Canada was conquered!

"Be true soldiers of Christ, to-day, as your fathers were true to their king and their country. Go and fight Rome as British men know how to fight. Go to the conquest of Canada with a British heart, a British intelligence, a British pluck and a British liberality, and Romanism will melt and disappear as the French colours had to fall and disappear at the roaring of the British lion on the Plains of Abraham, September thirteenth, 1759.

"But it is not with carnal weapons that we must fight Rome. It is not by hating or abusing the Roman Catholics we shall convert them. The only weapons which will give us the victory against Rome are the weapons of love which Christ has brought from heaven to save the world.

"The first weapon which will break the doors of the New Babylon and cause her strong walls to totter and fall into dust is the prayer of our hearts

"'Anything which you ask My Father in My name will be granted,' said our adorable Saviour. One of the great sins of the Protestants in Canada is that they do not pray as they ought for the conversion of the poor idolaters whom the Pope of Rome keeps enchained to the feet of his idols in Canada Oh! let the day come when every disciple of the Gospel, every true servant of God, among you will raise his supplicating hands to the Mercy Seat, and then the walls of the modern Babylon will crumble, and on their ruins the angels of God will sing, 'Praise the Lord, Babylon is fallen!'

"The second weapon is to send the Gospel of Christ into every family, through faithful and intelligent Christians.

"There is an irresistible power in the Word of God. As the dark hours of the night are changed into the bright hours of the day when the rays of the bright sun come down from from the skies, so the dark night of Popery will disappear, whenever you persuade our honest but cruelly deceived Roman Catholic countrymen to read the Word of God!

"The third infallible weapon to destroy Rome in Canada is, to give good example

"Let the day soon come when the Protestants in Canada will everywhere give examples of a holy and Christian life, and you will see how my dear Roman Catholic countrymen will soon break the heavy and ignominious yoke of Popery.

"The eyes of the Roman Catholics are sharper than you suspect When they look at you, they too often see your shortcomings. They see many who desecrate the holy day which the Lord has put aside to serve and glorify Him in. They see too often men who have a Christian name forget the respect they owe to themselves and to their God in the infamous saloons They too often hear of the dishonesty in the ranks and files of those who have a Christian name in your midst

"The result is that they say to each other 'Why should we leave our ranks in order to go among people who are as

bad as we are' Yes; the scandalous lives of too many Protestants in Canada constitute a wall so high and so thick
that my poor Roman Catholic countrymen can neither go
over nor through it.

"But let every disciple of the Gospel in Canada be true to
Christ, and give the example of a holy life, and very soon the
Roman Catholics will see it not only to admire, but to follow
you At the sight of your Christian life, my dear countrymen will say. 'How beautiful are thy tents, O Jacob, and
thy tabernacles, O Israel!'

"They will say to each other: 'Let us go into the midst of
that people, for surely the Lord is their shepherd.'

"They will come to you, brought by that irresistible attrac-
tion of your Christian virtues; and you will take them by the
hand to the feet of the Lamb who will make them pure with
His blood and free by His word And, after having given up
the false Christs of the Pope to follow the true Christ of the
Gospel during the few days of their earthly pilgrimage, they
will go with you to the Eternal Kingdom, where, during the
whole eternity, we will bless our God for having so much
loved the world that He sent His eternal Son, Jesus, to save
the world"

My last word had hardly gone from my lips when the Rev.
Mr Grant rose and addressing his people, said something to
this effect: "Now I understand why we almost constantly
hear of tumults and riots wherever the Rev. Mr Chiniquy
gives his lectures. His language is by no means soothing or
conciliatory towards Roman Catholics He has no right to
call them blind idolaters as he does . .   If I were a
Roman Catholic, after hearing him, I am not sure that I
could meekly accept his teaching I might even be glad if
he were silenced."

After a short tribute to my mission work in Montreal, Mr.
Grant sat down

I thought my duty was to answer him. I rose and said, as
calmly as I could·

"My dear sir, you are mistaken if you think that I shall accept in silence the judgment you have just passed upon me I believe with my whole heart what I have said; and I have not spoken in an unkindly spirit. Let me appeal to your people who have just heard every word that fell from my lips."

Then turning towards the multitude who had listened to my address with breathless attention, I said "Ladies and gentlemen, after listening to my address with such a kind attention, you have just heard the sentence passed upon me by your pastor. If you think that I deserve that public rebuke and that want of confidence, I will accept it as well merited. I want you all to give me your mind just as it is before God. Please let those of you who are of the same mind as your pastor lift up your hands, and, if you do it, I will confess guilty and ask pardon for what I have said. Please let those of you who are approving the censure which I have received in your presence lift up your hands."

But, though I requested that great gathering twice to lift up their hands in approbation of their pastor's views, not a single hand was raised:

Then I said: "Ladies and gentlemen, I appeal again to your Christian consciences and intelligences to know what you think of my address.

"Let those of you who disapprove the unfavourable sentiments uttered by your pastor raise their hands"

And all the hands, without exception, were raised. I then turned towards the Rev. Mr. Grant, and told him, "My dear sir, there is the sentence of your people, and I bless God for it. Please let us sing the Doxology· 'Praise God.'

And the Doxology "Praise God" was sung by the angels of God, I hope, as well as by that intelligent and noble people.

CHAPTER XXIX

On My Way to Australia, California, Oregon and Washington Territory

My sixty-nine years of age, with the incessant labours of the last four years in Montreal, had so much impaired my lungs, that my physicians advised a voyage on the Pacific Ocean as the only remedy which could give me a chance of working a few more years in spreading the Gospel among my countrymen. My noble Presbyterian Church, in 1878, granted me a whole year of rest. Without losing any time I crossed the vast plains of Illinois, Iowa, Colorado, Wyoming, Utah, Nevada and California to breathe the bracing atmosphere of the Pacific Ocean.

I will leave to others to speak of the innumerable marvels which the hands of God have sown, and which we meet at every step from the Mississippi river, so well called by the Indians the "Father of Great Waters," to San Francisco, that so young but already so mighty Queen of the West. It would require a large volume to give the history and description of that gigantic railway which encircles the whole of the United States and binds the Atlantic Ocean to the Pacific with steel chains; and it would take a more eloquent pen than mine to tell what the heart feels when the thundering iron horse, as rapid and daring as the eagle. carries us up to the very top of the Rocky Mountains, nearly 9,000 feet above the sea. How pure is the air we breathe, how beautiful are the blue skies, how everything takes new, strange, gigantic forms at that elevation! It is when soaring from the top of one of those giant mountains to the top of a still more gigantic one that man feels and realizes that he is created in the image of God—that the Almighty has breathed upon him the breath of an intelligence before which mountains and seas, winds and storms, light and lightning the whole earth, have to humble and submit themselves as to their legitimate king Ah! why is it that that mighty king so often forgets that he has himself an Almighty, Eternal King and Master to love and serve?

No words will ever give an idea of the magnificent spectacle of the mountains, whose tops are constantly covered with ice and snow, when they present their brow to the sun   The perfect peace and calm which surround them, the millions of glittering diamonds which cover their white robes, give more the idea of an angel of heaven, adoring his Creator and extending his wings over the earth to bless and protect it, than a cold and lifeless mountain.   No. this cannot be a heap of brute stones.   What magnificence is in that white satin mantle! What a grand, sublime, mighty being is there before me at the horizon! How reverently its noble brow looks to heaven above the highest clouds! Is not this one of the Seraphims whose twofold duties are to protect the earth and sing the eternal Alleluia?   Do you not hear his voice: "Come and see the works of God.   Who is like our God?   Let the nations praise Him   By His strength He setteth the mountains, being girt with power"?

But suddenly dark clouds rise behind the mountain; and, quicker than I can say it, the magnificent vision has disappeared, to be replaced by the most terrific one which the eyes can see.   The earth trembles under our feet; our ears are deafened by peals of thunder such as we never heard; our eyes are dazzled and blinded by such lightnings as we never saw.   It seems that the doors of hell are just opened, and all its armies hurled against the seraph whose silver wings were spread over the world   For more than half an hour we are the witness of a battle without mercy of all the elements against the mountain   Surely its flanks will be torn and blackened under the blows of the infernal artillery; the white snow will drift away, scatter and disappear before the

hurricane; the mountain will melt under the hail of brimstone and those torrents of fire which flow from the clouds.
With a breathless attention, through the closed windows of
the cars, we contemplate that sublime and terrible conflict.
But suddenly the noble mountain shows, again, its gigantic
head above the dark clouds. It has conquered The storm-
clouds are torn and broken into fragments; they roll at the
feet of their conqueror, to disappear in the plain below. The
white robe looks whiter than ever, and the rays of the sun
come as messengers of God to place on the conqueror's head
a diadem of gold, silver and precious pearls. And if your
soul has to pass through great tribulations—if you see dark
clouds at your horizon—even if you find yourself struck by
the hurricane, my Christian friend, you will surely hear a
sweet voice whispering into your ear, "Fear not, I am with
thee In the world ye shall have tribulations, but I have
overcome the world. Abide in Me, and I will abide in you
to be your strength and your joy and your life eternal "

I wish I had time and ability enough to describe the
wonderful walls, the high, strong towers, the marvelous castles
and the impregnable citadels—the works of the hands of
God—whose ruins are scattered all over those wonderful
Rocky Mountains. I would also like to say a word about that
marvel of marvels, "The Devil's Slide,' through which surely
his satanic majesty alone can pass without losing a liberal
portion of his apparel, and the "Hell Gates," and Col-
fax Mountains, which no traveler can see without losing his
breath. But I must hurry on, pass around Salt Lake, cross
the Mormon cities and villages—that dark spot of American
civilization—without saying a word, in order to take a
moment of rest at San Francisco. so well called the "Golden
City "

But here, again, I am at a loss what to say Shall I speak
of its magnificent banks some of them built of Chinese granite, imported from the "Flowery Land"? Shall I describe
the marvels of the "Safe Deposite Block," with its 4,600 steel

safes, built at the cost of more than two millions? Shall I
expose to the profane eyes of my readers the numberless gold
and silver vases, the gold and silver bars, the untold treasures, concealed behind the wall of that steel palace? Shall I
lead you, by the hand, through the numberless chambers of
that multitude of princely mansions, called hotels, one of
which, "The Palace Hotel," is almost a whole city by
itself?

Those giant works of a giant people must be seen to be
well understood. I will not, either, speak of the material
prosperity, or rather, the untold miseries, which the incalculable treasures of gold and silver, dug out from the mines of
this marvelous country, have produced. But I will not conceal my disappointment and sadness, when, lifting up the
deceitful gold curtain which the hand of man had spread over
everything here, I tried to find how many of my fellow-men
were really happy behind the shadow of those marble and
gilded walls.

Ah! do not come to San Francisco if you want to see cheerful faces and hear hearty laughs. You will, indeed, be more
lucky than I am, if you can find many in those multitudes
you meet in the streets, on the public squares, or in the
hotels, who look cheerful and happy. The deep furrows of
anxiety are traced on every brow; the sure indications of
trouble, if not of despair, are painted in almost every eye,
and the tortures of a broken heart have sealed and discoloured
almost every lip. Hour after hour I stood at the corner of
the most thronged streets, or the most frequented public
squares, to study that page of this wonderful people's
history; and I could hardly refrain from tears, when, alone
in my closet, in the presence of God, I recalled in my mind
the infallible marks of human misery and deep despair I had
seen on the faces of those beings whom God had created to
be happy, and for whom Christ died that they might forever
live with Him. Oh! how few of those multitudes I met
ever listened to the dear Saviour's voice: "Come unto Me, all

ye who are heavy laden, and I will give you rest." Nowhere, as here, have I seen, as written with letters of tears and blood on so many men's brows. "The love of riches is the source of every evil." There is probably not a single spot in this world where so many have suddenly passed from a state of comparative poverty to the height of fortune, and, in consequence, there is not a spot where all are so anxiously bent on the fortune's wheel with the hope of soon reaching its top. But, alas! how many, instead of rising to the summit of fortune, roll down, every day, to the bottomless abyss of the most hopeless misery. And among the few lucky ones, who have so suddenly become millionaires, how many, every day, see their treasures melt, fade away, and disappear almost as suddenly as they came.

When, in 1852, it became evident that my plan of forming a colony of French Canadian Catholics on the fertile plains of Illinois was to be a success, D'Arcy McGee, then editor of the "Freeman's Journal," the official paper of the R. C Bishop of New York, wrote me to know my views, and he immediately determined to put himself at the head of a similar enterprise in favour of the Irish Roman Catholics. He published several able articles to show that the Irish people, with few exceptions, were demoralized, degraded and kept poor around their groggeries, and how they would thrive and become respectable and rich, if they could be induced to exchange their city grogshops and low saloons for the fertile lands of the West. Through his influence a large assembly, principally composed of priests, to which I was invited, met at Buffalo in the spring of 1853 But what was his disappointment, when he saw that the greater part of those priests were sent by the Bishops of the United States to oppose and defeat his plans He vainly spoke with the most burning eloquence for the support of his pet scheme The majority coldly answered him: "We are determined, like you, to take possession of the United States and rule them; but we cannot do that except by acting secretly, and making use of the utmost wisdom. If our plans are known they will surely be defeated What does a skilful general do when he wants to conquer a country? Does he scatter his soldiers over the farm lands and spend their time and energies in plowing the field and sowing the grain? No, he keeps them well united around his banners, and marches at their head to the conquest of their strongholds—the rich and powerful cities The farming countries then submit and become the price of the victory, without moving a finger to subdue them. So it is for us. Silently and patiently we must mass our Irish Roman Catholics in the great cities of the United States, remembering that the vote of our poor journeyman, even though he be covered with rags, has as much weight in the scale of power as the millionaire Astor, and that, if we have two votes against his one, he will become as powerless as an oyster. Let us, then, multiply our votes; let us call our poor but faithful Irish Catholics from every corner of the world, and gather them in the very hearts of those proud citadels which the Yankees are so rapidly building under the names of Washington, New York Chicago, Buffalo, Albany, Troy, etc Under the shadow of these great cities the Americans consider themselves as a giant and unconquerable race They look upon the Irish Roman Catholics with the utmost contempt, as only fit to dig their canals, sweep their streets, and work in their kitchens Let no one awake those sleeping lions to-day, let us pray God that they may sleep and dream their sweet dreams a few years more How sad will be their awakening, when, with our out-numbering votes, we will turn them all, forever, from every position of honour, power and profit. What will those hypocritical sons and daughters of the fanatical Pilgrim Fathers say, when not a single judge, not a single teacher, not even a single policeman, will be elected, if he is not a devoted Irish Catholic? What will those so called giants think and say of their matchless shrewdness and ability, when not a single senator or member of Congress will be chosen if he is not submitted to our Holy Father the Pope?

What a sad figure those Protestant Yankees will cut, when we will not only elect the President, but fill and command the armies, man the navy, and keep in our hands the keys of the public treasuries! It will then be time for our faithful Irish people to give up their grogshops in order to become the judges and governors of the land. Then our poor and humble mechanics will leave their damp ditches and canals, to rule the cities in all their departments—from the stately mansions of mayor to the more humble, though not less noble position of school-teacher.

"Then, yes, then we will rule the United States, and lay them at the feet of the Vicar of Jesus Christ, that he may put an end to their godless system of education and sweep away those impious laws of liberty of conscience which are an insult to God and man."

Poor D'Arcy McGee was left almost alone when the votes were given. From that time the Catholic priests, with the most admirable ability, have gathered their Irish legions into the great cities of the United States, and the Americans must be very blind indeed if they do not see that the day is very near when the Jesuits will rule their cities, from the magnificent White House of Washington to the humblest civil and military department of this vast Republic.

They are already the masters of New York, Baltimore, Chicago, St. Paul, Milwaukee, St. Louis, New Orleans, Cincinnati, San Francisco.

Yes, San Francisco, the rich, the beautiful, the great Queen of the West, is in the hands of the Jesuits!

From the very first days of the discovery of the gold mines of California the Jesuits got the hope of becoming masters of those inexhaustible treasuries, and they laid their plans with the most admirable ability to succeed.

They saw, at first, that the immense majority of the lucky miners, of every creed and nation, were going back home as soon as they had enough to secure an honourable comfort to their families. It became evident that, of those multitudes

which the thirst of gold had brought from every country of
Europe and America and even Asia, not one in fifty would
fix his home in San Francisco and become her citizen The
Jesuits saw at a glance, then, that if they could persuade the
Irish Catholics to remain and settle, they would soon be the
masters and the rulers of that gold city whose future was so
bright and so great   And that scheme, worked day and night
with the utmost perseverance and wisdom, has been crowned
with perfect success

When, with few exceptions, the lucky Frenchman, who had
become wealthy, was going back to his " Belle France," with
a cheerful heart, and when the intelligent German, the industrious Scotchman, the shrewd New York and New England
diggers, or the honest Canadian, suddenly made rich, were
gladly bidding an eternal farewell to San Francisco to go and
live happily in the dear old home, the Irish Catholics were
taught to consider San Francisco as their promised land

The consequence is that where you find only a few American, German, Scotch, or English millionaires in San Francisco,
you find more than fifty Irish Catholic millionaires in that city
The richest bank of San Francisco, Nevada Bank, is in their
hands, and so are all the street railways   The principal offices of the city are filled with Irish Roman Catholics, almost all of the police is composed of the same class, as well
as the volunteer military associations   Their compact unity
in the hands of the Jesuits, with their enormous wealth, makes
them almost the supreme masters of the mines of California
and Nevada

When one knows the absolute and abject submission of the
Irish Roman Catholics, rich or poor, to their priest—how the
mind, the soul, the will, the conscience, are firmly and ir-
revocably tied to the feet of their priests—he can easily understand that the Jesuits of California form one of the richest
and most powerful corporations the world has ever seen

It is known by every one there that those fifty Irish Catholic millionaires, with their myriads of employees, are,

through their wives, and by themselves, continually at the feet of the Jesuits, who, here, more than in any other place, really swim in a golden sea.

Nobody, if he is not a Roman Catholic, or one of those so-called Protestants who give their daughters and their sons to the nuns and the Jesuits to be educated, has much hope of having a lucrative or honourable position in San Francisco.

Entirely given to quench their thirst for gold, the Americans of San Fransisco, with few exceptions, do not pay any attention to the dark cloud which is rising at the horizon of their country Though it is visible that that cloud is filled with rivers of blood and tears, they let the cloud grow and rise without even caring how they shall escape from the impending hurricane.

It does not take a long residence in San Francisco to see that the Jesuits have chosen this city for their citadel on this continent Their immense treasures give them a power which may be called irresistible, in a country where gold is everything

It is to San Francisco that you must come to have an idea of the number of secret and powerful organizations with which the Church of Rome prepares herself for the impending conflict, through which she hopes to destroy the system of education and every vestige of human rights and liberties in the United States, as she has repeatedly and bravely boasted in her most popular organs I might give hundreds of those extracts; but, to be brief, I will give only two:

"The Catholic Church numbers one-third of the American people, and if its membership increases in the next thirty years as it has for the thirty past, in 1900 Rome will have a majority, and be bound to take this country and keep it. There is, ere long, to be a state religion in this country, and that state religion is to be Roman Catholic

"The Roman Catholic is to wield his vote for the purpose of securing Catholic ascendancy in this country.

"All legislatures must be governed by the will of God, un-
erringly indicated by the Pope

"Education must by conducted by Catholic authorities;
and under education the opinions of the individual and the
utterances of the press are included. Many opinions are to
be punished by the secular arm, under the authority of the
Church, even to war and bloodshed "—Catholic World, July,
1870.

"While the state has rights, she has them only in virtue
and by permission of the superior authority; and that authority can only be expressed through the Church.

"Protestantism of every form has not and never can have
any right where Catholicity has triumphed; and, therefore,
we lose the breath we expend in declaiming against bigotry
and intolerance, and in favour of religious liberty or the right
of any man to be of any religion as best pleases him."—Catholic Review, July, 1870

In order to more easily drill the Roman Catholics, and
prepare them for the impending conflict, the Jesuits have
organized them into a great number of secret societies, the
principal of which are

Ancient Order of Hibernians.
Irish American Society.
Knights of St. Patrick.
St. Patrick's Cadets.
St Patrick's Mutual Alliance.
Apostles of Liberty.
Benevolent Sons of the Emerald Isle.
Knights of St. Peter.
Knights of the Red Branch.
Knights of Columbkill

Almost all these secret associations are military ones.
They have their headquarters in San Francisco, but their
rank and file are scattered all over the United States   They
number 700,000 soldiers who, under the name of U S A.
Volunteer Militia, are officered by the most skilled generals

and officers of the Republic For it is a fact, to which the
Protestant Americans do not sufficiently pay attention, that
the Jesuits have been shrewd enough to have a vast majority of Roman Catholic generals and officers to command
the armies and man the navy of the United States.

Who will be able to stand against a power supported by
700,000 soldiers, well drilled, armed with the best modern
arms, officered by the most skilful military men of the
country, and whose treasurers will not only have the keys of
the public treasuries of this vast Republic, but who will be,
in great part, the masters of the untold millions dug out in
the mountains of California and Nevada?

That you may know the Christian feelings of the Jesuits
of San Francisco towards Protestant England, I give you
here an extract of the address of Rev. Father Rooney on
St Patrick's Day:

"Irish Catholics, trust your priests, as you ever have, as a
nation, and when the propitious moment comes to settle the
accounts of brutal old England, the murderer of your priests
and forefathers, the murderous despoiler of your sanctuaries,
the pilferer of your possessions and the starver of your
people, those priests will bless the swords that you use, that
it may cut more keenly; the bullet, that it may perforate
more deeply; your hands, that they may wield the weapon
more powerfully; and your nerves, that you may the more
steadily avenge your injured mother and your noble ancestors. Never trust an enemy that has deceived us so often as
England, and violated every treaty made with us. You may
expect nothing from her except through the cannon's roar,
the whizzing bullets, and the flashing scimitar. But let us
be sure that we are ready and well prepared for the fray."

Though the Jesuits rule supremely in San Francisco, and
though the deleterious atmosphere of Romanism, which is
felt everywhere, coupled with that thirst for gold which
rages as a plague in almost every stage of society, are universally visible, the Lord has kept there for Himself many

faithful servants, and the great Captain of our salvation counts several intrepid soldiers of the Gospel around His banner. The Rev Messrs Hemphill, Fells, Taylor, Verrue, Stone, Guard, etc, are working with faithfulness in this deserted Gospel field, and they are gathering very precious fruits of their labours   Two missions have been established for the conversion of the Chinese, which God has already blessed by the conversion of more than one hundred souls Some of those converts have already gone to China to preach the Gospel to their countrymen.   Let us pray and hope that among those converts there will be a Paul whose voice will shake and pull down the old idols of that remarkable people   I have also found in San Francisco and Oakland a good number of my dear countrymen who have given up the errors of Rome to accept the Gospel of Christ.   Three of them are near relatives of the Roman Catholic Bishop of Canada.   By the great kindness of the Rev. Mr. Verrue, I have been able to give two addresses in French to the interesting congregation of French speaking people which his admirable zeal has gathered.   Rev. Mr. Verrue himself is a convert from Romanism, and his labours have been much blessed here.

But if San Francisco presents a sad spectacle to the eyes of the Christian, it is not so in Portland, the most thriving city of Oregon, through which I had to pass on my way to the prairies of Washington Territory.   I spent there what I can call one of the most delightful Sabbaths of my life.

After a voyage of three days from San Francisco on the Pacific Ocean, and one day on the magnificent river Columbia, I arrived in Portland, Oregon, on Saturday, the tenth of August.   It was late in the afternoon, and the Presbyterian pastor, the amiable, zealous and learned Mr. Lindsay, being absent, my heart was a little heavy and my mind cloudy, for I knew nobody in that city.   But when the steamer was just moored to the wharf, and as I was inquiring to know the name of the most respectable hotel, I saw a gentleman who was very actively engaged in looking for some one he wanted to meet I said to myself "Oh, if my merciful God had heard my feeble prayers, and sent that gentleman, whose face looks so kind, to be my guardian angel, and take me by the hand in this strange city!"

Just then I heard his voice addressing some one of the crowd of passengers, saying: "Is not Father Chiniquy here?"

"Yes, sir," I answered; "here I am."

"Well, please come this way," replied with a smile, my new, kind friend

A moment after I was by his side, in a beautiful carriage, drawn by two splendid horses, going to his mansion, about a mile up town. On the way I learned that the name of this noble hearted Christian brother was William Wadham, and when I entered his house it was easy to see that he was one of the most wealthy merchants of the State of Oregon. After he had introduced me to his wife, who is a descendant of the Pilgrim Fathers whom God has chosen as the fundamental stones of this great Republic, he introduced me to his mother-in-law, Mrs. Skinner, who has this last ten years lost the use of her eyes, but whose spiritual eyes see day and night the bright lights which flow from the bleeding wounds of the Lamb. I felt so overwhelmed by the floods of mercies which my heavenly Father was pouring upon His unworthy child that I asked that Christian family to kneel with me and bless Him But the words were half suffocated in the tears of joy and gratitude which I felt for having been taken into such Christian and good quarters.

The next day was a Sabbath I accepted the privilege of speaking of the mercies of God towards us poor perishing sinners. But what I want to say is what I have seen of the manner in which our Christian brother, William Wadham, spends his Sabbaths

After his breakfast, from eight to nine, he reads to his venerable mother-in-law some of the most interesting parts of the Scriptures, with the most edifying commentaries, and they talk together about the great truths of Christianity as I never heard any one talk. Every word they exchange together about the love of Christ is like burning coals brought by the angels of God from the altar which is before the throne.

At ten Mr. Wadham goes to prepare everything in the church for the Sabbath-school and the choir; for the Sabbath-school is his favourite work, and he is the leader of the choir. But we must see his cheerful face and the beam of joy which illuminates his eyes when he is going to and fro, almost running up and down the stairs, in order that everything may be in good order and ready for the hour of worship "I prefer one hour passed in Thy house, O Lord, to a thousand passed in the tents of sinners." During the singing at the Divine service, you constantly hear his beautiful voice, and you feel that his heart is in it. The public morning service is hardly finished, when you see him rushing to the large basement, crowded by the young people of every age and sex, for the Sabbath-school. It is there that he feels at home, surrounded by the teachers and pupils of the Sabbath-school. With what exquisite politeness and piety he addresses that multitude! With what Christian enthusiasm he leads the hymns and mixes his voice with the voices of his hundred pupils, old and young, to praise the Lord!

It seems as if that man had never done anything but that in his whole life   He is, there, in his element, as the eagle who soars on his wings to the sky.

After the Sabbath-school he hurries home to take a hasty dinner with his family   But the meal is hardly finished, when his carriage is at the door for a new excursion

"Have you any objection to coming with me, Father Chiniquy?" said he in his smiling way of talking

"Where are you going?" I asked.

"Fishing in the streets and lanes," he answered

"Yes, please take me with you; I am a fisherman also," I replied.

And quickly the splendid horses take us to the door of the Young Men's Christian Association.

"Please," said he, "go to the other side of the street; you will be in the shade; the sun is too hot here. And, to obey him, I crossed the street, not understanding what would come next.

But I had not waited there two minutes in the shade, when I saw coming over after me twenty or thirty young gentlemen and ladies, who surrounded him. After he had saluted and welcomed them in his unique and amiable way, he drew from his coat one of the Moody and Sankey hymn-books, and started, with his powerful and melodious voice: ' Rock of Ages, cleft for me," etc, which the others sang with him with a power and effect that I had never witnessed before.

You may imagine the magical power of such singing in the open street of a large and thriving city, crowded with strangers from every country, not only from America, but from Asia and Europe. Nothing could be more amusing and pleasing to me than to see the young and the old, the poor and the rich, the loafer and the half-drunken man, with the most pious ladies and gentlemen, running from every side to hear the beautiful concert in the street. Two hymns had not been sung before that street was literally filled with people drawn, some from curiosity, some by the mere example of others, some to take part in the songs and unite themselves with the choir.

After Mr. Wadham had sung half an hour at the head of that selected choir, which had more than doubled during that time, he stopped, and said: "Now, my friends, we have sung the praises of our God, let us go upstairs and hear what He has to say to every one of us Oh! do come and spend a few moments with us in meditation and prayer."

There is no need to say that five minutes later the large hall of the Young Men's Christian Association was filled to its utmost capacity by the multitude whom the Lord had brought there, from every corner of the globe, to speak to them words of love, peace and mercy.

And who was there again to preside over that new meeting and lead the choir? Mr. Wadham But this time his face was more than ever beaming with joy, and his voice had a power and a melody which seemed to me superhuman. That meeting, where a dozen short and very touching addresses were given, generally by new converts, lasted one hour, and was the most interesting one I ever attended. Among the speakers we heard three young sailors who had recently found their Saviour, and whose words fell on us with a power which very few can forget Oh! who could refrain their tears of joy, when we heard one of those young British sailors telling us that the whole crew of their magnificent ship, with their captain, had lately found the Saviour, how they had asked Him to tarry with them, and how, since, He had been their most precious treasure, their strength and their joy. I cannot sufficiently express to you my joy when I saw several of our dear French Canadian converts from Rome in that crowd of redeemed souls! One of those French Canadian converts, an old traveler of the Hudson Bay Company, a well-educated man, had been, during several years of his life, the most infamous and public scandal of Portland —a drunkard, a blasphemer, an atheist. He was looked upon as an incarnate demon, the terror of the Christians, the pillar and strong fortress of all the wicked doers of the country. But one day some Christian ladies said to each other: "Should we not do something for the conversion of this sinner? or shall we let him continue to spread the pest of his impiety and scandal without an effort to save him? Let us go and pay him a visit."

A few hours later, half a dozen of the most respectable ladies of the city knocked at his door

"Walk in, ladies, walk in," said the notorious man, "what is it you wish, I am at your service?"

"We come to see you, and pray with you, my dear sir," answered one of the visiting angels

"Pray with me! Pray with me! Ah! ah! ah! You are

mistaken, my good ladies. Here we don't pray, but we drink and curse and lead a jovial life; please go and pray with my neighbour."

"But we will pray here, and sing the praises of the Lord with you, my friend," sweetly answered one of the daughters of Christ. "You are too much of a gentleman to insult ladies in your own house, and turn them out."

And the ladies, on their knees, with their faces and hands raised to God, and burning tears flowing down their cheeks, made such prayers as Christian ladies only can send to the Mercy Seat.

The desperate sinner tried at first to make some jokes with some of his companions of debauch. He turned the ladies into ridicule, and laughed at them, in drinking to their their health

But nothing could stop the angels of mercy, who were on their knees, from sending the arrows of burning Christian love to the heart of the guilty man through their ardent supplications to the seat of mercy. Little by little, the crowd of drinkers left, one after another, and our prodigal son remained alone in the midst of that choir of seraphims who had taken possession of his house

When alone with these ladies, whose prayers and sublime hymns were filling his rooms, he tried in vain to shut his ears, in order not to hear but his ears were opened, and so widely that floods of new light were flowing through them on the hardened heart and the guilty soul.

"Is it possible," said he to himself, "that there is a God; that He has seen all my crimes and that He will sooner or later call me to account for them? But is it possible, also, that that God sends to me these praying ladies to call me to repent, and will forgive me?"

With these thoughts in his mind, he leaves the ladies and rushes to another room. He shuts the door, and, absolutely beside himself he falls on his knees, and, not daring to raise his eyes to God, but prostrating his face to the floor, he cries "Oh! my God! my God! If Thou art here to hear my cries, have mercy upon me   If Thou canst forgive such a sinner, forgive me   If Thou canst save me. oh do save me. I come to Thee "

He had no sooner finished talking these few words, than his heart burst.   Torrents of tears rolled on his cheeks.   A new name had been written in the book of life, and the angels of God were once more rejoicing in heaven over the conversion of a sinner.

But let us come back to our dear Christian brother Wadham and follow him the rest of his Sabbath day

The meeting in the Y. M. C. A. rooms ended at 4 P. M. Then, turning himself towards me, he said again, with a smile, " Would you be so kind as to accompany me in my visits to our poor, dear sick people?" " With pleasure," I answered.

And on we went through the city, drawn, again, by the splendid horses, in his beautiful carriage.

By the singular providence of God, the first poor sick man whom we visited was from Montreal, a very dear friend of mine, an Orangeman, who had been wounded when fighting hard one evening to prevent the Roman Catholics from killing me   He was then lying on a bed of suffering; but that bed, with the rest of the house, was a model of neatness   You may imagine his joy and mine, when we met together, there, so far from Canada.   On his right hand was his Bible and at his left the Weekly New York Witness, published by a venerable Christian.

After spending an hour in that way, exhorting the sick and dying to repentance, and praying with them, we had to come home to take our tea at about six   But this was hardly finished, when my Christian host said, with one of his unique smiles, "I hope you will not rebuke me if I ask you to accompany me to another meeting, where many like to prepare themselves for the evening service by praying and singing   As you will give us the evening address at 7:30, you will be on the spot and join with us in these preparatory exercises "

I went again with him to this last gathering of Christian men and women, where, for a whole hour, I saw and heard things that filled my heart with joy. Then I gave my address to one of the most crowded and intelligent audiences before which it has been my privilege to speak of the mercies of God. During the evening service it was still the magnificent voice of our devoted Christian brother which led the choir. It was nearly ten at night when we were back home I was in fear lest he should look broken down and exhausted after such a day of work But he never looked so happy and cheerful as at the end of such superhuman labour. He asked me to help him to thank God for His mercies towards us during that day.

Oh! when will the day come when, in every city of the United States and Canada, the rich and the wealthy will put themselves at the service of our Lord and Saviour Jesus Christ as completely as that Mr Wadham

In 1858, not long after the greatest part of my colony of Illinois had given up the errors of Popery, I heard that one of our most respected families was to leave Kankakee for the coasts of the Pacific, in the state of Oregon I did all that I could to dissuade them, but in vain. In those days there were no railways to cross the plains; there was no other way but to travel nearly 3,000 miles, a journey which generally occupied six months. I put before the eyes of my friend (his name was Joseph Goyette) the dangers of every kind for himself, his wife and young children, not only from the fatigue, but from attacks of wild Indians who were constantly lying in wait for the emigrants, to plunder and kill them. I showed him that he was not only exposing his life, but that he was ruining himself by that long and costly journey. He listened to my observations with a respectful and breathless attention, and answered me. "Mr. Chiniquy, you are right when you say that I expose my life and the very existence of my family; you are also correct when you say that the expense of crossing that immense territory will ruin me. but God knows the motives which prompt me to leave this place and go so far away from you, and I hope He will protect me   I will tell you those motives· so long that you were faithful to your oaths, and a good priest of Rome, you know I was among your most devoted friends, and nothing was more pleasing to me than your presence in my house.   I liked your company, and I was among the most punctual, with my family, to attend your church, but now you are an apostate.   I know very well that it is your intention to make us all Protestants   My family is already shaken. I feel myself unable to answer your sophisms and resist your efforts.   I see only one way of escape from your perverse influence and example. It is to put such a distance between you and me that I shall not hear any more of you.   When there will be the whole continent between us, I shall have nothing to fear from your proselytizing efforts.   If I lose my fortune, I shall save my faith.   If I have to die on the plains of the West, God, who knows why I go there, will give me and my family a better life."

Though my heart was broken at the deplorable illusions of that dear friend, I could not but admire his noble sentiments. I left him but day and night I prayed God for him and his family.   It seemed that they had become even dearer to me after that conversation   Two or three days before his leaving I paid him a last visit   I brought with me a Bible (the Roman Catholic edition, of Sacy), and presented it to him, saying·   "My dear Goyette, please accept from me this Bible as a last token of our long friendship   It is a Roman Catholic Bible; you are allowed to read it by your Church "   Looking at me, with visible marks of indignation, he answered. "It is because you have too much read that dangerous book that you are lost to-day.   I will never read it; you may keep it."

These words struck me as if they had been a two-edged sword.   I fell on my knees at the feet of my unfortunate

friend, and with tears trickling down my cheeks, I said:
" My dear Goyette, for God's sake. do not refuse such a gift.
It is the very testament of our Lord Jesus Christ Do not reject it " By the great mercy of God, my friend, with a trembling hand, accepted the gift, and in pressing our hands for the
last time. he mingled his tears with mine. One or two days
later, he left Kankakee for Oregon, and for many years I
heard nothing of him, except that on the way he was attacked by Indians, and that his horses and waggons, with his
furniture, had been stolen by the merciless savages. But
though I heard no news from him, I never passed a day with.
out sending my humble but ardent supplications to the
Mercy Seat for that so interesting family

How can I tell you my joy, when twelve years later. I received a letter from Mrs. Goyette saying· " Help us to bless
the Lord for His great mercies towards my husband and my
family. We have read the precious Bible you gave us before
we left Kankakee, and through that reading, the saving light
as it is in Jesus has come to us We have detected the
abominable errors of the Church of Rome, and we have given
them up. It is no more to the feet of the priests or the idols
of the Pope that we shall go to be saved, but it is to the feet
of Jesus. Not only my family have given up the errors of
Popery, through that Bible, but a great number of French
Canadians who are settled around us are shaken. They say
that if you would come and visit us they would also accept
the Gospel of Jesus Christ as the only rule and guide of their
lives. Can you not come yourself, or send us a missionary?
for we are here like sheep without a shepherd."

I have no words to tell you of my joy at the reception of
such glorious news In my answer I promised a visit, if in
my power; either to go and visit them myself or send them
one of our missionaries; but insurmountable obstacles had
constantly made the accomplishment of my desire impossible.

Year after year I had to postpone my so desired visit, till

the doctor told me that the best, if not the only, way of reno-
vating the strength of my exhausted lungs was to make a long
voyage on the Pacific Ocean   One of the principal reasons
which determined to turn my steps towards the Pacific Ocean
was that it might give me a chance to visit that family, with
the numerous neophytes they were preparing to follow Christ
When I was in San Francisco I learned that I had only to
travel north 800 miles to reach the settlement of the Goyette
family, and that five or six days navigation, on one of the
splendid steamers of the Pacific, would land me near the place
where they had gone with the hope that they would never
hear any more of the apostate Chiniquy, and that they would
be forever out of the reach of his pernicious influence   No!
you will never have any idea of their joy and mine, when I
entered their happy home and knelt with them to thank and
bless God for the great things He had done in their midst.
I spent thirteen days among those dear countrymen, going,
day after day, from house to house, to carry the good tidings of
salvation; and I do not exaggerate, when I tell you that these
days must be put among the happiest of my life   As the roads
were very bad in those new regions, I had to walk the greater
part of the time.   But to walk through those forests of giant
pine-trees, measuring more than twenty-five feet in diameter, and whose gum filled the air with such a perfume that
one stops at every minute to enjoy and express his admiration, is the most pleasant one can imagine   Several times,
the road bringing me along the shores of the Cowlitz river, I
had only to throw my line for a moment into the water to
catch some excellent trout, which were a welcome offering to
the families I was visiting.   Had I not all the manners of
the true apostle of old, when at the setting sun, I was knocking at the door of some of those dear countrymen, bearing a
Bible in my right hand, and a dozen fishes in my left?
What delicious hours— I should better say nights—I spent in
explaining the Scriptures and showing the mercies of God
who has so much loved us that He has sent His eternal Son,

Jesus, to save us by dying on Calvary. How can I tell you the breathless attention, the unspeakable joy, of those families in listening to the simple, but so sublime. teachings of the Gospel And when between two and three o'clock. after midnight, they were asking me, "What must we do to be saved? We reject forever the errors of Rome, and will accept Jesus as a gift. In that great gift alone we put our trust and salvation Let Jesus, the great gift of God, make us pure with His blood and eternally happy with His Word." Yes! when it became evident to me, not only by their burning words of faith, but by their tears of joy, that salvation had entered into that house just as formerly it did into the house of Zaccheus, and that their conversion was as prompt, as sincere, will you be surprised if I tell you that I was beside myself with joy?

CHAPTER XXX

On Board Steamer City of Sydney. Honolulu

I left San Francisco for Australia on the second day of September, on the magnificent steamer, City of Sydney That ship is one of the giants of the sea by her size and strength, measuring 334 feet, with engines of 3,000 horse power. She was commanded by Captain Dearborn, one of the most polished gentlemen and brave sailors who ever manned a ship. We were about three hundred fifty passengers on board, one hundred fifty of them on the first-class list

I have never seen anything more solemn and sad than the few moments which preceded our departure When the first signal was given to those who had followed their friends or relatives to leave and clear the deck, an indescribable scene of desolation took place which would have melted the hardest heart. There were not less than one thousand people on board then, in the midst of whom I was an absolute stranger As I was perfectly alone, and free to hear and see everything, I chose a commanding place from which, as much as possible, nothing could escape my eyes and my ears. Who can depict the sudden rush of that crowd into the arms of each other, when the whistle had given the orders to leave? Who can tell the tears and sobs, the convulsive embraces and the desolating separations of that hour?

Here, a tall lady, surrounded by half a dozen children, was bathing with tears the face of her husband as if she had no hope to see him again There, sisters and brothers were pressing each other to their bosoms, unable to speak except with their sobs and their cries. A little further on, a young married lady had her face almost buried on the breast of her desolated husband She could not utter a single word; but

326

the rivers of tears which were trickling down her cheeks told me more eloquently than any words that she would have preferred death to such a long separation. Very near to me a beautiful little girl about eight or nine years old was hanging convulsively to the neck of her pale and sickly mother, crying: "Dear mother! Dear mother! Oh, do not leave me alone here! I will be dead when you come back! Take me with you, dear mamma! I cannot let you go alone! I will never see you any more! What have I done that you forsake me to-day? You have always been so kind to me!" And the tears of the poor mother were mixed with the tears of her darling child when she was pressing her, evidently for the last time, on her heart. An elder brother, himself bathed in tears, had to take by force his little sister out of his fainting mother's grasp. Dear little girl! Unfortunate young man! You may weep and cry, it is more than probable that you will never see, any more, your loving mother on this side of the grave; for merciless death has already put on her face the signs of an incurable consumption. Old and young were parting from friends dearer to them than life No! Never a more touching spectacle can be put before the eyes of a man; and when that man himself has to leave, far away, behind, his own beloved children, his home, his friends, his country, that he fears lest, perhaps, he will never see them again, you may believe me, a very dark cloud comes over that man's soul. Happy is he, then, if, putting his trust in God his Father, he throws himself into His arms, and goes to shed his silent tears at the feet of the One who has said to the distressed children of Adam, "Come unto Me, all ye who are heavy laden, and I will give you rest"

The distance we had to run from San Francisco to Australia was more than seven thousand miles, over a sea where myriads of men have already found a watery grave through shoals, rocks, waves and storms, by which thousands of noble ships have been wrecked In vain the traveler who starts on such a voyage arms himself with a strong courage. In vain he hopes for the best. A sudden, a terrible vision of wrecks, storms and horrible deaths flashes through his mind in that touching hour

Slowly the giant steamer left her moorings, and with majesty she crossed the waters, which bathes the feet of the proud Queen of the Pacific, to turn her bow towards the ocean In less than half an hour we had passed the Golden Gates of the magnificent port of San Francisco. It was there that, three weeks before, when going to the Cowlitz prairies of Washington Territory, on the steamer Idaho, I was the witness of one of the most sublime and heroic deeds. The sixth of August, we were just entering the Pacific Ocean, when every one on board was struck, as by a thunder-bolt, by the cry "A man overboard!" And, indeed, there, in the midst of the furious waves, we saw the distressing spectacle of a man struggling to save his life, and calling for help The rapid steamer was going at full speed, and in a few minutes she had made a serious distance between us and that unfortunate man. The order was immediately given by the captain to stop the engines and launch the life-boat to the sea. But before this could be done, what was our surprise and admiration to see a young man, apparently feeble and powerless, throw down his overcoat, and jump from the upper deck into the foaming sea to save his perishing fellow-man. Oh! what a spectacle of unsurpassed grandeur and sublimity to see him fighting the furious waves, and swimming with superhuman efforts after the perishing one. The wind was very stormy and those who have passed the Golden Gates know how terrible and irresistible are the waves of the Pacific on that very spot. Again and again we were terror-struck as we saw, from the deck, those furious waves thundering and rolling like mountains over the young hero. Sometimes he disappeared from sight, and we thought he was drowned and forever buried under the roaring billows It was not surprising to see tears coming down the cheeks of the hardest men, nor to hear the heartfelt cries that came from all-both men and women. But suddenly, the hero's head was seen again over the furious waves, he was swimming with all his might to save the drowning stranger. He, really, like a giant, when raising his noble head above the white crests of the furious waves, was fearlessly struggling against the bottomless and raging Pacific Ocean to wrench a victim from its fury. But how our sentiment and admiration increased when we learned that that young man was newly married in England and immensely rich. He had then forgotten his fortune, his wife, his friends, his country; he had forgotten himself to save a stranger. But that stranger was a fellow=man—a brother—to him.

In vain we cried to him that the unfortunate man whom he was trying to save had sunk down and disappeared forever. The noise of the wind and the waves prevented him from hearing anything. He continued to struggle for half an hour till exhausted and out of breath, nearly perishing himself, he was rescued by the life=boat and brought on board   The name of that young English man was Thumburg Chopper.

So long as noble England will train her sons to such heroic deeds, she will be worthy to march at the head of the civilized world, and God will make her glorious flag respected and feared on every land and sea.

Honolulu, where we landed on the ninth, and stopped ten hours, means, "The Paradise of the Pacific," and it deserves its name. After seven days of seeing nothing but the blue sea and the skies, the traveler feels inexpressible sentiments of pleasure in going around the grand and majestic promontory of Diamond Head, and passing at the foot of the volcanic mountains, which border the ocean, to reach the "Earthly Paradise," which the mighty and merciful God has made there in the very midst of the ocean   Our steamer had to pass very near the coral reef. against which the ocean breaks her mighty waves with a thundering noise from one end of the year to the other, before we entered the narrow passage which

leads us into the port. I confess, here, my perfect inability
to do justice to the subject on which I have to write   One
of the first things which struck us was a multitude of objects,
which we took at first for the heads of big fishes swimming
around the ship   They moved with such rapidity, plunging
and coming to the surface with such amazing ease, that it
took some time before I could persuade myself that those
were not fishes, but young boys from twelve to eighteen years
old.   More than fifty twenty-five cent pieces were thrown by
ladies and gentlemen from the deck into the deep waters, and
not a single one of them was lost.   They had hardly touched
the surface of the sea when, as quick as lightning, every
swimmer plunged and disappeared, making the waters boil
over them as if a thousand big stones had been thrown into
them   But, within one minute, we were amazed by the sight
of the swimmers coming up to the surface with the twenty-
five cent pieces between their teeth.   At last I took two ten-
cent pieces, and threw them over their heads as far as I could,
thinking that the smallness of those pieces of money would
make it impossible to see and grasp them below the big waves.
But in less than half a minute two of the swimmers were
laughing on the surface with my ten-cent pieces between their
white teeth.

"You told me," I said to a gentleman of Honolulu who was
among the passengers, "that there are at least 15,000 people
in your city, but where are the houses to lodge so many people? With the exception of the steeples of two churches we
see almost nothing but trees."   He answered me with a smile
"It is just so   Our houses are invisible   They are so well
covered with flowers, and surrounded by shade-trees and
fruit, that you cannot see them   But come on shore and you
will find them "   And it was so, those houses were like the
humming-bird's nests, concealed behind a real forest of passion
flowers, roses, orange, banana and cocoanut trees; algoraba,
hibiscus, breadfruit, mango, umiola trees, and other trees
and flowers the names of which are unknown to me   Fair

city of the most happy homes! Bright and fragrant blossoms
of every clime unite to add charm to this gem of the Pacific.

Every one you meet in that city has a smile on his lips,
and kind words on his tongue, and a friendly wish in his
heart for you   I never saw such cheerful faces, never heard
such joyous laughter, never felt my hand pressed with such
warm-hearted feeling as in Honolulu   It seems there is a
smile on every flower you touch, on every fruit you taste, and
in every tree you see   Nay; you see or feel a smile in every
breath of air you breathe in Honolulu. The atmosphere is very
pure, the air from the sea and the mountains is very fragrant
and perfumed.   When one is in Honolulu with its heaps of
oranges, bananas, watermelons, muskmelons, strawberries,
apples, plums, pineapples and cocoanuts, with its air perfumed by flowers of every hue and color—rose, orange, car-
mine, and primroses blue as the sea, or white as snow,—
he is tempted to say with Peter   "Lord, it is good for us
to be here; let us build here a tabernacle"

It is said that these islands were discovered by Captain
Cook on the 19th of January, 1778, but it is well proved that
the intrepid Spanish sailors, Quiros and Manita, had visited
them in 1696   Nevertheless, it is well authenticated that the
celebrated Captain Cook was killed on one of these islands,
called Hawaii, on the 14th of February, 1779, a few days
after having consented to be worshiped as a god by the
heathen inhabitants in one of their temples   But if these
islands are remarkable for their incomparable beauty, salu-
brity of climate, the incredible fertility of their soil, the
almost infinite variety of their fruits, and the unsurpassed
grandeur and magnificence of their sceneries, and the terrible
and almost daily eruptions of volcanoes of their mountains,
they are still more remarkable for the marvelous evangelical
work which has made them Christian, to-day. when they were
all plunged into the darkest night of idolatry only seventy
years ago   The history of the conversion of that nation is
one of the most admirable pages of the history of the Church

of Christ. It has been my privilege to be the guest of one of the apostles of that nation, the venerable Mr. S. C. Damon, and I have heard from the very lips of that apostle of the islands the following thrilling facts. I am sorry that I cannot enter into the details of that marvelous transformation I must content myself to give a few extracts of the memoirs of one of the gospel ministers whom God had chosen for the instruments of His mercies towards that nation.

The islanders cast off their idolatry in 1819, but it was not till 1835 that Mr. and Mrs. Coan arrived in Hilo, where Mr. and Mrs. Lyman had been working day and night for some time, and had produced a marked change in the social and religious condition of the people. Mr. Coan was a fervid speaker and a strong man morally and physically. There were 15,000 natives, then, in the district of Hilo, and its extremities were one hundred miles apart. As there were no horses, the whole distance had to be traveled on foot or in canoes, which could not be done without perils of every kind to limbs and life. He had sometimes to climb with his hands and feet, or to be let down by ropes from tree to tree and from crag to crag in the mountainous district. Many times he swam across the rivers with a rope to prevent him from being carried away. His smaller weekly number of sermons was six or seven, and the larger from twenty-five to forty Before the end of the year Mr. and Mrs. Coan had made the circuit of Hawaii, a foot and canoe trip of 300 miles, in which he nearly suffered canoe wreck twice. In all, he had admitted into the Christian Church, by baptism, 12,000, besides 4,000 infants

But let us hear him speaking, himself, of the first communion he administered to his dear converts. "The old and decrepit, the lame, the blind, the maimed, the paralytic, and those afflicted with diverse diseases and torments, those with eyes, noses, lips and limbs consumed, with features distorted and figures deformed and loathsome, came hobbling upon their staves, or led and borne by others, to the table of the

Lord. Among the strong, you might have seen the hoary priest of idolatry, with hands but recently washed from the blood of human victims, together with thieves, adulterers, highway robbers, murderers and mothers whose hands reeked with the blood of their own children. It seemed like one of the crowds the Saviour gathered, and on which He pronounced the words of healing "

Now, let me give the history of the conversion of one of the most celebrated and blood-thirsty priests of the idols, in the simple but so interesting language of Mr. Coan "That priest was six feet five inches in height, and his sister, who was co-ordinate with him in authority, had a scarcely inferior altitude. His chief business was to keep Pele appeased— Pele being the goddess of the Volcanoes, the most merciless and revengeful goddess of the world. He lived on the shore, but went often to the top of the volcano Kilanea with sacrifices If a human victim were needed, he had only to point to a native, and the unfortunate wretch was at once strangled. He was not only the embodiment of heathen piety, but of heathen crimes; robbery was his pastime. His temper was so fierce and so marked that no native dared to tread in his shadow; for treading on his shadow was immediate death to the guilty one More than once he had killed a man for the sake of food and clothes not worth fifty cents He was a thoroughly wicked savage. Curiosity attracted him into one of our Christian meetings, and the giant fell under the resistless, mysterious influence which was metamorphosing thousands of Hawaiians. 'I have been deceived,' he said, 'and I have deceived others, I have lived in darkness, and did not know the true God I worshiped what was not God. I renounce it all. The true God has come. He speaks I bow down to Him I wish to be His son.'

"The priestess, his sister, came soon afterwards, and they remained here several months, for their instruction. They were then about seventy years old, but they imbibed the spirit of the New Testament so thoroughly that they became

as gentle. loving and quiet as little children. After a long
probationary period, they were baptized, and after several
years of pious and lovely living, they passed gently and lov-
ingly away.

"In 1867, the old church at Hilo was divided into seven
congregations, six of them with native pastors. To meet the
wants of the widely scattered people, fifteen churches have
been built, holding from 500 to 1000 people. The present
Hilo church, a very pretty wooden one, has cost about
$14,000. All these have been erected mainly by native
money and labour."

Now, let me give you a most touching fact which was told
by the Rev. Mr. Lyman, and published in the interesting
series of letters of Miss Isabella Bird "In 1825, five years
after the first missionary had landed, Kapiolani, a female of
high rank, while living at Kaiwaalea, where Captain Cook
was murdered, became a Christian. Grieving for her people,
most of whom still feared to anger Pele (the merciless goddess of the volcano Kilanea), she announced that it was her
intention to visit Kilanea, and dare the fearful goddess to do
her worst. Her husband and many others tried to dissuade
her, but she was resolute, and taking with her a large retinue,
she made the journey of one hundred miles, mostly on foot,
over the rugged lava, till she arrived near the crater. There a
priestess of Pele met her, threatened her with the displeasure
of the goddess if she persisted in her hostile errand, and prophesied that she and her followers would soon perish miserably. Then, as now, ohelo berries grew profusely around the
terminal wall of Kilanea, and there, as everywhere, were consecrated to Pele; none being allowed to eat any of them, till
he had at first offered some of them to divinity. It was
usual, on arriving at the crater, to break a branch covered
with the berries, and turning the face to the pit of fire, to
throw half the branch over the precipice, saying· "Pele,
here are your aheolos; I offer some to you, some I also eat."
After this, only the natives had permission to eat that fruit

Kapiolani gathered and ate the berries without this formula, after which she and her company of eighty persons descended to the black edge of the volcano, called: 'Hail, man, man!' There in full view of the fiery pit, she thus addressed her followers· 'Jehovah is my God. He kindled those fires. I fear not Pele If I perish by the anger of Pele, then you may fear the anger of Pele, but if I trust in Jehovah, and He should save me from the wrath of Pele, when I break and despise her tabus (laws), then you must fear and serve the Lord Jehovah. All the gods of Hawaii are vain Great is Jehovah's goodness in sending teachers to turn us from these vanities to the living God and the way of righteousness!'

"Then they sang a hymn and you can fancy the strange procession winding its way backward over the cracked, hot lava sea, the robust belief of the princess hardly sustaining the limping faith of her followers, whose fears were not laid to rest until they reached the crater rim, without any signs of the pursuit of the avenging deity."

Is not this more sublime than Elijah's appeal on the soft, green slopes of Carmel?

Not only have these islanders become Christians, but they have become the instruments of the mercies of God towards the heathen of the numberless Polynesian islands. Many of them have become ministers of the Gospel, and have gone through many perils to preach Christ to the people of, at least, fifty islands, with the most admirable success

Though my stay in Honolulu was very short, I consider it a great privilege to have been allowed, by the good providence of God, to make the acquaintance of several of those modern apostles whose labours have been so abundantly blessed.

There is a college in Honolulu where many natives have been trained to the holy ministry, and who have become as remarkable by their eloquence and talents as by their sincere piety.

CHAPTER XXXI

On My Way to Australia. Sights on the Pacific

Everywhere, and in whatever circumstances of life one is providentially placed, he is sure to find in the Psalms of David the most practical and sublime thoughts and advice suited to his position. But it is when one "goes down to the sea" and does "business in great waters," that I invite him to take with him his Book of Psalms. He will surely find in them not only a faithful adviser, but a most elegant and interesting companion and friend.

Before this long voyage on the ocean, I had many times read with benefit and pleasure the inimitable and Divine songs of the royal prophet; but I had never understood their profound philosophy and their superhuman beauties as during those few weeks on the Pacific. It is evident that David had extensively traveled on the sea; that he had often admired its wonders, contemplated its grandeurs, and felt its dangers. His soul had surely been thrilled by the roaring waves, and he had heard the noise of their thundering billows, when he wrote "The voice of the Lord is upon the waters, the God of glory thundereth; the Lord is upon many waters; the Lord sitteth upon the flood, yea, the Lord sitteth forever."

Though our great and merciful God is everywhere, and the Christian meets and sees Him in all His works on earth, there is no place like the sea where He speaks to us of His infinite greatness, majesty, wisdom, power and mercy. Oh! who will ever be able to tell the magnificence of the setting or rising sun on the vast ocean? How many poems have I not read on that subject? But how far they all are from the mark! How pale are their colours, when put side by side

336

with the glorious rays of light which, in torrents, overwhelm everything, when the sun comes out of its mysterious night chambers!

When alone on deck, almost every morning, at the rising sun, I contemplated the glories and the magnificence of that spectacle, how many times I have tried to find expressions sufficiently noble to tell my friends the splendours, the grandeur, the ravishing magnificence of that spectacle. But, then, how I felt myself confounded, utterly confounded, by my impotence of speaking worthily of what my eyes saw, my heart and my soul felt, in the presence of the untold and unutterable beauties which the merciful hand of my mighty God was spreading before me. It was only in the Psalms that I could find words in which I wanted to tell my impressions, my admirations and my joys at being allowed to see, with my own eyes, such wonderful things: "The heavens declare the glory of God; and the firmament showeth His handiwork. Day unto day uttereth speech, and night unto night showeth knowledge. There is no speech nor language where their voice is not heard. Their line is gone out through all the earth, and their words to the end of the world. In them hath He set a tabernacle for the sun, which is as a bridegroom coming out of his chamber, and rejoiceth as a giant to run a race. His going forth is from the end of the heaven, and his circuit unto the ends of it; and there is nothing hid from the heat thereof. The law of the Lord is perfect, converting the soul· the testimony of the Lord is sure, making wise the simple. Let the words of my mouth, and the meditation of my heart, be acceptable in Thy sight, O Lord, my strength and my redeemer."

How many times these so simple and sublime words fell on my soul as a dew from heaven to gladden and raise it from these low and earthly regions to the foot of that throne of glory and mercy on which our great and eternal God reigns, and from which His mercy, light and life are manifested everywhere. "Oh that men would praise the Lord for His goodness, and for His mercies to the children of men! And let them sacrifice the sacrifice of thanksgiving, and declare His works with rejoicing They that go down to the sea in ships, that do business in great waters, these see the works of the Lord and His wonders in the deep" Does not the prophet plainly say, here, that when a man wants to understand the works of the Lord, it is among the wonders of the deep that he must come to study them? It is true that the Christian does not take a step on earth without meeting witnesses which speak to him of the power, wisdom, love and mercy of his God. But on the sea, those witnesses take larger proportions. They pass before our eyes as giants, by their number and their size. Their voices roar and thunder. as becometh the embassadors of the great and mighty God. whose throne is in the heaven and whose hands have dug the bottomless basin of the ocean.

How many times, before the rising sun had yet come out from the deep on his chariot of light and fire, did I remain mute with admiration at the sight of hundreds of whales playing about our ship! How majestic the motion of those gigantic citizens of the ocean! With what inconceivable agility they glide above the waves! Does not the great Pacific Ocean seem to be proud to bear in its bosom those mighty creatures of the deep? How quickly it opens its doors to let them come out to the surface. that they may speak to us of the great God who created them! And when the first rays of the sun meet those mighty giants, how suddenly they are covered with a mantle of silver and gold! How they glitter with diadems of most precious pearls and radiant emeralds! Do they not even change the breath of their nostrils into as many rainbows, which seem crowns of glory and honour put on the foreheads of those unrivalled monsters of the deep? And when they majestically raise their heads above the roaring waves toward heaven, crowned with those rainbows. and covered with the brilliant mantle of gold and silver, pearls and rubies, sapphires and emeralds which the rays of the sun have just laid upon them, do they not look like angels of the deep, which come to unite themselves to the exiled sons of Adam, to adore and praise the eternal God, before whom all the creatures, all the worlds, must prostrate themselves in ceaseless adoration? I then called the prophets of old to help me to express the feelings of admiration and joy by which I was overwhelmed   Job was the first to fill my soul with the music of his Divine poetry.

"Canst thou draw out Leviathan with an hook, or his tongue with a cord which thou lettest down? Canst thou put an hook into his nose, or bore his jaw through with a thorn? Will he make many supplications unto thee? Will he make a covenant with thee? Wilt thou take him for a servant forever? Who can open the face of his garment, or who can come to him with his double bridle? His scales are his pride, shut up together as a close seal. By his neesings a light doth shine, and his eyes are like the eyelids of the morning. Out of his mouth go burning lamps, and sparks of fire leap out. Out of his nostrils goeth smoke, as out of a seething pot or caldron. His breath kindleth coals, and a flame goeth out of his mouth. In his neck remaineth strength, and sorrow is turned into joy before him   His heart is as firm as a stone. When he raiseth up himself, the mighty are afraid. The sword of him that layeth at him cannot hold   He esteemeth iron as straw, and brass as rotten wood! The arrow cannot make him flee; sling-stones are turned with him into stubble   He maketh the deep to boil like a pot. He maketh a path to shine after him; one would think the deep to be hoary   Wilt thou play with him as with a bird, or wilt thou bind him for thy maidens? Shall the companions make a banquet of him, shall they part him among the merchants? Canst thou fill his skin with barbed irons, or his head with fish spears? Lay thine hand upon him, remember the battle, do no more. Behold, the hope of him is in vain: shall not one be cast down even at the sight of him? None is so fierce that dare stir him up; who then is able to stand before me? Upon earth there is not like him who is made without fear. He beholdeth all high things, he is a king above all the children of pride."

With what power and solemnity the voice of Job, passing through forty centuries, came to me on this deck to say that those leviathans of the deep were sent there to me as the ambassadors of my God, to make my ears ring with the solemn questions which constantly fill the echoes of heaven and earth, "Who is able to stand before me?" Oh! blessed is the man who does not shut his ears to those words which God addressed us from the south and the north, from the west and the east, which on the ocean come from the flash of lightning, the clap of thunder, the howling of the waves, the moaning of the hurricane, the blowing of the whales! "Who is able to stand before Me?" But believe me, when those voices of the prophet come to us, rolling on the big waves of the boundless ocean, they have a power which no human words can express. And when all the chords of my soul were still vibrating under the voice of Job, how can I tell you what I felt, when, alone, in a retired corner of the deck of our noble ship, having the infinite heaven above my head, the infinite ocean before my eyes, at my right hand and my left, the infinite before and behind me, I listened to the celestial poetry of David "Bless the Lord, O my soul. O Lord, my God, Thou art great, Thou art clothed with honour and majesty. Who covereth Thyself with light as with a garment; who stretchest out the heavens like a curtain. Who layeth the beams of His chambers in the waters; who maketh the clouds His chariots, who walketh upon the wings of the wind. Who maketh His angels spirits, His ministers a flaming fire. Who laid the foundations of the earth, that it should not be removed forever. Thou coverest it with the deep as with a garment; the waters stood above the mountain. At Thy rebuke they fled, at the voice of Thy thunder they hasted away. They go up by the mountains, they go down by the valleys into the plains Thou hast formed for them. Thou hast set a bound that they may not pass over, that they turn not again to cover the earth. The young lions roar over their prey, and seek their meat from God. The sun ariseth, they gather themselves together, and lay them down in their dens. Man goeth forth unto his work and to his labour until the evening. O Lord, how manifold are Thy works. In wisdom hast Thou made them all. The earth is full of Thy riches. So is this great and wide sea, wherein are things creeping innumerable, both great and small beasts These wait all upon Thee, that Thou gavest them they gather· Thou openest Thy hand; they are filled with good. Thou hidest Thy face, they are troubled. Thou takest away their breath, they die, and they return to their dust. Thou sendest Thy Spirit, they are created, and Thou renewest the face of the earth The glory of the Lord shall endure forever· the Lord shall rejoice in His works. He looketh on the earth and it trembleth. He toucheth the hills and they smoke. I will sing unto the Lord as long as I live, I will sing praise to my God while I have my being. My meditation of Him shall be sweet, I will be glad in the Lord. Bless thou the Lord, O my soul Praise ye the Lord." I would have to write a whole volume on my impressions and feelings at the marvelous things which the hand of the Lord has scattered everywhere on the broad ocean, that the traveler may not forget Him, and that he may praise Him day and night. But it is when we study those marvels with the lights of the Divine songs of David in our hands that they appear to us in all their grandeur and ravishing beauties. Who, when crossing the ocean in the darkest hours of the night, has not remained mute with admiration at the marvelous bright and innumerable sparkles of light which follow the track of the ship around her sides, and crown her bow as with a garland and a crown of stars? We are told by the learned and scientific men of this day that these lights are nothing else but myriads of small animals covered with a robe of phosphorus But are not all these infinitely small beings, whose robe is fire

and light, as many witnesses who cried to me not to forget
that my God also is light and life; that it is only through
Him and in Him that I can breathe, move, and live. Those
animals are so small that the eye of man cannot see them.
But, though infinitely small, do they not spread, all around,
such a beautiful light that the darkest night is changed into
the brightest day. Why should not every Christian try to
shed light all around him as these admirable animalcule.
Are not these marvelous beings there to repeat to us the solemn words of the Son of God. "Let your light so shine before men that they may see your good works, and glorify
your Father which is in heaven Ye are the light of the
world, etc."? But if from these marvelous little beings,
which God has evidently put there on every inch of that
great ocean that we may not forget Him, we turn our eyes
towards the innumerable islands with which the Pacific
Ocean is studded, how can we express our sentiments of awe,
when we see that many of those islands, at a period more or
less remote, were submarine volcanoes which vomited torrents of lava and threw toward the sky, day and night, whole
mountains of molten iron, stones, sulphur, etc   The fact is
that this Pacific Ocean was once nothing but a seething
caldron, or rather, steaming furnace, where all the elements which compose the earth were mixed, boiled, burnt,
and melted together with a fire whose power cannot be expressed with human words   Yes, from this very ocean flames
have come out whose blasts were irresistible; fires burnt and
raged in an inconceivable manner, clouds of darkening smoke
covered the whole world earthquakes shook the earth to its
foundations   Whole continents were created, innumerable
islands were formed by the burning stones, melted iron, lead,
gold, silver, lava, which were vomited from the craters of the
numerous volcanoes whose proud heads seem again to threaten
the world   Not only many of the islands of the Pacific are
evidently of volcanic formation, but we know that several
islands have entirely disappeared with their unfortunate

inhabitants Some years ago, two or more well-known
islands, between New Zealand and Tahiti, suddenly sank down
with the thousands of men, women and children who inhabited them. No vestige, except the top of a few naked rocks,
have remained to indicate where those volcanic islands were
situated When the traveler sees, as I do, now, from the deck
of this ship, those marvels with his own eyes; when he knows
he is just crossing those fiery regions, his ears are ringing
with the prophetic words of Peter, " Whereby the world that
then was, being overflowed by water, perished· but the
heavens and the earth which are now, by the same word, are
kept in store, reserved unto fire against the day of judgment
and perdition of ungodly men. But the day of the Lord
will come as a thief in the night; in the which the heavens
shall pass away with a great noise, and the elements shall
melt with fervent heat, the earth also and the works that
are therein shall be burned up."

The appearance of the greatest part of those volcanic islands is really formidable, with their black peaks shooting
up over the dark clouds, with their large craters still reddened with the torrents of burning lava, which not only
filled the basins of the ocean at a depth of 3,000 or 4,000 feet,
but raised mountains of more than 14,000 feet in height over
the seething waters Sometimes our ship had to pass very
near those huge remains of days of inexpressible horror.
The roaring waves were beating them as if they wanted to
roll them down into the deep, but it was in vain. Those
rocks of melted granite, iron and sulphur dared with an
apparent contempt the rage of the winds and the waves
They looked like witnesses posted there by the hand of our
Almighty God to make the traveler remember His infinite
power. The deafening voice of the roaring ocean, breaking
on the immovable base of those desolated rocks, was repeating to my soul the words of the royal prophet "Then the
earth shook and trembled the foundations moved and were
shaken, because my God was wroth There went up a smoke

out of His nostrils, and fire out of His mouth; fires were kindled by it He bowed also the heavens and came down, and darkness was under His feet And He rode upon a cherub, and did fly, yea, He did fly upon the wings of the wind. He made darkness His secret places; His pavilion round about Him were dark waters and thick clouds of the skies. The Lord also thundered in the heavens, and the Highest gave His voice; hailstones and coals of fire; yea, He sent out His arrows and scattered them; He shot lightning and discomfited them Then the channels of water were seen, and the foundations of the worlds were discovered, at Thy rebuke, O Lord, at the blast of the breath of Thy nostrils. He sent from above, He took me; He drew me out of many waters." I had been told that the many days passed on the ocean would be tedious and lonesome ones; but this was a mistake. There is not a day, I dare say, nor an hour, when our merciful God does not present new wonders to admire His power, bless His mercy and adore His majesty. What can be more singular and interesting, for example, than those thousands of porpoises which so often come alongside the ship, as to run a race with her' That fish, which is much larger than a kingfish, seems to be proud of its elegant form, its bright and rich robe, and its incredible agility. He comes as near as possible to the ship, that we may see and admire him Though we were often going at the rate of twelve knots an hour, those fishes were swimming much faster. With what sentiments of admiration we were following their swift and elegant motions, particularly when, reaching the top of the foaming billows, they leaped out of their liquid element, to plunge five or six yards below into the bottom dug by the receding waves before them! Who gave to this singular fish the instinct of coming alongside the ships which cross this boundless ocean, and so often refresh us poor prisoners of the deep with one of the most amusing and wonderful spectacles which can be seen? Is it not the mighty and merciful hand of God which has given them those singular habits, with the evident view of breaking the monotony of the long hours spent in crossing those boundless oceans? Had we not, then, good reasons to say with David· "Your hearts shall live that seek God; for the Lord heareth the afflicted, and despiseth not His prisoners. Let the heavens and earth praise Him, let the seas and everything that moveth therein. He shall have dominion from sea to sea Thy way is in the sea, and Thy path in the great waters, and Thy footsteps are not known For God is my King of old, working salvation in the midst of the earth. Thou didst divide the sea by Thy strength; Thou breakest the heads of the leviathan in pieces, and gavest him to be meat to the people inhabiting the wilderness. If I take the wings of the morning and dwell in the uttermost parts of the sea, even there shall Thy hand lead me, and Thy right hand shall hold me. Praise the Lord from the earth, ye dragons from all deeps. O Lord, our Lord, how excellent is Thy name in all the earth, who hast set Thy glory above the heavens! When I consider Thy heavens, the works of Thy fingers, the moon and stars which Thou hast ordained, what is man, that Thou art mindful of him, and the son of man that Thou visitest him? For Thou hast made him a little lower than Thy angels, and hast crowned him with glory and honour. Thou madest him to have dominion over the works of Thy hands; Thou hast put all things under his feet. The fowls of the air, and the fish of the sea, and whatsoever passeth through the paths of the sea."

CHAPTER XXXII

On My Way to Australia The Dangers of the Deep

By the great mercy of God, we entered the port of Sydney, one of the finest seaports in the whole world.

Our voyage had been one of the shortest on record, and it would have been one of the most pleasant ever made if, when three hundred miles from the shore, we had not been assailed by a hurricane, which very nearly sent us to wait the great Judgment day in a watery grave

Till then, we had always had fine weather and fair winds. Even when crossing the tropics, and when over the equator, we had not met anything but the most pleasant weather and fair winds We had not even had a single day of that extreme heat which is so dreaded by the traveler.

A strong, fresh breeze from the east had constantly blown over us, filled our sails, and given us a spring atmosphere But when we reached the south latitude, between the 34th and 35th degrees, the skies began to be covered with dark and threatening clouds. Lightnings such as I had never seen, and claps of thunder such as I had never heard, accompanied with such torrents of rain as fall only in these parts of the globe, told us that our bright and sunny days were at an end, and that we had to prepare ourselves for a change of scenery, thoughts and aspirations. It was evident that we were just encountering the equinox gale so much feared even by the most expert and tried mariners

On the 28th, at about 3 P M, our noble ship began to groan under the blows of the furious waves, in a way that would strike with terror the bravest hearts. She began to go up to the top of the waves, and to plunge into the profound abyss dug before her by the receding seas, in the most fearful manner.

It soon became absolutely impossible for anyone to stand on his feet without being hurled, with the most tremendous violence, if he were not well tied with a rope, or if he had not his hands grasping some well-fastened object.

Though, in my two voyages to Europe, I had seen pretty big waves, nothing could be compared with the mountainous, tumbling billows which rolled over us with such terrific noise and such irresistible power on this never-to-be-forgotten day. But the more furiously the hurricane roars above and around, the more sublime is the grand spectacle before our eyes. Every aperture and door on the windward were, at first, firmly shut to prevent the waves from entering and filling the ship. Only one door, on the leeward, remained open for some time, at my earnest request, that I might see and admire to my full heart's content, the unspeakable grandeur and terrible beauties of the most fearful storm I had ever seen.

During the last fierce conflict which took place in our Canada Presbyterian Church about instrumental music, one of the opponents said that God Almighty had evidently formed the human throat as the only instrument of music to proclaim His majesty, His power and His mercies. No doubt that good brother would have changed his mind had he been near me, there, on that steamer. For, every part of the noble ship had a voice; every rope and string had a voice; every wave had a voice; every clap of thunder had a voice to speak to us of the power and majesty of God as no human throat ever spoke. Yes, when the united sounds of the roaring hurricane, the thundering waves, the moaning billows, the whistling ropes, the cracking ribs of the ship, the breaking of the chairs and tables of the dining saloon, hurled on every side, mixed with the constant claps of thunder, struck the chords of our soul, the irresistible and infinite power of God was revealed to us as it could not be revealed by any man's throat.

In fact, were not, then, the very angels of God striking the strings of convulsed nature to sing with David. 'Who is so great a God as our God? Thou art the God that doeth wonders; Thou hast declared Thy strength among the people The waters saw Thee, O God, the waters saw Thee; they were afraid: the depths also were troubled The clouds poured waters, the skies sent out a sound; Thine arrows also went abroad. The voice of Thy thunder was in the heavens, the lightnings lightened the world; the earth trembled and shook Thy way is on the sea, and Thy path on the great waters; and Thy footsteps are not known."

I never felt as then how we are disposed to form different judgments about the same thing according to the different emotions or passions of the moment. That noble steamer which had appeared so large with her 334 feet length, and so strong with the iron and steel material with which she is entirely built—that steamer, which looked so like a giant of the seas when we went aboard of her in the calm basin of San Francisco, looked as a powerless bundle of straw when tossed about and attacked from every side by the furious waves of the raging Pacific Ocean.

It soon became evident to the most as well as to the least expert that we were in imminent danger of perishing At any moment we expected that some part of the engine would give way, or that the axle of the screw would break, or that the fires would be put out by the torrents of water which every wave was throwing into the doomed ship. At about 4 P. M one of those waves had struck me in the breast and hurled and rolled me more than thirty feet from the leeward towards the windward side, without more ceremony than if I had been a straw. After this I crawled to my room to change my clothing, but it was to find it flooded with water, and to see my floating trunks tossed about me as if they were in the midst of a deep and rapid river

Unable to continue our course without an evident danger of foundering, the captain ordered the course of the ship changed, and put her bow instead of her side to the hurricane. In that position, the mountains cf water, hurled upon us with such tremendous power, might roll over the ship without upsetting her entirely. We had the hope that, at the setting sun, the hurricane might subside a little, as is sometimes the case; but we were to be disappointèd The terrible storm, instead of subsiding, increased its fury at the approach of the night, and the foaming mountains of the furious ocean struck more and more mercilessly the bow, and often even the sides of the ship. The frightful flashes of lightning seemed more and more to wrap us as in a sheet of fire; the continuous peals of thunder, with the rolling billows beating constantly against us, as bomb shells, caused our model steamer to reel, tremble and shake at every shock, as if the angel of death had struck her with the avenging sword. To add to the terrors of our situation, at the setting sun we saw that the captain had ordered the crew to have the life boats ready at a moment's notice to be launched to the sea, as the last resource when the steamer would sink. I hope that not a single one of our friends who will read these lines will ever personally experience the horrors of that hour, when the terrible night spread her mantle over us all Oh! what sublime pages I would write, if I could describe, in their plain grandeur and solemnity, the episodes of the six hours which passed over us from the beginning of the night till three o'clock next morning, when we heard the Good Master's voice telling us, " Fear not, I am with you " Human language is inadequate and powerless to tell of those terrible, but at the same time superhumanly grand and sublime things. In those solemn hours, how the silent prayers which escape from the recesses of the heart and the soul are fervent, humble, pressing! How the merciful Saviour's voice comes as celestial music to the redeemed sinner's soul: " I go to My Father to prepare you a place. When it is ready, I will come and take you with me, and where I am there shall you be also."

From the very first day of the voyage, I had made it one of my most important duties to find out among the multitude of travelers those whom the Saviour of the world had selected for His own, and, by the great mercy of God, I had found them. They were not very numerous, but how sublime and simple, how ardent and sincere was their faith and their love for the Lamb who had been slain for them, and in the blood of whom they had washed their robes! How many times they had drawn my tears of joy, when, gathered together every day, at 3 P. M., they had raised their supplicating hands to the throne of mercy! As soon as the danger had become imminent, the greater part of the fervent Christians gathered with me in a corner of the splendid upper saloon, and, shall I tell it? Yes. When I found myself in the midst of those praying brethren and sisters, almost every idea of danger went out from my mind. But at about two o'clock, after midnight, the hurricane seemed again to increase its fury; the claps of thunder became more terrible, and the raging billows seemed to make a supreme effort to dash into pieces the iron sides of our vessel then half-filled with water. A wave now struck with such tremendous force that it seemed to me, and to everyone, that the steamer was broken into two pieces. The small window before me having been smashed, allowed me to see the most terrible and magnificent spectacle which can be given to man to contemplate. Literally the sea did not look any longer like a sheet of water, but an ocean of fire. Every wave, every billow looked like the pines of the forest when the devouring element is burning their noble heads during the night. Before those fires the darkness of night had almost entirely disappeared. The heavens above seemed also to be an ocean of fire, by the constant flashes of lightning. The phosphorous lights of the sea, brought to the surface and beaten by the hurricane, seemed to have transformed the Pacific Ocean into a seething caldron of burning elements, on which our half-wrecked ship was hopelessly struggling for life.

After I had had a glimpse of that marvelous and awful vision, I turned towards those of my praying friends who were nearer to me, and I said: "It is a miracle that we are not already perished; our merciful God wants to try our faith, but He wants also to save us Oh! let us go to Him and pray as the apostles went to Him and prayed, when they awoke Christ at the very moment they were perishing "

And I heard, then, prayers such as I had never heard For a whole hour cries of faith and love, cries of hope and joy, went from this little band of children of God to the Mercy Seat, such as the spirit of life and light alone can give.   Yes; there was a struggle that night, on that little corner of the raging Pacific Ocean, in which love and mercy were again to win the day against the justice and wrath of God.

A few minutes after three, a young and very dear sister, the widow of an English officer, said to me: "Do you not feel that the storm is not so strong, and the ship is not so terribly tossed about as one hour ago?" "Evidently," I answered, "the Lord has heard the voice and the humble supplications of His poor, perishing servants.   Let us bless Him."

And, falling on our knees, we together sent from our hearts and lips to the throne of mercy the sublime hymn of David. " Bless the Lord, O my soul, and forget not all His benefits; who forgiveth all thine iniquities, who healeth all thy diseases; who redeemeth thy life from destruction; who crowneth thee with loving kindness and tender mercies; who satisfieth thy mouth with good things, so that thy youth is renewed like the eagle's The Lord executeth righteousness and judgment for all that are oppressed The Lord is merciful and gracious, slow to anger and plenteous in mercy; Who will not always chide, neither will He keep His anger forever He hath not dealt with us after our sins, nor rewarded us according to our iniquities For as the heaven is high above the earth. so great is His mercy to them that fear Him.   As far as the east is from the west, so far has He removed our transgressions from us.   Like as a father pitieth his children, so the Lord pitieth them that fear Him.   For He knoweth our frame; He remembereth that we are dust.   As for man, his days are as grass; as a flower of the field, so he flourisheth. For the wind passeth over it, and it is gone, and the place thereof shall know it no more.   But the mercy of the Lord is from everlasting to everlasting upon them that fear Him, and His righteousness unto children's children, to such as keep His covenant, and to those that remember His commandments to do them.   The Lord hath prepared His throne in the heavens, and His kingdom ruleth over all. Bless the Lord, ye His angels that excel in strength, that do His commandments, hearkening to the voice of His word.   Bless ye the Lord all ye His hosts, ye ministers that do His pleasure. Bless the Lord, all His works, in all places of His dominion! Bless the Lord, O my soul!"

It was then nearly four in the morning. The threatening voice of the thunder was silenced, and the hurricane had visibly lost more than half its strength.   We were all chilly and exhausted.   We left each other, to take some rest.

At seven, I was awakened by the warming rays of the bright sun shining upon me through the broken window of my room. I was soon on the deck to gaze again on that treacherous Pacific Ocean, which seemed so well disposed a few hours before to bring me below its bitter and angry waves.   Though the roaring billows were still very high, it was evident that the One who commands the storms, and they are still, had passed by us, and heard our humble but ardent supplications.

I joined my voice with the voice of all His creatures, the wind and the sea, the sun and the light, the earth and heavens, to praise and bless Him; and I went to the captain to know if our noble ship had sustained any serious damage. "Not much," he said, "she has admirably fought the terrible battle.   But so sudden a cessation of that hurricane is one of the most extraordinary things I have seen in my life.   Those equinoctial storms generally last three days, and they very often keep us a whole week suspended by a thread between life and death" "Ah," I answered, "you were not aware that you had on board some of the children of those fishermen who caused Christ to stop the storm on the Sea of Galilee?" "I wish," he answered with a smile, "that I would have always on board some of those Galileean fishermen's children."

With the fair wind and big waves to push us towards the long wished for shores of Sydney, we arrived in the evening about eight o'clock

As soon as the anchor was let down, as the sanitary laws of the country prevented us from landing immediately, I went among the passengers to request them to come and pass that last Sabbath evening in hearing what our friend David had to tell us about the storm of the previous night, and they gladly gathered to listen to the sublime words of the royal prophet, which I read and commented upon "Oh! that men would praise the Lord for His goodness and His wonderful works to the children of men; And let them sacrifice the sacrifice of thanksgiving, and declare His works with rejoicings. They that go down to the sea in ships, that do business in great waters These see the works of the Lord, and His wonders in the deep For He commandeth the stormy wind, which lifteth the waves thereof. They mount to the heaven. they go down again to the depths, their soul is melted, because of troubles They reel to and fro, and stagger like a drunken man, and are at their wits' end. Then they cry unto the Lord in their troubles, and He bringeth them out of their distresses. He maketh the storm a calm, so that the waves thereof are still Then are they glad because they be quiet, so He bringeth them unto the desired haven Oh that men would praise the Lord for His goodness, and for His wonderful works to the children of men! Let them exalt Him also in the congregation of the people, and praise Him in the assembly of the elders."

No! I have never seen anything like the profound and deep impression of those words of the Divine Book when they fell on my companions, who had, with me, just come out from that watery grave dug under our feet by that terrible hurricane Both Jews and Christians, Romanists and Protestants, atheists and infidels, as well as fervent disciples of the Gospel, vied with each other in praising and thanking God with cheerful heart, singing the most beautiful hymns of the Moody and Sankey collection

This last Sabbath service which we had on board was one of the most solemn and most touching episodes of my life, and I am sure that it will never be forgotten by those who took part in it.   We had begun at eight P. M., and it was ten before we could put an end to it   For every one wanted to praise the great and merciful God who had seen their tears, heard their prayers, silenced the storm, made the furious waves still, and saved them   Every one felt and proclaimed that, indeed, our God is a prayer-hearing God.

CHAPTER XXXIII

Australia

Our noble steamer laid her anchors in the calm and magnificent harbour of Port Jackson, on the 29th of September, at 7 P. M., after her narrow and almost miraculous escape from the hurricane of the previous night. The first thing we did was to thank God for having brought us safely into our "desired haven", and from eight to ten P M, the walls of the great saloon echoed with the sincere expressions of our gratitude.

At half past ten I had retired to my room and was preparing myself for the night, when I was not a little puzzled by the distant sounds of a great multitude of voices singing the beautiful hymn,

> "Ho, my comrades, see the signal waving in the sky;
> Reinforcements now appearing—victory is nigh "

My windows were opened; and when these words, gliding over the still waters of the sea, ten times reverbrated by the surrounding heights, struck my ear, and when the perfect stillness of the dark night was broken by the melodious verses and tune repeated by several hundreds of powerful voices,

> " Hold the fort, for I am coming
> Jesus signals still,
> Wave the answer back to heaven—
> By Thy grace we will."

my soul was thrilled with such sentiments of surprise, admiration and joy that no words can adequately express.

"What does that mean?" I said to myself. But the voices came nearer and nearer. "Are we not yet seven miles from Sydney? These voices cannot, then, come from that city. Do they come from the near shore around us? Impossible! for on one side is the quarantine hospital, at the feet of which we must remain till we have our clearance, to-morrow morning, from the health officer. Surely, the few unfortunate sick people who are behind the walls of that hospital cannot make the echoes of the night resound with such powerful and melodious tunes. Besides that, the other side of the shore is a perfect wilderness—naked rocks—where no human being can think of passing the night in singing. Evidently that multitude of Christian singers are on a steamer, for I hear the noise of her wheels slowly approaching. There, I see her blue and red lights moving through the darkness towards us."

The night was very dark, which made the numerous lights of our mysterious visitor look still brighter.

Suddenly the voices stopped, and the whistle of the strange steamer filled the air, to call our attention. When the black hull of the unknown steamship was about fifty feet from us a profound and perfect silence succeeded the noise of the whistle and the songs. Every one on our steamer had their eyes fixed on the dark object which was silently rocking on our leeboard, and every one whispered to his neighbour, "What does it mean?" when a loud voice was heard, "Is not Father Chiniquy on board?" Twenty voices answered, "Yes, Father Chiniquy is on board."

"Tell him to come on deck, his friends of Sydney want to see him," rejoined the first voice. "We are here on this steamer to give him an Australian welcome."

I could hardly believe my own ears. I felt so confounded at such an unexpected and unmerited public expression of kindness that it seemed, at first, as if I were dreaming. But no, it was not a dream, it was a reality. My merciful God had prepared for His unprofitable servant one of the most de-

licious hours of his life. When I was just saying to myself
"Is it not a rash and foolish act on my part to have come alone
to this distant land, where I have only one friend whom I
know? Is it not a want of discretion and wisdom in me to
have accepted the invitation of that friend to come and rest from
my labours in his house? Will I not be a burden to him and
his family? Is it not ridiculous, with the burden of my
seventy years, to have crossed the whole hemisphere to come
to Australia? Will I not be the first subject of the scorn of
the whole world for such a rash action at the very end of my
life? Will not God, to punish me for this act of folly, make
such a solitude around me here in this distant land that I will
weep as I remember the fatal hour when I left' my
missionary field of Canada to recruit a bodily strength which
cannot be recruited at such an age?"

But these fears soon vanished away from my mind, when
in the presence of that great mercy of God. The less I deserved and expected so solemn and so great a mark of
kindness on the part of my unknown friends and brethren of
Australia, the more I felt overwhelmed by it. My emotion
was so great that I might have fainted under its burden, had
not big tears of joy gushed out of my eyes and rolled down
my cheeks, when kneeling for a moment in my cabin to say,
"O my God, may Thy name be forever blessed for Thy mercies towards me, Thy unprofitable servant." I was soon on
deck to answer, "May God bless you all, noble Christians of
Sydney, for your kindness to your old unknown friend,
Chiniquy Here I am to thank and bless you all "

"Do you not recognize the voice of your old friend, George
Sutherland?" asked one of the crowd

"Yes, I recognize your friendly voice, dear and kind Mr.
Sutherland, and I bless you, here, again, for all you have already done for my dear missions."

"But it is not enough to hear you; we must see you," said
several voices "Get some light around your head that we
may see your face."

These words had hardly been uttered when some of the kind stewards of the steamer brought around me some of their big and bright lanterns.

"Very well! very well!" cried several hundred voices "We are satisfied We have heard and seen you. That is all we wanted To-morrow we will be on the wharf of Sydney, where you will land, to give you another Australian welcome. It is now eleven o'clock You want some rest after the terrible hurricane of last night. Go and take that rest. Good night God bless you."

"May God bless you, noble and kind-hearted friends," I replied

Three rousing cheers were given, and the national anthem, "God save the Queen," was sung to tell us that the noble friends whom God had given me in Australia were as loyal to their queen as they were devoted to their God. It was the signal for the steamer to turn her bow towards Sydney and leave me absolutely overwhelmed with emotions of surprise, joy and gratitude which no human words can express. But some will ask, "Who is that Rev Mr Sutherland who seems to be at the head of your friends in Australia?" As this question, which is a very natural one, will give me an opportunity of presenting one of the most admirable and striking evidences that our God is a prayer-hearing God, who never deserts those who put their trust in Him, I will answer

When, in the spring of 1858, the bishops of the United States and Canada saw that I had definitely broken the iron chains by which I was like all other poor priests of Rome, tied to their feet, they wanted to make of me such an example of misery and desolation that no other priests would ever dare to follow my example, Not satisfied with excommunicating me publicly in all their cathedrals, in their synodical meetings in their great cities, as well as in the humblest churches of their most insignificant villages, they spread everywhere the most horrible calumnies against my honour and my character During a whole year a real deluge of denunciation—calumnies of the vilest kinds—were poured on my devoted head from all the pulpits and through all the weekly and daily journals of the Roman Catholic clergy of America. But, not satisfied with these things, they engaged men to drag me before the civil and criminal courts and summoned false witnesses, who accused me of crimes for which I would have been, if not hung, at least sentenced to the penitentiary for life, had they been proved   Though perfectly innocent, I was sure to be found guilty and to be condemned, if I had not defended myself.   I had then to engage the best lawyers to defend my honour and to protect my life against my accusers. Among those lawyers was Abraham Lincoln, the martyred President, who fell under the hands of the Jesuits, through their tool, in 1865

During more than a year I was left alone to fight my battles against the giant power of Rome   No hope could come to me from my old Roman Catholic friends; they were bound in conscience to curse and destroy me.   And no help could be expected from the Protestants, whose ears were, from morning to night, filled with calumnies spread everywhere against my honour, and who were under the impression that I was a disguised Jesuit, who intended to deceive them.

Though I was always, by the great mercy of God, enabled to prove myself innocent before the civil and criminal courts, these suits were costing me great sums of money, and my small private resources were soon exhausted.   I had even soon to mortgage everything which was mine to pay the witnesses and satisfy the lawyers   When the time came to pay and redeem those mortgages, I was unable to do it.   Then the sheriff of Kankakee took everything in my possession, even my bed, my chairs, my last cow, my library, of which I kept only my dear Bible; all was sold by the sheriff at the door of the public court of Kankakee.   I was absolutely ruined that day.   I had not a pillow on which to rest my head, and that night I had to sleep on the naked floor.

This was a very dark hour indeed in my experience, but I

knew for whom I was suffering all those things, and my hope was that the great Captain of my salvation, under the banner of whom I was fighting, would sooner or later come to my help, for I had put my trust in Him and Him alone.

The very next morning, when I was on my knees, crying to God for mercy and help, a letter was handed to me from Prince Edward Island with $500 in it "to strengthen my hands and cheer up my heart." That letter was signed, George Sutherland

So it was that the very same noble-hearted Christian brother whom God had chosen as the instrument of His mercies to strengthen my hands and cheer up my fainting heart in my first struggles against Rome, in 1859, was the very same one whom He had sent there to cheer me up again guide and protect me in this distant land of Australia, in 1878

How many times when working in England, Scotland, Ireland, the United States and Canada I have understood that a true friend is the greatest treasure which God can give to man. But how I realized the value of that most precious of treatures when it was again presented to me by the hands of my merciful Heavenly Father, when alone at a distance of ten thousand miles from my home, I was standing on these distant but hospitable shores of Australia

"O sing unto the Lord a new song, for he hath done marvelous things His right hand and His holy arm hath gotten Him the victory   He hath remembered His mercy and His truth toward the house of Israel, all the ends of the earth hath seen the salvation of our God   Let the sea roar and the fullness thereof, the world and they that dwell therein   Let the floods clap their hands, let the hills be joyful together " (Psalm 98.)

Four months having passed since I had landed in Sydney, by the great mercy of God, my bodily strength had been so perfectly restored, that I had given eighty-two lectures and preached fifty sermons since the day of my arrival

In this strange antipode land everything seems to work

by contrary laws from those of the northern hemisphere. Such a work ought to have put me down, but it was the contrary. There was such an elasticity in the pure air we breathed, there was such an exuberance of life coming from those evergreen forests and those everlasting flowers; there was such a balm spreading from those enchanted gardens, which were bathing in the light and the breeze of an eternal spring, that my threescore and ten years were passing without leaving any of the usual ugly traces of their passage. The only thing that I did not absolutely enjoy was to see and feel the thermometer marking, quite frequently, from 140 to 143 degrees in the sun and 110 in the shade. Such a heat seems almost incredible to my readers, and I would hardly believe it possible, had I not experienced it myself. But, strange to say, that burning state of the atmosphere, which would be intolerable, and which would kill people in Canada, is perfectly bearable there.

However, it was my intention to go to some cooler part of the new continent, and as I had received many kind invitations to visit the great cities of Melbourne, Ballarat, Geelong, Adelaide, etc., in the southern part of Victoria, I intended to avail myself of that providential chance to know something more of our terrestrial globe. Those regions are some 800 miles nearer the eternal ices of the southern pole, and I was told that there the southern breezes of the sea were unsurpassed for their healthy influence on the people who had the good luck to breathe their perfumes.

I purposed to return to New South Wales at the end of the hot days of the Australian summer, which meant that I intended to come back to Sydney at the end of April or May, for one must not forget that there the summer months are December, January and February. The autumn months are March, April and May. The spring months, September, October and November. How upside down the world appeared to the exiled son of Canada!

The short limits of a chapter will not permit me to relate

all that I saw of the visible manifestations of the mercies of God towards several Roman Catholics who attended
my lectures in Sydney.   I will give only one or two facts.

A well-educated Catholic lady had come, through curiosity,
to hear my second address on "Auricular Confession," though
her priest had strictly forbidden her to do so.   In order not
to be known by the spies the priests had at the doors of the
hall to report the names of their disobedient children, she had
so well disguised herself that nobody could recognize her
She listened with breathless attention from the first to the
last words, though she was uncomfortably crushed in her seat
by the multitude which was crammed around her.   But instead of smiling and laughing with the rest of the crowd, she
was weeping all the time; for her personal experience of the
abominations of Auricular Confession were almost word
for word the awful repetition of what she was hearing

When she went home she fell on her knees, took a Gospel
book and read the chapters which I had cited, and which she
had taken down in her note-book.   She found what I had
said was true, that it was not at the feet of a miserable, sinful
man, but only at the feet of the Lamb that sinners had to go to
find peace, life and pardon.   She did not want any one to
tell her that, far from being purified and sanctified by pouring
into the ears of her confessor the sad history of her sins, she
had always come out of the confessional more guilty and miserable by the questions put to her and the answers she had to
make.   After a couple of days of anguish, tears and prayers,
the voice of God was heard in her soul with such a power
that she determined to do what I had advised her, to look to
Christ and to Him alone for pardon and peace.   With Magda-
lene, she went to the dear Saviour's feet, bathed them with the
tears of her love and repentance, and, like that model of penitents, she heard the sweet voice of Jesus telling her, "Thy
sins are forgiven, for thou hast loved Me much."   Her joy
and happiness were unspeakable at this first experience of her
regeneration.   There was only one thing which marred her

happiness· "What will my dear Emma say when she hears that I have left the Church of Rome to become a Protestant? That dear sister is so devoted! She is so fond of her father confessor! She is scrupulous to go to mass every morning, and receive the communion every Sabbath and every festival day of the blessed Virgin Mary! How angry she will be against me!"

Such were the fears of our interesting new convert about her younger sister. When, five or six days later, she received her visit as usual, she threw herself into her arms and kissed her with the most sincere affection. But, after a few minutes of conversation, her young sister said to her· "My dear Mary, allow me to ask you the cause of that unusual embarrassment which I notice in you. Though you have received me with your usual love and kindness, there is something strange in your voice and manners which I cannot understand. You look distressed and uneasy. What does that mean?"

"You are not mistaken, Emma, when, for the first time in my life, you find that I am a little uneasy and distressed with you. I have a secret to tell you which I fear will make you feel bad against me. But I have prayed our merciful God to grant you the same favour He has granted me, and I hope He will hear your elder sister and most devoted friend's prayer. I must tell you I am no more a Roman Catholic. I have forever given up that Church in order to follow Christ and Him alone."

"Is it possible?" exclaimed Emma. "And how long is it since you have given up the religion in which we were both reared?"

"Since I heard the lecture of Pastor Chiniquy last week I found that what he said of the polluting and damning influences of Auricular Confession was so perfectly like what I know by my own personal experience, that I am sure he was true and honest in all that he said. I have read the Gospel with the utmost attention this whole week. I have so earnestly prayed the Author of every perfect gift to direct and

guide me, that I feel sure to be in the true religion of Christ
when I put my trust only in His blood shed and His life
given up on Calvary to save my soul."

"May Almighty God be forever blessed," answered Emma,
with a cry of joy, and tears trickling down her cheeks   "I
was at that same lecture on Auricular Confession, and, like you,
I felt and knew by my own sad experience that Auricular Confession is a school of perdition   Like you, I have given up
the Church of Rome, and I have found at the dear Saviour's
feet a joy and a peace that passeth understanding."

The two sisters fell into the arms of each other, and, bathing each other's faces with the tears of unspeakable joy, they
blessed the merciful Saviour who had made them free by
His Word, and pure by His blood.

CHAPTER XXXIV

Visit to Hobert Town. Account of the Disturbances. Closing Lecture—
Dramatic Scenes.

During my stay in Australia I spent some time in Tasmania. This is about three-fourths the size of Ireland, and has nearly fifty islets surrounding it. It has a great variety of surface, and much grand scenery. Its former name was Van Diemen's Land. It has lofty mountains, one of which, Ben Lomond, is 5,500 feet high, and several large lakes and rivers.

Hobert Town is the chief place and contains 30,000 people. The principal square in the city is called Queen's Domain, and there is a town hall which cost $60,000 The place is well supplied with schools, churches and newspapers

I arrived at Hobert Town on Saturday, June 21, 1879, and was received by a number of clergymen, among whom was the Rev. R. Maclaren Webster, of the Chalmers Presbyterian Church, who had arranged for my entertainment at his pleasant home On the Sabbath I preached in the Chalmers Presbyterian Church, and in the afternoon in the Melville Wesleyan Church On the latter occasion I spoke on the duties, responsibilities, privileges and glories of the Christian In my discourse I expressed a fear that some of the soldiers composing the army of Christ, instead of being on the aggressive, were more inclined to come to terms of peace with the enemy at any price. I pointed to the valour and achievements of the British nation in subduing other powers; contended that, whenever Great Britain had been engaged in a conflict in which Romanism was involved, the British had gained a victory, and referred to the overthrow of Rome, not by carnal weapons, but by a spiritual warfare, and at the same time disclaimed being an enemy of Roman Catholics, whose honesty, earnestness and fidelity I spoke of in favourable terms   I contended, however, that with all those qualities they were a deluded class of religionists and that it was the duty of Protestants to effect the opening of their spiritual sight, so that they might be enabled to realize the blessedness of the Christian religion.   I alluded to the parable of the rich man and Lazarus, and in its application showed that the rich man was represented by Christians who were in the possession of the Bread of Life, but neglected to supply the spiritual wants of their Roman Catholic brethren, who stood in the relation of Lazarus

I had arranged to deliver a series of lectures to be given during the whole week, the Town Hall having been definitely engaged for that purpose; the first lecture to be given on Monday evening

The large hall on that evening was filled, and on the platform were several of the leading clergymen of the city After the usual devotional exercises, I began my lecture. There were several attempts to create a disturbance and the police present seemed to have little control, but the general body of the audience being orderly, peace in every instance was soon restored.   However, this was only the beginning of the disturbance and the persecutions which were to come on the following evenings   Romanism is the same there that it is in all other places; it demands liberty for itself, but refuses it to those who differ from it   Its loud talk about liberty of conscience in any proper sense is all hypocritical and false.

On Tuesday evening I was to lecture in the same place. A letter appeared during the day in a newspaper called the *Mercury,* published by a leading Romanist whose name was Hunter, and who had a great influence on his fellow-religionists in their subsequent conduct   He expressed surprise that I should be allowed the use of the town Hall for holding such "orgies," as he expressed it

The hall on this evening became the arena of an extraordinary and disgraceful scene   I pass over here some of the details of that stormy meeting, where the elements of bedlam and pandemonium seemed to be combined.   It was found that the lecture could not be given.

It was at last resolved, on the motion of Mr. Scott, seconded by Mr. Napier, that all legitimate means, inclusive of our appeal to the police, having failed to enable the meeting to be carried on, it be dismissed   After the lapse of ten minutes, during which the rowdies sang "John Brown," and "We won't go home till morning," the audience gradually dispersed at about half-past nine o'clock.

On Wednesday evening the rioters had mostly their own way, so that the meeting could not go on.   The particulars of this I pass over

On Thursday preparations were made for the struggle in connection with the meeting in the evening.   Both parties were quite active   The party in favor of the law and order sent a committee to the acting Colonial Secretary, Hon H. L. Crowther.   The Roman Catholics sent a deputation to the Mayor to remonstrate against my utterances in the Town Hall   A special meeting of the City Council was held in the afternoon to consider the situation and decide what might be best to do.   The motion that the Council be prepared to maintain peace and order was carried.   The Romanists were not idle in the meantime   Having failed through their deputation to the Mayor to secure the cancellation of my engagements in the Town Hall, they resolved to hold a mass meeting outside on Domain Square. the burning of Chiniquy in effigy to be a part of the programme.   To make a greater impression, it was decided to summon friends from the country around.   The general intention, though not expressed, was evidently to make a violent assault on the Town Hall.   Late at night the Bishop, who had been apparently inactive, forbade the meeting by a pastoral letter.   He was evidently afraid of bloodshed, and concluded to interfere as a matter of policy.

Friday came, and the authorities determined to take steps to put down the law breaking, while the action of the Romanists was doubtful The Bishop, fearing the terrible results which would be likely to follow a collision between his people and the authorities, went to the meeting in the Domain at six o'clock and implored the assembly to disperse, and not commit any breach of the peace The result was that the second lecture in the course was given on Friday evening without disturbance.

There was a call by the Mayor, through the papers, for special constables This was largely responded to, and two hundred and fifty were sworn in. The information having been received that a most alarming riot would be likely to take place, the government in the afternoon decided on securing the assistance of the volunteers, and word was sent to the officers and men that there would be a parade at the barracks at five o'clock. The military force thus suddenly called and prepared amounted to the number of four hundred and thirty-nine men.

In the meantime all the influence of the Romish clergy was used to prevent the meeting in the Domain. They visited members of their church with great zeal to persuade them not to attend the meeting in the evening. and to remain in their houses. The Bishop and his clergy resolved to visit the meeting in the evening and urge those present to retire to their houses, and avoid serious consequences

I give here a copy of the letter which the Bishop issued on Friday

"To the Catholics of Hobert Town. Seeing that your efforts to prevent the City Council letting the Town Hall for the purposes to which it has been devoted during this week have failed, and being informed that further demonstrations on your part in that direction will be resisted by the force of law, leading probably to rioting and bloodshed, I most earnestly request that you will have the good sense to abstain from making any further attempts to vindicate, on the present occasion, your rights as citizens and ratepayers, and to absent yourselves from the precincts of the Town Hall this evening My only object in thus appealing to you is to prevent injury to persons and property, and to induce you to show your respect for yourselves as Catholics and loyal citizens.

" Daniel Murphy,
"Bishop of Hobert Town.
" Hobert Town, June 27th, 1878."

This letter of the Bishop is very significant and suggestive. He, of course, knew what was going on in connection with the rioting of the Romanists, and the breaking up of the meetings at the Town Hall. There was a direct violation of law and order before his eyes, but he never remonstrated against it But when the government proposes to interfere by armed force, he appears on the scene His letter does not appeal to any motives of conscience or obedience to law, peace, and good order. He sees that the argument to protect the rights of British subjects, to be resorted to after all arguments addressed to reason and conscience, is that of armed force. He trembles and fears results, and urges his slaves to be quiet lest they be shot down. What a position this letter puts him in, and what a black reflection on the system he represents!

At a large meeting held shortly after by Protestants, there was strong action, called out by this letter of the Bishop which I here record Rev B Butchers, after stating at the meeting that he had an unpleasant duty to perform, remarked that they were, of course, aware that during the last two or three days a pastoral had been issued by the Roman Catholic Bishop relating to the disgraceful disturbances, and it was laid upon him, by Pastor Chiniquy's committee, to enter a very earnest and very solemn protest against the spirit and sentiment of the pastoral letter It would be altogether against the dignity of the committee of the pastors, and alto-

gether beneath the dignity of such an influential and repre-
sentative meeting as that, to have taken any notice of any
individual utterances of Bishop Murphy, his clergy, or any
other gentlemen in the city. But it is not beneath the dignity of that, or any other assembly, to take notice of the calm
deliberate, and official utterance of the highest ecclesiastical
dignitary of the Roman Catholic Church in the city and in
Tasmania More especially was this the case when the sentiment and principle contained in that official utterance was
such as to be subversive of civil and religious liberty, and it
was on that ground that the protest he was about to read, and
which he imagined would be endorsed by that meeting, had
been drawn up.

THE PROTEST

"This meeting having heard read Bishop Murphy s letter
to his flock, desires to record its most earnest and solemn protest against it, on the following grounds, viz:—

"First Because it begins with a statement which is at
variance with truth, inasmuch as it is beyond dispute that
while an organized band of Catholics by lawless violence, on
three successive nights, prevented Pastor Chiniquy, his committee, and the citizens generally from using the hall, after it
had been let by the Town Hall committee, and that also a
large and influential deputation of Roman Catholics waited
upon the Mayor and City Council for the avowed purpose of
inducing them to break through their contract with Pastor
Chiniquy's committee, no 'efforts' whatever were made by
Roman Catholics to 'prevent the City Council from letting
the Town Hall for the purposes to which it has been devoted
during the week.'

"Secondly Because the Bishop, in affirming that 'further
demonstrations on the part of his flock in that direction will
be resisted by force of law, leading probably to rioting and
bloodshed,' ignores entirely the notorious fact that serious
'rioting had already taken place, and that bloodshed 'had

only been averted by the Christian forbearance of the law-abiding and lawful occupants of the hall, and most unjustifiably throws the entire responsibility of prospective 'rioting and bloodshed,' not on his riotous flock, but on the civil authorities who were determined to repress such lawless 'efforts' by the 'force of law.'

"Thirdly Because Bishop Murphy does not in his pastoral letter express the slightest regret or indignation on account of 'efforts' which the Mayor of Hobert Town officially and justly designates the 'late disorderly and unlawful proceedings at the Town Hall'

"Fourthly Because, in earnestly requesting his flock to 'have the good sense to abstain from making any further attempts to vindicate their rights as citizens and ratepayers,' Bishop Murphy, so far from condemning and reproving the 'late disorderly and unlawful proceedings,' officially justifies and sanctions and applauds them.

"Fifthly Because, in stating that his 'only object' in thus appealing to his flock 'is to prevent injury to persons and property, and to induce you to show your respect for yourselves as Catholics and loyal citizens,' the Bishop entirely and disloyally ignores the supreme obligations which he and his flock are under, not only in respecting persons, property and themselves. but also the laws of the land and their legitimate administrators.

"Sixthly: Because, in expressly limiting his request to the 'present occasion,' Bishop Murphy does not only not forbid, but directly invites similar 'disorderly and unlawful proceedings' at some future and more favourable season."

After reading the protest, Mr Butchers said if the meeting endorsed it they would manifest it by rising to their feet.

The meeting rose almost unanimously.

The Rev. Mr. Webster then rose and said he had the honour to be deputed to read an address to me presented by the committee.

The address stated that prior to leaving Hobert Town after

the exciting and historical disturbances of the past week, the committee were desirous of recording a very sincere, earnest and emphatic opinion respecting my character, so far as known to them   They did not forget that I came into their midst sufficiently accredited by my sacrifices, sufferings and labours, as well as by the indisputable fact of my being a minister of the Canadian Presbyterian Church, bearing trustworthy credentials commending me to the confidence and respect of Christian men, wherever the providence of God might direct my steps.   They desired further to say that so far as they had had an opportunity of testing my facts, proofs and arguments, they had always found them trustworthy, and they here expressed their most decided opinion that if my facts could be disproved, if my quotations were garbled or false, and my arguments inconclusive, it was imperatively incumbent upon my opponents, in the best interests of morality, to discharge this public duty   They further desired to testify that, during my present visit, and amidst the extraordinary irritation and excitement that had prevailed, I had uniformly both in my public and private deportment a spirit of moderation and Christian charity toward those from whose communion I had severed myself, such as to command their admiration and esteem, and they desired now to take an affectionate farewell of me, commending me and my noble mission to the grace of that God who had so marvelously enlightened, guided, protected and blessed me during my past life and work, and who, as they fervently prayed, would continue the same mercy to the end.

The address was signed by the committee

On rising to reply, I said I could not sufficiently express my gratitude and admiration for what I had seen and heard, not only that day, but during the whole week   I had been providentially brought into their midst, trusting to find here true liberty and Christianity, and I had not been mistaken. By the great mercy of God, I had found not only what I expected, but much more   I thanked my committee for the

address they had presented to me.   It had come from friends
who had stood in my defense as soldiers of liberty, and who
proved themselves as true sons of England, and worthy of her
glorious freedom, which made her so great in the world.
These friends had stood by me in a time of danger.   I felt
no danger because they stood as a wall before me, protecting
me from the pistols and daggers of my enemies, who would
have had to pass over their bodies to harm me   They were
stronger than the walls of the strongest fortress, for there
was nothing so strong as a fearless heart.   I had come there
to speak, not trusting in my own strength, but in Divine
help.   I was but weak and faltering, but, aided by God, I
might be the instrument of giving them light.   I am a
British subject, and claim the rights and liberties of English-
men   Born under the British flag, like those before me, I
know perhaps better than you the danger which menaces that
flag   From having been for twenty-five years in the camp of
the enemy, I was able to study their plots and machinations,
and now I can raise my feeble voice in warning against the
threatening danger   What I am about to say here I have
said in England, in Scotland, in Ireland and in America, and
I thought it was my duty to come to Australia to tell you of
it too   The Australians are young in years, but from the
marvelous rapidity of their growth they are giants in strength
and development, a mighty people, but you are sleeping upon
a volcano—and you do not suspect it.   There are great
dangers ahead for Great Britain and its colonies, dangers as
vast as the ocean which is around the beautiful Tasmanian
shores, as deep as the Pacific seas we have to cross to reach
each other.   Yes the danger is great and near, and yet you
do not suspect it.   Having been raised in the atmosphere of
a Christian household, fed on the bread which Christ had
bought with His blood, there is a spirit of honesty, kindness
and Christianity in you which prevents you from suspecting
the danger which is at your doors.   Even when I tell you the
truth, you will suppose it to be an exaggeration, for the

Church of Rome is so wise and skilful in her ways, her plots are so well laid against your liberties, your constitution and Queen; it does all this with such ingenuity, making it appear like patriotism, fair play, and Christianity, that it is really difficult for any one to understand the dangers. But I have asked for help to-day from God, and I hope that guided by His Spirit I shall be able to throw some light on that great subject

The dangers ahead for England and her colonies come first from the corruption of Rome, and that corruption is caused chiefly by the practise of Auricular Confession. I then spoke of the practise of confession carried on in the Episcopalian Church, even in Hobert Town, where I knew from good authority that it was practised privately I spoke at length of confession as the destruction of morality, and therefore as one of the greatest dangers that was menacing England.   It was the death of honesty, the death of purity, the death of holiness.

There was another danger. Not only were honesty and holiness the foundation of a Christian state, but education The Church of Rome was the enemy of education and light. That Church could thrive only by the ignorance of her people, and for that reason she made every effort to keep the people in ignorance, to destroy intelligence It was true that in the Church of Rome there were houses of education, and great sacrifices were made by the Church in order to build and support them, and to have men and women to teach, but the education of the Church of Rome was a deception This I established by several arguments drawn from facts, from history and from the very nature of Romanism.

I alluded to Bishop Smith's pastoral to prove that the education Roman Catholics receive from their superiors is conducive to intolerance and treason.

"How could it be otherwise?" I said "The Church of Rome is led by the Jesuits, and the Jesuitical creed placed the Pope's authority before that of the Queen "

Then on my request a part of the creed of the Jesuits was read by the Rev Mr. Butchers as follows:—When Pope Clement XIV. issued a bull in 1773, abolishing the order of Jesuits, annulling its statutes, and releasing the members from their vows, its constitution was made public, and embraced the following oath:—" I, A. B , now in the presence of Almighty, God. the Blessed Virgin Mary, the Blessed Michael, the Arch-angel, the Blessed St. John Baptist, the Holy Apostles St Peter and St. Paul, and the saints and sacred host of heaven, do declare from my heart, without mental reservation, that Pope Gregory is Christ's Vicar-general, and is the only true and only head of the Universal Church throughout the earth; and that by virtue of the keys of binding and loosing, given to His Holiness by Jesus Christ, he hath power to depose heretical kings, princes, states, commonwealths and govern-ments, all being illegal without his sacred confirmation, and that they may safely be destroyed, therefore, to the utmost of my power, I will defend this doctrine and His Holiness, rights and customs against all usurpers of the heretical, or Protestant authority whatsoever, especially against the now pretended authority and Church of England, and all adherents in regard that they be usurped and heretical, opposing the sacred Mother Church of Rome. I do renounce and disown any allegiance as due to any heretical king, prince, or state named Protestant, or to any of their inferior magistrates or officers I do further declare the doctrine of the Church of England, of the Calvinists, Huguenots. and other Protestants, to be damnable, and those to be damned who will not forsake the same. I do further declare that I will help, assist, and advise all or any of His Holiness' agents in any place where-ever I shall be, and do my utmost to extirpate the heretical Protestant doctrine, and to destroy all their pretended power, legal or otherwise. I do further promise and declare, notwith-standing that I am dispensed with to assume any religion heret-ical for the propagation of the Mother Church's interests, to keep secret and private all her agents, counsels, as they entrust

me, and not to divulge, directly or indirectly, by word, writing
or circumstance whatsoever, but to execute all which shall be
proposed, given in charge, or discovered unto me, by you my
ghostly father, or by any of this convent. All of which I, A. B,
do swear by the blessed Trinity and blessed sacrament, which
I am now to receive, to perform, and on my part to keep in-
violable; and do call all the heavenly and glorious hosts of
heaven to witness my real intentions to keep this my oath.
In testimony hereof, I take this most holy and blessed sacrament of the Eucharist, and witness the same further with my
hand and seal, in the face of this holy convent"

"You have in this solemn oath of the Jesuits," I added, "a
sworn document which tells you more than my words that a
true Roman Catholic priest and layman must be a traitor in
your camp   For it is to the Pope that he must be obedient
in civil as well as religious matters. After such an oath to
the Pope, the oath of allegiance to the Queen is only dust
thrown into your eyes, as you may see by the following extract from the *Dublin Tablet* of July 26, 1851.—'Neither in
England nor in Ireland will the Roman Catholic obey the
law. It is not a law. It is a lie   The law of God, that is,
the Pope's command, will be carried into effect; the Parliament's law will be spit upon and trampled under foot
Rather than our loyalty to the Holy See should be in the
least degree tarnished, let ten thousand kings and queens
(Queen Victoria included) perish; let them be deposed from
their thrones   When the Pope and the Queen are placed in
antagonism to each other, and it is intimated that Her Majesty would not accept a divided allegiance, we are compelled
to say plainly which allegiance we consider the more important, and we would not hesitate to tell the Queen to her face.
that she must either be content with this divided allegiance,
or none at all   Let us never forget that whatever her boasted
authority may be, it is as nothing compared to that of the
Vicar of Jesus Christ'

"I thank God that my coming here has forced Rome to take

away her mask and show her horns. How many among you, before these last few days, were sincerely and so earnestly believing that the priests, the Bishop, and the people of Rome were a law=abiding people; that the oaths they had made to obey the Queen were the oaths of honest Christians, real gentlemen and true patriots. But to=day you have read with your eyes, and heard with your own ears, that one of the greatest crimes which can be committed against the laws of the Queen of England, is not a crime in the eyes of the Roman Catholic Bishop, when it is committed to destroy liberty of speech and conscience. The very men who have forcibly broken the doors of your house with the avowed intention to slaughter you and me, if we would dare to enjoy the most sacred rights of a British subject—the right of conscience and speech—have been publicly approved and publicly told that it was their right to do it.

"Protestants of Hobert Town and Tasmania, what have you to do now? Your eyes are opened, you know that by 'liberty of conscience' Rome means that she has a right to cut your throat and blow out your brains if you do not ask her permission about the orators you want to hear and the subjects you want to have discussed in your presence.

"Shall I advise you to retaliate and petition England to withdraw the Emancipation Bill, and put again the chains of slavery around the necks of those poor deluded men? No: let them be free to worship their wafer=christ and to prostrate themselves before those gods made with their own hands; let them continue to go to confession and listen to the damning and polluting questions which Dens, Ligori, Débreyne and all the theologians of Rome force the confessor to put to his male and female penitents; let the Roman Catholics be free as the birds of the air in the practise of their religion But after you will have told the Roman Catholics, 'You are free to worship God according to your conscience,' tell them: 'You will not rule our dear and beautiful Tasmania. It is not the Pope, but it is our gracious Queen who will govern us. It is not the Holy Inquisition, but the glorious British flag which will forever float to the breeze over the sublime mountains and the magnificent valleys of Tasmania '

"Read your Bible and you will see that the greatest crime a nation can commit is idolatry   See how God visits the idolators in His terrible justice.   What a difference between a Christian country and an idolatrous one! how weak, poor, wretched the latter looks when compared with the former! How the power of an idolatrous people melts like snow before the burning rays of the sun, when coming in contact with a Christian one!   But what is Roman Catholicism?   Our great and glorious Queen (may God bless and keep her many years more at the head of Great Britain), our glorious Queen Victoria herself answers my question by telling us that, before she put on her royal head the most glorious crown in the world, she swore that Romanism is 'idolatry,' and our glorious Queen Victoria is not a perjured queen   No· the words which fell from her lips on the solemn hour of her coronation rolled over all the mountains and plains of her vast empire, they crossed the boundless oceans over which her glorious flag floats without a rival to deny its untarnished glory, or contest its irresistible power   The words of our glorious Queen Victoria, when she swore that the mass of Rome is 'idolatry,' were repeated by all the echoes of heaven and earth.

"Rome is not only idolatrous, but her idolatry is the most degrading, impious and damning mode of idolatry the world has ever seen

"When the Persians adore the rising sun, they give their homage to the most glorious object that is presented to our human vision   That magnificent orb, which rises like a giant every morning from behind the horizon, to pass over the world and pour everywhere his floods of heat, life and light, cannot be contemplated without feelings of awe and admiration.   Man must raise his eyes to see that glorious sun, he

must take the eagle's wings to follow his giant march throughout the myriads of worlds which surround him as a king.   It
is easy to understand that poor, fallen and blind humanity
may take that glorious object for God.   And when I see the
Persian priests of the sun in their magnificent temples, waiting with their gold censers in hand for the appearance of
his rays, to chant their melodious hymns and sing their sublime canticles to his glory, I know their error, but I understand it; I was going to say that I can almost excuse it.   I
feel an immense compassion for those poor deluded idolaters,
but at the same time I feel that they are raised above the
dust of this earth, and that their minds can be filled with
sentiments of gratitude and adoration   Their souls cannot
but receive some sparks of light and life from the inexhaustible focus of light and life.   But the poor deluded Roman
Catholics! are they not a thousand times more worthy of our
compassion when we see them abjectly prostrated before this
small 'wafer-god,' baked by a servant girl between two well
heated irons in her kitchen?   It is impossible to see a spectacle more ignominious and lamentable than a multitude of
men and women prostrating their faces to the dust to adore
a god that the rats and mice have many times dragged and
devoured in their dark recesses!   Where are the rays of light
and life from this contemptible little cake?   Instead of being
enlarged and elevated in the presence of that ridiculous
modern divinity, is not the human intelligence paralyzed and
struck with idiocy and death at its feet?

"There is great danger for England from that idolatry.
For it is of no use to shut your eyes to the truth   England,
which had evidently been chosen by God to put down the
idols of Rome, is everywhere not only relieving them, but
she helps with her own money to spread and support their
impious worship.   She raises the colleges and universities
where the priests of Rome learn how to preach and perpetuate
their idolatrous religion.

"How God Almighty blessed England and made her great

and glorious when she cast off the yoke of Rome and demolished her idolatry, and kept herself pure from her idols! But
how the same God will quickly withdraw His protecting arm
from England, and let her lose her past glory, if she pros-
trates herself again at the feet of the idols of the Pope!

"Who does not feel his heart saddened at the awful apostasy of so many ministers of the Episcopal Church of England, who have lately deserted the standard of Christ, and
passed over to the camp of the enemy? But who is not
still more saddened by the perfidy of a still greater number
of disguised Jesuits, who, under the name of Episcopal ministers and bishops of the Church of England, are at work to
destroy her by introducing one after the other the idolatries of
Rome into the temples of God?

"But no! our dear Great Britain will never bend again
her knees before the idols of Rome, she will never bow down
again her noble head to the feet of the great impostor who is
insulting God on the crumbling throne of the Vatican. Let
us hope and pray that all over the world the sons and daughters of England will rally with more fervour than ever around
the banners of Christ, in order to go to the conquest of the
world   Let every Protestant from the northern shores of old
England and dear Scotland, to the beautiful southern hemisphere which you have chosen for your home, remember the
tears and the blood shed by their ancestors to break the humiliating yoke of Popery, and conquer the glorious liberty
and privileges which have made them the first nation of the
world . . .   However, when I ask you in the name of
your heroic ancestors to remain true to the flag on which they
wrote with their blood, 'No surrender,' I adjure you to remember that you have a duty to perform towards the Roman
Catholics   It is to love them and to prove that love in doing
all in your power to show them the fatal errors which make
them the abject slaves of men   Show your love to the Roman
Catholics by telling them the truth, bravely, incessantly, every
time the good providence of God will allow you to do it

Not only pray for them constantly, but do all in your power
to partake with them the pure bread of the children of God,
the Word which gives joy and life to those who possess
it, give them the waters which flow from the fountains
of eternal life, and which are so sweet to those who drink
them.

In order that my Christian readers may understand how
Roman Catholics understand liberty of conscience and of
speech, I will give them an illustration. On the second night,
as has been stated before, the lecture could not be given in
the Town Hall on account of the rioting. This is a specimen
of some of the dramatic scenes which occurred during my
visit at Hobert Town, as reported in the press of that city:

"The Town Hall was the arena of an extraordinary and disgraceful scene. It was given over to uproar and riot. Pastor Chiniquy was silenced by brute force by an organized
mob of Roman Catholics. The storm might have been brew-
ing from the time the doors of the hall were opened. Numbers of rough-looking characters, armed with sticks, entered
early and formed a compact body in the back of the hall.
But there was deceitful calm. The audience was as quiet as
a Sunday congregation. The Pastor, who was advertised to
lecture on 'Rome, and Liberty of Conscience,' occupied the
platform supported by the Revs J. Cope, B Butchers, J. Scott
and Webster.

"There was hushed silence till Mr. Webster rose to propose
that the chair should be taken by the Rev. J Cope. This
was the prelude to lawless fury. At once there rose a deep,
tempestuous swell like the bursting of a thunderstorm. There
was no mistaking its tone; it was that of a roused and wrath-
ful passion. Yells, groans, loud expletives, hisses and fierce
shouts rent the air, accompanied by a deafening clatter of
sticks and boot heels, drowning every attempt at proceeding
with the object of the meeting. There was immediately a
scene of wildest confusion. The greater part of the hall was
filled with a respectable audience, partly women, who were

terrified at these demonstrations of violence. All started to
their feet. The ladies rushed toward the platform as if to
seek safety there; the cushioned crimson seats were trampled
under muddy feet; the clergy besought order from the police,
of whom there were at first five or six, gathered round the
rioters, and tried, but in the mildest manner, to quell the disturbance, but in vain. The clangour sounded louder, hoarser,
with all attempts to subdue it. Volleys of epithets were
showered upon the Pastor, to the rallying cry, 'Tally ho!
Tally ho!' which resounded from the lusty throat of a stout
and elderly Irishman. The disturbers would not be quieted.
All appeals from the platform were met with derisive cheers.
The Rev Mr Webster asked for fair play in vain, hoots
and loud cries were the only response. The police were
inactive. The supporters of the meeting were indignant.
'Why don't the police do their duty?' 'Send for more
police;' 'arrest them;' were the cries heard from all sides
The Rev. B. Butchers, Mr. Russell Young, and C. D.
Haywood, went into the midst of the peace disturbers
to try and induce them to stay their clamour They might
as well have tried to hold back the billows of the ocean. The
whooping chorus grew the louder The blood of the disturbers was hot and unappeasable. A disputation, a push, and
blows were struck, a *mêlée* ensued; combatants and police
interlocked in confusion—a struggling, surging mass, grap-
pling and fighting among the forms in the body of the hall
It was a critical moment; a general *fracas* was imminent.
The Pastor sought shelter near the organ seat No arrests
were made, and, by the intervention of some civilians aiding
the police, a momentary lull ensued, then an attempt was
made to go on with the meeting The rabble drowned all
sounds in a tempest of malignant cries of, 'Turn him out,'
'Three groans for the apostate priest,' 'Three cheers for the
kicked-out priest,' and unrestrained opprobrious and coarse
abuse From time to time the ministers begged a fair hearing
'Truth,' they said, 'would not suffer from speech, let Pastor

Chiniquy be heard; those who disagreed with him might leave the hall' But the turbulent rioters would not leave. Drawing breaths at intervals, their ferocity was not to be turned aside, and delusive moments of quiet were followed by a still more tumultuous outbreak of passion In the midst of this mob, a rumour went round that the Mayor was coming; the word passed that he had been sent for, and it was hoped that he would be able to restore something like order But he did not come; and the Rev Mr. Webster made another effort to carry on the meeting He begged the people to be seated. He said the meeting must be carried on, and he asked the police (who had, by this time, been reinforced) to do their duty. Shouts of defiance from the rioters greeted him They had, they said, paid for the hall, and it was an insult to allow the Pastor to speak there, they would not allow him; they would hear anyone but him 'Then.' said Mr Webster, 'we will sing a hymn.' The mob then commenced singing, 'God save the Queen' in bantering style and tune, but all was quiet when the respectable portion of the audience began singing, 'There is a Fountain Filled with Blood,' which was given out by Mr. Webster The reverend gentleman asked once more that the Pastor should be allowed to be heard. A voice: 'If he does not say anything offensive' Mr Butchers: 'Who is to be the judge of that?' Mr Webster said he would take care that nothing offensive was said, there was no fear of that. A voice· 'We were insulted last night.' Mr Webster said he had heard the Pastor s address, and there was not a word in it to which exception could be taken. (Derisive cries, and 'No, no.') Mr Webster appealed for fair play A voice· 'Any other gentleman but Chiniquy' Mr. McPherson (who was on the platform) vehemently 'Why don't the police do their duty? they are paid for it by the public Why don't you take Fay in charge?' (Fay, the person alluded to, had been a prominent disturber throughout) Mr. Webster· 'No, no We don't want any one taken in charge. You are an English audience. As such you must love fair play Give the Pastor fair play; let us hear his address.' (Uproar) A voice ' He is defaming our religion, he is insulting us ' Mr Webster said he would be the very last one to listen to an insult, he would be the first person to protest against it. But he would hear every man. He would listen with great delight to Cardinal Newman, for example, if he were to come there to speak. A voice. ' He does not attack your religion.' (Cheers.) A voice. 'What is one man's food, is another man's poison ' (Cheers and laughter) ' We will listen to you all night, Mr. Webster, but not to the Pastor.'" And so on, till the meeting was dismissed, as stated before

The other few days of my stay in Hobert Town were devoted to sight-seeing and to the organization of a Protestant association whose object was the defense and fostering of Protestantism. I visited all the points of interest about the city with the greatest delight and admiration, and on the Saturday afternoon of that eventful week, I left by the steamer Tasman *en route* for New South Wales and Queensland

CHAPTER XXXV

Ballarat and Horsham. Riots—Narrow Escapes. A Woman Spits in My Face to Obey Her Father Confessor. The Muddy Ditch

Ballarat is one of the most remarkable and thriving cities of New South Wales, situated in a very rich and beautiful plain, where an enormous amount of gold has been found The population, when I was providentially called to spend three weeks of evangelistic labour among its people, was about 35,000

Unfortunately the Roman Catholic population was very strong, composed, as it is in too many places, largely of drunkards, thieves and murderers. The goal was filled almost exclusively with them, and they had furnished a great number to the penitentiary.

As soon as they heard of my going to their city, they determined, as they have done in so many other places, to prevent me from addressing the people, even if they had to murder me.

But, by the great mercy of God, the intelligent and Christian Orangemen of the city knew all their plans, and they were determined, at any cost, to defeat them.

My greatest difficulty, on my arrival, was to find a house to dwell in. The rumor was spread that that house would surely be destroyed by the slaves of the Pope.

At last, a respectable widow, who was living honourably by keeping boarders, offered me her best room and I accepted it But my trunk had hardly been placed in the house, when a multitude of furious men surrounded it, pulled down the doors and broke the windows

This was done whilst I was delivering my first lecture.

My first words to my friends after the lecture were, " Have

385

you saved my trunks?' They answered, "Yes, sir, they are all safe in the hands of a friend."

"Have you selected another house where I can be lodged without any more trouble?" I asked

"Not yet, sir; but this will soon be done. But come and take some refreshments at a friend's house and then we will see where you can spend the night and the rest of your time among us, without any danger to your life, it not absolutely in peace; for you see the war is begun by the priests; it will be a war to the knife But we are a match for them, if they want blood they will have it to their hearts' content We cannot consent to be their slaves in our own dear city of Ballarat"

We had not proceeded far when furious cries were filling the air all around us Multitudes, armed with sticks and stones, were issuing from every side street to surround us

"Boys," cried a loud voice near me, "be calm and steady If you have to strike, see that every blow leaves its mark Do not begin the fight, but let them begin it at their risk and peril"

Had I not seen that spectacle many times before, it would have been enough to fill me with terror. But I had seen that in Quebec, Montreal, Ottawa, Charlottetown. Many times I had had the opportunity of witnessing the heroic courage and the admirable intelligence and sang-froid of the Orangemen in presence of danger. And I knew my God was by me, I felt that His mighty and merciful hand would protect us all

In that very moment, on our left, a numerous band of Irishmen, filling the air with cries of fury, rushed at us. At their head, a tall woman, brandishing a stick, ran towards me with the evident intention of striking me, but a terrible blow, struck on her face with a hard stick by my nearest Orange friend, brought her down on the pavement of stone.

It was a horrible sight to see that miserable woman, evidently half drunk, with her hair spread in the dust and her face awfully wounded and bleeding. She was crying like a wild beast, "Murder! Murder!"

At that very moment my nearest friend whispered

" My dear Father Chiniquy, we are on the eve of a terrible and bloody encounter. Please do not remain here. There is too much danger for your life. Follow me through this narrow alley, my home is at the end of it. In the present tumult nobody will see us going that way. You will spend the night in a secret room where you will be absolutely safe from any danger, so long as there is a drop of blood in my veins."

Without losing a single moment, I followed him through that narrow and dark alley, and I found everything as my kind, noble-hearted friend had promised me.

The next morning the city was filled with the noise of that terrible riot. Nobody was killed, but there were many broken noses and black eyes.

The rumor, at first, was that I had been killed, but they soon learned that I was safe in the house of a popular and worthy Presbyterian minister of the Gospel, the Rev. Mr. Quick

At first, the ministers of the city had determined to ignore me during my evangelistic work in their city, on account of the evident and terrible dangers which would accompany me wherever I might lodge.

But the wife of that worthy minister of Christ had told him at breakfast, "It is a burning shame to let Father Chiniquy expose his life in helping us to confound and fight the greatest enemy of the Gospel We ought to give him a shelter under our Christian roof. Please go and ask him to come and spend the whole time he will be in Ballarat, with us "

That noble Christian lady came nearly paying with her life for her charity towards me.

That same evening, a moment after my coming back from lecturing. she was standing by the window, when her husband remarked that that was a dangerous place. " My dear," said he, " so long as Father Chiniquy is our guest, do not stand at night before the windows, for a pistol shot or a stone can come to show your imprudence "

Strange to say, she had hardly left the window to sit in a

safe place, when a volley of big stones went through that window, broke every part of it, crossed the room and smashed into fragments a mirror at the other end of the parlour.

It would be too long and tedious to give the details of that mission in Ballarat. Suffice it to say that it was blessed by fifty Roman Catholics who left their Pope to follow Christ

I must not, however, omit saying that all our meetings were attended with more or less troubles of a dangerous character, and that the Orangemen put a guard of twelve fearless men to protect us every night.

But I cannot omit to mention a striking act of the priests of Rome against us.

The day I left, I learned, when at the railway station, that the trains were half an hour behind time.

When patiently waiting in the midst of many friends who had accompanied me to give me their last farewell, I saw a tall lady, splendidly dressed, advancing towards me at a double-quick pace.

My first thought was to move a little to the left side and let her pass, but she turned with me, and she was soon face to face with me. I thought she was a half crazy woman who wanted to kiss me. I felt ashamed and made a back step.

But she soon filled the distance I had put between her and me. Quicker than I can write these lines, she was again face to face with me.

Then, without giving me time to make a new back step, she threw from her mouth an immense quantity of dirt and spat it in my face.

I felt absolutely blinded, my eyes were utterly filled, and my face was completely covered with dirt.

In a moment she disappeared, running full speed

The reader may imagine the surprise and indignation of my numerous friends at such a public and daring insult Some of them went to get some fresh water and a towel to wash and cleanse my face, while other friends, with a policeman, were running after the strange woman

Ten minutes later my face was cleansed, but my eyes were very dim. However, I could see enough to observe the indignation of the crowd

The tall lady, trembling and pale as death, was standing by me, in the midst of the multitude by whom I was surrounded

My secretary told me: ' Here is the miserable woman who has just now so cruelly insulted you. What do you wish us to do with her?"

Looking at her, I said: "Is it not your Father Confessor who ordered you to do that action?"

With trembling voice she answered· "Yes, sir. It was my Father Confessor who ordered me to do that "

Then looking to the people by whom I was surrounded, I said:

"Did our Saviour order those who spat in His face to be punished? No. But He forgave them, so I do not wish this woman to be punished. Let her go back home in peace "

I forgave her what she had done me.

A few minutes later I departed on the next train.

After a few days of evangelistic labour in some of the thriving towns and villages around Ballarat, the good Mr Cameron, of Horsham, persuaded me to go and spend a couple of days in his interesting town about one hundred miles distant

All along the way I had again to admire the vast and so well cultivated fields, the splendid cattle, many thousands of sheep, waiting for the scissors of the shearers or the cruel knife of the butcher.

The splendid cottage of Mr Cameron was fitted with all that good taste and wealth could offer to make a home pleasant and healthful I really felt delighted when receiving the noble hospitality of that gentleman and his accomplished lady in that distant land He took me at night to the church where I was to deliver my lecture. The distance was not more than two miles.

When on the way he told me, " We have nothing to fear, here, this evening from the Roman Catholics. Their village

is more than five miles distant from ours   They surely will
not travel such a long distance to trouble us, and the few who
live with us have always been peaceful "

"You must not rely too much on those circumstances to
hope for peace this night," I answered him. "The Irish
Roman Catholics, like the wolves of the prairies, can travel
more than five miles to quench their thirst for mischief and
blood.   Though naturally good, intelligent, brave, hospitable
and religious, they are turned into wild beasts by their monks
and priests, not only in Ireland, but everywhere they go.   Let
us pray God to protect us this night, if your good minister
and his people have done nothing to prevent the Irish from
giving us new tokens of their cruel fanaticism.   For such wild
beasts, half drunk, it would not take much time to travel five
or six miles to disturb our meeting if it is their priest's mind
to do it."

My address was not yet finished when a volley of stones broke
all the windows, struck me and many of my hearers.

Let the reader understand the horror of our situation
when I tell him that, relying on the distance of the Irish
village, not a single one had taken any weapon, not even a
cane, to comfort and protect himself   We were absolutely
in their hands and at their mercy, for they were evidently
all armed with stones, sticks, etc.

Their usual furious and beastly cries were filling the air
"Kill him! Kill him!" was heard from all sides around
the church   Inside the church the cries of the ladies and
the supplications of many Protestants were the sad and only
music in my ears, after my address.

Mr. Cameron came to me and whispered in my ear· "Do
not go out of the church, for they are watching you, and
they will surely kill you if they find an opportunity   The
only way to escape I see is in a secret back door, of which,
providentially, I have the key with me.   They know nothing
about that door.   Go through it and walk straight on till you
find a large and deep ditch, usually half filled with mud and

water. When there, walk the best you can towards your left Keep your head down as much as possible, for though it is very dark, they might see you when they will cross the ditch in search of you. Walk nearly half a mile in that ditch, and then you will meet me with my carriage. I will be there in the dark, with Mrs. Cameron, waiting for you, and I hope by the mercy of God I will take you safely to my home."

A few minutes later I was in that ditch, which I shall never forget, though I might live a thousand years. I found it deeper and filled with more water than I had expected. In many places I had to crawl on my hands and knees in order not to be seen, for I was constantly hearing voices saying· "Where is he? Where is he?" when my would=be murderers were jumping over it some times at a very short distance from me.

Though I had hardly a mile to walk, or rather crawl, I found the way very long and exhausting. I was absolutely out of breath when I found myself at the end of it. I surely looked more like a frog than a man when they helped me to my seat in the carriage.

But we were not yet at the end of our journey How can I tell you what our feelings were when we found that during our absence the beautiful and richly furnished cottage had been visited by my would=be murderers? When those faithful servants of the Pope had found that we were not there, and could not kill us, they had destroyed everything they could lay their hands on. The rich and beautiful piano was destroyed, the fine glasses on the walls, and the chairs and sofas were broken into fragments. They did not set fire to the house only for fear that the light would make them known when moving away from the spot.

CHAPTER XXXVI

Abbe Fluet's Conversion, Temptation and Final Triumphs.

The 10th of July, 1881, I received the following letter:—

"Sandwich.

"Dear Mr. Chiniquy·—

"My dear father is very sick. He has not many days to live. He wants you to be by his side in these solemn days to help him to prepare himself to die, as he has lived, a true Christian.

"Please grant us that favour

"Respectfully yours,

"(Signed) MARY WILLIAMS,

"née Fluet."

The reader will ask me, "Who is that Fluet who wants you by his bedside when at his last hour of life?"

My regret, when answering that question is that I have only a short chapter to offer, when I could write such an interesting volume on that remarkable man, the first French Canadian Roman Catholic priest whom I have known brave enough to throw off the heavy and ignominious yoke of the Pope to follow Christ.

In the year 1831, when a professor of belles-lettres in the college of Nicolet, the director, Rev. I. Leprohon. used very often to show his friendly feelings in sitting by me during the hours of recreation, under the shadows of the giant pine-trees, which made an earthly paradise of that never-to-be-forgotten spot.

That venerable man was my benefactor. I loved him as a father and I venerated him as a saint.

Though many times he expressed his desire that I should become his successor as director of that college, I refused to consent. The principal object of his conversations was to initiate me into the numerous little mysteries, difficulties and responsibilities of his position He was often speaking of the difficult art of knowing the characters of the men by whom we are surrounded, in order to become a source of blessing and usefulness to them

This caused me one day to put him the following question·

" As you have been the director of this college for more than twenty years, you have had to deal with a great number of professors; is it an indiscretion to ask you whom you consider the best among the many ecclesiastics and professors who have laboured under you while the director of the college at Nicolet? "

He answered me " Your question is a very delicate one, and the answer you want is still more delicate and difficult Give me twenty-four hours to think and I will answer you."

My curiosity was not a little stimulated by that promise I was longing for the moment when I would know the name of the most worthy man who had served as professor and teacher in that college of Nicolet which was so dear to me.

I was not a little pleased, when, the next day, I saw him coming to me with such a smiling face that I could see I was not to be disappointed.

After the most mature consideration, he said " The best professor and the most perfect ecclesiastic I have known in the college of Nicolet is Mr. Fluet I have never seen a man so gifted with all the virtues which make a true Christian and a perfect gentleman. As you were his most intimate friend, you remember how he was constantly referring to his New Testament on almost every subject of conversation. The name of Jesus, so often on his lips, was the sure indication that he was keeping himself as perfectly united to our Saviour as a man can be. His knowledge as a theologian and a philosopher was above everything I have seen among my acquaintances. To those moral qualities, the good providence of God has given him some of the highest physical qualities of the body   He was one of the most handsome men, and he had one of the sweetest and most melodious voices I have ever heard."

"I then can answer your question of yesterday by assuring you that Mr. Fluet was the most accomplished professor the college of Nicolet ever had.   I have not known any one who gained the esteem and commanded the respect of all in our college as Fluet did

"The day he left us to be ordained a priest and go as a missionary to Sandwich, was a day of universal sorrow.   But we consoled ourselves of his absence by the knowledge of the good he is doing in the vast missionary field of the west of Canada where he is working since he left us.

"The details he gives me in all his letters of his missionary labours very often draw my tears of admiration and gratitude to God.   It is surely an honour and blessing for the college of Nicolet to have given such a priest to the Church "

I answered Mr. Leprohon "You have not exaggerated the good qualities of Mr. Fluet.   As I had been his most intimate friend when he was with us, the more I knew him the more I admired him."

This conversation had done me much good.   I felt happy to see that my respected superior was sharing my views about my friend   My last thought when going to bed at the close of that day was to thank God for having given me such a friend.

The next day was a stormy day, which I could never forget should I live a thousand years   Two of our noblest pine-trees had been shattered into fragments by the lightning and brought down by the hurricane with a terrible noise.

It seemed impossible to get any mail in such a storm, but in this we were to be happily disappointed; for our long-wished-for letters arrived, though six hours later than usual.

However, I was among the disappointed of that day.   No letters for me.   My business was then to look at the more lucky ones whose eyes were running from line to line of the messages they had received   My attention was particularly riveted on our good director, Mr Leprohon, who, convulsively raising his hands towards heaven, was crying. "My God! My God! This is not possible. This cannot be!"

Suspecting that he had received the sad news of the death of some dear friend or relative, I kept silent to show my respect for his grief.

But after a few moments of unspeakable grief, turning towards me, he said, "Dear Chiniquy, I have just received the most deplorable, the most incredible news   I do not dare to tell it to you. It is incredible. My God! This is not possible! I cannot consent to give you such a deplorable message   Try to find it out   But you cannot"

After a moment of silent anxiety and surprise I answered, "You have just received the saddest, the most incredible news which could come to you and to me, and you want me to guess at it? Well! Well! The most incredible and the saddest news that can come to me is that Mr. Fluet has become an apostate, and that he has turned to be a Protestant."

"How can you say that?" replied Mr Leprohon, with an accent of terror and unmistakable sorrow.

"Because it comes to my mind as a flash of lightning as being the most incredible and the most desolating news I can receive." I answered

"This is more than strange," replied Mr. Leprohon. "You are correct; Fluet is an apostate. He has just publicly abandoned our holy religion. He is a Protestant"

This news spread like a thunderbolt all over Canada And it created unspeakable surprise and sorrow wherever it was told

No French Canadian Roman Catholic priest had left our Church for more than sixty years   The humble people of the country, as well as the highly educated ones of the city, had almost come to the conclusion that their religion of Rome was on such sure foundations that nothing could shake it

Of course since my conversion, they had a good opportunity to change their minds, as hundreds of priests and monks have left the Pope to follow Christ, in America

The following facts were also calculated to give them more correct views.

In the spring of 1851, just twenty years later, the Bishop of Chicago, my Lord Vandevelde, having asked me to go to the State of Illinois in order to direct the tide of the French speaking emigrants from France, Belgium and Canada towards the magnificent plains of that state, in order to form a new France, I went to ask the benediction of my Lord Bourget, Bishop of Montreal.   After receiving it I told him "My Lord, you know that I cannot go to Illinois without passing through Sandwich, which is on this side of the River St Clair, the dividing line between the United States and Canada Allow me to tell you that I cannot pass by Sandwich without saluting my old friend, the Rev. Mr Fluet, and making an effort to help him to come back to our holy Church, of which he has been so long one of the most devoted and respected priests   I have invited the Rev Mr Brassard, curate of Longueuil, to accompany me, for he was one of the most devoted friends of Mr. Fluet.   I hope that our united efforts, with the help of God, will determine that stray sheep to come back to the true fold."

"Oh!" cried Bishop Bourget, "yes, go and bring back that stray sheep.   I will do anything to help you in this holy work. I will immediately write to all our priests and good nuns to unite in prayer, that you may succeed   Oh! what a victory over the enemy of our holy Church if you can persuade Mr. Fluet to come back to us   I have known him personally and I had such a high opinion of his piety, his zeal and his matchless capacity "

"Yes, my Lord," I answered, "this is all right, but you must not forget that Mr Fluet is married, that he is poor and that he has at least three or four children.   It would be more than ridiculous and unbecoming to invite him to let that woman and those children starve by deserting them in that cowardly way. We cannot extend to him a helping hand out of the bottomless pit into which he has fallen without presenting to his wife and children the means of an honest living."

"You are right, Mr. Chiniquy, you are perfectly right,' said the Bishop. ' We cannot invite Rev. Fluet to let his wife and children starve, after his conversion. How much do you think that we must offer him for the support of his family?"

" We cannot offer him less than $10,000,· I answered

"Though it is a pretty big sum to give, I will ask the advice of my secretary and my other counselors, and if they are of the same mind with me, you shall have the money you want. Ten thousand dollars are nothing to our holy Church compared with the loss of a priest like Mr. Fluet."

To the honour of the counselors of the Bishop, I am happy to say that in less than half an hour, the $10,000 were safe in my little purse, and I was on my way to Lachine to the steamer which was to take us to Detroit. Three days later we were in the beautiful parlour of Mr Baby, the judge of Sandwich, on the Canadian shore. A few years before I had made the acquaintance of that gentleman in Quebec, and I had known from his own lips that he used to employ Mr. Fluet as his legal advisor, and had business to transact with him almost every day. He had said to me, "The only defect of Mr Fluet is that he is a Protestant. Apart from that he is a true gentleman, and one of the most honest men I have ever known."

No words can give an idea of Judge Baby's surprise when Mr. Brassard and I told him that we were the most devoted admirers of Mr. Fluet while in the Seminary of Nicolet, and that we had come to Sandwich to make a supreme effort to bring him back to our holy religion.

"My impression is that you would easily succeed if he were alone. Though a Protestant and an apostate, he is not such an enemy of our holy Church as people think. He is the best gardener of Sandwich and you will find in his garden

the most beautiful flowers which can grow in Canada. And
do you know what he does with a part of those flowers? I
would not believe it had I not seen it with my own eyes.
Once and often twice a week he makes one or two splendid
bouquets with them which he asks his young daughters to put
on the altar of our Church. The greatest difficulty you will
meet is his poverty. His wife and children would surely
starve if they had not the modest income derived from his
daily work among us as notary."

I then showed him my cheque of $10,000 for the support of
Mrs Fluet and her children in case they would all consent
to become Roman Catholics, and let her husband make his
peace with the Church he has denied.

"This $10,000 may be a great factor in your holy mission,"
said Judge Baby, "but I see a more formidable obstacle in
the character of Mrs. Fluet. She is a most honourable lady,
but her character and her will are formed of granite of the
hardest quality. She sincerely loves and respects her husband, and she is one of the most dutiful and loving mothers I
have ever seen. Like a furious lioness, she will tear the hand
which will take her children from her and she will demolish
those who will try to deprive her of her husband."

I met the objections of Judge Baby by saying that I
knew the success of our mission required a true miracle of
the grace of God, but my faith was strong enough to hope
that that miracle would be wrought. "The first thing we
have to do," I said, "is to meet Mr Fluet. He knows nothing
of our presence here. He would at once come here if
you had the kindness to address him a short note saying that
you want him for an important business. You have told us
that he is your notary. No doubt he is accustomed to come
and see you often about his legal business."

"That is just what I will do. Remain in the parlour waiting for Mr Fluet, who will be here in a few moments." An
hour later Mr Fluet was knocking at the door, expecting to
meet Judge Baby

Though he had not seen us for just twenty years, he recognized us at once.

With a cry mixed with joy and surprise, he exclaimed, "Merciful God! Brassard and Chiniquy here!" Half fainting with his uncontrollable emotion, he threw himself into our arms, without being able to utter any other words than " Brassard and Chiniquy here!" Torrents of tears which ran down his cheeks helped him to come to himself. Bathing our hands with his tears he was crying, " Is it possible they think of me and still love me in Canada?" " Yes, we think of you and we still love you in Canada. You see it in our presence here. It is in the name of your former friends, the priests and the Bishop of Montreal, that we come to salute you and to press you to our hearts."

After at least an hour of the most friendly conversation about his old acquaintances in Canada, I introduced the delicate and real subject of our mission, but in such a friendly manner that he could not be offended.

"I understand and respect the object of your visit," he said " My only surprise is that you have so long delayed it. But do not forget that I am married and that I have four children St Paul says marriage is a great mystery It makes only one of two human beings We must be one, not only in body, but in mind and aspirations I cannot tell what I can do without consulting Mrs Fluet. I am going back home at 4 P. M. and I will give you my answer, rather her answer," he added with the most amiable smile.

The $10,000 note I had shown him had not drawn from him the expression of gratitude I expected. He had refused to touch it, and only said when looking at it. " It is very kind and generous on the part of the Bishop and the priests of Canada "

The hours from 10 A M. to 4 P. M seemed to me as long as a century. My heart was throbbing between the hope of success and the fear of disappointment

At last the clock struck four and our friend was again pressing us to his bosom.

The preliminaries of this last conversation were short, and to my anxious question, "What news do you bring us?" he answered·

"I never saw anything like the wrath and indignation of my wife, when I told her the message you had brought from Canada for us both 'Is it possible,' she said, 'that the priests of Rome are so degraded and so blind as to believe that their money could tempt me to break the sacred and most blessed ties that unite me to you? Go and tell them that there is not gold enough in Canada, nor in the whole world, to tempt me to trample under my feet the honoured and blessed crowns of wife and mother which the great God that governs this world has given me. I love you, Mr Fluet; you know it, but do not forget it, it is my conviction that there are not tortures enough on earth to punish you as you deserve if you were deserting me to go back and wallow in the mire in which the priests of Rome are living To split your head with an ax with my own hands would be too mild a vengeance for the crime you would commit in deserting me to obey the precepts of a church which I know, as well as you is the masterpiece of the devil, etc.'

"Please do not ask me to give you in detail all the compliments she paid you for your friendly message. You now hear enough to show you that it is absolutely impossible for me to break the sacred ties which have made me the happy father of children, who with me will bless the good God of heaven during all eternity for their existence. But I hope that this stern determination of Mrs. Fluet will not break the blessed ties of friendship which united us together."

With these words he shook hands with us and went back to his happy home

"It is just as I expected," said Judge Baby. "Mr Fluet's family is one of the most happy and respectable at Sandwich He is not rich, but he has enough for the every day wants Though he is not an aggressive man, in that he does not preach against our holy religion, his example does a great injury to our Church. Our priests have made a terrible mistake by publishing that he was a drunkard, a wicked man who was beating his wife They know that these reports are vile calumnies, for Mr. Fluet is a perfect example of sobriety, being one of our most faithful teetotalers."

Though I failed in my efforts to persuade him to make his peace with the Church of Rome, I kept up a course of friendly letters with him when forming my French colony in Illinois

The reader may imagine his joy when I wrote him all about my conversion. He answered me with a letter bathed with tears of joy.

CHAPTER XXXVII

The Truth Proclaimed at Montague. Narrow Escape. Brutally Struck Whilst on the Steamer. I Forgive My Aggressor.

The 6th of August, 1886, I arrived at Montague, one of the most interesting towns of Prince Edward Island The weather was splendid. Mr. McLeod who gave me hospitality in his house, after extending to me a most hearty welcome, said: "There is great excitement in the town on account of your coming, but we have a good number of Orangemen here, and with the help of God we will protect you.

At the evening meeting the fine new church was crowded to its utmost capacity. Among the crowd were many Irish Roman Catholics and some French Canadians. The address was on the idolatry of the Church of Rome, which worships a god made with a wafer To my great joy several Romanists came to shake hands with me at the close of my address, saying· "Thank you, you have said the truth we will no longer worship a god made by the servants of the priests."

I blessed God for the result of that address, and my hope was that my humble labours there would be fructified by the God of the Gospel

When my hostess showed me to my room at night I remarked that it was very near the street. and that it was too much exposed to the stones of the rioters, if there should be any trouble in the night. Then the good lady gave me another room which could not be exposed to the stones from the street. We went to bed after asking God to protect us during the night. He had heard our prayer and granted our humble petition.

At about twelve o'clock—the night was very dark—I was awakened by a frightful noise. Evidently the window of

402

the first room which the good lady had prepared for me was smashed to pieces, and stone after stone was pouring into the room I kept as quiet as possible in my room that they might not see their error. Of course no one was hurt, as there was no one there. The reader may imagine the excitement in the morning when the people came to see the broken window and the many big stones on the floor and on the bed, every one of which could have killed a man I had to thank God for having inspired me not to take that room, for I surely would have been killed there Many friends came during the forenoon to congratulate me on my narrow escape, and I joined my thanksgiving to theirs, to the God of the Gospel who had so visibly protected me. Several friends proposed to make legal inquiries to find out the rioters and the would-be murderers, but I prevented them, saying that the best thing we could do was to follow the example of our Saviour, " Forgive and forget "

As I was to give an address that same evening in another place, I prepared myself to take the steamer which was to leave at noon, but when on the boat I saw that I had made a mistake; I found that the steamer instead of leaving at noon, was to leave only at 2 P M. The captain and his crew were on shore taking their dinner I had dismissed the friends who had accompanied me to the steamer and I remained alone with a few passengers I took a chair and sat on the rear of the deck reading my Bible I had not been there long when I heard rapid steps approaching me, and, looking up, I saw a giant man, with rough face, walking up to me and uttering terrible imprecations, saying " D—— apostate! this is your last day!"

My first thought was that it was his intention to throw me overboard. I cried to my God for help But I was mistaken. Instead of trying to throw me into the water, he raised his terrible arm and gave me a blow evidently intended for my left temple. By the mercy of God he missed his aim, for he would surely have killed me instantly had he struck the temple His fist struck the cheek-bone, one of the strongest parts of the human body. I fell unconscious on the deck, where I suppose I remained two or three minutes When I came back to myself I found three good ladies washing my face with cold water and crying "My God! my God! he has killed him!" My mouth was filled with blood and my nose was bleeding profusely, trying to speak I felt that one of my teeth was broken. Quite a crowd of friends surrounded me and helped me to stand upon my feet, expressing their indignation at the brutal attack of which I had been the victim.

A few minutes later another crowd arrived, having in their midst my would-be murderer. These were Orangemen who were working on the shore near the steamer, and who had seen him when he struck me. Quick as lightning everyone of them had armed himself with sticks and was running after the faithful servant of the Pope. Having overpowered him they forced him to march back to me in order that I might have him punished as he deserved One of them said "Here is the infamous coward who has just struck you, we saw him from the shore, and we have brought him back to you that you may tell us what to do with him and he be punished as he deserves." I answered him· "My dear friends, when our dear Saviour was struck on one cheek, did He ask His Father or His apostles to punish and strike his enemies? No. On the cross where He was nailed He prayed to His Father for those who had crucified Him, saying 'Father, forgive them, for they know not what they do.' Well, the only thing we have to do is to dismiss the man, and to pray our Heavenly Father that He may help him to know the Gospel truth, and to give up the errors of the Church of Rome which has made him so blind and so cruel. Give me his name and let him go" They told me that his name was Wm S Monds

The empty place of the missing tooth is a daily witness of what I have suffered for my dear Saviour's sake, and I bless Him for it.

CHAPTER XXXVIII

A Vindication

I am become a fool in glorying, ye have compelled me. 2 Cor. 12:2.

Paul, being calumniated by false disciples, felt bound to vindicate himself and to show how fully his apostolic position was evidenced by his life and his fruitful labors.

False disciples having yet the same method of attack as those in the time of Paul, must be fought with the same weapons as those of the apostle

Again and again since my conversion to Protestantism I have read in the Roman Catholic press that no respectable Protestant would have anything to do with me Such slanders were specially current about the year 1892, and formed a part of a great scheme plotted by the Roman Catholic clergy of Canada, no doubt the evident purpose of which was to take away my honour, to kill me morally, seeing that the various attempts to take away my life had been frustrated.

It was so manifestly the case that even newspapers could not help noticing it.

If you look in the file of the *Montreal Witness* for the year 1892. you can read in an editorial of the 10th of March the following item:

"We see by an Iowa paper that Mr. Chiniquy is lecturing there and that he is pursued by carefully concocted slander of the vilest kind, which would appear to have been furnished by some slander bureau in Canada

"Such attacks, when publicly made where Mr. Chiniquy is known, are comparatively harmless, as he is well able to shame his slanderers, and they only furnish him with a more effective text.   It is a sufficient answer to such abuse that though he has been similarly vilified ever since he left the Church of Rome, he is still, as he has been for over twenty years, a minister in good standing of the Presbyterian Church of Canada."

A Roman Catholic under the name of *Kentucky Ben* having published in that same paper similar stupid slanders, I thought I was in duty bound to write and publish an answer. As many new facts and events of my forty years in the Church of Christ are brought out in that answer, I judge it proper to insert it in this book.

"Editor of *The Witness:*

"Sir —If your Protestant readers have had as much pleasure as myself in perusing the last article of my Roman Catholic friend, 'Kentucky Ben,' they will unite with me in addressing him our public thanks   For that correspondent does not touch a single point of the subject of the controversy. In order to enjoy the pleasure of personal abuse and slander, he has not only given to your readers the best proof that my arguments were unanswerable, but he has also shown what kind of honesty and truthfulness we must expect when arguing with a Roman Catholic

"Yes! let your readers see again his first article and my answer, with his last reply, and they will find that no attempt has been made to touch a single one of my arguments And why so?   It is simply because Roman Catholics, being unable to meet us on the fair ground of argument, are forced to shift the questions, and they resort to abuse, of which they always have a rich stock   Finding himself utterly incapable of denying or of refuting the blasphemous and idolatrous teachings of his Church, which I had copied word by word from his most approved authors, he thought that he would forever crush me into atoms by calling me 'apostate,' and by assuring you that 'No respectable

Protestant . . would associate with him' (Chiniquy) But, as he has not deigned to give any proof of my public degradation and rejection from the company and intercourse with respectable Protestants, I will fill that gap and give you a few facts which will show that not only 'Kentucky Ben,' but that all the Bishops and priests of Canada, with the whole Roman Catholic press of Montreal and Quebec, are honest when they proclaim from morning till night these last thirty years that the apostate Chiniquy is so degraded that 'No respectable Protestant would associate with him.'

"Surely, they will be grateful to me for giving them the unanswerable proofs of that supreme degradation, under the burden of which I am crushed to the ground.

"*First Fact* A few months after my conversion from Romanism to the truth as it is in Jesus Christ, my people of St. Anne, Illinois, were visited in 1859 by a terrible calamity. They lost their crops, and they had not enough to live on two months The ministers and people of Washington, Baltimore, Philadelphia, New York, Boston, Plattsburg, Springfield, Chicago, Lafayette and many other cities, having heard of that calamity, invited me to go and address them During the three months I spoke to these people, the large churches and the immense halls were never large enough for the multitudes who wanted to hear me Those multitudes not only wanted to have a little talk with the infamous apostate Chiniquy—but they wanted to press his hand—and when pressing his hands, they let $75,000 slip into them as a public token of their horror and contempt for him. Those $75,000 not only saved my dear colony of St Anne from a sure ruin, but they became the first irrefutable proof that Chiniquy was so degraded that no respectable Protestant would associate with him

"*Second Fact:* The next year, 1860 was the three hundreth anniversary of the Protestant Reformation of Scotland. An evangelical festivity such as the world had never seen was prepared in Edinburgh, to which the most prominent Protestant ministers and laymen were invited. The committee appointed to make those invitations in the name of the Scotch people were Rev Doctors Guthrie, Cunningham and Begg These gentlemen wrote me a most polite invitation to go and attend their grand meeting in Edinburgh. When I arrived in the midst of that venerable assembly, there were such cries of joy, such clapping of hands, such stamping of feet, such manifestations of joy that, for a long time, it was impossible for me or anybody else to say a word. Though the rule had been passed that no orator should speak more than once, I was asked and forced to speak three times After the assembly, four hundred of the principal ministers pressed me to go and address their people and I spent six months lecturing in the cities of London, Glasgow, Liverpool, Birmingham, Bath, Manchester, Brampton, Sheffield, Oxford, Edinburgh, Armagh, Kingstown, Queenstown, York, etc   To show me further their supreme contempt for my person and my work, as proclaimed by Mr. 'Kentucky Ben,' they gave me $25,000 before I left their noble country, for my humble labour.

"*Third Fact*.   When I was lecturing in Glasgow, the richest merchant of that city, John Henderson, invited me to his magnificent mansion that I might take a few days of rest The second day he invited a great number of the ministers of Glasgow to a soirée, at the end of which he presented me with a purse filled with $2,000 in gold, that Mr 'Kentucky Ben' and the whole Roman Catholic people might understand and publish that 'the apostate Chiniquy was so degraded that no respectable Protestant would associate with him.'

"*Fourth Fact*   When I was lecturing in Great Britain, the Synod of the Free Protestant Church of France, which was held at St. Etienne, invited me, through their illustrious president, Frederic Monod, to attend their meetings. I accepted that honour. I went to St Etienne and addressed that venerable Church of France twice, that I might give a proof to **Mr.** 'Kentucky Ben' that no respectable Protestant would have anything to do with the infamous apostate Chiniquy

"*Fifth Fact·* When I went back to my colony of St Anne, Illinois, in 1861, I was the witness of the terrible civil war between the North and the South of the United States As I was the personal friend of President Abraham Lincoln, I used to visit him every year in his grand white mansion at Washington. and that illustrious man each time overwhelmed me with the marks of his esteem. But the last time he gave me such a grand proof of it that I think it is my duty here to tell it. It was on the 8th of June, 1864, he told me·

" 'To-morrow afternoon I will receive the delegation of the deputies of all the loyal states sent to officially announce the desire of the country that I should remain the President four years more. I invite you to be present with them at that interesting meeting. You will see some of the most prominent men of our Republic, and I will be happy to introduce you to them. You will not present yourself as a delegate of the people, but only as the guest of the President, and, that there may be no trouble, I give you this card with a permit to enter with the delegation. But do not leave Washington before I see you again. I have some important matter on which I want to know your mind.'

"And the next day that infamous apostate Chiniquy was put the first at the right hand of the Protestant President of the United States, and introduced by him to the most illustrious Protestants of that great Republic, that my friend, 'Kentucky Ben,' and all his compeers in the Church of Rome might have the right to proclaim to their people, that the 'apostate Chiniquy is so degraded that no respectable Protestant would associate with him'

"*Sixth Fact·* In 1874 the whole Protestant people of England wanted to congratulate the German Emperor and his Prime Minister, Bismarck, for the noble rebuke they had given to the Pope, when he (the Pope) had so insolently written to the Emperor that, because he had been baptized, he ought to consider himself a spiritual subject of the Pope

"A grand meeting was convoked at the splendid Exeter Hall of London, when the best Protestant orators of the time were selected to speak and prepare the address which was to be put into the hands of the German ambassador for his Emperor

"Well, the committee of organization of the memorable assembly requested me in a polite letter to go again to England to address that meeting, and I went I spoke there twice in the presence of all England's noblest Protestant sons and daughters.

"These providential and surely unmerited honours were given me that the Bishops and priests of Rome might proclaim with all their trumpets and through Mr. 'Kentucky Ben,' that the 'apostate Chiniquy was so degraded that no respectable Protestant would associate with him'

"*Seventh Fact* · I forgot to mention that the first time I addressed the people of London in their immense Exeter Hall, the crowd was so great that thousands of people had been unable to enter That the Rev Mr Spurgeon had introduced me to the people of that great metropolitan city of England, and that the Viceroy, one of the greatest heroes of India, Sir John Lawrence, had consented to act as the president of that meeting. These three facts prove to a certainty that the priests of Rome and Mr. 'Kentucky Ben' are perfectly honest when they assure their people that the 'apostate Chiniquy is so degraded that no respectable Protestant would associate with him.'

"*Eighth Fact* · The second time I was invited to go to England in order to congratulate the Emperor of Germany, in 1874, two hundred ministers requested me not to leave their country before addressing their people on the errors and idolatries of the Church of Rome And I spent again six months in lecturing on those sad subjects in one hundred and twenty of the cities of Great Britain. The noble Protestant people gave me again $28,000 as the expression of their Christian sympathies, that the whole world might know that the priests of Rome and Mr 'Kentucky Ben' are perfectly honest when they say that I was so degraded in the eyes of the Protestants that no respectable person would have anything to do with me

"*Ninth Fact:* When I returned from that second excursion to England the grand Presbyterian Church of Canada wanted me to leave my dear mission of Illinois in order to preach to my French-Canadian countrymen of Canada. They rented a good, comfortable house in Montreal for me and my family, and gave me a sum of money much above my merit for my work. In unity and under the supervision of that grand Presbyterian Church, I laboured from 1874 to 1878 in Canada with such an admirable success that four thousand French-Canadians of Montreal and vicinity left the errors and idolatries of Rome to accept the Gospel of Christ, and they formed several congregations of converts I stopped that work only when, being quite exhausted, I was ordered by my physician to go and take the bracing air of the Pacific Ocean in 1878.

"During these four years almost all the ministers of Montreal had requested me to address their people, and it was my privilege to speak in Montreal, Toronto, Kingston, London, Guelph, Sarnia, Windsor, Quebec, Halifax, St. Johns. N. B., Peterboro, Muskoka, Ottawa, Bothwell, Belleville, Brockville, Dundas, Hamilton, and two hundred and fifty other cities and towns.

"These facts are evidence again that the priests of Rome and 'Kentucky Ben' are perfectly honest when they proclaim and publish that I was so degraded that the Protestants who have any respect for themselves would have nothing to do with me

"*Tenth Fact.* In 1878, when preparing to go and breathe the bracing atmosphere of the Pacific Ocean, I providentially received a kind letter from the Rev George Sutherland, D D., pastor of one of the richest and most influential congre-

gations of Sydney, New South Wales, Australia   He invited
me in the name of the Protestant people of that distant land
to go and visit them   There was a bank-note in that letter of
$500 to help me to pay my traveling expenses, and to help
Mr "Kentucky Ben" and all the priests of Rome to prove
that the infamous apostate Chiniquy was so degraded that
no respectable Protestant would associate with him.

"*Eleventh Fact* When the principal Protestants of Sydney
heard that the steamer which was taking me to their young,
but already so grand country, was in sight, they engaged a
steamer to come and receive me in triumph, at a distance of
twelve miles, that the honest priests of the Church of Rome,
with 'Mr Kentucky Ben,' might have a good opportunity to
publish that the apostate Chiniquy's moral degradation is so
well known to the whole world that 'no respectable Protestant would associate with him '

"*Twelfth Fact*. I spent two years in Australia, Tasmania,
and New Zealand   All that time the Protestant ministers and
people overwhelmed me with public and personal tokens of
the kindest Christian respect and feeling. I dare say they
took me in triumph from one extremity to the other of their
vast countries. Having known from the most reliable
sources that there was a plot among the Roman Catholics to
murder me, they put a guard, almost every night for more
than a year, of twelve and twenty men to protect me. Their
large churches and halls were never large enough for the
multitudes who wanted to see and hear me. Several times
they fought like lions, and several were wounded when they
wanted to repulse the blind Roman Catholics sent by the
priests to kill me. In Hobert Town, they requested the
Governor of Tasmania to use a militia force in order to protect and save my life. I gave seven hundred addresses,
lectures and sermons to those dear and noble Protestant
friends whom my God had given me in those distant lands,
and they gave me $40,000 as a token of their kind feelings
when I was in their midst; and it is in the presence of those

public facts that Mr. 'Kentucky Ben' repeats what he hears every day from the lips of his priests and what he reads in their daily and weekly press. "That the apostate Chiniquy's moral degradation is such that no respectable Protestant would associate with him."

"*Thirteenth Fact*· At the June meeting of the General Assembly of the Presbyterian Church of 1889, some members having said that in a few days Father Chiniquy was to celebrate his eightieth anniversary, there was such a burst of applause as I never heard before. Rev. Dr. MacVicar, president of the Presbyterian College of Montreal, and Rev. Dr. Warden, secretary-treasurer, moved that the whole assembly should give me a vote of congratulation as a public token of their esteem. After that vote was unanimously given he asked the General Assembly to invite me to write a new book under the name of "Thirty Years in the Church of Christ," as a sequel to my last book, 'Fifty Years in the Church of Rome,' and this vote was passed unanimously in the midst of the greatest enthusiasm and good feelings I ever saw. And it is only a few days after such public facts that all the echoes of the Church of Rome proclaim what the priests and the Bishops and their press say with Mr. 'Kentucky Ben': 'that the apostate Chiniquy's degradation is so complete that no Protestant who has any self-respect would associate with him.'

"*Fourteenth Fact*· When in England in 1860, great receptions were given me by some of the most eminent Protestants of Great Britain. I will mention only a few for the edification of the Bishops and priests of Rome, who constantly assure their people that my degradation is as complete among the Protestants as it is among the Roman Catholics. The first invitation was from Dr. Tait, Lord Bishop of London, who was soon after named the Primate of England and raised to the highest dignity of the Church of England by being named Archbishop of Canterbury. That grand reception was given me in the historical Palace of

Lambeth, where I was surrounded by some of the most prominent men of the Protestant Church, among whom was the Right Rev. Dr. Thomas, now Bishop of Geelong, Australia. The second reception given me which I will mention was by Lord Gainsborough, whose wife was the first attending lady of the Queen of England. At his table and in his magnificent salon I was surrounded by the elite of the nobility of Great Britain. They spent the evening by questioning me about the superstitions and idolatries of Rome, and the hope I had of seeing the dear people of Canada following the example of England by breaking the heavy and ignominious yoke of the Pope; they really overwhelmed me with the tokens of their kind and Christian feeling. In the course of the evening, Lady Gainsborough invited a young duchess to go round her noble guests to receive the offerings they wished to give me for the support of my mission among my countrymen, and she brought me two hundred and fifty gold guineas, that Mr 'Kentucky Ben,' and all the Bishops, cardinals and priests of Rome, with their truth loving press, might have good reasons to publish that the apostate Chiniquy was so degraded that no Protestant who had any self-respect would have any thing to do with him.

"I might speak of the other receptions given me by Lord Roden, by Sir Arthur Kinnaird, M. P. for Edinburgh, and many others, but I suppose that my intelligent readers have got proofs enough to convince them that the priests and Bishops of Rome with Mr 'Kentucky Ben' are real gentlemen and most honest, fair-play-loving men, when they tell you that the infamous apostate Chiniquy is so degraded that no respectable Protestants have ever consented to have intercourse with him since he left the Holy(?) Catholic(?) and Apostolic(?) Church of Rome.

"*Fifteenth Fact*. However, there is another fact which so clearly shows that the Bishops and the priests of Rome, with Mr 'Kentucky Ben,' are honest, reliable and lovers of truth when they speak of the apostate Chiniquy, that I cannot omit it.

"Since my God has opened my eyes to the corruption, superstitions and idolatries of Rome, I have considered it my duty to publish, not all—it would be too horrible—but a part of the mysteries and iniquities which I saw when within the walls of that modern Babylon, and I have written a good number of pamphlets and books—among the principal of which are· 'The Priest, the Woman and the Confessional'; and 'Fifty Years in the Church of Rome' Well, to prove their supreme contempt, the Protestant nations of Europe and America have translated my books into their languages, and they have bought a prodigious number of them They have been translated into the languages of Italy, France, Spain, Denmark, Sweden, Germany, and Bohemia.

"The 'Priest the Woman and the Confessional' is in its fiftieth edition, though it was published for the first time in 1874; and 'Fifty Years in the Church of Rome' is at its twentieth edition, though published in 1884 Two hundred thousand copies of my lectures have already been sold, and more than 100,000 copies of 'The God of Rome Eaten by a Rat' have been bought in England, and still more on the continent of America. More than a million, then, of my books and pamphlets have been purchased by the Protestants within twenty years, to show to the priests of Rome that they are perfectly true, honourable and honest, when they assure you that the apostate Chiniquy's degradation is so well known that no Protestant who has any self-respect would have anything to do with him.

"*Sixteenth Fact:* When in the month of January, 1883, I was lecturing in London, I received the visit of Lord Shaftesbury, who presented me an invitation from the committee of the British and Foreign Bible Society, to attend their grand meeting on the 5th of February. When a priest of Rome very often I had read the encyclicals of the infallible Pope of Rome, assuring me that the Bible Society was one of the most infernal inventions of the devil; that the men engaged in circulating the Bible were the instruments of the devil, and that next to the devil they were the enemies of God, and I had to believe it then, just as Mr. 'Kentucky Ben' with all his priests has to believe it now   Had I had any self-respect or a spark of religion, I would have rejected with horror a message coming from such degraded men, particularly when it was brought to me by such a vile Protestant as Lord Shaftesbury   But, alas, I was then as degraded as I am to-day, and I accepted the invitation.   The 5th of February, 1883, I was in the midst of those infamous heretics who, according to His Holiness, the infallible Pope of Rome, are so blindly the enemies of God and His Son Jesus Christ that they circulate His soul-destroying word all over the world.   I gave them an address, of which they ordered 100,000 copies to be scattered all over Great Britain   Through that address, finding that I was as depraved as they were themselves in reference to the Bible, they, by unanimous vote, elected me one of the governors and rulers of the British and Foreign Bible Society, and now you can see my name in the very midst of those wicked men.

"After such a proof of my degradation, I hope your readers will easily admit that Mr 'Kentucky Ben,' his Bishops and priests are true gentlemen and lovers of the truth, when they have proclaimed these thirty years, throughout the whole world, that the apostate Chiniquy is so degraded that no honest Protestant would have anything to do with him.

CHAPTER XXXIX

Conversion of M. J. A. Papineau to Protestantism. Senator Tasse's Dasardly Attack Against Me Answered.

Brighter sunshine of Christian joy never beamed in my soul than at the reading of the following message which I received on the threshold of the year 1894

"Monte Bello, January 1, 1894.

"My Revered Friend:

"Through the grace of God I have come to see that it is my duty to break openly with Romanism, in which I have ceased to believe these last thirty years But so far I have not had the courage of following your heroic example in giving up before the world the errors of the Pope to embrace the truth of Christ as we find it revealed in the Gospel. However, to-day, with the help of my Divine Master, I wish to do so, and I come to ask you what steps I have to take to become a member of the Presbyterian Church; and as I consider you the Luther of Canada and as the reading of your works has greatly helped me in coming to my present resolution, I beg the favour to be admitted by you into the great, noble Protestant family.

"Your sincere friend and admirer,

"L. J A PAPINEAU."

Louis Joseph Amédée Papineau bears the most illustrious name of Canada. He is the eldest son of Louis Joseph Papineau, whose memory will be forever dear to the French-Canadians, for it is to the ardent patriotism, the indomitable energy and the remarkable eloquence of that great patriot that they are indebted for the enjoyment of all the British franchises

The son had inherited the patriotism of the father, he followed him throughout that glorious campaign of agitation and revendication during the year 1837   To help more effectively the great movement of political reforms he founded the society of the *Fils de la Liberté*.   But one of the greatest obstacles in the way was the Roman Catholic clergy, who saw in those reforms a threat to their power

The rebellion of 1837 having failed, Mr Papineau took refuge in the United States, where being welcomed in a Christian family he learned to know something of the glorious liberty of the children of God.   After having been admitted to the bar in New York, he visited France, his mother country, the researches he made there into his family tree proved to him that his ancestors were Protestants and that they were only restored to the Church of Rome through bloody persecutions.

He returned to Montreal in 1843, and being yet desirous of devoting himself to the welfare of his countrymen he organized an association called *Société des Amis*, which was the forerunner of the *Institut Canadien* destined to vindicate so bravely the right of the people to think for themselves   At the same time he used his pen in giving lessons of political economy which were published in the *Revue Canadienne*. In 1844 he was appointed protonotary of Montréal, an office which he filled worthily during thirty-two years, when in 1875 he resigned and retired to private life in the historic *manoir* of the seigniory of Monte Bello, bequeathed to him by his father.   There, in the quiet of a delightful country abounding in grand sceneries, Mr Papineau, in the presence of his God, pondered most earnestly over the religious question with the ultimate result set forth in his letter

It was my great joy and privilege on Wednesday evening, the 10th of January, 1894, in St. John's French Presbyterian Church, to admit that brother into the fellowship of the

Christian Church before a great concourse of attentive and respectful people composed very largely of Roman Catholics

The ceremony was grand in its simplicity and solemnity

Eloquent addresses were delivered by some pastors of the French Protestant Churches of the city, and by Rev. Dr. MacVicar, who wished also to honour us with his presence on this occasion. Before extending the right hand of fellowship to Mr Papineau, the following questions were put to him, to each of which his answer was clear and firm, testifying his deep conviction that the course he was pursuing was the proper one:

1. Do you believe with all your heart in God your Creator and Father, in Jesus Christ, His Son, who has redeemed you, and in the Holy Ghost, who has sanctified you?

2. Do you believe that the Word of God, which you have been taught, is the perfect revelation of His will and can alone instruct you to safety? Are you so persuaded of the truth of the Gospel that you understand that it is better to suffer all things than to abandon the profession of it?

3 Do you put all your confidence in Jesus Christ as your only Saviour and do you seek in Him your safety and your justification?

4. Do you repent of all your sins and do you confess them to God with a sincere heart? Do you ask pardon of the Lord and will you in return renounce sin to live according to temperance, justice and piety and to offer yourself to God in holy living sacrifice, which is your proper and reasonable service?

After his formal reception, Mr Papineau, trembling slightly with emotion, slowly mounted the platform and expressed his gratitude to God for that glorious day In his present step he had consulted no one but his own conscience. At the age of eighteen he had been driven from his country into exile He had seen priests refuse the last consolations of the Church to his friends who had fallen in the rebellion of 1837.   The priests had in this way done more to defeat and crush the cause of the patriots than all the English bayonets brought against them.   Forced to expatriate themselves as a result, he was warmly welcomed in a Presbyterian family in the United States   Here he first learned to think that salvation could be found outside of the Catholic Church   He had asked himself· "Are we not all children of God?" He commenced to reason; naturally doubt followed.   At the age of twenty-five he had ceased the practise of the Catholic religion.   After a long study he had reached the conviction that the only pure source of Christianity and the only rule of faith was the Bible.   In barbarous ages the clergy succeeded in introducing into the belief and ceremonies of the Catholic faith a host of legends until it had lost all resemblance to the true faith of Christ.   Only recently had the council of the Church surrendered its supremacy in favour of the Pope. To-day the Pope was a spiritual czar   He had arrived at the conclusion that the most evangelical Church was the best, and hence he had resolved to cast his lot with the Presbyterians, who were the spiritual heirs of the Huguenots, his ancestors.

The conversion of Mr. Papineau called from the dark abyss loud thunders of maledictions and gave the Roman Catholic newspapers the occasion to prove once more to the world that Romanism is a school of intolerance teaching that, as the end justifies the means, it is then legitimate to get rid of an adversary by slander and calumnies, and, if law allows, by sword and fire.

The Minerve, a French daily of Montreal considered as the organ of the Roman Catholic clergy at the time, signalized itself above all others by its slanderous attack against Mr. Papineau and myself.

The editor of that paper was then a Mr. Tassé, a senator of the Federal Government, a very pious man, devoted to his Church, a mere tool in the hands of the clergy.

Under the heading, "The Apostate Papineau," he published

an article on the 11th of January, 1894, which I consider proper to put before the eyes of my readers to give them a sample of the style of controversy the converts from Romanism have ordinarily to contend with

"Louis Joseph Papineau, the famous tribune, brought up in the atheist school of the encyclopedists of the eighteenth century, ended his career ignominiously   It would have been better for him to have never been born than to have such an end! His indomitable pride brought him to the threshold of eternity without asking pardon from the One who had created him. Papineau set a terrible example, which, alas! has deleterious fruits   'Woe to him through whom scandal cometh!' saith the Holy Scriptures   We find to-day a sad application of these words.

"The father had defied God on his death bed   He grieved, filled with terror and scandalized all those who believed in eternal truth

"The son has just abjured the faith of his fathers. He has put upon himself an indelible stain.

"Both have placed between themselves and the race that so long followed the former, an impassable gulf. Nothing is wanting in the shame of the son of the agitator.

"The one who presided at last night's ceremony, in the St. Catherine St Presbyterian Church, amidst the sound of hymns, is that white-washed sepulchre, that prevaricating priest, rotten to the very marrow of his bones, that shameless high liver who broke all his vows, who soiled those around him while at the same time saying his mass, who preached temperance in order the better to wallow in licentiousness, who, in the confessional, learned the secrets of human failings only to make use of them, who, having no other means left of blackmailing but apostasy, has ever since been constantly carrying his crimes through every clime and vomiting insult upon the holy religion of which he was for a long time the unworthy defender

"It is unnecessary for us to say that his name is Chiniquy,

that this reprobate man has become an object of horror among our people, and that he never treads lower Canadian soil, a soil covered with the blood of martyrs, but holy water is sprinkled to wipe off his diabolical footsteps.

"A Papineau becomes the victim, the prey of Chiniquy, what a debasement, what a gloom for us, what a national humiliation! Let us bow down our heads and cover ourselves with ashes. Let us pray and ask pardon from God for having drawn upon us such a terrible punishment."

I thought it was my duty to reply to such vituperations, as they came from a man who occupied such an exalted position in this country, but Mr Tassé, as it might well be anticipated, denied me the justice to publish my vindication in his paper. It then found its way into the Protestant press of this city.

As it is an answer to repeated attacks against my character found current among Roman Catholics, I consider it binding upon me to include it in this book.

"To the editor of *The Minerve.*

"Sir.—You expect, no doubt, that your article against me, in your issue of yesterday, will not be left unanswered, and you will not be disappointed.

"You cannot find words vile enough to express your contempt for my priestly life.

"Well, I must confess before God and man, to-day again, what I have confessed a thousand times before the disciples of the Gospel, not only on this continent of America. but all over Great Britain and in the Australian colonies, that during twenty-five years I was a priest of antichrist, when it had been my intention and the ardent desire of my heart to be the priest of Christ.

"I had to learn by heart the infamous questions which the Church of Rome forces every priest to learn by heart.

"I was, in conscience, as all your priests are, bound to put into the ears, the mind, the imagination, the heart and the souls of females, questions of such nature, the immediate and direct tendency of which is to fill the minds, the memory and hearts of both priests and penitents with thoughts, phantoms and temptations of such a degrading nature that there are no words adequate to express them.

"Pagan antiquity has never known any institution more polluting to the soul and body than the Roman Catholic Auricular Confession. No, there is nothing more corrupting under heaven than the law which forces a female to tell her thoughts, desires, and most secret feelings and actions to a bachelor, an unmarried man. Let him be called a priest or a monk, it makes no difference Your priests may deny that before you; but they will never, never dare to deny it before me.

"Now, my dear sir, if you look upon me as a degraded priest, because my heart, my soul, my mind, as those of all your priests, were plunged into those bottomless waters of iniquity which flow from the confessional, I confess guilty I was polluted, and I was polluting the souls of my female penitents just as every priest has to do every day

"It has required the whole blood of the great Victim, who died on Calvary for you and for me and for all sinners, to purify me. And I pray that you and all your priests who are required to live in the same pestilential atmosphere may be purified through the same blood.

"But now that, by the great mercy of God, I have been taken away from the ways of perdition in which Rome was forcing me to walk with all her priests, I have no fear to be confronted with you, or any other of my small or big slanderers. Many times since that, I have challenged my bitterest enemies to find anything in my life for which an honest man must blush.

"Without any boasting I can say that there has never been any priest in Canada so constantly cherished, honoured and respected by the priests, the Bishops and the people as I was It is a public fact that I was carried in triumph from one parish to the other from the remotest part of lower Canada to the shores of Lake Huron.

"There is not a great city, not a small town, not a cathedral in the province of Quebec or Ontario, to which the Bishops have not invited me to address the people, and the churches, even your immense Notre Dame Church of Montreal, were never large enough to receive the people who wanted to hear me   I do not say these things in boasting, but only to show to you and your readers how our dear countrymen, people, priests and Bishops, were kind to me.

"The powers given to me to hear confessions and to preach everywhere were greater than those given to any other priest   In 1850, after I had been a priest seventeen years, two years after I had left my parish of Kamouraska, in order to establish the temperance society all over Canada, when the Bishop of Quebec, the Right Rev Baillargeon, went to Rome, he came to meet me in Longueuil and requested me to address a letter with my book on temperance to the Pope, through him, that he might present it himself to the Sovereign Pontiff—and when he had presented it he wrote me a letter, which is still in my hand, and which I will be much pleased to show you, if you desire to see it.   In this letter my Bishop tells me these very words:

"'Rome, Aug , 10, 1850.
"'Sir and Dear Friend:—
"'It is only to-day that it has been given me to have a private audience with the Sovereign Pontiff.   I have taken the opportunity to present to him your book, with your letter, which he has received, I do not say with that goodness, which is so eminently characteristic, but with all special marks of satisfaction and approbation, while charging me to send to you that he accords his apostolic benediction to you, and to the holy work of temperance which you preach

"'I esteem myself happy to have had to offer on your behalf, to the "Vicar of Christ," a book, which, after it had done so much good to my countrymen, has been able to draw from his venerable mouth such solemn words of approbation of the temperance society, and of blessing n he one who is its apostle, and it is also for my heart, a very sweet pleasure to transmit them to you.

" 'Your friend,
" 'CHARLES T. BAILLARGEON.'

"Do you believe that such approval could have been given by my Bishop, if, as my slanderers say to-day, my previous conduct had been that of a vile man, when I left my dear parish of Kamouraska, in order to spread the principles of temperance all over Canada? Then, that Bishop would have been the vilest man. But if you will ask me, with many of my other slanderers· 'Were you not interdicted in 1851 by the Bishop of Montreal, a few days before you left Canada for the United States?'

"I will tell you, Yes, sir; the Bishop of Montreal pretended to have suspended me then. But I will allow you to judge if that event is not one of the most glorious of my life, and one for which I must bless God forever. For my integrity has never been more clearly shown than in that circumstance

"The sham interdict, which was a nullity by itself—for its want of form, of justice and of foundation, had been kept by the Bishop, and for good reasons, a secret in Canada as well as in the United States. By his immediate and subsequent acts the Bishop has given me the evidence that he was regretting his error, and was trying to repair it and make me forget it. But not long after I left the Church, to my surprise, the Bishop of Montreal said that he had interdicted me, and that he was inviting me to publish the reasons of my interdict. It was the best opportunity that the providence of God had offered me to prove my innocence. and the incredible ·excess of folly and tyranny of this Bishop of Rome Without delay I accepted the challenge, and published through the French=Canadian press the following letter, which forever confounded the poor Bishop He has

never been able to reply, though it was so important for his
honour, and the interests of his Church, that he should have
replied to it:

"'St. Anne, April, 18, 1857.

"'To Bishop Bourget:

"'My Lord:—

"'In your letter of the 19th of March you assure the public
that you have interdicted me, a few days before my leaving
Canada for the United States, and you invite me to give the
reasons of that sentence. I will satisfy you. On the 28th of
September, 1851, I found a letter on my table from you, telling me that you had suspended me from my ecclesiastical
offices, on account of a great crime that I had committed, and
of which I was accused. But the name of the accuser was
not given nor the nature of the crime. I immediately went
to see you, and, protesting my innocence, I requested you to
give me the name of my accusers, and to allow me to be confronted by them, promising that I would prove my innocence. You refused to grant my request.

"'Then I fell on my knees, and with tears, in the name of
God, I requested you again to grant me to meet my accusers
and prove my innocence. You remained deaf to my prayers
and unmoved by my tears; you repulsed me with malice and
with airs of tyranny which I had thought impossible in you.

"'During the twenty-four hours after this, sentiments of an
inexpressible wrath crossed my mind; I tell it to you frankly.
In that terrible hour, I would have preferred to be at the
feet of a heathen priest, whose knife would have slaughtered
me on his altars to appease his infernal gods, rather than be
at the feet of a man, who, in the name of Jesus Christ, and
under the mask of the Gospel, should dare to commit such a
cruel act. You have taken away my honour—you have destroyed me with the most infamous calumny—you have refused me every means of justification. You have taken
under your protection the cowards who were stabbing me in
the dark!

"'Though it is hard to repeat it, I must tell it here publicly. I cursed you in that horrible day.

"'With a broken heart, I went to the Jesuit College, and I showed the wounds of my bleeding soul to the noble friend who was generally my confessor, the Rev Father Schneider, the director of the college.

"'After three days, having providentially got some reasons to suspect who was the author of my intended destruction, I sent someone to ask her to come to the college without mentioning my name.

"'When she was in the parlour I said to Father Schneider· "You know the horrible iniquity of the Bishop against me— with the lying words of a prostitute he has destroyed me; but please come and be the witness of my innocence"

"'When in the presence of that unfortunate woman, I told her "You are in the presence of God Almighty and two of His priests They will be the witnesses of what you say! Speak the truth. Say, in the presence of God and of this venerable priest, if I have ever been guilty of what you accused me to the Bishop.'

"' At these words the unfortunate woman burst into tears, she concealed her face with her hands, and, with a voice half suffocated with her sobs, she answered· "No, sir, you are not guilty of that sin!"

"'"Confess here another truth," I said to her; "Is it not true that you had come to confess to me more with the desire to tempt me rather than to reconcile yourself to God?"

"'She said, " Yes, sir, that is the truth." Then I said again, " Continue to say the truth, and I will forgive you and God also will forgive your iniquity Is it not revenge for having failed in your criminal design, that you have tried to destroy me by that accusation to the Bishop?"

"'"Yes, sir, it is the only reason which has induced me to accuse you falsely."

"'And all that I say here, at least in substance, has been heard, written and signed by the Right Rev. Father Schneider, one of your priests and the director of the Jesuit College That venerable priest is still living in Montreal; let the people of Canada go and interrogate him. Let the people of Canada also go to Mr. Brassard, who had also in his hands an authenticated copy of that declaration.

"'Your lordship gives to understand that I was disgraced by that sentence, some days after when I left Canada for Illinois. Allow me to give you my reasons for differing from you in that matter.

"'There is a canon law of the Church which says: "If a censure is unjust and unfounded, let the man against whom the sentence has been passed pay no attention to it. For, before God and His Church, no unjust sentence can bring any injury to anyone. Let the one against whom such unfounded and unjust judgment has been pronounced even take no steps to annul it, for it is a nullity by itself."

"'You know very well that the sentence you have passed against me was null and void for many good reasons, the first, because it was founded on a false testimony. Father Schneider is there ready to prove it to you, if you have any doubts.

"'The second reason I have to believe that you yourself had considered your sentence a nullity and that I was not suspended by it from my ecclesiastical dignity and honours, is founded on a good testimony, I hope, the testimony of your lordship himself.

"'A few hours before my leaving Canada for the United States, I went to ask your benediction, which you gave me with every mark of kindness I then asked your lordship frankly to tell me if I had to leave with the impression that I was disgraced in your mind You gave me the assurance of the contrary.

"'Then I told you that I wanted a public and irrefutable testimony of your esteem

"'You answered that you would be happy to give me one, and you said, "What do you want?" "I wish," I said, "to have a chalice from your hands to offer the holy sacrifice of the mass the rest of my life." You answered, " I will do that with pleasure," and you gave orders to one of your priests to bring you a chalice that you might give it to me But that priest had not the key of the box containing the sacred vases; that key was in the hands of another priest, who was absent for a few hours.

" 'I had not the time to wait, the hour of the departure of the train had come. I told you, " Please, my lord, send that chalice to the Rev Mr. Brassard of Longueuil, who will forward it to me in a few days to Chicago." And the next day one of your secretaries went to the Rev. Mr. Brassard, gave him the chalice you had promised me, which is still in my hands. And the Rev Mr Brassard is there, still living, to be a witness of what I say—and to bring that fact to your memory if you have forgotten it.

" ' Well, my lord, I do believe that a Bishop will never give a chalice to a priest to say mass when he knows that that priest is interdicted. And the best proof you know very well that I was not interdicted by your rash and unjust sentence, is that you gave me that chalice as a token of your esteem and of my honesty, etc.

" ' Respectfully,

" ' C. Chiniquy.'

"Ten thousand copies of this terrible exposure of the depravity of the Bishop were published in Montreal! I have asked the whole people of Canada to go to the Rev. Mr Schneider, and to the Rev. Mr Brassard, to know the truth. The Bishop remained confounded. It was proved that he had committed against me a most outrageous act of tyranny and perfidy; and that I was perfectly innocent and honest, and that he knew it, in the very hour that he tried to destroy my character, sending this wicked woman to corrupt me Probably the Bishop of Montreal had destroyed the copy of the declaration of my innocence and honesty, and he thought he would speak of the so-called interdict after I was a Protestant. But in that he was cruelly mistaken.

" By the great mercy of God, three other authenticated copies had been kept, one by the Rev. Mr. Schneider himself, another by the Rev. Mr. Brassard, and another by one whom it is not necessary to mention—and then, he had no suspicion that the revelation of his unchristian conduct, and of his determination to destroy me with the false oath of a prostitute, were in the hands of too many people to be denied. The Bishop of Chicago, whom I met a few days after, told me what I was well aware of before: " That such a sentence was a perfect nullity in every way, and that it was a disgrace only for those who are blind enough to trample under their feet the laws of God and man to satisfy their bad passions. And no doubt you will be of the same mind if you are an honest man."

"But to show you that the Bishop of Montreal himself never thought that his unjust sentence had any effect, and that he himself never lost his good opinion of me, I also publish for your perusal the letter he gave me the day that I left Canada. These are his words:

" 'October 13th, 1851.

" 'I cannot but thank you for what you have done in our midst, and in my gratitude towards you I wish you the most abundant benediction of heaven. Every day of my life I will remember you. You will always be in my heart, and I hope that in some future day the providence of God will give me some opportunity of showing you all the gratitude I feel for you.

" 'IGNACE,
" ' Bishop of Montreal.'

" I ask you, 'Will ever a Bishop say to a priest, in a written document, signed with his own hands, ' I cannot but thank you for what you have done in our midst,'—if that priest had been an immoral, a bad priest?

" Does not the Bishop who writes such words acknowledge

that he was wrong in his previous and hasty and unfavorable judgment?

"Would the intelligent editor of *The Minerve*, if he were the Bishop of Montreal, write to a priest, 'I cannot but thank you for what you have done in our midst; in my gratitude towards you I pray God to pour His most abundant blessings upon you,' if he knew that that priest was an immoral and wicked man? No, never; nor would you give a chalice to an interdicted priest to say mass with the rest of his life

"Is it so that, as long as a priest is in your midst, he may be a most depraved man, a public scandal, a murderer of souls, yet the Bishop will like him, honour him and overload him with every kind of public and private mark of respect? But when he leaves them to become a Protestant, then they pour out on him their scorn and abuse! By their own confession have they not done this to me? If I were an immoral man when a priest of Rome, how is it that the Bishops have known it only after I had left the Church? And if I were an immoral man when in their midst, why is it that the Bishops from the beginning to the end of my career, gave me so many public and private marks of esteem and respect? If they have done so, are they not confessedly worse than what they called me?

"In 1848 the Bishop of Montreal, in a public document, puts me in the most exalted position in which a priest has ever been placed. He calls me 'The Apostle of Temperance of Canada,' and one of his best priests. The same year he induces the Pope to send me a magnificent crucifix In 1850 he invites the people of Montreal from his pulpit in his cathedral to come with the Hon Judge Mondelet to present me with a gold medal, as a public token of his respect and gratitude to me. In 1851, the day that I left Canada, he writes me that what I have done in his diocese, when working under his eyes, has filled him with gratitude! And the same man, after I had left the Church of Rome, says that I was an immoral priest—an interdicted and suspended priest!—and that, on the testimony of a prostitute, who afterwards declared that she had made a false oath to revenge herself because she had not been able to persuade me to commit a crime with her!

"If what I declare of the infamous conduct of the Bishop had not been correct, and if the recantation of that unfortunate woman in the presence of the Rev. Father Schneider had not been correct also, how easy it would have been for the Bishop to confound me forever by bringing the superior of the Jesuit College as a witness of my imposture And how it would have been the imperative duty of Father Schneider, when he saw his name in the public press committed with a fact so degrading to the Bishop, to come forward and publish that what I had said was forgery!

"Then Chiniquy would have been forever and so easily confounded! But such was not the case. The poor Bishop had to pay publicly for his infamous conduct towards me, and he was left without any chance of escape. If you are honest it is not on Chiniquy that you will turn your scorn; it is on the man who, forgetting all the laws of justice, of God and men, had united his efforts to those of a perjured prostitute, to destroy his innocent victim. And if you are not honest enough to see and understand this, what have I to care about your scorn?

"Now let us say a word about the interdict by Bishop O'Regan. And I tell you boldly, that if anything can be considered an honour by any man, it is to have deserved the wrath of so publicly depraved a man. Though he never interdicted me (he only threatened to do it) he found fit to publish that he had done it. But in his letter of November 20, 1856, where he publicly gives the reason of that so-called sentence, he somewhat disturbs the plan you have contrived, my dear sir, to make people believe that it was on account of immorality. In that letter the Bishop says: 'His obstinate want of submission and his excessively violent language and conduct obliges me to suspend him!'

"I thank and bless God who gave me the strength to say some great truths to that most immoral and tyrannical Bishop.

He was such a wicked man that several priests, among whom I was one, wrote to the Pope about his bad conduct; and the Archbishop of St. Louis, and many other Bishops, having brought also serious complaints against the man, his diocese was taken away from his hands, and he got a bishopric 'in partibus infidelum,' which you very well know means a bishopric in the moon—and the place was just fit for the man.

"The sentence was never served on me in any way. The Church allowed me to pay no attention to it; and the subsequent excommunication having been brought by three priests who at the time were beastly drunk, and not being signed by the Bishop nor any of his grand vicars or known deputies, I was bound by the laws of the Church not to pay any attention to it. The Rev Mr Desaulniers and the Rev Moses Brassaid, having come some time later from Canada to inquire about those matters and reconcile us to the Bishop, declared before more than five hundred people that we 'could not be blamed for having paid no attention to that sentence, which was evidently and publicly against all the known laws of the Church'

"But I have no bad feelings against that unfortunate man, who died five years after. It is the contrary. His abominable life, his vices, his complete want of principles which forced the Bishops of the United States to denounce him to the Pope, who condemned him at the end, have helped me much, by the mercy of God, to know what the Church of Rome has been, what she is, and what she will be till the great day of God shall open the eyes of her poor slaves and bring them to the feet of Jesus, who will make them free with His Word and pure with His blood.

"Read the following declaration of the same Bishop to four deputies sent to him by the people of St Anne just two days before our excommunication. That declaration, signed by four Roman Catholics, is under oath before the civil tribunal of Kankakee;—it is the best refutation of your slanderous article against me.

" Bishop O'Regan gave the deputation a written response. which was published in Canada at the time in the leading newspapers.

" The Bishop was waited upon the 27th day of August, 1856, and presented the following reply:—

" '1st. I suspended Mr. Chiniquy on the 19th of this month.

" '2d. If Mr. Chiniquy has said mass since, as you say, he is irregular; and the Pope alone can restore him in his ecclesiastic and sacerdotal functions.

" '3d. I take him away from St. Anne, despite his prayers and yours, because he has not been willing to live in peace and in friendship with the Revs. M. Lebel and M. Cartevel, although I admit that they were two bad priests, whom I have been forced to expel from my diocese.

" '4th. My second reason for taking Mr. Chiniquy away from St. Anne to send him to his new mission south of Illinois, is to stop the lawsuit Mr. Spink has instituted against him; though I cannot warrant that the lawsuit will be stopped at that.

" '5th. Mr. Chiniquy is one of the best priests of my diocese, and I do not want to deprive myself of his services; no accusations against the morals of that gentlemen have been proved before me.

" '6th. Mr. Chiniquy has demanded an inquest to prove his innocence of certain accusations made against him, and has asked me the names of his accusers to confound them; I have refused them to him.

" '7th. Tell Mr. Chiniquy to come and meet me—to prepare himself for his new mission, and I will give him the letters he needs to go and labor there.'

" 'Then we withdrew and presented the foregoing letter to Father Chiniquy.

" 'Frs. Bechard,
" 'J. B. L. Lemoine,
" 'Basilique Allair,
" 'Leon Mailloux.'

"Now, my dear sir, before taking leave of you allow me to give you a little friendly advice.

"When you argue with a Protestant, even one whom you call an apostate, never make a personal question of a principle, if you wish to make people think that you have the right side, and that the irrefutable arguments are in your favour. For the very moment that you give up the arguments on the question to drag your adversary on the ungentlemanly and unchristian ground of personal injuries and slanders, you lose your cause in the mind of an intelligent people. A man who has good reasons to support his cause and strong arguments has never recourse to those personalities and hard names which you have used.

"The question is not to know who has committed the most sins against the Decalogue, but whether it is true or not that the Church of Rome has forsaken the Word of God, the Gospel of Christ, in order to preach her lying traditions.

"If you could prove that when I was a priest of Rome, I was as criminal as David, and as weak as Samson, a perjurer as Peter, or a blind persecutor as Paul, this will not at all prove that I have not done well to leave the Pope in order to follow Christ. It is just the contrary. The more wicked I was in the Church of Rome, surrounded as I was, and as you are to-day, by the most pestilential atmosphere, and having before my eyes the example of a concealed though most horrible corruption in high quarters, as well as among my equals, the more imperative was the duty for me, as for you, to go out of those ways of perdition.

"Do you know, my dear sir, to what I have been tempted when writing this letter? The thought has come to my mind to publish, not all (for it would be too terrible) but a part of what I know of the inside, and almost incredible corruption of Rome! To give, for instance, a part of the history of that Grand Vicar who was guilty of an unmentionable crime and was never interdicted; of that other dignity whose conquests were so numerous in Montreal that the ground became too hot for him, and who was not interdicted but kindly invited to go to another place; the history of that good Bishop, also, who, for five years kept a fine young man in his house as his confidential friend, and who had to send that faithful servant, with five hundred pounds, to the United States, when a very interesting circumstance proved that the fine young man was a fine young girl! 'Honi soit qui mal y pense.' I was also tempted to give to the public some very interesting details from the memoirs, not of poor Father Chiniquy (though he has some memoirs also), but from the memoirs of one of the most respectable Bishops of Rome, Bishop de Riccy, where it is often said and proved 'that the nuns of Italy are the wives of the priests.' Happy celibataries indeed! I had some very interesting things also which you have known, no doubt, of those three good priests in a diocese not many miles from here, who made a very interesting voyage with three young ladies, and were so kindly treated by the holy Church of Rome, that one of them is now hearing the confessions of the good nuns of the City of Three Rivers, and the two others are in a very exalted position in the diocese of Montreal.

"My intention, after having given you the correct history of those respectful and venerable priests of Rome, was to ask you, in a friendly way, without bitterness, why the Bishops should have been so hard against me, when they were so kind to others?

"No living man knows better than I do the clergy. I have been fifteen years traveling amongst them. I have seen the inside as well as the outside of your walls. For many years I have been a serious observer of men and things; and everyday I have put down in my note-book that which would make many knees shake in the midst of the priests of Rome. I do not say that they are all wicked and depraved. Thanks be to God I have found among them men who would have been almost as pure as angels, if the confessional had not been there as a snare to pollute their noble hearts. But

I have known enough to startle the world, if I had not more charity for my old friends of Rome than many of them have shown to me, since God in His infinite mercy has given me the light and the truth as it is in Jesus. If you honour me with an answer, I will be proud and happy to meet you as a gentleman on some of those high grounds of historical and theological truths and errors about which we differ But give up that unmanly and unchristian way (which is too much the use of Roman Catholics) of speaking of the real or supposed sins of an opponent We are all more or less great sinners, and are too apt to see the straw in the eyes of our poor neighbour, while we do not see the beam which is in our own

"Though you have been a little hard on your old country-man, I feel grateful to you for having given me the opportunity of explaining many things which I hope it will be good to my friends to hear.

"Now, farewell, au revoir Allow me to call myself your fellow-sinner and your devoted brother in Christ."

CHAPTER XL

Futile Efforts. Priest's Efforts to Reach My Bed of Sickness Frustrated. Challenge to Archbishop not Accepted

After a month of hard missionary labour in New England, during the fall of 1894, having caught cold, I returned to Montreal quite exhausted and sick, and consequently was laid up for nearly two months.

During that long illness the Roman Catholic clergy made special efforts to reach my bed, in order, evidently, to have some seeming pretext or ground to announce to the public that I had become reconciled to their Church. But their plan failed.

Suspecting what might happen, I had given strict orders, as I generally do in such cases, not to allow any priests or their agents to enter my room.

One day, however, in October, a lady by the name of De la Rousselière, of very respectable appearance, presented herself at the door of my house, and in a polite note begged an audience with me. As she seemed so much in earnest, and persistent, her request was granted. When ushered into my room, where my wife, one of my daughters and a friend were present, she asked to be allowed to see me alone. I told her that I did not wish to hear anything that she could not tell me in the presence of my family and that friend. Meanwhile, the door-bell rang again; and on opening, the servant saw a priest who seemed to be in a great hurry, and who said at once:—" Is there not a lady who has just come in? Please take me where she is; I must see her immediately." But the faithful servant said she could not do that, and directly she called my son-in-law, the Rev Mr. Morin, who on coming downstairs found himself face to face in the hall with a stout, jovial priest "I am Abbé Marre of Notre Dame Church," he said, "and as I have heard that Mr. Chiniquy is very sick, I thought I would stop and see him; for we do not forget that he is a priest, and as such, he is considered to belong to our parish." Mr. Morin told Abbé Marre about the strict orders I had given not to allow any priest to come into my room, —but that he would be welcomed should he call on me when I had recovered

Meanwhile, Miss De la Rousselière was entreating me to pray to the Virgin Mary, to be reconciled to the Holy Church, and to accept the ministry of a priest, etc. I told her that Christ was sufficient for me; He was my only Saviour and my only Mediator, and that I had no need of the intervention of any priest; that I had a horror mingled with pity for those poor slaves of the Pope.

On hearing that, she rushed out of the room and went down double-quick where she met Abbé Marre, and quite excited, exclaimed: "Oh Monsieur le curé, do not go to see him; he says he has a horror for your black gown!" The priest began to laugh, and went out, leaving the witnesses of that scene under the firm impression that the whole thing had been planned beforehand, but that the plot had been victoriously defeated.

Soon after that clerical stratagem, I was besieged by other zealots of the Pope, especially women, whose avowed aim was my return to the Church of Rome.

As all these attempts failed, the Jesuits, who consider themselves, and rightly so, the shrewdest servants of the Pope, thought they should also try their hand at my conversion. So they set about it, using likewise a woman for their agent, pretending that through her I had asked for their spiritual assistance, all this appears in the two letters I here insert The first one was addressed to me on the 4th of November by Father Hamon, being as follows:

"College St. Marie. Montreal.

"Dear Sir:

"Mrs. F. X. Trudel tells me that you would gladly receive the visit of a father Jesuit, and she has shown me an envelope signed by Mr. J. L. Morin, appointing for an interview the first Sunday of November at half past two o'clock.

"Unfortunately at that hour I must preside at a meeting of the *Catholic Union;* but if it is convenient for you, I can be at your place at half-past four.

"Yours truly,
"G. J. M. HAMON, S. J."

Mr. Morin, on receipt of the Jesuit's letter, perceiving that Rev. Mr. Hamon had been apparently misled, wrote at once the following reply:

"65 Hutchison St., Montreal, Nov. 5, 1894.
"To Rev. G. J. M. Hamon, S. J., College St. Marie,
"Sir:

"Mr. Chiniquy requests me to acknowledge the receipt of your letter, and to tell you that he never expressed to Mrs. Trudel the desire to receive the visit of a father Jesuit during his sickness; on the contrary, he told that lady last Saturday that it was sufficient for him to have the presence of Jesus; that he had no need of the presence of a Jesuit to die in the full assurance of his salvation.

"As to that interview I am said to have appointed for the first Sunday of November, here is the fact about it. That good Mrs. Trudel, who has put forth a great deal of untimely zeal to bring us back to the Church of Rome, began to extol to me last Sunday the great advantages of ecclesiastical celibacy. I then took the liberty to allude to the several irregularities and disorders occasioned in all ranks of papal hierarchy by compulsory celibacy, and I further pointed out to her that the Apostle Peter was married, that the Roman Catholic clergy followed his example in that respect during several centuries, and that there are even to-day Roman Catholic priests who have their legitimate wives. All these assertions of mine appeared to her as so many errors and heretical propositions, that I could not defend in the presence of a priest or a Jesuit, she said. 'As well as in your presence,' I replied 'In that case,' she added, 'will you allow me to bring here a Jesuit next Sunday to discuss those questions with you?' 'I have no objection if you wish it,' I answered.

"She then asked me to write on an envelope, which she held in her hand, the day and hour of that meeting and to sign my name, 'for I fear that my memory would fail me,' she said This I did. But you see that Mr. Chiniquy is not involved in any way in all this affair, and I do not conceive how Mrs. Trudel could mislead you so much as to tell you that it was Mr. Chiniquy who had appointed an interview with you.

"However, if you are very anxious to know what Mr. Chiniquy thinks of the Church of Rome, what faith and joy he possesses in his Divine Saviour. you have only to tell me, and when he is well enough I will notify you.

"Of course I am disposed to defend the propositions which have horrified that poor Mrs. Trudel, and should you wish to come for that purpose, I would ask you to choose another day than next Sunday, for I will then be engaged.

"Yours truly,

"J. L. MORIN."

To be sure that this letter would reach its destination, Mr. Morin, accompanied by a friend, took it himself to the St Mary's college and gave it to the doorkeeper of that institution, who said that Father Hamon was in, and that he would deliver it to him personally.

We thought that we had heard the last of that affair, but we were mistaken. True to his promise in his note, Father Hamon called on Sunday at half past four—to see me accord-

442 Forty Years in the Church of Christ

ing to the appointed engagement, he said. When told by Mr. Morin that he had written him a letter explaining all, he said that he had not received it, that the messenger must have miscarried it. "But I left the note myself at the college," said Mr. Morin. After such a hit, an ordinary man would have lost his countenance: Father Hamon was not disturbed by *so little.* After a very amicable conversation, he took leave of Mr. Morin, excusing himself for the intrusion—and feeling, doubtless, that *honesty is the best policy,* even in the conversion of heretics.

When God in His mercy had restored me to health, I thought it was my duty to send to the Archbishop of Montreal the following letter, which appeared also in the press at the time:

"Montreal, 65 Hutchison St., December 8, 1894.
"To My Lord Fabre, Roman Catholic Bishop of Montreal.
"My Lord:—

"Your besieging me with your priests and priestesses during my last sickness is the reason for my addressing you this letter.

"I am perfectly cured, my lord: my bodily strength is so perfectly restored that I write you this letter without the use of any spectacles, and my hand does not shake more than when I was only thirty years of age, though I am in my eighty-sixth year.

"Yes, my lord, I am cured, perfectly cured, though I have not had a single drop of your waters of Notre Dame de Lourdes and without going to the good St. Anne de Beaupré!

"I am cured, in spite of the maledictions and excommunications of the Bishops and the priests of Rome!

"And, what will puzzle you the more, I am cured, perfectly cured, without having accepted any one of your medals or scapularies—without even having bought any of your blessed candles which I might have bought from you for fifteen cents.

"But to prevent you from suspecting that the devil alone or some witches could have healed such a bad man as I am, I must give you the secret of that cure.

"May our merciful God grant that you may have recourse to the same remedy with the multitudes of our dear countrymen you are leading in the perishing ways of Rome.

"From the very day that I broke the chains which were tying me to the idols of the Pope, I put myself under the care of the best Physician the world has ever seen.

"His name is Jesus!

"He is both the Son of God and the Son of Man

"He came from Heaven more than eighteen hundred years ago, to save us from all our spiritual and even bodily miseries.

"But His condition was, that those who wanted to be cured by Him, should not invoke any other name but His own. For His Apostle Peter wrote in His Testament those very words—'There is no other name under heaven given among men whereby we must be saved ' Acts 4: 12

" His Testament is called 'The Gospel '

"These last eighteen hundred years, all the echoes of heaven and earth are repeating His sweet words.—'Come unto Me, all ye who are heavy-laden, and I will give you rest.' Matt 11·28

"'Whatsoever ye shall ask in His name, that will I do, that the Father may be glorified in the Son.' John 14.13.

"'If ye shall ask anything in My name, I will do it.' John 14 14.

"'If a man love Me he will keep My words; and My Father will love him, and We will come unto him, and make Our abode with him.' John 14 23.

"'I am the True Vine; ye are the branches.

"'Abide in Me, and I in you.' John 15· 1, 2, 3, 4.

"'If I be lifted up from the earth, I will draw all men to Me.' John 12: 32.

"From the day I gave up the Pope to follow Christ, I have found more and more every day that the greatest joy, the greatest happiness in this world, is to love and serve Him. I have kept myself then united to Him with all the faculties of my heart and my soul, as being my only Light, my only Strength, my only Wisdom, and I have always found Him true to His promises.

"But when I found that it was good to be united to that mighty and merciful Friend in the days of prosperity, I have found that it was still more to my interest to be united to Him in the days of trial through which I had to pass.

"He was my Shield when I was attacked by the thousands of assassins whom you or your priests have so often sent to take away my life, either with their pistols, or with their murderous sticks, or with their sharp stones.

"When those stones were falling upon me as hail in a stormy day, in the streets of Montreal, Quebec, Halifax, Charlottetown, Antigonish, Ottawa, etc., I was throwing myself into the arms of that mighty and loving Friend, I was pressing myself on His heart, and I felt secure as a little child when in his loving mother's arms. I was invoking His Almighty Name, and it seemed I was feeling His merciful arms around me to protect me. I was hearing His sweet voice telling me: 'Fear not, I am with thee!'

"And when I was escaping from my would-be murderers' hands bruised, wounded, bleeding, I felt happy for having suffered something for the sake of that beloved Saviour who, on the cross, had shed His blood for me.

"But it is when I was attacked by the last terrible sickness that I felt the necessity of having that mighty and merciful Friend near me as my Physician. With Peter I cried, 'Lord, save me.'

"And you may come and see with what merciful and mighty hand He has come to my help and cured me!

"You may readily imagine my surprise and sadness when at that very time I saw your priests and priestesses coming to tell me that I was out of the way of salvation, and that I was to be damned if I would not come back to the Church of Rome, of which you are a Bishop.

"For what had these priests of Rome to give me to take the place of that Divine Friend and Physician, Jesus, the Son of God, that I might forget that He was my only Hope, my only Life, my only Saviour, my only Refuge?

"What did they offer me to prevent me from saying with Paul. 'I do not want to know any other but Jesus and Him crucified'?

"They had nothing but a few rags, called scapularies, and some idols of copper, iron and silver, probably found in the crumbling remains of the temples of Venus, Minerva, Bacchus and Jupiter!

"Yes! what had your priests to give me that I might forget and forsake that dear Saviour Jesus, whose presence in my heart was, very often. making me so happy that I was not only forgetting my terrible sufferings, but was changing those sufferings into feelings of unspeakable joy?

"They had to offer me a little god, only about one inch in diameter. made with a little cake baked by their servant girls between two heated irons

"Be not surprised, then, if I have repelled those ambassadors of Rome with the utmost indignation and pity.

"Here, my lord, allow me a few remarks

"Since more than thirty years that I separated myself from the Church of Rome, I have hardly been a single day, when in good health, without asking, supplicating, even challenging you and your priests to come and show me what you call my errors.

"Thousands of times I have told you that I would, with pleasure, go back to the feet of your Pope and submit myself to his authority, if you had the kindness to show me, before the world, that the Apostle Peter has ever been in Rome, that the present Pope is his legal successor, and that Peter with all your Popes has received from Christ the power to rule over His whole Church

"I have requested you many times and I do request you again to-day, to show me, in a public conference, that your

Auricular Confession is a sacrament established by Christ, and that it has been always practised as it is to-day in your Church; and I pledge myself to show, from the authority of your best Roman Catholic authors, that it is of pagan origin, and that it is in use in your Church only since the dark ages.

"In that public conference, I will also ask you to show me the text of the Gospel which allows you to let the poor people burn in the flames of purgatory, because they have no money, when you so quickly draw out of that burning furnace the rich, who fill your hands with the gold which very often they have stolen from those very poor people.

"I will have another favour to ask you in that public conference.

"It will be to show me a Gospel text which allows you to send to hell, as guilty of a mortal sin, the poor man who in Lent has eaten a piece of pork not bigger than my thumb, and that you allow him to go to heaven as a true Christian, if he eats that piece of pork when it is melted in his soup.

"When at that conference, I will also ask you to show me the text of the Gospel which authorizes you to advise, if not to force, so many men and women (priests, monks, and nuns) to make vows of celibacy, and to promise they will never marry, when God Himself in the Bible is so evidently opposed to such vows, as you may see by the following texts:

"'And the Lord God said: It is not good that man should be alone. I will make him a helpmeet for him.' Genesis 11: 18.

"'To avoid fornication, let every man have his own wife; and every woman her own husband.' 1 Cor. 7: 2.

"'Now the Spirit speaketh expressly, that in the latter times some shall depart from the faith, giving heed to seducing spirits and doctrines of devils . . . Forbidding to marry, and commanding to abstain from meats which God has created to be received with thanksgiving of them which believe and know the truth.' 1 Timothy 4: 1, 2, 3.

"You have never been brave enough to come and discuss those matters with me so long as I was in good health and able to answer you. The only answer you have given has been to send murderers with sticks, stones and pistols to kill me. But as soon as you hear that I am so sick that I can hardly move my head on my pillow, you become brave, you besiege me with your priests under the pretext of showing me my errors and bringing me back to the Church of Rome.

"But do you not fear that even your schoolboys will see that there is a lack of courage in you? Will they not feel that you have no confidence in your own cause?

"When I was sick and unable to argue with your ambassadors, I refused to see them. But to-day, thanks be to God, I am well and able to meet and answer you; hence I challenge you.

"If you were sincere in your efforts to bring me back to your Church, come to-day, and show me my errors. I will open you the doors of my house, and I will be the most happy man to receive you in my humble home, and to give you all the honour and respect due to your high position, and according to my own personal esteem for you.

"We will meet and discuss as true gentlemen.

"Bishops and priests of Canada, if you grant me the favour of that public discussion, I will also ask you to show me the text of the Gospel which told you to hang our heroic patriots of 1837 and 1838.

"For the French-Canadian people have not forgotten that it was the desire of General Colborne to let them live, when the Bishop of Montreal, Lartigues, said· 'Hang them!'

"You had excommunicated and cursed them before the battles! As much as it was in your power, you had tied and paralyzed their strong arms when on the battle-fields that they might not conquer, and not satisfied with that—when they were defeated, you ordered them to be hanged!

"What crime had they committed, to be so cruelly, so unmercifully treated by you?

"Ah! they had so much loved their dear country, which is yours and mine, that they thought it worth shedding their blood to make it free!

"The stern voice of historical truth tells you that a handful of insolent tyrants had taken the notion that the French-Canadians were good only to draw their water and cut their wood. More and more every day they were trampling under their feet our most precious and sacred rights; they were not concealing their minds, that just as the negroes of the Southern States were destined to serve their white masters, so the children of the French-Canadians, conquered on the plains of Abraham, were fit only to serve their conquerors.

"The only crime of our heroic patriots was that they considered it better to die free men than to live slaves.

"Has not noble England, after the bloody days of St. Charles and St. Eustache, taken the defense of our patriots? Has she not applauded when her most eloquent parliament orators with Lord Brougham, Lord Durham, etc., declared that the French-Canadian patriots were among the noblest men of our age; that they had fought and died for the defense of their rights—and to prove it, has not that noble English nation granted to us all the rights and privileges for which those heroic countrymen of ours fought and died?

"Are you so blind and so ignorant of the history of your own country as to ignore those facts?

"Among the heroes who shed their blood in those days for you and for me, there was one who was the bravest among the brave. The pages of ancient and modern history have no record of any more daring and devoted soldier of liberty than Chenier.

"But why is it that the very name of Chenier still fills your hearts with fear and rage?

"Not satisfied with cursing that French-Canadian hero in his life and in his death, you want to degrade his memory, you want his body to be buried in the open fields with the carcasses of the brute animals!

"Why so?

"It is only because the name of that heroic patriot is forever mingled with the love of liberty!

"You hope that by destroying the first you will make the people forget the second, for it is only slaves you want and only slaves you can rule.

"But you are mistaken.

"Wherever there is a French=Canadian heart on the borders of our majestic St. Lawrence River, it beats with a holy emotion at the spotless names of Papineau and Chenier. Every true French=Canadian, in spite of your fulmination, is proud of having had such an eloquent apostle of liberty in the first one, and such a heroic martyr of liberty in the second one.

"In spite of you the seeds of fraternity, equality and liberty which Christ has brought from heaven to save the oppressed nations from the hands of their tyrants, are bearing their blessed fruits in Canada.

"Whilst you trample under your feet those sacred seeds of liberty, the hour is coming fast when the French=Canadian people, with the holy Gospel in their hands, will settle their accounts with you.

"In that day your high citadels will crumble in Canada as they have crumbled in England, France, Germany, Mexico, etc.

"That day the French=Canadians will accept the Word of God to guide them; and that Word will make them free!

"Truly and respectfully yours,

"C. CHINIQUY."

CHAPTER XLI

My Fourth and Last Visit to Europe in 1896. The Challenge of Father
Begue Accepted. The Roman Breviary. Discussion at Oban

So many Christian friends from England and Scotland had
of late invited me to visit again their country, that I thought
my duty was to grant their request. They wanted me, they
said, to help them to fight the ritualists, whose deplorable
success was more and more, every day, a cause of anxiety to
the true disciples of the Gospel.

Though eighty=seven years of age, my health was so good
that I thought the invitation of those friends was the voice
of God.

After having received from the grand and noble *Protestant
Alliance Society,* through their secretary, Mr. A. H. Guinness, a promise that they would map out and guide my tour
through Great Britain, and arrange the details of my addresses on the different subjects on which they wished me to
speak, I took my passage to England on the steamship
Laurentian, the 10th of September, 1896. But before leaving
Canada I thought my duty was to address the following letter to my countrymen:

"The good Master calls me again to go and work among
our Christian brethren of England for a few months. But before leaving the enchanted shores of our beloved Canada,
allow me to address a few words to our dear countrymen of
every origin and creed on the great question of the day—the
separate schools. More than eighty=seven years have passed
over me. Every day of that long experience has taught me that
one of the greatest calamities which can fall on a country is
the separate schools, established under the pretext of religious
differences. If you put the stupid, unpatriotic, unchristian

walls of religious division to separate the children from each other when in the schools, it will be as impossible to make of them a united, strong and happy people, as it would be to make a strong rope with grains of sand. Yes, if you allow a part of the children to say to the other part, born under the same skies, 'We are too holy to sit on the same school benches with you; we are too holy to kneel before the God of heaven and earth with you,' you sow seeds of contempt, hatred and division which will make it absolutely impossible to reap the blessed fruits of unity, esteem and respect for each other, without which men are very little superior to the wild beasts of the forests. Yes, if you allow a part of the people to say to the people of the other part in the school, 'You are so contemptible in our eyes, you are so much the enemies of God; you are so completely damned that we cannot allow our children to breathe the same atmosphere in the school, etc,' you at once form two camps of implacable enemies of all your boys and girls, and those implacable enemies, when young, will, for the greater part, remain implacable enemies when old. Those boys and girls who will never see, know or love each other when young, will not be likely to know and love each other when men and women. Surely, no person should be asked to give up his religion under the pretext of sending his children to school Liberty of conscience is one of the precious fruits of modern civilization—a fruit bought by too many rivers of blood to be given up on any consideration Nothing must be done or said by the teacher which may hurt the religious feelings of any one of his pupils; but, thanks be to God, there are a thousand things which are common to all Christian denominations, on which the teacher can speak without hurting any one's feelings. If any one objects to the speaking on any religious subject by the teacher then let the children learn their catechism and their Bible at home and in their Sabbath-schools rather than go to separate schools during the week. But I hope that the Roman Catholic Bishops and priests in Canada have received enough of the bright light of our age to allow their people to read the Bible, and that the time has also come to them to know that they have not the right to prevent the people from bathing in the rays of that grand and divine Light which heaven has given to earth—the Bible. They will not object any more to the reading of the Bible in the schools, provided the teacher will not be allowed to make any comments thereon.

"I have another favour to ask my dear countrymen before I leave my dear Canada. It is that they go no more to Rome to ask the Pope how to rule Canada. Let the men whom we have selected to guide and rule us give in their resignation if they do not find themselves wise and learned enough to fulfil their duties. But by no means let us hear any more of consulting the Pope how to rule Canada. The Pope has no more business here in our legislative affairs than the Emperor of Constantinople. The Pope and the grand Turk are two great gentlemen, surely, but they have business enough at home to be released from the burden of ruling such a distant country as Canada. Besides that, let us remember the white breeches of Mercier! What a price we have paid for those breeches! What disasters and humiliations were in store for that great patriot and all his friends, through those white breeches!

"My last request to my kind friends is that they pray for me when I will be working in that precious part of our Lord's vineyard—Great Britain. Let them ask our common Saviour that He may so constantly guide me in everything I will do and say in England, that it may be all for His glory and the good of the precious souls for whom He suffered and died on the cross."

After a pleasant voyage I reached England on Thursday, September 22d. A deputation was in readiness to receive me, embracing several of the prominent officers of the Alliance. After warm congratulations had been exchanged, I was informed that the applications from churches and societies for my services were much more numerous than could possibly be entertained, and that my great age had been borne in mind, and that I would not be overworked while in England. In my reply, I said. "That is very kind of you, but you see, when I am in Canada I am lecturing almost daily, and when I had so many pressing invitations to visit England, I thought at last, 'Well, if it be the Lord's will that I should go to England, I shall only be doing there what I should do if I remained in Canada, and the voyage will do me good.' Although I am convinced that Rome will never again get the upper hand in England, yet you have a battle to fight in England against Romanism, and you in England do not know what Rome is, and so I am coming to tell you that her system is not Christianity Why, when I was in the Church of Rome, I had to repeat the following prayer from my Breviary 'Mary, thou art the only hope of sinners' That is not Christianity. It is paganism and idolatry. The christ of Rome is a false christ, and not the Christ revealed in God's Word."

I could but little anticipate that the few statements I made before these friends, and which the press reported more or less correctly, were to have the importance that circumstances gave them. As the readers will see hereafter, they led to a challenge of a priest and an exciting controversy

On Wednesday the Protestant Alliance held a reception in the drawing-room of the National Club, for the purpose of giving me a welcome, and of affording an opportunity for many old friends to renew the acquaintances formed on previous visits. The drawing-room was far from large enough to accommodate the ladies and gentlemen who had accepted the invitation.

Mr T. A Denny occupied the chair, and after a prayer by Canon McCormick, he referred to having presided for *Pastor Chiniquy* many years ago in Exeter Hall, when the meeting proved a somewhat stormy one, owing to the presence of an opposing element in its midst. He maintained that the cause of Protestantism was by no means dead, and that, despite the progress of Romanism in some quarters, it would be a large undertaking to kill the Protestants to be found in the country. He deprecated the false charity which was only manifested on one side and instanced the declaration of the Pope as to the "invalidity" of Anglican orders as showing that the demand of Rome is " all or nothing."

Mr. Guinness, secretary of the Alliance, read a long list of influential names in clerical, military and other circles who sympathized with the object of the meeting, but were prevented from being present. Among these were Archdeacon Sinclair, Canon Tugwell, Prebendary Webb-Peploe, the Duchess of Manchester, the Countess Tankerville, and Lord Roden. It was encouraging to see such an intelligent and sympathetic audience. In my address I remarked:

"I do not come as a learned man or as a teacher, for there are very many able to occupy such a position better than I; but I come from Canada at the request of many English friends to do what I can to open the eyes of the English people to the dangers to which they appear to be drifting. Not long ago, in the United States, a train heavily laden with passengers was proceeding at full speed towards a bridge which had just collapsed. A man who had seen the disaster ran back to stop the train. I am like that man, and my desire is to do something to prevent the country from committing itself to the broken bridge of Romanism. For twenty-five years I was a priest in that Church, and honestly desired to serve God. It is a mistake to suppose that all Roman Catholics are not honest. Many of them are thoroughly so, though they are mistaken, and, having been brought up in that system, it requires almost a miracle to open their eyes to their true position. During my stay among you I hope to have the opportunity of addressing meetings in many parts of the country. It is not my desire to abuse Roman Catholics, for I have known many noble and honest hearts among them, but it is our duty to give the truth to those who have it not. I am sorry to find, so far as my observation goes, that Protestants are too silent, and lose in that way many converts who might be won if as Christians they had more zeal You are too much on the defensive. Do you fear the future? Christ is in the boat, though the tempest is raging, and though the machinery of the Romish Church may be powerful, yet 'the race is not to the swift, nor the battle to the strong,' but the side on which God is will have the victory "

In the midst of my work, a letter containing a challenge appeared in the *Catholic Times* of October 2, 1896, by the Rev. F. Begue of the Pio Cathedral, Oban This is the letter:

"I read in the *Rock* of September 25th the following statement by Pastor Chiniquy, who, I understand, is on a visit to England. 'You in England do not know what Romanism is, and so I am coming to tell you that I know that her system is not Christianity.' 'Why,' continued the Pastor. 'when I was in the Church of Rome I had to repeat every day the following prayer from my Breviary· *Mary, thou art the only hope of sinners.* That is not Christianity. it is paganism and idolatry' Now, sir, I beg to challenge the statement italicized, and I defy Mr Chiniquy or any of his friends to give chapter and verse, i. e, the place where the said prayer is to be found in the Roman Breviary, which I suppose the gentleman in question must have read in by-gone days And I hereby offer to hand over to him a cheque on the Nottingham and Notts Bank for £150, being all I possess in this world, if he can make good his assertion "

After the challenge was read to me the officers of the Alliance thought it hardly possible that a priest should issue such a challenge if the prayer were not in the Breviary. They seemed to fear that I had put myself in an inextricable predicament by asserting what I could not prove. I told them that there was just one way by which they could become perfectly sure about the matter, which was to get the book and see for themselves. I told them to send for the book and I

would show them the prayer addressed to Mary—"Quia tu es
spes unica peccatorum."

The secretary of the Alliance immediately sent to Wash-
bourne's for a copy of the Breviary and a copy was purchased that had been issued in the year 1895, "Jussu Editum,
Clementis VIII. Urbani VIII. et Leonis XIII.

I then told the secretary to take the volume entitled
"Pars Autumnalis" and to turn to page 331, which he
did, and, to his great surprise, as well as that of the other
friends present, read the very words: "Quia tu es spes unica
peccatorum."

Seeing the prayer with their own eyes, the officers of the
Protestant Alliance said that they were fully satisfied that I
was right.

I accepted of course the priest's challenge, and after subsequent correspondence with Mr. Begue, I sent the following
letter to the press:

" Protestant Alliance, November 5, 1896.
" Sir:
"In reply to the Rev. Father Begue's letter, which letter
is of the 28th of October, he states that 'with regard
to my challenge to him he reasserted his previous statement
as to the prayer we priests are (falsely) said to be under the
obligation of reciting every day 'to Mary, our only hope.'

" I beg to state that I have not reasserted anything of the
kind; what I did say was, that the 'Breviarum Romanum'
was a prayer-book, a part of which the priests of Rome had
to read every day; and in the 'Romanum Breviarum' these
words occur, in Latin: 'Thou art the only hope of sinners,'
which statement is addressed to Mary. The Rev. F. Begue
must know that there are four volumes of the Breviary—
Spring, Summer, Autumn and Winter.

" The challenge that I accept, as stated by the Rev. F.
Begue, is as follows:
" 'And I defy Mr. Chiniquy or any of his friends to give

chapter and verse, i e., the place where the said prayer is to be found in the Roman Breviary, which I suppose the gentleman in question must have made use of in by-gone days, and I hereby offer to hand over to him a cheque on the Nottingham and Notts Bank for £150, being all I possess in this world, if he can make good his assertion.'"

I should state here that a letter containing Priest Begue's challenge had been sent to clergymen in the districts in England where meetings were being held in connection with the Protestant Alliance, no doubt with the motive of discrediting my statements in the eyes of the public. Priest Begue in all probability had no expectation that his challenge would be accepted in view of my great age (it being then in the midst of winter), and the great distance from England to Oban, in Scotland. He did not evidently think that he ran any risk of losing his £150 under the circumstances. In this he found his mistake; for the Protestant Alliance took immediate steps to meet the challenger, and the Argyllshire Hall in Oban was secured for a meeting on the 17th of November.

As the Breviary is prominently named in connection with the Oban controversy, most readers are not supposed to have a knowledge of it, except in name.

This is the handbook, or, as it is sometimes called, the prayer-book of the priests. There are lessons in it for the different days of the year, and every priest is required to devote considerable time to its perusal every day; a neglect to do that is classed among mortal sins, and cannot be forgiven except on severe conditions. This book must have a great influence on the minds and characters of the priests. This is in reality their Bible. They are bound to believe everything in it as infallibly true. This fact alone ought to be sufficient to open the eyes of any one to see that Popery is a system of superstition and downright fraud Truly it is a system of lying wonders This book, a modern writer has remarked, "is the most vulnerable point of attack on the Roman system, and is really indefensible."

This book was sanctioned by the Council of Trent, and was revised by Pope Clement VIII., and printed in 1602 at the Vatican. In 1631, Urban VIII. revised it, and this seems to be the authentic Breviary, which is of course in Latin. It is a work of great magnitude. There are in it biography, hymns, passages from the Psalms, prayers and lessons covering all the days of the year. Miracles, or "pious frauds," constitute a prominent feature. An English translation was made some years ago by the present Marquis of Bute, in two large volumes. The work passed under the supervision of a learned Jesuit, to whom the Marquis expresses his obligations. He says in his preface, "that if the translation itself or the foot-notes, should contain anything which a faithful Catholic ought not to have written, he has written such passages inadvertently."

The work contains many absurdities and lies, and any one to accept them must be either dishonest or blindly credulous, or I may say insane. In it there are things stated which no man using ordinary reason can accept.

Let us now mention a few of these. Holy children spoke when five months old. St. Philip Beniti at that age scolded his mother for not giving alms to some begging friars. Bells sometimes rang of their own accord when saints were born.

There is quite an account of St. Rose, in connection with whom there were miraculous manifestations from her earliest childhood. Her face took the form of a beautiful rose. She was born in Lima, South America, in 1586, and the only native of this continent ever canonized by the Pope. At the age of five years she uttered a vow of perpetual virginity!

The translation of the story of that saint by the Marquis differs considerably from the original. A copy of the passage from the Latin is this: "Quinquennis votem perpetuae virginitatis emisit." But the translator gives her age as fifteen, instead of five as found in the original, when she took this step. He either makes a great mistake, inadvertently or by design, to make the act seem more reasonable. How many more inadvertencies, mistakes or alterations he has made to tone down the absurdities, it is hard to say. St. Rose wore a garment of rough haircloth into which she inserted small pricks. She wore day and night under her veil a crown, the underside of which was made of pricks. In imitation of Katherine of Sienna, she girded her loins with a three-fold iron chain. She had a bed of knotty sticks, and filled the gaps with broken pieces of pottery. She lived in a wretched hut and subjected herself to fastings, whippings and sleeplessness. She was visited by departed spirits or ghosts.

St. Reymond on one occasion being on a certain island, and wishing to go to Barcelona, spread his cloak upon the sea and passed over the waters, accomplishing the whole distance of sixty leagues in six hours, and finally entered his convent through the closed door! Thirty miles an hour was good speed. No modern steamships have come up to that yet. Why not cross the Atlantic Ocean at the present day by some such arrangements and dispense with costly and cumbersome steamships? There is an account of the holy house of Lorett in Italy, which was brought centuries ago through the air by angels over the seas from Jerusalem. This was the house in which the Virgin Mary and Joseph lived. This beats all the modern improvements in house moving. One saint stuck his staff in the ground and it developed into a fig-tree covered with fruit. One nun found herself short of bread, having only a few crumbs of crust, but the fragments became loaves of bread so that she and those with her had an abundance. Pope St John went on a journey to Corinth, and was furnished with a horse by the lady of a nobleman, which was her favourite animal. The horse after being returned was unmanageable, and kicked in the hands of its mistress so violently that she parted with it, and gave it to the Pope. The horse was then perfectly tractable with its master, having become so proud that it would serve no one of less dignity than the Holy Father. St. Dionysius was beheaded and walked off with his head under his arm to Paris, and entered the present Abbey of St. Denis in that position. St. Jannarius was thrown into a red-hot furnace, and was not even singed. The next day all the beasts of the amphitheater came crouching before him. The body of this saint once extinguished the flames of Vesuvius. Rome ought to supply saints to extinguish some of the terrible fires that break out in our great cities. Such might bring millions into the Pope's treasury. Of course the liquefaction of the blood of this patron saint of Italy is not passed over in the Breviary. St. Francis de Paulo crossed the Strait of Sicily on a cloak taking another monk as a passenger. St. Hyacinth, a Pole, prosecuted a long voyage in a similar way, taking his companions with him.

St. Ferdinand is most highly praised for his defence of the Catholic faith. The Breviary states: "This he performed in the first place by persecuting heretics, to whom he allowed no repose in any part of his kingdom; and for whose execution, when condemned to be burned, he used to carry the wood with his own hands."

The Breviary records a sort of penance which was prominent, and tended to spiritual purification—that of self-flagellation. This absurdity is strongly recommended. The greatest saints found the application of scourges specially conducive to holiness. Xavier, Bernard, and many other eminent saints were in the habit of lashing themselves. Xavier used an iron whip, which at every blow was followed with copious streams of blood. Teresa used freely this kind of purification, but she was not satisfied with this; she sometimes rolled herself on thorns, and the Breviary tells us that the holy nun, by this means, "was accustomed to converse with God." Her body, we are told, after her death becoming "circumfused in a fragrant fluid, remains till the present day, the undecayed object of worship."

January 10th is the festival of the identical chair used by Peter. For many years the chair was exposed for the adoration of the faithful. In 1662 an unfortunate thing happened. While the chair was being cleaned the twelve labours of Hercules appeared, so that the genuine chair of St. Peter suddenly vanished. The chair is not now on exhibition, the fraud being so barefaced that the material thing had to be kept out of sight.

In the lesson for May 26th, "St Philip Néri was so smitten with the love of God that he continually languished, and his heart boiled with such ardour, that when it could not be contained within its own boundaries the Lord wonderfully enlarged his breast by breaking and elevating two of his ribs."

Under the date of December 3d: ",St Francis, by the sign of the cross, turned so much salt water into fresh, that for a long time he supplied 500 sailors who were at death's door for thirst, and, being carried into various countries, many were cured by it."

January 15th, we are assured, "When Anthony visited Paul, the hermit, in a cave in the desert, he found him dead, and when he had not an implement to dig the ground for a grave, two lions came with rapid course from the innermost parts of the desert to the body of the blessed old man in such a manner that it was readily understood that they expressed their sorrow in the best way they could, then eagerly tearing up the ground with their paws made a hole which would conveniently hold the man." April 2, about Francis of Paola, we are told that, "God was pleased to attest the sanctity of His servant by many miracles, of which the most celebrated was, that being refused a passage by sailors, he crossed the Straits of Sicily with his companions, on his cloak spread upon the waves."

I might go on multiplying the lies contained in the Breviary, which the priests are bound to believe as facts. The translation, which was the result of a work which lasted several years under the supervision of Father Swiney of the Jesuit order, is in two volumes, 8 vo, of over 1200 pages.

The Breviary reminds one of the sacred books of India

which abound with stories similar to those we find in it
There are the accounts of gods (saints) to be worshiped,
abounding with superstitious lies and absurdities, but no
greater than are found in the Breviary.

In a long article on Buddhism in the Encyclopedia
Britannica, the writer, in speaking of the form of this system
in Thibet, makes a very significant statement: "Lamaism, with
its shaven priests, its bells and rosaries, its images and holy
water, its popes and bishops, its abbots and monks of many
grades, its processions and feast-days, its confessional and
purgatory, and its worship of the double Virgin, so strongly
resembles Romanism that the first Catholic missionaries
thought it must be an imitation by the devil of the religion of
Christ; and that the resemblance is not in the externals only
is shown by the present state of Thibet—the oppression of all
thought, the idleness and corruption of the monks, the despotism of the government, and the poverty and beggary of
the people."

In view of the stuff found in the Breviary, with the stamp
of papal infallibility which the priests are required to
saturate their minds with every day, their low intellectual
and moral grade is what might be expected. It is no wonder
that such men never elevate the people, and the condition of
the people in Italy, Spain, Quebec and Ireland is what might
be expected.

The Romish missionary goes forth with his Breviary,
stuffed with superstition, lies and idolatry. The Christian
missionary goes out armed with the Holy Scriptures, given
by inspiration of God.

I proceed now to speak directly of the controversy at Oban
which had been decided upon. I went to Oban and learned
that Father Begue refused to meet me. I then suggested
that three arbitrators should be chosen on either side to settle
the disputed points. This Priest Begue refused in the following letter:

"Bishop's House, November 17, 10·15 A. M

"Dear Sir:—

"The very nature of my challenge, *which I hereby repeat,* precludes the possibility of any discussion or controversy on the point. It is a mere matter of fact. *On what page of the Breviary are the words quoted by Mr Chiniquy?* The meeting is to be public, and I will attend with Breviary at 7·30, and on his *publicly* making good his assertion I will hand him the cheque. No further correspondence is needed on the subject.

"Yours truly,
"F Begue, Priest."

He thus agreed to attend the public meeting and prove his point At the appointed time I attended the meeting accompanied by deputies from the Scottish Protestant Alliance,—Mr M C Maughan, chairman of the directors of that society and the Rev. A. Townshend, of St. Silas Episcopal Church, Glasgow. There were also on the platform· Rev. Alex. Duff, Rev Ewan Macleod, Rev James Hutchison and Rev. James Forbes Campbell of Dunstaffnage, who briefly introduced the proceedings. Scripture was then read and prayer offered. after which Mr W C Maughan read to the meeting the terms of the challenge which, he said, had led me at the great age of eighty-seven to undertake a journey to Oban, he read also a letter from Father Begue of the same day's date, in which he said. "The very nature of my challenge, which I hereby repeat, precludes the possibility of any discussion or trifling with the point. It is a mere matter of fact on what pages of the Breviary are the words quoted by Mr. Chiniquy. The meeting is to be public and I will attend with my Breviary at 7:30, and on his publicly making good his assertion I will hand him the cheque." Mr Maughan stated that Father Begue had refused to attend a meeting specially called for, at which three arbitrators on each side who understood Latin should give their translation of the prayer which appeared in the Breviary, and, therefore, they brought the matter before the public meeting.

The Rev. Mr. Begue, who ascended the platform carrying an armful of Breviaries, while Mr. Maughan was speaking, said he had read in the *Rock* of the 25th of September my words referred to, and he had challenged the statement and did so again. They were going to be told by Mr. Townshend that there was one passage in the Roman Breviary, where the words occur in Latin, "*Maria, tu es sola spes peccatorum,*" but he would say—"these words occurred only once a year, or perhaps twice. Mr. Chiniquy said these words were a prayer, and were to be said daily in the Roman Breviary." That was the statement he challenged, and none else.

Rev. Mr. Townshend rose to reply to Rev. Father Begue. He said the challenge as set forth in *The Catholic Times* was different from that set forth by Father Begue that night. That challenge was, that Father Begue "defied Pastor Chiniquy or any of his friends to give chapter and verse—the place where the said prayer was to be found in the Roman Breviary." Rev. Father Begue had also sent a letter to Rev. Mr. Macleod of Oban, in which he said: "It is a mere matter of fact on what page of the Breviary are the words quoted by Mr. Chiniquy." He (Rev. Townshend) would now read from the Breviary, and as he was only a poor Irishman, he hoped they would listen to him as he read them. He had with others that morning visited Father Begue, who received them most kindly—and he must thank Father Begue for the courteous manner in which he treated them—and he admitted that in the Roman Breviary, for the 9th of September, they did find words similar, quoted by Pastor Chiniquy. The reverend gentleman then read out of a copy of the Breviary the words referred to, upon which there was prolonged applause. If they were not satisfied with his reading from that Breviary, he could, he said, read the words from any other they liked. There were the words as distinct as could be.

Rev. Mr. Townshend added. "Without going into the question of whether Pastor Chiniquy said every day or not, I only again refer to the letter of Father Begue, who said distinctly: 'I defy Mr. Chiniquy or any of his friends to give chapter and verse—the place where the said prayer is to be found in the Roman Breviary' I have done that"

Rev. Father Begue again pressed his point that the words did not occur daily, and that they were in a sermon, not a prayer

At this stage the Rev. Mr Kennedy, of Loch Ranza, who occupied a place at the back of the platform, stepped forward and asked permission to make a remark. He said they had not come to ascertain whether the prayer was a daily one or not. They were concerned with the substance, and if Father Begue admitted that once a year he prayed— "Mary, thou art the only hope of sinners," that was the crux of the question, and nothing else.

Rev. Father Begue said he maintained that the words in the Breviary were not a daily prayer. That was the term of his challenge He maintained that if the words occurred, they were in a sermon of St Augustine, and were not a prayer Now, as he asserted this to be a matter of fact, Father Begue started to leave the platform, and said, "I wish you good-night. You won't have the £150" There were, on his leaving the platform and going out of the hall, booing, laughter and cries of "Shame! Shame!"

Rev. Mr. Townshend said he thought they had the right to decide that I was the victor in that matter. Father Begue had said he defied me and my friends to give the place where the prayer was to be found in the Roman Breviary, and said if that was done he would hand over £150 "I have shown," said the reverend gentleman, "that Pastor Chiniquy is right and that Father Begue is wrong, and he has gone and taken his cheque with him"

I then spoke, and in the course of my discourse I said that the £150 was nothing to me; I cared only about the truth. I showed my hearers that I had offered through friends to settle the question with Father Begue in an amicable way, but this offer had been refused three times. I had never said that the prayer was repeated every day; although that statement had appeared in the newspaper, I never said so. There were different prayers for every day, and the same one was not said every day.

In response the Rev. Messrs. Townshend, Duff and Macleod intimated that they had read the prayer in question, in the Breviary.

Rev. Mr. Townshend in a letter to one of the public papers a short time afterwards, gave the following statement: "On receipt of this letter, arrangements were made for Father Begue to attend the public meeting in the Argyllshire Hall. The terms of the challenge having been stated by Mr. W. C. Maughan, Father Begue endeavoured to cover a retreat by affirming that he offered the £150 only on condition that the prayer could be pointed out *daily* in the Breviary. Producing his own letter, I read to the meeting his own words—'It is a mere matter of fact. On what page of the Breviary are the words quoted by Mr. Chiniquy?' I then read from an authorized edition of the Roman Breviary the following prayer, occurring on September 9th:—'O beata Maria . . . accipe quod offerimus, redona quod rogamus, excusa quod timemus; quia tu es spes unica peccatorum.'

"And I invited any one in the hall to inspect the passage. Without disputing the truth of my assertion, Father Begue then left the hall. Pastor Chiniquy at once proceeded to appeal to the following gentlemen: Rev. E. Macleod, Rev. A. Duff, Rev. J. Hutchison, and Mr. W. C. Maughan, whether the prayer was to be found in the Breviary or not. These gentlemen, representing different Churches, replied in the affirmative; and finally the following resolution was carried by acclamation by the whole meeting: 'This meeting is satisfied that Pastor Chiniquy has most conclusively answered the challenge of Father Begue, and they are of the opinion that Father Begue is now in honour bound to pay over the sum of £150 ' "

As Father Begue tried to escape from his predicament by quibbling, I notice this to show and illustrate the Jesuitism of the enemy we have to deal with. His resorting to such subterfuges only went to prove the truth of what I asserted in regard to the prayer of the Breviary.

As to the fact of the prayer being such and where I asserted, was as plain as anything could be. This accords with what we find in several of the most prominent Romish books. "The Glories of Mary," by St. Liguori, is one of these books sanctioned by the highest popish authorities. The general drift of the book accords with the prayer I have proved to be in the Breviary. I might give almost any number of passages to show this. This writer represents John Damascus as thus addressing Mary· "Oh lady, in thee I have placed all my hope and my firm confidence I look to thee for my salvation." St. Thomas is represented as saying that, "Mary is all the hope of our salvation." St. Ephrem prays, "Oh most holy Virgin, receive us under thy protection, if thou wilt see us saved, since we have no other hope of being saved but through thee."

St. Liguori writes further: "Do you not know that she (Mary) is the only city of refuge, and the only hope of sinners?" St. Augustine has called her "the only hope of sinners"; "Unica spes peccatorum." He speaks in another place of a red ladder upon which Jesus Christ was standing, and a white one upon which was His holy mother. The persons who attempted to ascend the red ladder rose a few steps, and then fell, they ascended again, and again fell. When they were exhorted to ascend the white ladder and obeyed, they succeeded, for the Blessed Virgin offered them her hand and took them directly into paradise.

A volume might be filled with similar statements from Romish writers.

The attempt of Father Begue to escape by saying that the

idea asserted in the prayer is found in a sermon by St. Augustine, borders on the ludicrous. If the power ascribed to Mary in a prayer is ascribed to her in a sermon, it is a doctrine, and such a prayer would be consistent with, and based upon the doctrine. It is not likely that Augustine had advanced so far towards popery that he taught any such doctrine or prayer. But be that as it may, what is ascribed to him, is endorsed in the Breviary as infallible.

I quote a passage from the " Banner of the Covenant " that is here in point:

"The most stirring incident of his visit (Dr. Chiniquy's) was connected with a challenge sent by a Father Begue of Oban, to prove in the Roman Breviary the use of the blasphemous expression, 'Because thou art the only hope of sinners,' etc., with a prayer to the Virgin. The existence of the words was proved, the priest himself admitting it in one or two places. The meeting declared Chiniquy the victor, and entitled to the £150 which the priest was to give him if successful. But Begue gathered up his Breviaries and disappeared with the money. The discussion has, however, created considerable interest in Oban, and friends there, greatly astonished to find such blasphemous sentiments attributed to the great Augustine, Bishop of Hippo, desired us to verify the words. It was certainly a very difficult task to search for these words in twelve huge Latin folio volumes. A slight reference to Dr. Pusey's *Eirenicon* attributed the expression to sermon eighteen, by this Father. The ordinary editions of his works are no help, but on referring to the best and most reliable, that edited by the Benedictine Fathers at Louvain, there was a surprise. Where sermon eighteen was to be, there was a blank. It was found, however, in an appendix and numbered 194. It was removed as spurious from the authentic works of the Father, the learned editors adding a note that, 'in the judgment of the Louvainenses, it is the work of an uneducated man.' "

Thus another fraud is laid bare, not by Protestants, but by

Benedictines, on which the idolatry and superstition of the Roman Breviary is built up. It may interest others as well as friends in Oban.

The Oban debate resulted, under God, in a grand triumph for the cause of truth. I can see the hand of my Heavenly Father in it. The influence of it for good was manifested not only in Scotland, but in Ireland and England. The hand of the same God that was in the struggles of Luther and Knox, was shown in this. To His name be all the glory.

CHAPTER XLII

My Fourth and Last Visit to Europe—Continued. Severe Illness and Recovery. Invitation to Lecture in Holland Accepted. A Week in Paris. Germany Visited. The Pulpit and Tomb of Luther. Return to Canada. The Close of this Book and of Life's Voyage.

I cannot undertake to give a detailed account of my work in Great Britain during my last trip there; suffice it to say that eight days after my arrival, more than a hundred invitations had been received from my English friends, to go and deliver them the message which the good Master wanted me to proclaim.

On December 22, 1896, I had already given eighty-two public addresses to multitudes which very often could not be accommodated in the large halls or churches where I spoke in London, Glasgow, Edinburgh, Brighton, etc.

But on December 22d, after two days of lecturing in Norwich, it was the will of God to stop my humble labours with a severe cold, which kept me in bed till April 22d, —just four months. Several times during those months my doctors told me: "We would hope to cure you very soon, if you were not so old. But with your eighty-eight years of age, the best thing you can do is to prepare yourself for the better life which is in store for the children of God."

These words were very wise, and I would have been very imprudent not to pay attention to them. However, it was the will of God to restore my health again, and on April 30th, I was enabled to give two lectures, without feeling any fatigue, to more than three thousand people, in the immense Queen's Hall of London, on the occasion of the annual meetings of the Protestant Alliance of England.

But the physicians told me that for a thorough restoration

of my health, I needed a change of atmosphere, and as I was consequently contemplating my return to America, I received an invitation from the Rev. H. J. Schouten, of Ommeren, Holland, to visit his country, where he said I had many friends desirous of hearing me. This invitation, which was not in the least anticipated, seemed to me providential, affording me the three-fold opportunity of proclaiming the truth, of following the advice of my physician and of visiting that interesting people whose grand history I had so greatly admired, especially in connection with the struggle for the cause of civil and religious liberty, when the mighty and tyrannical Philip II. of Spain failed to crush that small but heroic people. It was then my privilege and my unspeakable joy to address the disciples of the Gospel who filled with their multitudes the immense and beautiful churches of Rotterdam, The Hague, Harlem, Amsterdam, Utrecht, Anhalt, Apeldorn, Leyden. I was thus lecturing among that most hospitable, kind and earnest people during the whole month of April, speaking sometimes through an interpreter, and part of the time directly to the audience in French or in English, many of the people of that country being highly educated and speaking three languages. The ministers seemed to vie with each other to manifest tokens of respect and friendship

I owe a special debt of gratitude to the Rev. Mr. Schouten, who put forth such earnest efforts for the extension and success of my work, and also to his worthy brother, a lawyer who resides at The Hague.

At that time there was quite a political campaign going on in Holland. One of the parties to which the Romanists mostly belonged, hoped to influence the Protestants that belonged to another party to join them, so that they would be sure to win the day. But in that the Romanists failed, and they themselves ascribed that result to the influence of my lectures

But on the 31st of May, some important affairs in the in-

terest of the Gospel having called me to Paris, I was obliged
to go from Holland to France.

When in that brilliant capital of the French people, I had
the joy to meet my daughter Rebecca and her husband, the
Rev. Mr. Morin, who had come to that great centre to enjoy
the educational advantages it affords.

I spent a week with my dear children, and during that
time, besides sight-seeing and many visits to places of interest, I addressed the Coligny Society of Colonization
which is especially interested in promoting the immigration
of Protestants to Algeria. By special request, I spoke of my
colonization in Illinois. My few remarks aroused patriotic sentiments among the members of that society when
they learned that one of my primary objects in founding that
colony was to foster the interest of the French nation in
America. I was, on the spot, elected an honourary member
of the society.

One of the most pleasant recollections of my short stay in
Paris this time is the great pleasure I had in meeting Mr.
Eugène Réveillaud, whom I found to be a most warm and
attentive friend. He took great pains in entertaining us at
Versailles, where he resides. He arranged for meetings upon
my return to Paris in July, but, as it will be seen, hereafter I
could not fulfil these engagements on account of previous
invitations in England.

As many German friends had invited me to go and visit
them, I left Paris on the 7th of June for Germany. The
next day it was my privilege to see and admire the marvelous
Cathedral of Cologne, and on the 9th of June I enjoyed the
Christian hospitality of one of the most learned and pious
ministers of the Gospel in Germany, the Rev. A. Schneider,
in the celebrated city of Magdeburg.

It is known that that city had been destroyed and entirely
burned by the Jesuits in the days of the Reformation, to
punish its inhabitants, who had broken the yoke of the Pope
in order to follow the Gospel which Luther had given them.

But since that time they have rebuilt it on a more splendid scale

A public open=air meeting had been prepared in that city to hear the Gospel message they had asked me to give.

It seemed, at first, a great imprudence to deliver a long address in an open=air meeting, in the very heart of the city; but though my address lasted an hour, no injury came to me. It was the contrary—I have never enjoyed better health since I gave to those multitudes the Gospel food my God had ordered me to dispense to them

The next day it was my joy—my unspeakable joy—to go and visit the tombs where Luther and Melancthon are resting from their labours, at Wittenberg How can I express my feeling and emotion when in that beautiful and cele-brated church, where the hero whom God had chosen to strike down the modern Goliath, had so often made his thundering voice heard!

No; no words can tell what I felt when in the very pulpit of Luther I made the echoes of the church repeat the beautiful words of David "O my soul, bless the Lord, and let all that is within me bless His holy name."

It seemed I heard from the tombs of Luther and Melancthon a mysterious voice uniting to mine, saying: "O my soul, bless the Lord, and let all that is within me bless His holy name."

I would have to say many things about what I have seen with my eyes and touched with my hands in that celebrated city of Wittenberg, the blessed cradle of the Reformation, but it would be only the repetition of the story which all the tourists have to tell who have seen the same city However, I may say that I did not like to leave that historical spot without carrying with me, as a precious relic, some of the earth I had taken from the tomb of Luther

I had to hasten my return to England, as the Rev Mr. Sterling and other friends had arranged for a few lectures they wished me to give before my departure for Canada

My passage, with that of my daughter and son-in-law, was secured for the 8th of July on the "Parisian." What joy I anticipated at seeing again my dear and beautiful Canada after more than ten months absence!

But before leaving England I thought it proper to publish an address of farewell to my Christian friends there, together with those of Scotland and Ireland, part of which I insert here:

"I cannot leave your hospitable shores without thanking and blessing you for the numberless acts of kindness by which you have overwhelmed me these last ten months. Our merciful God alone can pay the debt of gratitude I owe you. May that merciful heavenly Father pour upon you the richest treasures of His mercies for what you have just done to me, His old, unprofitable servant.

"I will not leave your hospitable shores without telling you again: Beware of the Jesuits! and still more, beware of the traitors in your midst under the name of Ritualists or High Church party! they are the agents of the enemy of your liberties to bring England back under the heavy and degrading yoke of Popery. If you want to bequeath to your children the glorious Gospel which your heroic ancestors have purchased with their own blood, gird your loins and fearlessly prepare yourselves to fight again the battles of the Reformation.

"The Pope of Rome, with his armies of Jesuits, priests, nuns, cardinals, approaches you to-day with smiling lips and honeyed words,—just as Delilah did with Samson,—but do not forget how this giant of old was punished for trusting himself to the perfidious Philistine girl.

"Rome has not changed: she cannot change. The Rome of to-day is the Rome that planned the Gunpowder Plot, built and manned the 'Invincible Armada,' and reddened your soil with the blood of your noble ancestors.

"But to fulfil your grand and sublime mission, it is not enough to fight Rome; you have something better to do: it is to convert the Roman Catholics.

"Do not forget that you have a whole nation in Canada which God Almighty granted you to conquer that you might bring them to the dear Saviour's feet. You have already done much to help our Canadian missions to reflect the light of the Gospel into the midst of the terrible darkness with which Popery has covered my dear native country— Canada But the work is not yet finished. It is true that we feel an unspeakable joy when we consider that there are at least 30,000 French-Canadian Roman Catholics who these last fifty years have broken the heavy yoke of the Pope to follow Christ. But we have still more than two millions who are at the feet of the idols of Rome, and who are adoring a god made with a wafer baked by the servants of the priests of Rome.

"Divided we perish; united we stand. Let us unite our prayers as well as our efforts, and the God of the Gospel will give us the victory over the common foe   The stronghold of Popery in Canada will be brought into dust, the French-Canadian people will be wrenched from the hands of the enemy, and we will, during all eternity, bless the Lord for having granted us the privilege and honour of doing something for that glorious and blessed work "

After a most enjoyable voyage, brightened by a beautiful sun and enlivened by most pleasant company, we arrived in Montreal on the 18th of July, experiencing the truthfulness of the most touching English song.—

Home' home! sweet, sweet home!
There's no place like home'

Now, dear readers, I bring my book to a close.

In it I have endeavoured to state and enforce the truth as I find it in the Gospels and the writings of the inspired apostles

This truth I have been preaching for forty years, ever since I received the full light.

I loved the truth as such from the bottom of my heart and I have not consciously varied from it a particle in my teaching.

Nothing can do us the highest good except the simple truth as revealed in God's Holy Word. This is the medicine and food of the soul, not the traditions and inventions of fallible men. The blessed Saviour prayed: "Sanctify them through Thy truth; Thy Word is truth." We cannot be saved by mere *churchianity* but by Christianity.

As to matters of fact stated in this volume, I have not knowingly varied in the least degree from the truth. My readers can judge for themselves, and arrive at conclusions.

My work on earth is now coming to an end, and I must soon appear before my Judge, who knows all things, and who will do just right. My entire trust for salvation is in Christ as my Redeemer and Mediator.

I am now about to cross the river, I am just at the end of life's pilgrimage, rich with the unspeakable gift which has been given me, and pressing my dear Bible to my heart as the richest treasure, I hasten my steps with unspeakable joy towards the Land of Promise. I hear the angel's voice telling me: "Come, the Master calls thee."

My life has been lengthened out much beyond the average, being now in my ninetieth year. This has been prolonged by the good mercy of my Heavenly Father, so that I could do something in the cause of my Saviour, who has done so much for me.

I ascribe my long life under God to my abstaining from the use of intoxicating liquors, and general observance of the laws of health. No doubt my habitual state of mind has had a great influence on my bodily health. My strong confidence in my God and the peace and joy I have felt, springing from an abiding evidence of my acceptance with Him, have tended to promote health and length of days.

I am now ready to depart and be with my Lord. All my labours and trials seem insignificant in comparison with that eternal weight of glory which awaits me. I have no fear of death—it has no sting for me. Thanks be to God who gives me the victory over the last enemy through our Lord Jesus

Christ, I can adopt the words of Paul: " I am now ready to be offered and the time of my departure is at hand. I have fought a good fight, I have finished my course, I have kept the faith henceforth there is laid up for me a crown of righteousness, which the Lord, the righteous Judge, shall give me at that day; and not to me only, but to all those that love His appearing."

CHAPTER XLIII

The Final Triumph. Requiescat in Pace.

I

THE LAST MESSAGE OF FATHER CHINIQUY—HIS ANTE-MORTEM
DECLARATION OF FAITH, SIGNED AND ATTESTED SIX DAYS
BEFORE HIS DEATH.

REASONS WHY HE COULD NOT RETURN TO THE CHURCH OF
ROME.

On this 10th day of January, in the year of our Lord
1899, at the special request of the Reverend Charles Chiniquy,
of the city of Montreal, evangelist, minister of the Gospel,
Doctor of Divinity, etc., I, George R. Lighthall, the under-
signed Notary Public, practising in the city of Montreal,
aforesaid, in the province of Quebec, accompanied by
William Grant Stewart, of the said city of Montreal, Esquire,
Doctor of Medicine, a witness to these presents, expressly
called, went and repaired to the domicile, in the said city of
Montreal, of the said Rev. Charles Chiniquy, where being,
and finding him in poor health of body, but of sound mind,
as appeared to us, said notary and witness, by his actions,
conversation and demeanor, he hath made and published,
and has declared to us, said notary and witness, as follows:—

"Believing that my earthly life is drawing to its end, and
that I am about to die and enter into the presence of God
Almighty and of my blessed Saviour, our Lord Jesus Christ,
I, before God Almighty, declare the following to contain the
faith in which I die, and some of the express reasons why I
still, and will refuse to return to the yoke of the Pope or of
his Church, which is commonly called the Roman Catholic

478

Church, of which Church I was at one time, and for years, a priest in good standing.

"I commend my soul into the hands of Almighty God, my Creator, through the sole infinite merits of Jesus Christ. my Divine Redeemer.

"I hereby expressly declare myself to be a Protestant, protesting against the many damnable errors of the Roman Catholic Church, and in the Protestant faith I have, once and for all, accepted Jesus Christ for my only Saviour, believing that God has forgiven all my sins for His sake, and I accept His Holy Word for my only guide.

"I can never return to the yoke of the Church of Rome, for, amongst others, the following reasons:—

"1. The dogma of the apostolic succession from Peter to Leo XIII is an imposture   There cannot be found a single word in the Holy Gospel to show us that Peter passed a single hour in Rome. The superiority or pre-eminence given by the Roman Catholic Church to Peter over the whole apostles is another imposture. Every time that our Saviour was asked by His twelve apostles who would be first, the leader, the Pope, He always answered that there would not be such first, leader or Pope in His Church   More than that, He positively answered the mother of Zebedee's children, that He had not received from His Father the power to establish one of His apostles over the others. 'To sit on My right hand or My left, is not Mine to give.'   (Matt. 20. 23.)

"We have an irrefutable and infallible proof that our Saviour never put Peter at the head of the apostles as the first, the leader or the Pope, in the dispute that occurred among the apostles a little before His death   'And there was also a strife among them, which of them should be counted greatest.' (Luke 22. 24.)   Such a dispute would never have occurred if Jesus Christ had established Peter as the greatest, or the first of them. They would surely have known it, and Jesus would have answered, 'Have you so soon forgotten that Peter is the greatest among you, that he is the first among you from the day on which I appointed him the fundamental stone of My Church?' But far from answering thus, the Son of God rebukes His apostles and tells them positively, 'The kings of the Gentiles exercise lordship over them . . . But it shall not be so among you.' (Luke 22: 23-25.) Not only that modern forged primacy of Peter had never been acknowledged by any of the apostles, but had been openly and positively denied by Paul. 'For He that wrought effectually in Peter to the apostleship of the circumcision, the same was mighty in me towards the Gentiles.' (Gal. 2: 8.) 'And when James, Cephas, and John, who seemed to be the pillars, perceived the grace that was given unto me, they gave to me and Barnabas the right hand of fellowship, that we should go unto the heathen, and they unto the circumcision.' (Gal. 2: 9.) Here Peter is named only after James, a thing that never would have been done by St. Paul if he had known anything of the marvelous superiority and primacy of Peter over the rest of the apostles.

"The following are the words of St. Paul: 'But when Peter was come to Antioch, I withstood him to the face, because he was to be blamed.' (Gal. 2: 11.) It is evident that Paul had not the least idea of any kind of superiority of Peter over him when he withstood him to the face; and still more when he wrote these lines. It is clear that the Holy Ghost inspired Paul to give us the history of his so stern withstanding to the face of Peter, that we might not be seduced by the grand imposture of the supremacy of Peter, which is the corner-stone of the apostate Church of Rome.

"2. I will never be a Roman Catholic, for the Roman Catholic Church is idolatrous. It worships God? Yes, but the god whom it worships is made with a wafer—it is a wafer-god that is on its altar. Every hour of his priestly life a priest is guilty of the crime which Aaron committed when he caused the Israelites to worship a golden calf. The only difference between him and Aaron is that Aaron's god was made of gold, and that of the priest is made of some dough baked by nuns or servant girls between two well-polished and heated irons.

"The Roman Catholic Church has a christ on its altars. Yes, and it is very devoted and truly pious towards that christ, or rather, these christs: it praises their powers and their mercies; it sings beautiful songs in their honour; but the christs whom they worship are spoken of by our Saviour in the 24th of Matthew: 'There will be false christs, and they will show great signs and wonders, insomuch that if it were possible they should deceive the very elect. Wherefore if they say unto you, behold He (Christ) is in the secret chambers, believe it not'

"Now I see that terrible prophecy is accomplished by the Church of Rome every time its people prostrate themselves before these christs made in little cakes and put in the secret chambers of its Church. Its people believe in those christs of the secret chambers, when the Son of God tells them 'Believe it not.' They go there to adore the wafer-god, when the true Christ says, 'Go not there.'

"In vain it tells us that Christ gave its priests the power to make its god with the engraven wafer. I answer that Christ Himself had not the power to make God and make Himself with an engraven wafer; for His Father had forbidden such an absurd and idolatrous act when, on Mount Sinai, in the midst of thunders and lightning, He said: 'Thou shalt not make unto thee any graven image, or any likeness of anything that is in heaven above, or that is in the earth beneath, or that is in the water under the earth: thou shalt not bow down thyself to them, nor serve them· for I the Lord thy God am a jealous God, visiting the iniquities of the fathers upon the children unto the third and fourth generation of them that hate me.'

"Christ came to accomplish and not to break His Father's commandments. He could not give the Church of Rome the permission or the power to break them by ordering it—as it pretends He did—to make an engraven wafer, turn it into

God, and bow down before it, for this is idolatry   When
Christ told us to eat His body and drink His blood, He was
speaking in the same figure as when He said He would eat
the Passover   Though Christ said, 'I will eat the Passover,' he was not able to eat the Passover, for the simple
reason that the passage of the exterminating angel over
Egypt could not be eaten.   But the lamb which was eaten in
remembrance of the Passover would be eaten, and that lamb
was called the Passover because it represented a Passover.
By the same figure of speech the body and blood of Christ
would not be eaten.   But the bread which represented that
body would be eaten, and the bread had then to be called the
'body' for the same reason and by the same rule of language that the lamb was called the 'Passover' though it was
not the Passover; just in the same way and by the same rule
of language that when we look at the marble statue of Queen
Victoria we say, 'This is Queen Victoria,' though it is not
Queen Victoria at all.

"3.   I will never be a Roman Catholic because every Roman Catholic Bishop and priest is forced to perjure himself
every time he explains a text of the Holy Scriptures.   Yes,
though it is a very big word and a hard word, it is the truth
From the day that he has sworn when he was ordained a
priest to interpret the Holy Scriptures *only according to the
unanimous consent of the holy fathers*, he has seldom
preached on a text of the Holy Scriptures without being
guilty of perjury, for, after having studied the holy fathers
with some attention, I am ready to prove that the holy
fathers have been unanimous in only one thing, which was to
differ on almost every text of the Scriptures on which they
had written.   For instance, the priest cannot say that the
books of the Maccabees are inspired without perjuring himself, for the greatest part of the holy fathers say that these
books are not inspired.   A priest cannot, without perjuring
himself, say, when Christ said to Peter, 'Thou art Peter,
and upon this rock I will build My Church,' it signified that

Peter was meant by this rock, and that he is the corner-stone of the Church, for the priest knows very well that St. Augustine and many other holy fathers said that Christ meant Himself when He said, 'Upon this rock I will build My Church'

"4 I cannot be any more a Roman Catholic, for I know that Auricular Confession is a diabolical institution, as I have amply shown it to be by my book called, 'The Priest, the Woman, and the Confessional.'

"5. I will never be a Roman Catholic, for I have seen with my eyes the inside of the walls of the churches, and they are filled with all the abominations of the world The priestly celibacy is of diabolical institution Purgatory, with the poor souls that burn in it, and are saved by paying the Church so many dollars, is of diabolical institution The waters of La Sallette and Notre Dame de Lourdes which are sold in the Roman Catholic Church, are of diabolical in-stitution. The Roman Catholic Church's forbidding to eat meat on certain days is of diabolical institution Its infalli-ble Pope and immaculate Mother of God are of diabolical institution.

"6 With the help of God I will never think of making my peace with the Church of Rome, for her priests, Bishops and Popes have shed the blood of millions of martyrs. from John Huss to our dear brother, Hackett. On the Pope's hands I see the blood of 75,000 Protestants slaughtered on the night of St. Bartholomew, and the blood of half a million of Chris-tians slaughtered in the mountains of Piedmont.

"7. I will never be a Roman Catholic, for its Church is the implacable enemy of the laws of God and of the rights, liberties and privileges of man Its Church has degraded and brought into the dust and mud all the nations it has ruled

"I might give many other reasons why I would never be a Roman Catholic, but I hope that these are sufficient to show to my dear countrymen, who are so cruelly kept in ignominious ignorance and slavery, that, having once accepted Christ and

His holy Word for my guide, I cannot bow down any more before idols and wafer-gods.

"It is my wish and desire that publicity be given to this my declaration of faith, and to that end I hereby instruct and appoint my son-in-law, the Rev. Joseph L. Morin, of said city of Montreal, minister of the Gospel, to cause these presents to be published in the newspapers of the French and English languages as he may think best, and to take such other means for the publication thereof as in his opinion may be advisable. I also hereby instruct him to forward a duly certified copy hereof to the Roman Catholic archbishop of Montreal, for the time being, at the time of my death."

"Executed at the domicile of the said Rev Charles Chiniquy on the day and date aforesaid, under the number three thousand five hundred and sixty-six, and signed by said declarant, witness and notary, after due reading hereof.

"(Signed)   C. CHINIQUY.
"W. GRANT STEWART,
"GEO. R. LIGHTHALL, N.P.

"A true copy of original hereof remaining on record in my office.

"(Signed)   GEO. R. LIGHTHALL, N. P."

II

ADDRESS DELIVERED AT THE FUNERAL SERVICE OF FATHER CHINIQUY, ON THURSDAY, JANUARY 19, 1899, BY THE REV. C. E. AMARON, D. D., PASTOR OF ST. JOHN'S FRENCH PRESBYTERIAN CHURCH, OF WHICH THE DECEASED WAS A MEMBER.

The solemn duty of saying a few words at the tomb of the illustrious man of which the French Protestant Church and Christendom have just been bereft, has been entrusted to me by my brethren. I feel unequal to the solemn duty.

If I followed the promptings of my heart, if I did not conquer my feelings, with the afflicted family, with this vast
concourse of people, come from far and near, to honour the
memory of the valiant defender of the truth who has ceased
his labours, with a multitude from the ranks of the humble
and poor of the world. whom he always aided and succoured,
I would bow my head in sorrow and allow my tears to flow

We deplore the great gap that has been caused We feel
the loss we have sustained, and all the more because we were
not prepared for it.

It had seemed to us that the mighty wrestler of so many
years, who, like the oak of the forest, had withstood so many
storms, and whose admirable physical frame had so often
triumphed over sickness, would once more be conqueror to
continue the great work to which God had called him. But
our fond hopes have been disappointed, and with the prophet
of Israel we are constrained to cry aloud " Howl, fir tree,
for the cedar has fallen "

I need not dwell here on the leading features of the history of the distinguished reformer whom God has called
away

Born in the Church of Rome when she was all-powerful in
Canada, Father Chiniquy became one of her leading priests.

Miraculously guided and illumined by the teachings of
God's Holy Word, he was impelled by the Holy Ghost to
abandon the religious system that could no longer satisfy the
wants of his soul and the promptings of his conscience, to
accept the religion of the Gospel.

No one ignores the sacrifices which were involved in such a
step, not to speak of the dangers. For conscience sake
he voluntarily divested himself of those supernatural powers
which every priest is supposed to possess, and he forfeited the
immense influence which he had already acquired, and made
the sacrifice of greater riches and honours in store for him.

He did not hesitate to come down from that lofty pedestal
of ecclesiastical and worldly glory, to become a simple minis-

ter of the Gospel, should we not rather say, to ascend to the dignity of the honourable servant of Jesus Christ.

He was well aware that outrages, persecutions and dangers awaited him on all sides. He felt conscious that there would be strong misgivings as to the character of the work of intellectual and moral emancipation, which would absorb his thought, and to which he felt called to devote his life. Beforehand he knew he would be despised, hated and cursed by the powerful Church from which he was withdrawing, and he would be suspected by Protestantism.

But the voice of duty prevailed over all others, and inspired by the cry of this illustrious forerunner, John Calvin, "God wills it, God wills it," with that energy, with that indomitable courage which ever characterized him, born of strong convictions and faith in Christ, like the Apostle Paul, that noble apostate of the Jewish Church, he forsook all to unfurl the banner of the Christian faith. In view of the extraordinary influence which he wielded among his countrymen, the responsibilities which God entrusted to him were very great.

Would he be faithful to his sacred trust? Would he prove worthy of it? Would he proclaim to the end the principles of evangelical Protestantism? Having been a priest of Rome, would he dare to face the messenger of death without the ministry of the priest? Thousands of his fold who so often unjustly accused him of pride, predicted again and again his return to Rome at the solemn hour. Likewise did others, who did not cease to love him, while regretting his conversion. Those who had previously experienced saving faith, and who had knowledge of his, who knew him intimately, who had witnessed his piety, and who had occasion to become acquainted with the motives which prompted him even in his most scathing discourses against that which for him was error and idolatry; those who had shared his great moral and religious struggles, never doubted his sincerity and fidelity. He had failings, yes, and who is without these? Those with which he could in a special manner be reproached, must be charged to the inadequate and positively harmful clerical education he had received, and which he in after years so vigorously combated.

Possessing strong convictions, Dr. Chiniquy remained faithful to the Protestant faith to the end, in public and in private he proclaimed the virtues of Him who had called him out of darkness into His marvelous light.

During his last illness of fifteen days, his strong faith sustained him One week previous to his death, after hearing the reading of the letter from the Archbishop of the Roman Catholic Church of Montreal, who offered him the help of his ministry, the sick man, still strong and in the full enjoyment of his intellectual powers, asked those who had made him acquainted with the intentions of the Archbishop to express to him his sincere thanks for the interest he had manifested in his spiritual welfare, and said in substance· "I am grateful to the Archbishop . . . but I have definitely withdrawn from the Church of Rome. I am perfectly happy in the faith in Christ Jesus. God and Jesus suffice me. I long to depart."

In an interview which I myself had with the Archbishop, I promised him that if Dr Chiniquy expressed a desire to see him, his liberty of conscience would be respected. On several occasions I asked the distinguished patient if the faith which had sustained him during the last forty years of struggles proved sufficient at the supreme hour. With uplifted hands he replied· "The road which leads me to heaven is straight; it is Jesus Christ"

Two days later he said to me: "It is beautiful to reach the end of the voyage. Heaven opens before my wondering eyes. What more could be offered me? How could I miss the road when Jesus the only Saviour guides?" My brethren, if a man who dies with such a faith is not saved. there is no salvation possible. And thus did this noble life come to a close, a life of intense Christian activity and charity.

Calmly and peacefully he fell asleep; the celestial messengers carried his soul, ransomed in the blood of the Lamb, to the city of God, and at this solemn moment his peaceful countenance reflects the calm rest of heaven.

During his life, he proclaimed to thousands of souls salvation through the merits of Christ alone. He placed Jesus and His ministry of grace and pardon ever above that of man.

By his triumphant death he now lifts the veil which has concealed the truth from thousands of timid souls, men and women, who, whilst having lost faith in the religious system which he combated, have never had the courage to embrace the evangelical faith. He says to them that he who forsakes all to accept Christ, the Saviour, is happy during life, and receives the crown of immortality at the hour of death.

Servant of the living God, we do not bid thee adieu, but farewell; thy pains and griefs and labours are ended. No more shall we hear the accents of thy sympathetic voice. The noises of the earth for thee are now hushed in silence, and thou art at rest under the shadow of the tree of life.

We give the rendezvous in the Jerusalem above, the eternal city, the holy palace where dwells the great King, the abode of the ransomed, faithful soul.

While we weep for thee, in the mansions of God all is joy and peace; the vaults of heaven resound with loud hosannas. There, no more sorrows, no more pains; all tears are dried.

> Sleep thy last sleep,
>   Free from care and sorrow;
> Rest where none weep,
>   Till the eternal morrow;
> Though dark waves roll o'er the silent river,
>   Thy fainting soul Jesus can deliver.
>
> Though we may mourn
>   Those in life the dearest,
> They shall return,
>   Christ, when Thou appearest;
> Soon shall Thy voice
>   Comfort those now weeping,
> Bidding rejoice,
>   All in Jesus sleeping.   Amen.

III

MEMORIAL SERVICE.—SERMON PREACHED BY THE REV. A. J.
MOWATT, IN ERSKINE CHURCH, MONTREAL, ON SUNDAY
MORNING, JANUARY 22, 1899.—THE APOSTLE OF FRENCH
EVANGELIZATION.

" I have fought the good fight, I have finished my course,
I have kept the faith, henceforth there is laid up for me a
crown." 2 Tim. 4. 7, 8.

I see Paul yonder writing his last letter, putting on record
his dying words. He knows it. Death faces him. The lion
that had been kept at bay is now ready to spring upon him.
The sword leaps from its scabbard that is to slay him. What
will he write? How do things look to him now? It is one
thing to see them with life and all its promises before one,
and it is another thing to see them when life and all it has
failed to be lie behind one. Is he sorry now that he broke
with his old faith and all the brilliant prospects it held out to
him? Does he now see that the great light that flashed upon
him in the way was not a light that he should have followed?
Does he regret the zeal that swept him from city to city,
shore to shore, preaching Christ crucified? He remembers
what he has had to suffer and sacrifice for the Gospel's sake
The loss of all things it means to him, the times he had
been whipped and stoned and imprisoned, the perils it had
dragged him into and through, and for what? Here he is,
a poor old missionary, deserted of his friends forsaken of
those who should stand by him when he needs them most
Oh, it is sad, it is all a mistake; "so let apostates die!" his
enemies are saying. But Paul does not regret Read his
dying testimony, and if words mean anything, he counts his
life not a failure at all, but a splendid success, a triumph·
" I am already being offered, and the time of my departure is
come. I have fought the good fight, I have finished my
course, I have kept the faith. henceforth there is laid up for

me a crown of righteousness, which the Lord, the righteous Judge, shall give me at that day: and not only to me, but also to all them that have loved His appearing."

I stood here on Thursday, where I am standing now, and I looked into Father Chiniquy's dead face as it lay before me, and there were some questions suggested that seem to me worthy of our most earnest consideration. It may have been fancy on my part, but his face seemed to smile up into mine, and to say something like this: "I am already offered, and my departure has come. I, too, have fought the good fight. I, too, have finished my course. I, too, have kept the faith. And for me is the crown that was the apostle's crown, the crown of all who have loved the Lord's appearing."

I want to ask this to-day, first of all, with his dead face still before me, if it was a mistake, one of the blunders of a great life, such as his has been,

TO BREAK WITH THE CHURCH OF ROME?

Men do make mistakes. They blunder their lives. Great men do that. Wise men do it. Did Father Chiniquy do it, when, at an important crisis in his life, he broke with his own past record of some fifty years standing, broke with the faith that had done so much for him, broke with the Church of his fathers, the Church that had nourished and cherished him as a mother nourishes and cherishes her child; that had baptized him, that had taken him into her bosom and had put him among her children, that had educated him and then had ordained him, that had opened a brilliant future for him and honoured him with her honours—did he, I ask, do a great wrong, make a mistake, blunder his life, blunder so much?

Now, it is easy for some, looking at things from their particular standpoint, to say: "Yes, he did wrong." And so they call him an apostate. Others again find it just as easy to say: "No, he did nothing wrong; he did right." And so they call him an apostle and extol his virtues.

We listen to these and they speak well, we listen to those and they speak well. too, or seem to And yet both cannot be right If Chiniquy was an apostate, he cannot be an apostle; if he was an apostle in any proper sense, he cannot be an apostate Where, then, are we?

I need not dwell on the particulars of his life; these have been sufficiently dwelt upon. A lovelier childhood could hardly be. We see mother and child bathed in one another's tears as the one teaches and the other learns the sweet Gospel story of the Saviour's love, and there is nothing to be desired If that is in any measure a sample of what is going on in Roman Catholic homes, it shames many a Presbyterian home Then, later, we see him entering upon his public duties with a holy, burning zeal. The way he championed the temperance cause, and sought to lift up the people in that respect, cannot be too highly praised. And so it goes on with him till a complication of circumstances arise in connection with the gigantic colonization scheme he is at the head of, that drives him to choose between obedience to God and man. It is solemn moment with him, a real garden of Gethsemane. Who can enter into that darkness? Who can estimate the agony of a true soul as it is led to tear itself away from a past so sacred, and venture upon a future so dark and ominous? But when he took from his breast-pocket his little French Testament and read. "Ye were bought with a price; become not bond-servants of men," that settled it. He fell on his knees and yielded himself to Him who had bought him with His blood—bought him to make him free Henceforth let no one lord it over him When a Church, whether the Church of Rome or the Presbyterian Church, usurps the place of God, and seeks to bind men to her as slaves are bound, she is to be broken with Thus was Father Chiniquy led, driven, compelled, as he looked upon it, to break with the Church of his fathers, to free himself from what he felt to be, on her part, tyranny, spiritual usurpation.

There was Paul—he broke with his Church the tyrannous and persecuting ecclesiasticism of his day. I ask, did he do right? You find him in full sympathy with her bitter persecuting spirit. A fiery zeal burned in his great soul and swept him on. But he saw a great light. It flashed upon him from heaven. He was not looking for it. It came looking for him. And in its light how differently things looked from the way they had looked to him before! And then he heard a voice as well as he saw a light—the voice of Jesus the Crucified. The voice and vision so changed things for him that he would not go back to what he had been. You see him on his knees in the little room. It is his Garden of Gethsemane. Who can enter into the awful experiences of those three days? But he emerged a new man. They called him an apostate for turning his back on his Church and people and all he had been. They said all manner of hard things about him. And was there not good reason for it? Had he not in all good faith accepted a position and commission, and bound himself to stand by the mother Church? Yes. No sooner, however, is he out of sight of the authorities that had sent him and trusted him than he broke faith with them and went over to the other side to be as strong there. What shall be said of such a man? Apostate shall we not call him? And yet, he is no apostate, but an apostle. He had been wrong, and he came to know it. His Church had been wrong, and he came to know it. Her priests and high priests and ecclesiastics were all wrong, and he came to know it. With his fuller light then, what else, as an honest man, could he do if he would be true to himself, true to the truth, true to God, but break with his Church, change his faith, apostatize—shall we not call it? I tell you the world would be the better and the Church would be the purer if there were more of such apostates as Paul and Chiniquy.

I look again into the dead face of Father Chiniquy as he lay there and I ask myself and ask you here to-day if he did a thing unworthy of him to give himself with all the intensity of his great soul, with all the fire of apostolic zeal, and with all the eloquence with which he was endowed so richly, to

THE CAUSE OF FRENCH EVANGELIZATION

Look at Paul and see what he did As we have seen, he broke with the Church. In the new light that had come to him he could not do otherwise. And not only did he break with his Church, he turned right round, and was as hard against her as he had been for her He gave himself to the Gospel, to its promulgation and extension, with all the might that was in him. He went into the synagogues of the land with his new faith and pleaded there the cause of the Gospel, and thus divided them, sowed dissension, set them on fire, overturned things. He found men living at peace with one another, doing their duties in the old way, and after he had spoken, they were all at variance, some holding to the old faith still, others siding with the new, and the very foundations of things ready to be broken up. Do you wonder then that such a firebrand of a man as he was, was mobbed in the streets, stoned, imprisoned, driven out from one place and pursued to another, the most hated and abused of his kind?

And yet he was gentleness itself, as kind as love could make him, seeking only men's highest interests, willing to lay down his life, if in that way or in any other way at all he could be a help to them. It was the truth as he preached it that set them on fire, and so whenever he came preaching the Gospel there was hot work,—hot words, hot hearts. "Let us have peace," men said And the Gospel is peace. But how can truth and error be at peace together? Peace indeed! I tell you it is a dead state of things with both of them where there is peace. Put a dead wolf and a dead lamb together in the same fold and all will be peace—the peace of the dead But let there be life, and where then is the thing men call peace?

Many could not see what the old fight was all about.   The old Jewish Church and the new Christian Church—are not both, the one as well as the other, seeking to lead men to the one and same place?   Let there be no quarrel between them. But there was all the difference between truth and error. The one had the Gospel and the other did not have it.   The one rejected Christ, crucified Him; the other received Him, crowned Him.   Paul, with his light, saw all the difference in the world between them, and so he preached Christ, and in preaching Christ he went full tilt against the Church of his fathers.   There was nothing else for it, and so the smoke of battle arose.

Now, as with Paul, so with Father Chiniquy.   And I hesitate not to compare them.   The Gospel Paul preached, Chiniquy preached.   It was Christ crucified with Paul, and it was Christ crucified with Chiniquy.   It was salvation by grace through faith with Paul, and it was salvation by grace through faith with Chiniquy.   It was everything to Paul to preach the simple Gospel, and it was everything to Chiniquy to do it, too.   If Paul was the apostle to the Gentiles, Chiniquy was the apostle of French evangelization.

What is French evangelization?   It is simply the Gospel to the French people.   Paul felt it his duty and privilege to go to his countrymen with the Gospel, and Chiniquy felt it his special call and mission to go to his countrymen with the Gospel.   You see Paul rising from his knees and with his soul on fire going forth to tell his co-religionists of Jesus. And you see Chiniquy rising from his knees and hastening home to his beloved people; he tells them with a tongue all on fire what a blessed light had broken upon him, and the people, one and all, hailed him and followed where he led them.   It was another day of Pentecost yonder.   That was forty years ago, but the memory of it can never fade, the light of it never go out.

French evangelization—some do not like it.   They speak against it, call it hard names.   It filled the streets of Mon-

treal with a howling mob in other days, stoned Chiniquy
and his friends, it must be a bad thing. It kindles up
strife and controversy, casts firebrands; it must be a bad
thing. It enters once happy homes and sets one against
another; the husband against the wife and the wife against
the husband, the parent against the child and the child
against the parent; a thing that does that must be a bad
thing.

But is that so? Why cannot we see that that is the very
thing that is wanted? Why cannot we see that in so far as
it does that it is the old Gospel Christ preached and Paul
preached and Luther preached? The Gospel, as Christ
preached it, mobbed Him and at last crucified Him. The
Gospel, as Paul preached it, threw him into prison, and at last
martyred him. Think it not a strange thing then, if the apostle
of French evangelization could not fulfil his mission, do his
work without a fight. When French evangelization or any
other evangelization ceases to be a firebrand in the land, it has
outlived its usefulness, its day is done, it has lost its power.
It is time to give your money, your support, to something
else, something better.

I asked here to-day—and that old face with the light still
in it is before me as I try to speak—if it was his one great
mistake, the maddest and foolhardiest thing a man of his
ability ever set himself to do, to give the best forty years of
his life to a thing so utterly hopeless as French evangelization? If he had remained true to his Church he might have
occupied the proudest positions at her disposal, and died full
of her honours And yet despise not French evangelization
It is still a little thing in the land—a little thing ecclesiasti-
cally, socially, politically. And now its apostle and champion
has fallen, and its friends are asking what is to become of it
now.

But let us not fear for it As I saw the thousands come to
look on his face, and heard the words that fell from their
lips, this was made very clear to me, that the movement has

taken a deeper root in the hearts of the people than many of us are aware of. It is not man's work, but God's, and that being the case it will go on, slowly it may be, and not without a struggle, but in the end it will triumph. The Church of Rome cannot put it down.

Some see no necessity for it. They tell us the French people do not want it. They are satisfied with their Church and she is all right. Why should we encourage schismatics and firebrands such as old Chiniquy was? But that was just the way men talked about Christ and His work, Paul and his Gospel. They were not wanted, it was said. Things were well enough as they were; let them alone.

The truth is, however, the Church of Rome is not right. She is standing in the way, as she has ever done, of the country's progress and the people's good. Patriotism calls upon us as well as piety to push as we have never done the claims of French evangelization. As soon as the people know what it is, the Gospel there is in it for them, they will hail it. Already the leaven of doctrine is at work, and there is a waking up all over the land. A movement is developing, taking shape and working out, the extent and value of which we cannot foresee. There is hope for Quebec, but not in what the Church of Rome can do for her, but in the direction of Chiniquy's labour. It is still the Gospel of Christ crucified that is to save and lift up the people, not ultramontanism. Give the people the Word; sow the seed of truth among them with a full hand; teach them of Jesus; inspire them with faith, and they will awake as from sleep, and put on strength.

Oh! great Chiniquy, we shall not soon see thy like again. Thou wert a greater man than we knew, a mightier force for good than we realized. The Lord raised thee up to lead forth an exodus, and although it is still in the wilderness, and the land of promise still afar off, it will yet get there and possess the land. In that day it will be seen as it is not to-day what it was thine to do, what a seed of faith it was

thine to plant, and what a crown it will be thine to wear
Rest from thy labours, O great worker, and let them follow
thee. Hero of many battles, thou didst fight well in the cause
of truth, and now it is the victor's crown. We saw thy faults
when thou wert with us, but now we see thy virtues, and we
honour thee, for the Lord honoured thee above many. Fare
thee well, apostle of French evangelization, till the day when
it will be ours to greet thee in glory to come, shining amid
the shining ones near the throne. Amen.

IV

RESOLUTIONS OF THE PRESBYTERY OF MONTREAL, OF WHICH
FATHER CHINIQUY WAS A MEMBER.
AT MONTREAL, 14TH DAY OF MARCH, 1899.

The Presbytery of Montreal of the Presbyterian Church in
Canada met *inter alia*. The Rev Principal Mac Vicar, D D.,
LL. D., on behalf of the committee appointed to propose a
suitable minute on the death of the late Rev Charles Chiniquy, D. D., submitted the following, which was unanimously
adopted by the Presbytery:—

"The Rev. Charles Chiniquy, D D., was naturally endowed
with talents of an exceptionally high order. The knowledge
of God's Word imparted to him in childhood by his mother
exerted a powerful moulding influence upon his character and
subsequent career In early manhood he was educated for
the priesthood in the Church of Rome, in connection with
which he continued during fifty years As a priest he enjoyed in an extraordinary degree the confidence and veneration of the people, and received from his ecclesiastical superiors, including the Supreme Pontiff, special marks of approbation and favour. As 'the Apostle of Temperance,' he accomplished a great, beneficent and patriotic work, and gained
unique distinction in his native province and far beyond it.
Forty years ago, for reasons drawn from the Word of God, he
withdrew from the Church of Rome, publicly renouncing her

distinctive dogmas, and entered the ministry of the Presbyterian Church, in which office he continued in good and regular standing till his demise. His unfaltering faith in the Scriptures of the Old and New Testaments as the only infallible rule of faith and practise, his intense love of his French compatriots, his burning missionary zeal, his heroism in fighting the battles of truth and freedom, and his persuasive eloquence in the pulpit and on the platform, were conspicously recognized in the Old and New World, as well as in New Zealand and Australia   His labours to the close of his long life were most abundantly fruitful, being mainly directed to the enlightenment of his French=Canadian countrymen, among whom he was spared to see that signal growth of a spirit of toleration and great advancement in their enjoyment of the blessings of the Gospel and in the exercise of their civil and religious rights as citizens of the British Empire   In his ninetieth year he peacefully fell asleep in Jesus, trusting in Him as the only Saviour and Mediator between God and man."

Extracted from the minutes of the Presbytery of Montreal,

JAMES PATTERSON,
Presbytery=Clerk.

understand this also - 6ᵈ
r ethical award That 14
th. confession 8 r
man forgiving sin
denomination based 12ᵈ

CPSIA information can be obtained at www.ICGtesting.com
Printed in the USA
LVOW120322020113

313949LV00006B/135/P